All that glitters...

Even the stars

All things precious...

Even your life

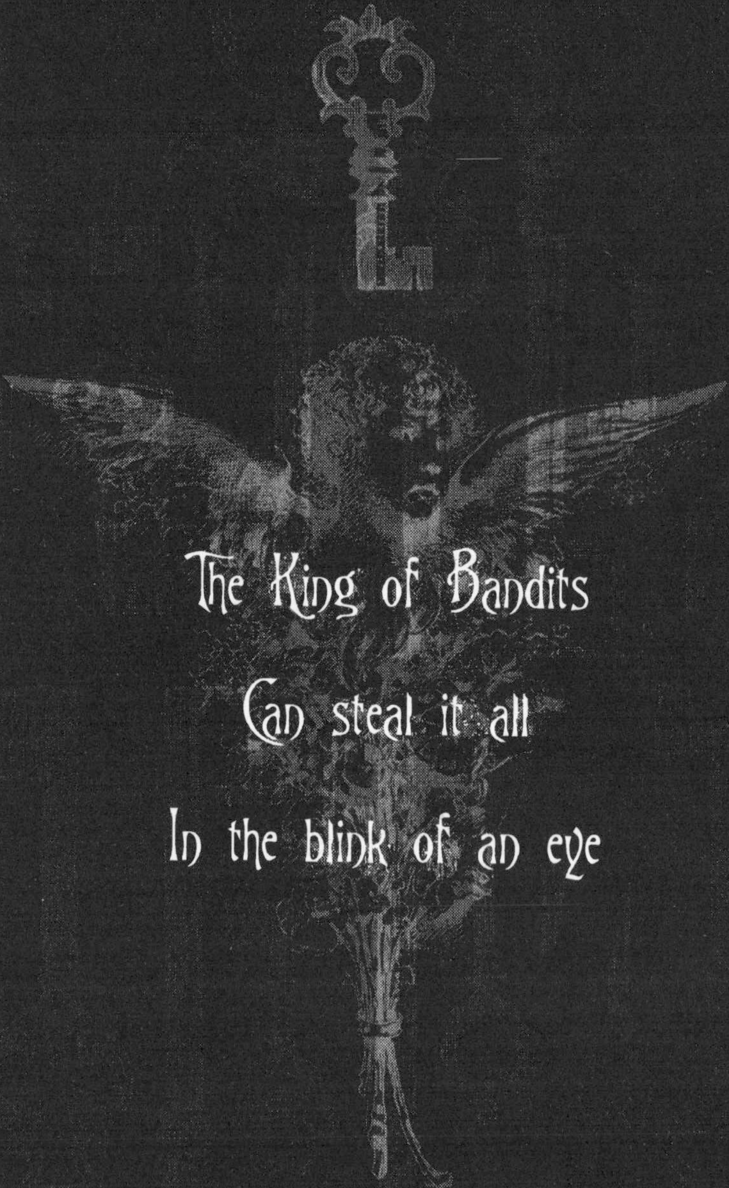
The King of Bandits
Can steal it all
In the blink of an eye

王ドロボウ
JING
新装版
FIVE

jing&stir

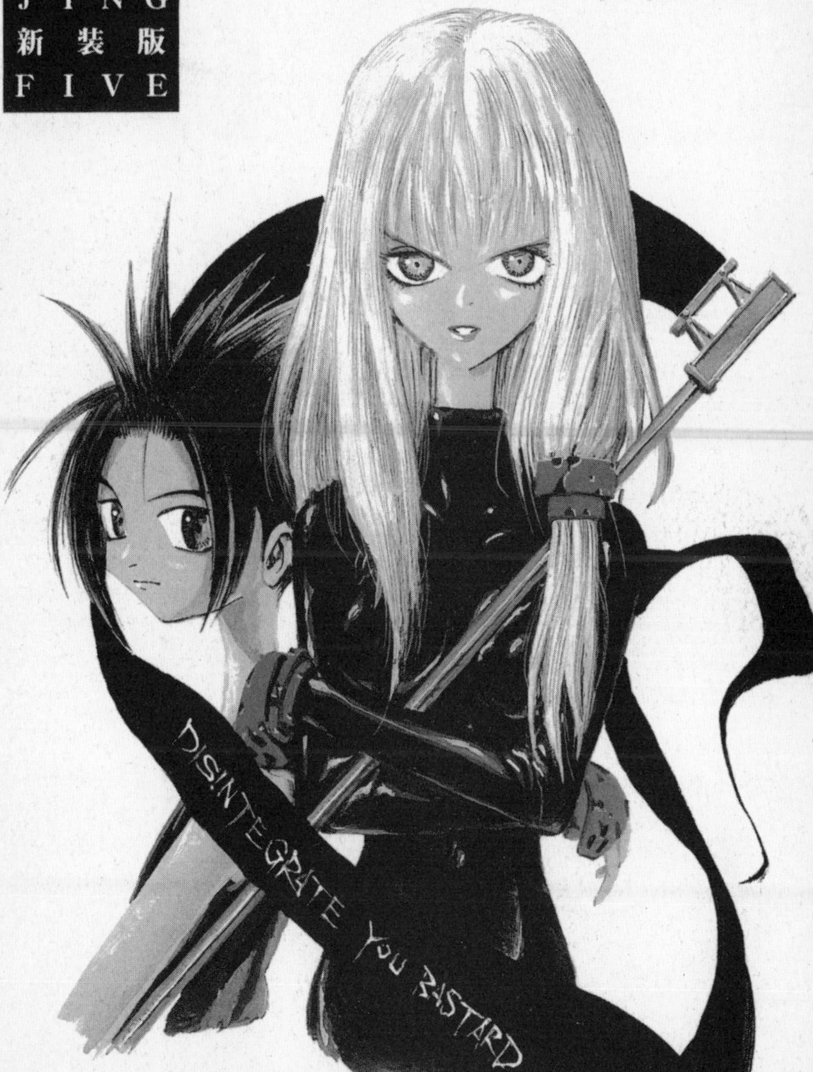
DISINTEGRATE YOU BASTARD

Translator - Kong Chang
English Adaptation - Carol Fox
Copy Editor - Tim Beedle
Retouch and Lettering - Yoohae Yang
Cover Layout - Gary Shum

Editor - Paul Morrissey
Managing Editor - Jill Freshney
Production Coordinator - Antonio DePietro
Production Managers - Jennifer Miller & Mutsumi Miyazaki
Art Director - Matthew Alford
Editorial Director - Jeremy Ross
VP of Production - Ron Klamert
President & C.O.O. - John Parker
Publisher & C.E.O. - Stuart Levy

Email: editor@TOKYOPOP.com
Come visit us online at www.TOKYOPOP.com

A  Manga

TOKYOPOP Inc.
5900 Wilshire Blvd. Suite 2000
Los Angeles, CA 90036

Jing: King of Bandits Vol. 5

ISBN: 1-59182-466-4

First TOKYOPOP® printing: March 2004

10 9 8 7 6 5 4 3 2 1
Printed in USA

KING OF BANDITS JING

VOLUME 5 OF 7

STORY AND ART BY
YUICHI KUMAKURA

TOKYOPOP®

Los Angeles • Tokyo • London

Once upon a midnight dreary, a thief named Jing was weak and weary,
Many strange and forgotten lands he did traverse and explore.
His companion was a bird named Kir, his black wings a-flapping,
While Jing nodded, nearly napping, Kir saw booty galore.
"Wake up, Jing," Kir muttered, "all around us is loot galore."
Treasure from ceiling to floor!

Thus, this ebony bird's wiling, sent Jing's sad face into smiling,
For Jing could steal the stars from the sky, thievery he truly did adore.
The albatross sat proudly on Jing's placid bust, his beady eyes did implore,
One more thing Kir did utter, his feathers all a greedy flutter, his voice a roar,
Quoth the albatross, "Let's steal some more!"

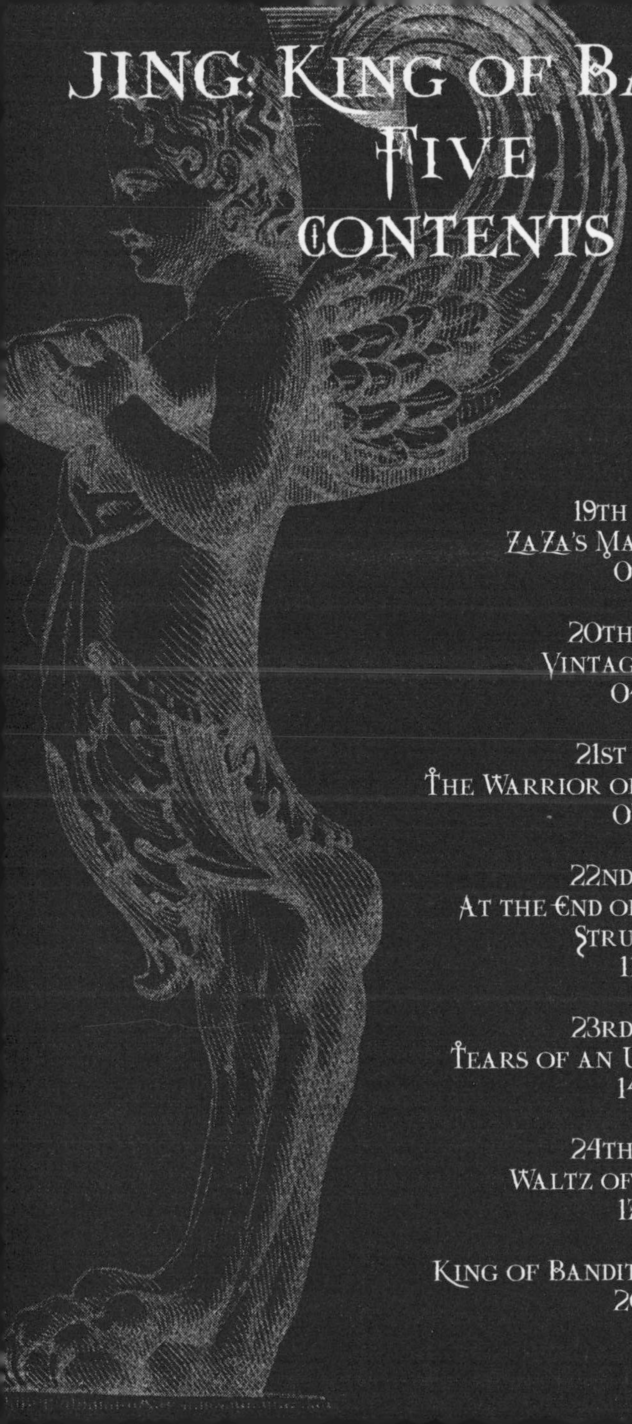

JING: King of Bandits
Five
Contents

jing in a rage

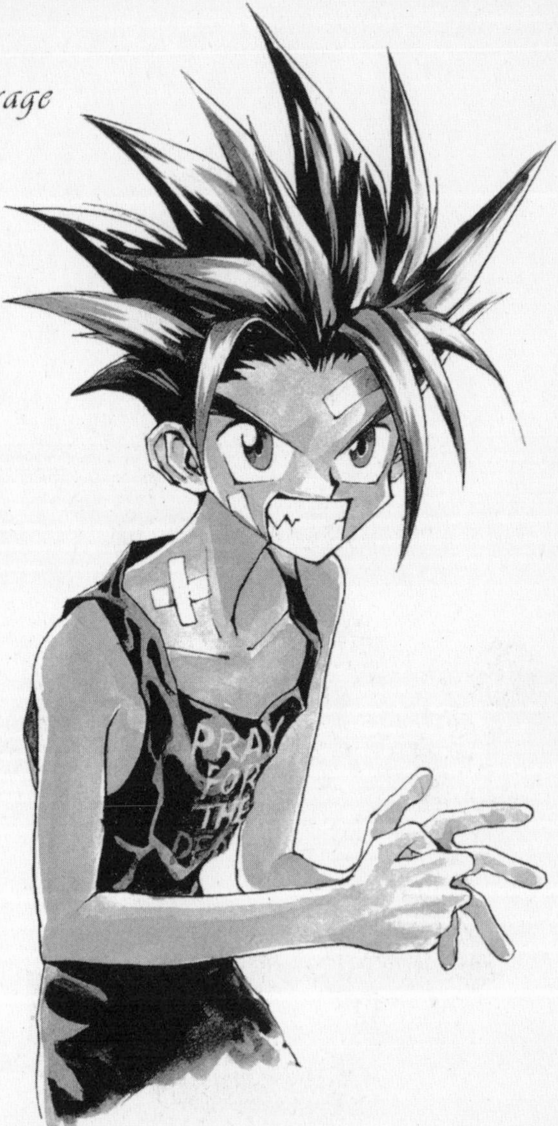
PRAY
FOR
THE

juggling the dreams

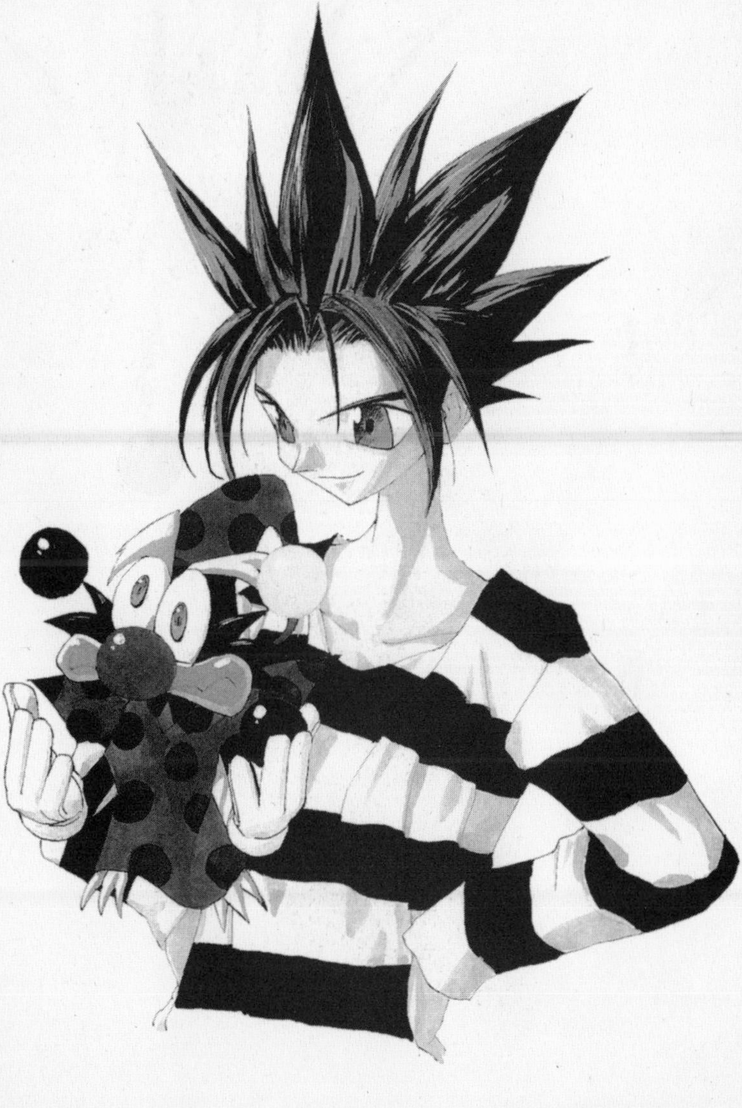

over the top of zaza

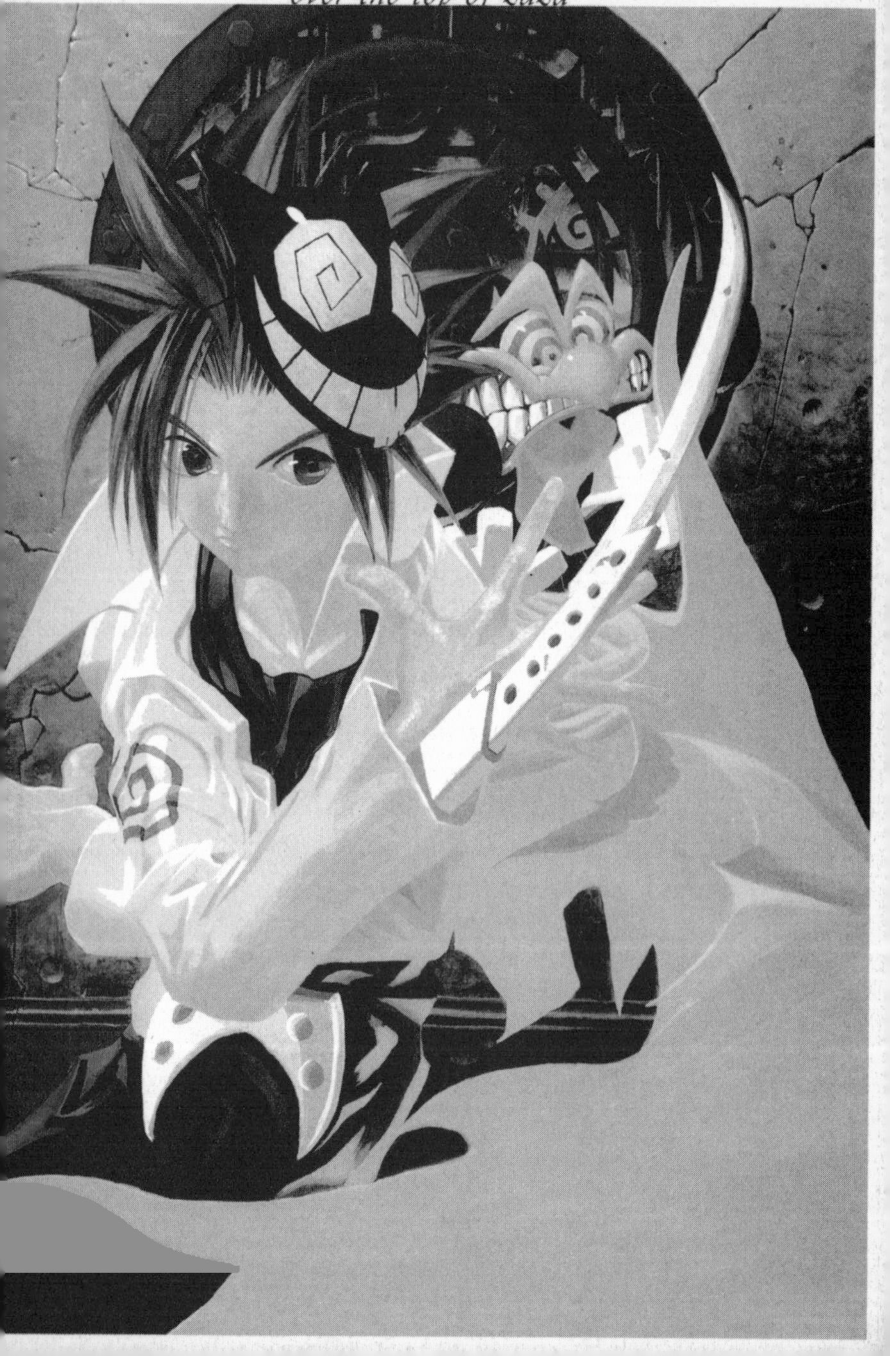

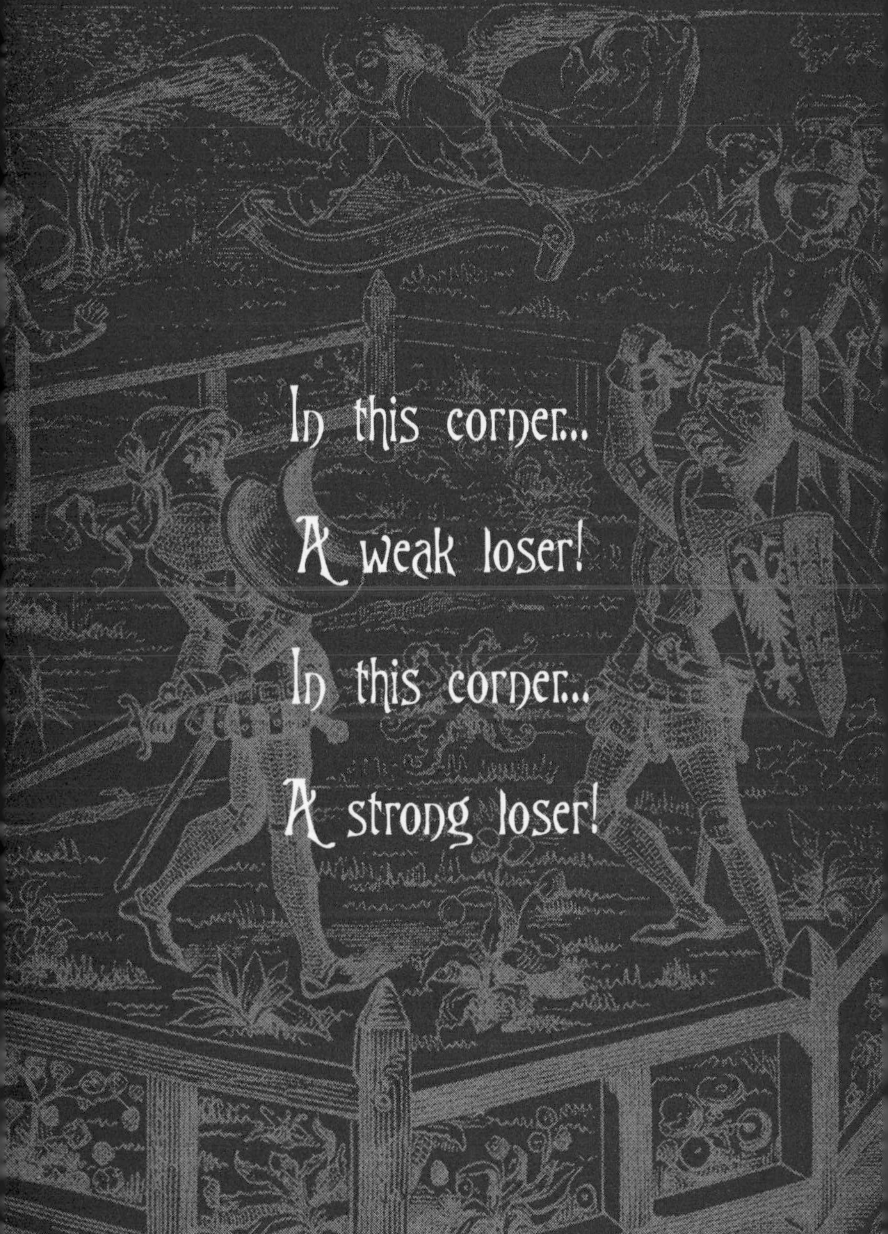
In this corner...
A weak loser!
In this corner...
A strong loser!

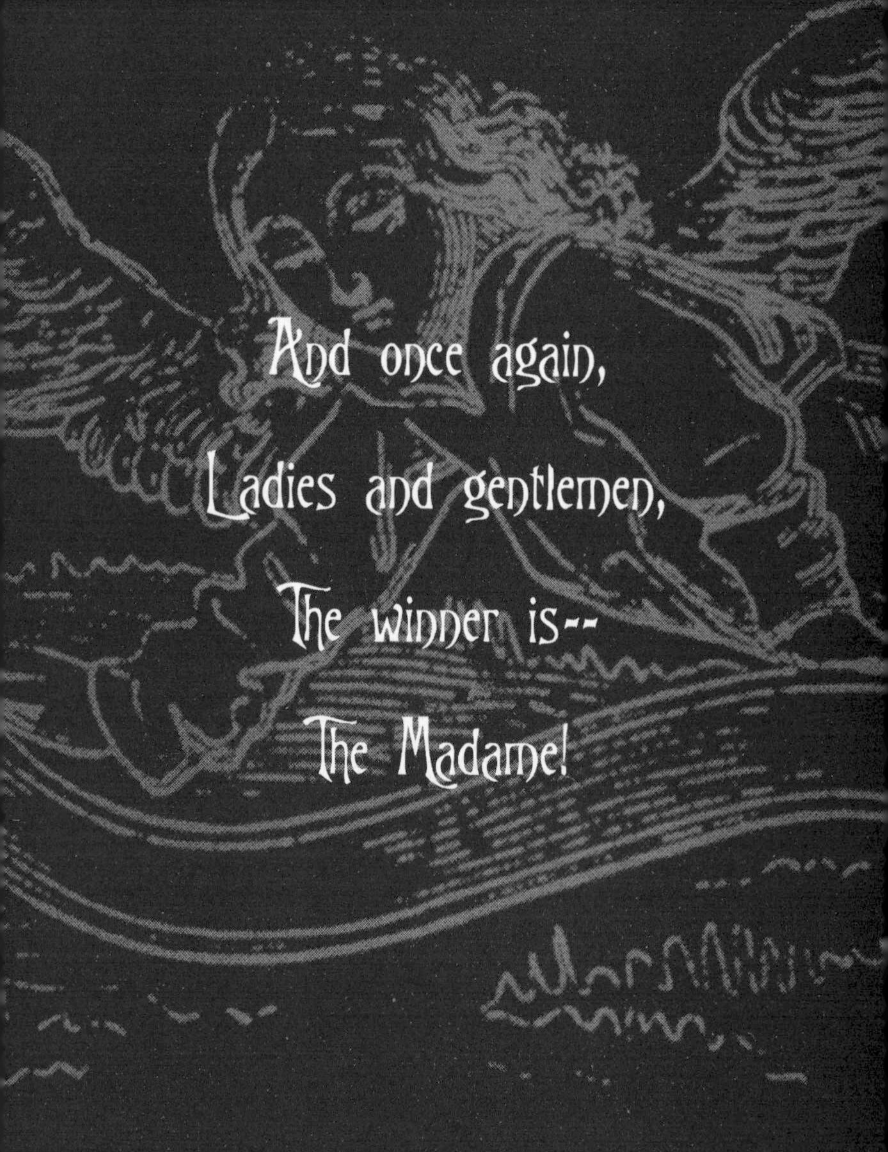
And once again,
Ladies and gentlemen,
The winner is--
--The Madame!

ＺＡＺＡの仮面舞踏会編

19th SHOT - ZAZA'S MASQUERADE

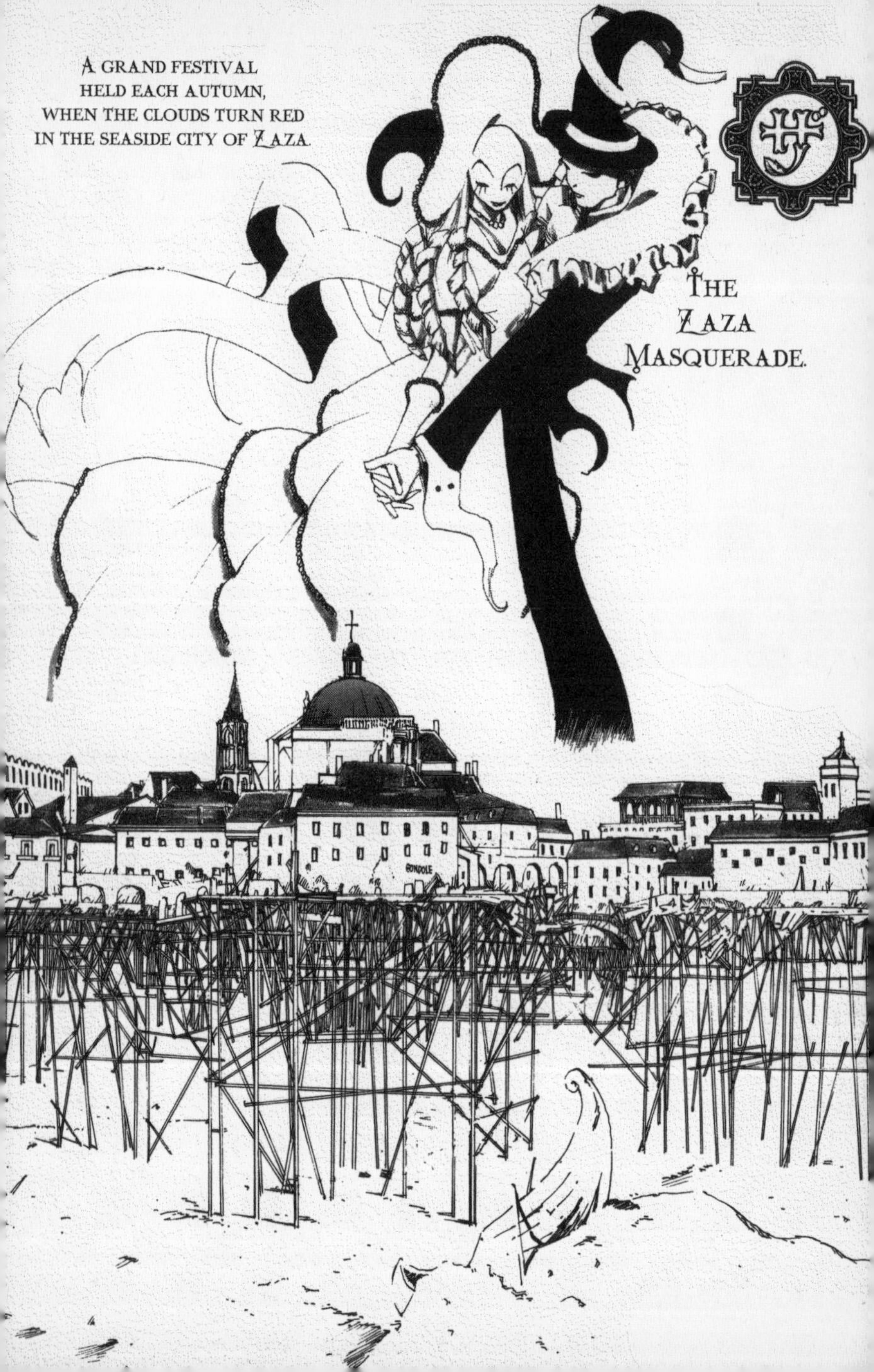
A GRAND FESTIVAL HELD EACH AUTUMN, WHEN THE CLOUDS TURN RED IN THE SEASIDE CITY OF ZAZA.
THE ZAZA MASQUERADE.
GONDOLE

As its name implies, the festival requires each of its over five hundred thousand participants to wear some sort of mask. In fact, one of Zaza's more remote suburbs makes its entire living by trying on masks to be used for this ball. The origin of the masquerade, a term which has come to be understood worldwide as a masked ball, is not certain. However, rumor has it that the practice actually hails from this town's original philosophy of fellowship: that when masks are worn, the distinctions of race and social standing are eliminated. Ironically enough, the festival has today become synonymous with spectacle. The city's labyrinth-like streets now overflow each year with the exchange of ornate masks and fantastic jewels with which festival participants may adorn themselves to vie for the distinction of most splendid, a competition that is becoming increasingly common...

— From A Moveable Feast Guide, Parabola Knights Edition

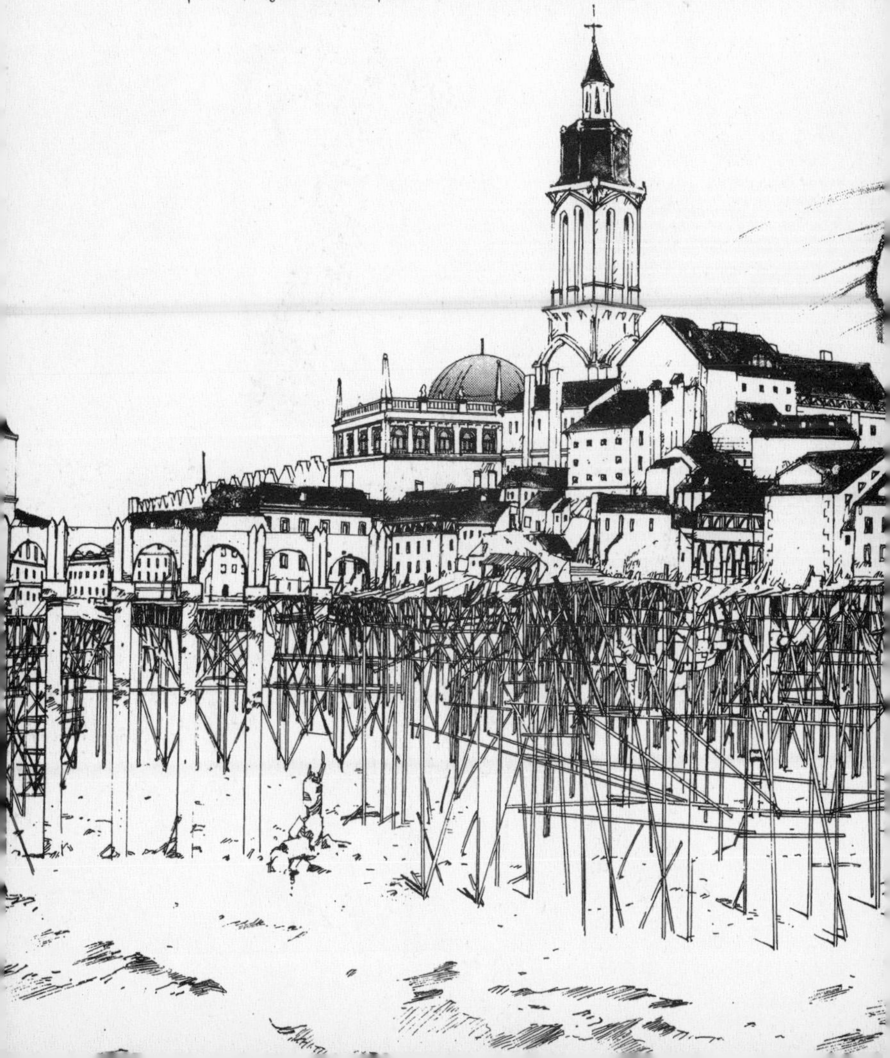

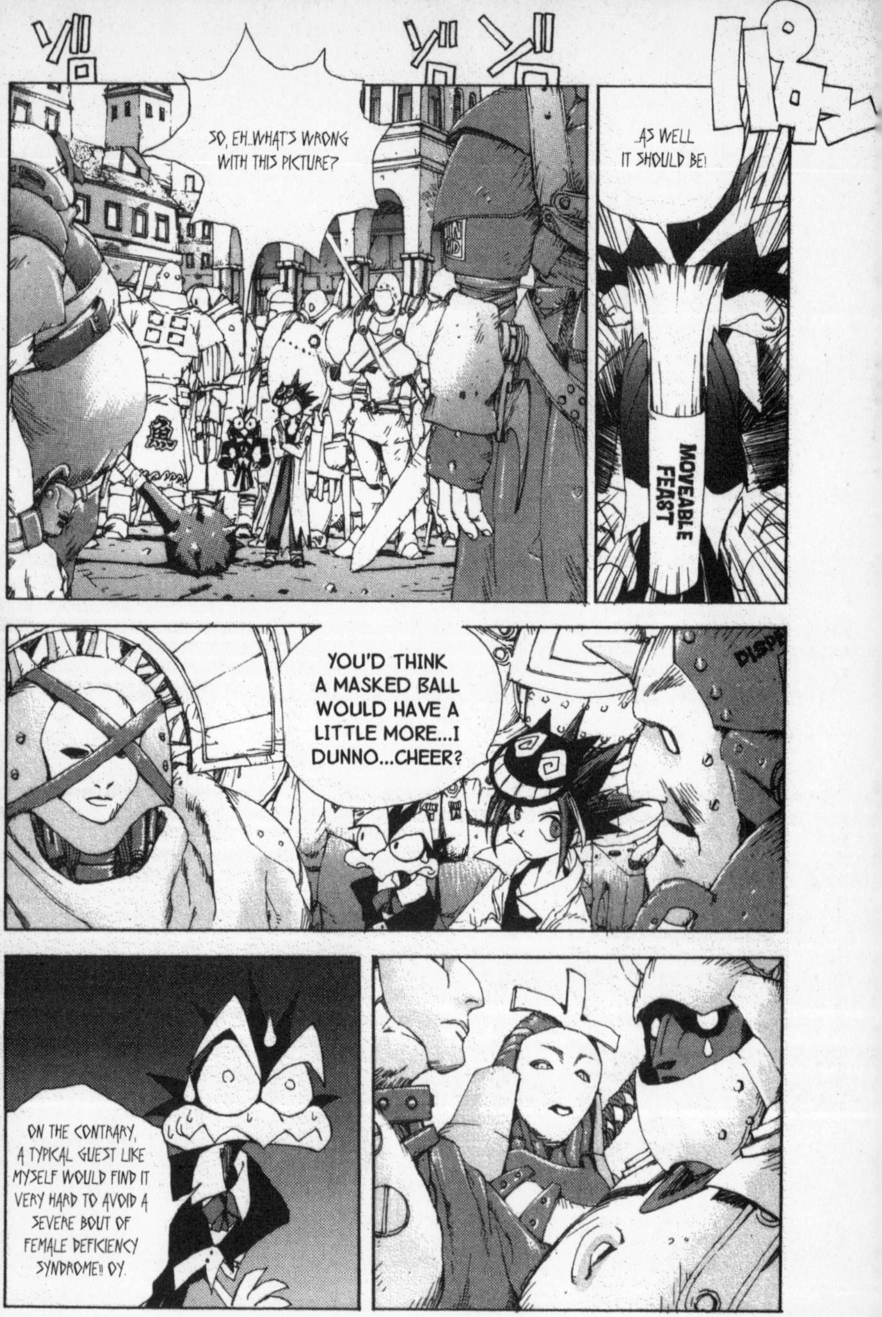
...AS WELL IT SHOULD BE!
MOVEABLE FEAST
SO, EH...WHAT'S WRONG WITH THIS PICTURE?
YOU'D THINK A MASKED BALL WOULD HAVE A LITTLE MORE...I DUNNO...CHEER?
ON THE CONTRARY, A TYPICAL GUEST LIKE MYSELF WOULD FIND IT VERY HARD TO AVOID A SEVERE BOUT OF FEMALE DEFICIENCY SYNDROME!! OY.

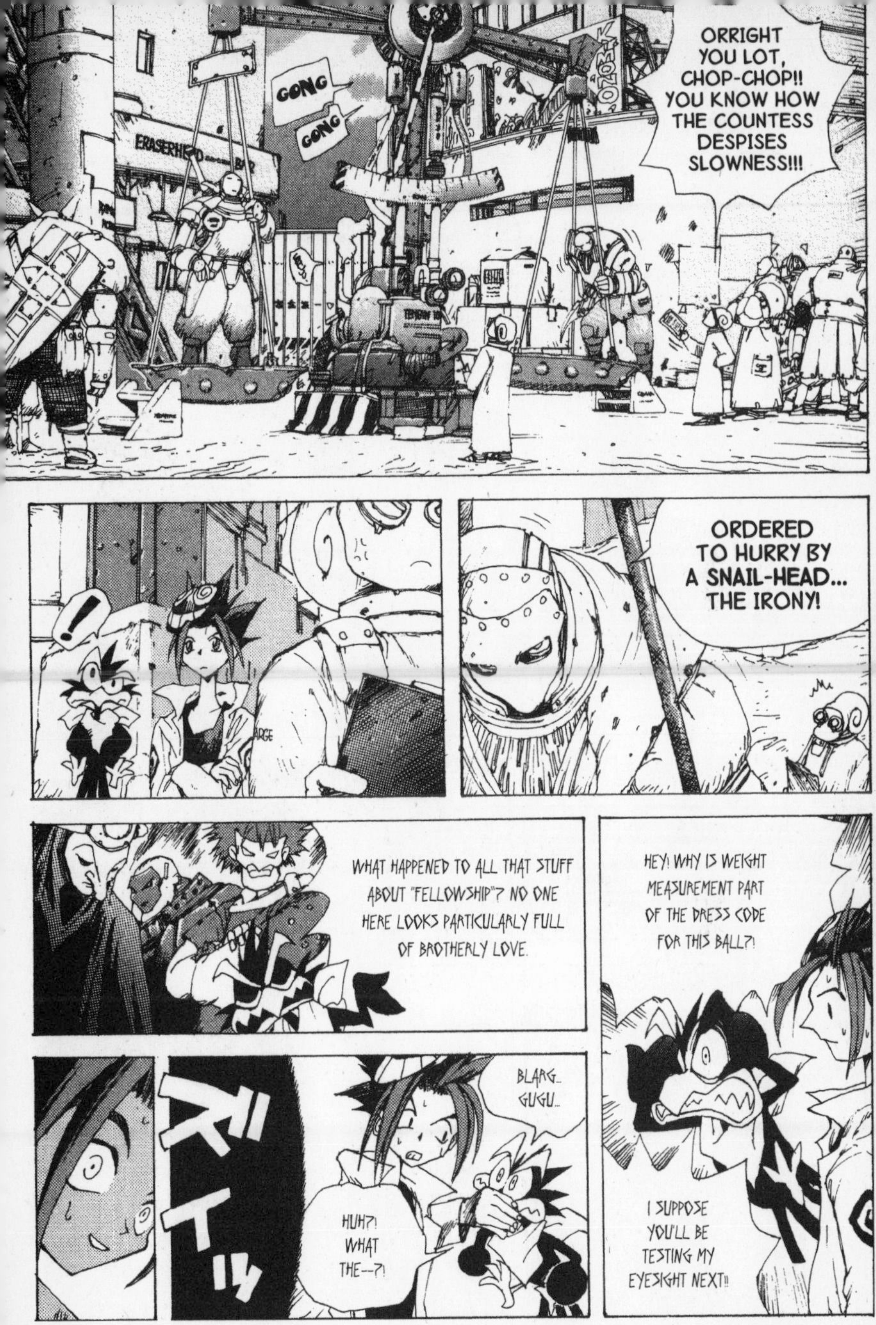
GONG
GONG
ORRIGHT YOU LOT, CHOP-CHOP!! YOU KNOW HOW THE COUNTESS DESPISES SLOWNESS!!!
ORDERED TO HURRY BY A SNAIL-HEAD... THE IRONY!
!
HEY! WHY IS WEIGHT MEASUREMENT PART OF THE DRESS CODE FOR THIS BALL?!
I SUPPOSE YOU'LL BE TESTING MY EYESIGHT NEXT!!
WHAT HAPPENED TO ALL THAT STUFF ABOUT "FELLOWSHIP"? NO ONE HERE LOOKS PARTICULARLY FULL OF BROTHERLY LOVE.
BLARG.. GUGU..
HUH?! WHAT THE--?!

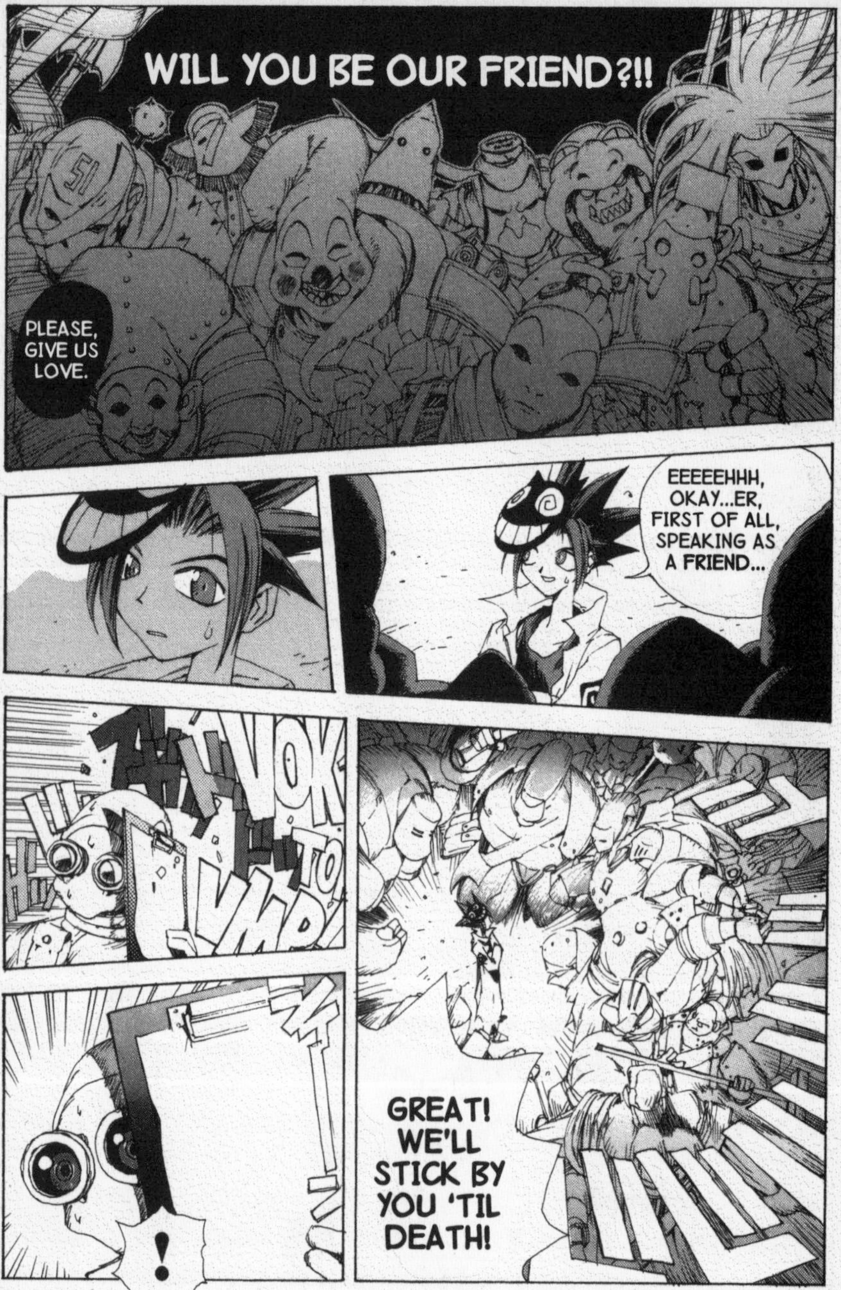
WILL YOU BE OUR FRIEND?!!
PLEASE, GIVE US LOVE.
EEEEEHHH, OKAY...ER, FIRST OF ALL, SPEAKING AS A FRIEND...
GREAT! WE'LL STICK BY YOU 'TIL DEATH!
!

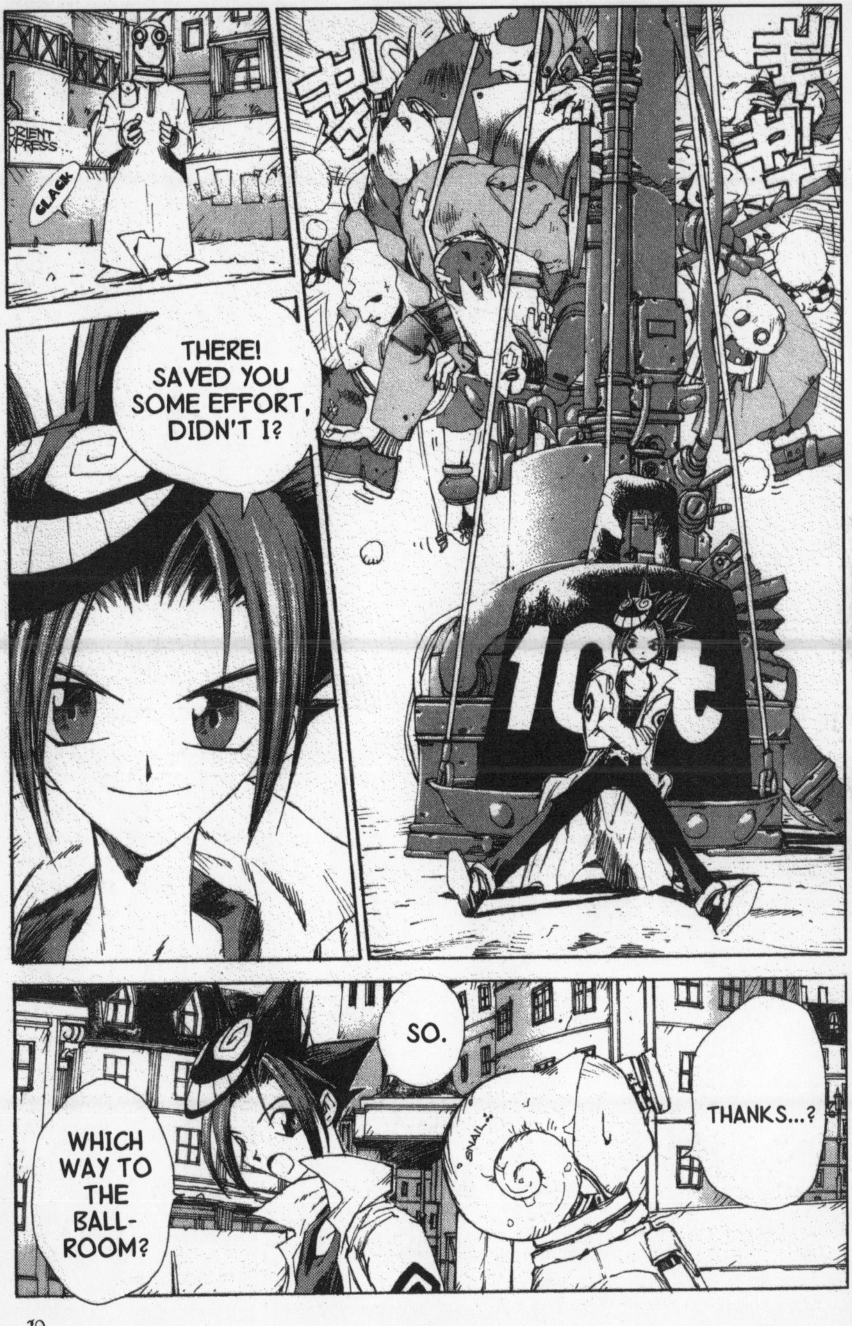
10t
ORIENT EXPRESS...
CLACK
THERE! SAVED YOU SOME EFFORT, DIDN'T I?
THANKS...?
SNAIL
SO.
WHICH WAY TO THE BALL-ROOM?

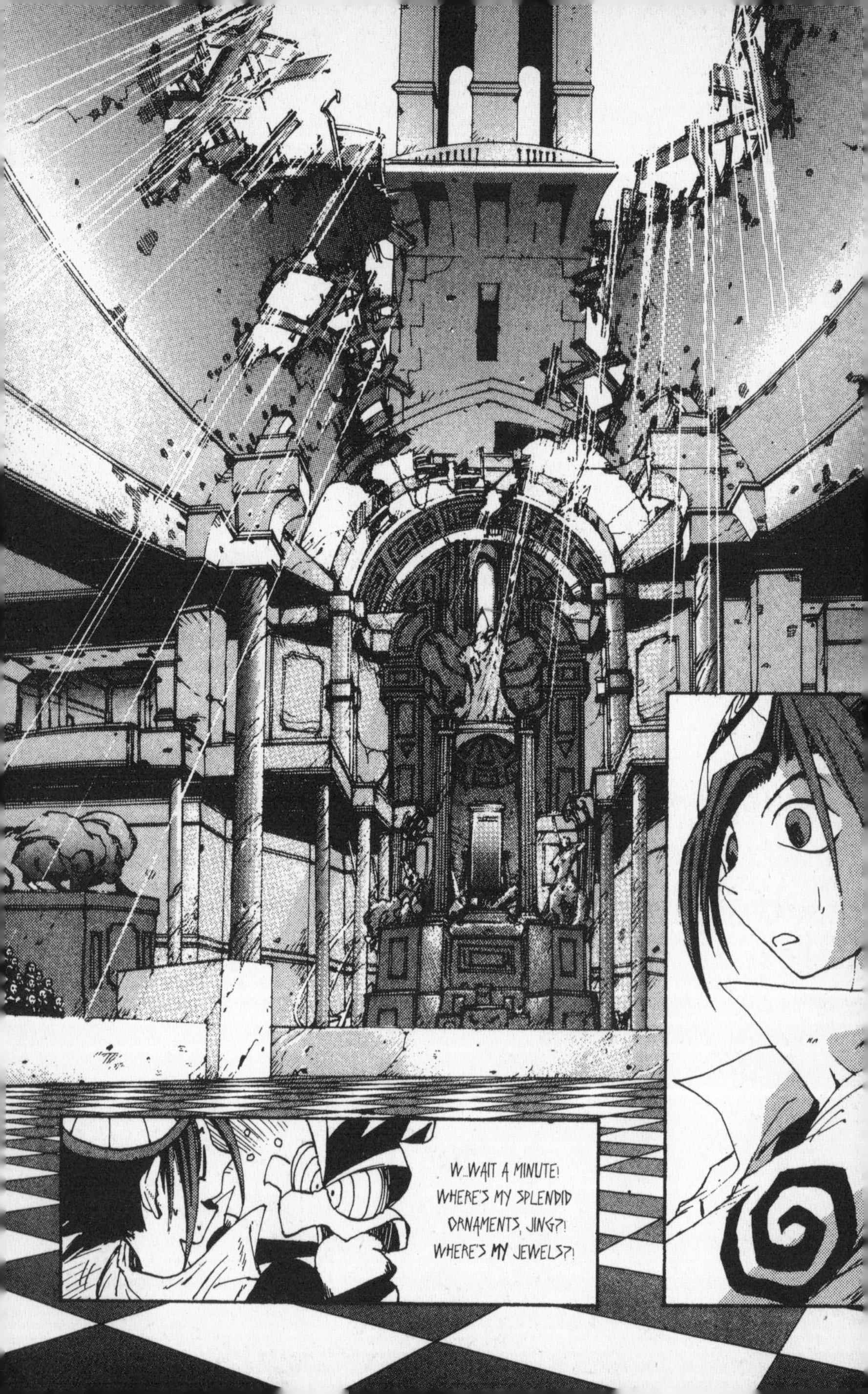
W...WAIT A MINUTE! WHERE'S MY SPLENDID ORNAMENTS, JING?! WHERE'S MY JEWELS?!

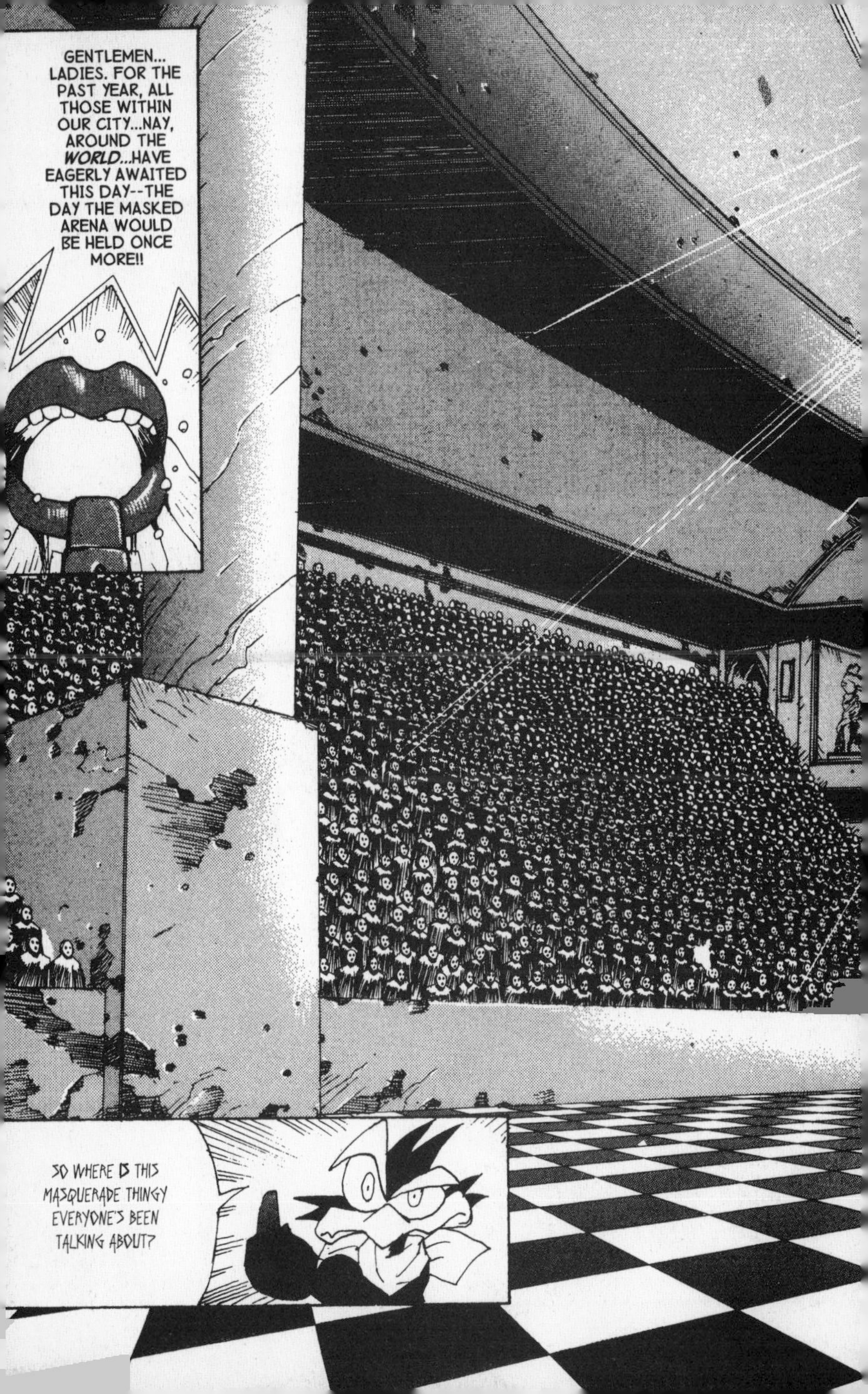
GENTLEMEN... LADIES. FOR THE PAST YEAR, ALL THOSE WITHIN OUR CITY...NAY, AROUND THE *WORLD*...HAVE EAGERLY AWAITED THIS DAY--THE DAY THE MASKED ARENA WOULD BE HELD ONCE MORE!!
SO WHERE IS THIS MASQUERADE THINGY EVERYONE'S BEEN TALKING ABOUT?

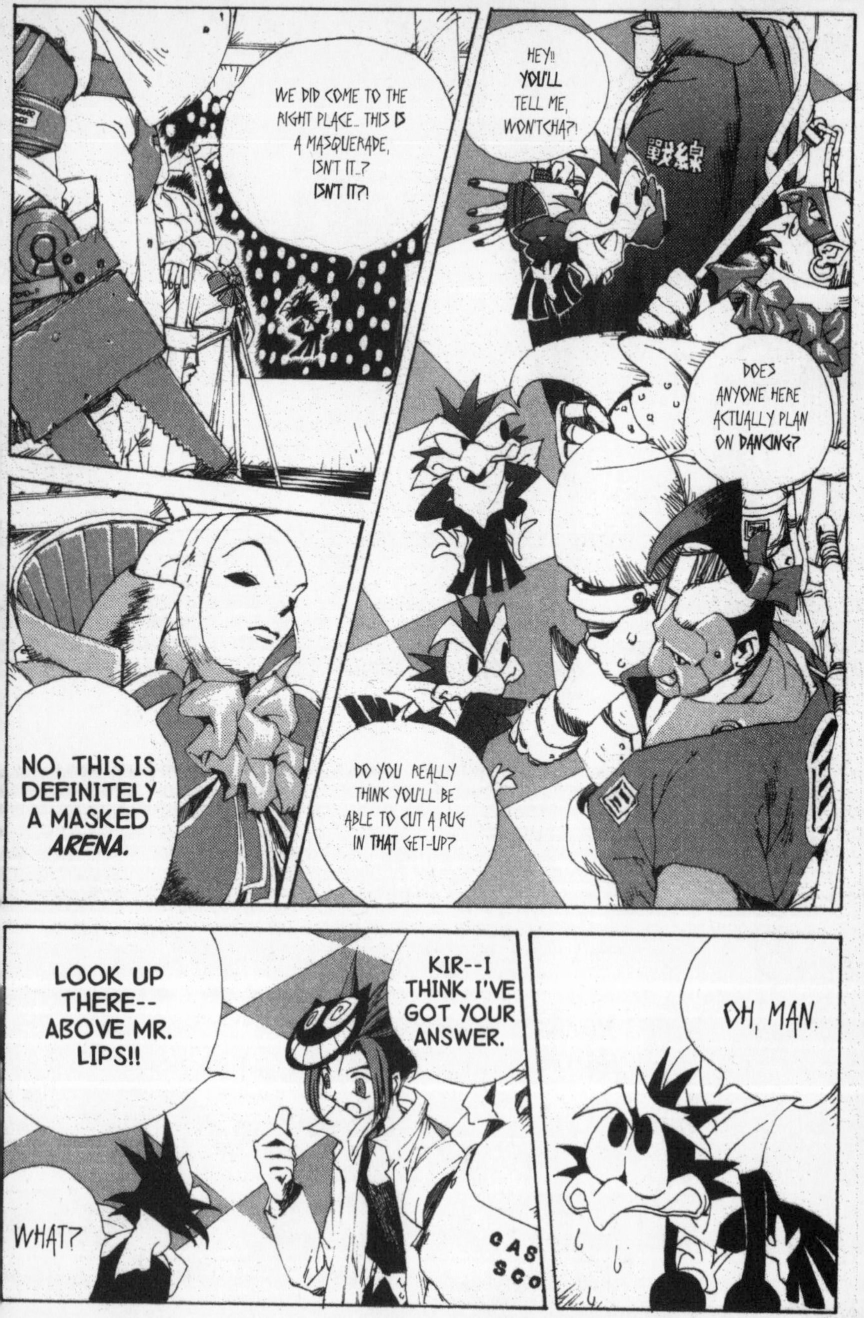
HEY!! YOU'LL TELL ME, WON'TCHA?!
DOES ANYONE HERE ACTUALLY PLAN ON DANCING?
DO YOU REALLY THINK YOU'LL BE ABLE TO CUT A RUG IN THAT GET-UP?
WE DID COME TO THE RIGHT PLACE... THIS IS A MASQUERADE, ISN'T IT...? ISN'T IT?!
NO, THIS IS DEFINITELY A MASKED ARENA.
OH, MAN.
KIR--I THINK I'VE GOT YOUR ANSWER.
LOOK UP THERE-- ABOVE MR. LIPS!!
WHAT?

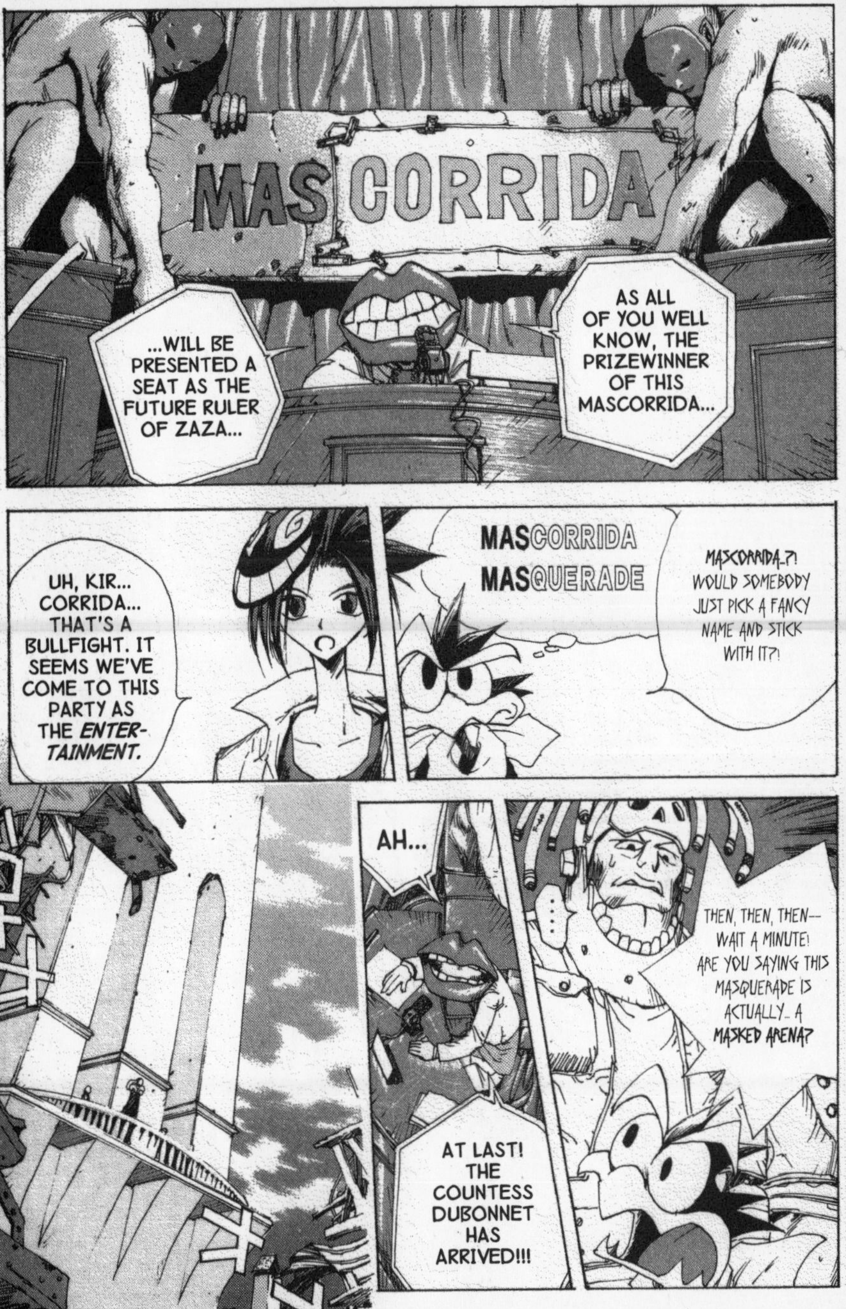
MAS CORRIDA
AS ALL OF YOU WELL KNOW, THE PRIZEWINNER OF THIS MASCORRIDA...
...WILL BE PRESENTED A SEAT AS THE FUTURE RULER OF ZAZA...
MASCORRIDA..?! WOULD SOMEBODY JUST PICK A FANCY NAME AND STICK WITH IT?!
MASCORRIDA
MASQUERADE
UH, KIR... CORRIDA... THAT'S A BULLFIGHT. IT SEEMS WE'VE COME TO THIS PARTY AS THE *ENTERTAINMENT*.
THEN, THEN, THEN-- WAIT A MINUTE! ARE YOU SAYING THIS MASQUERADE IS ACTUALLY... A **MASKED ARENA?**
AT LAST! THE COUNTESS DUBONNET HAS ARRIVED!!!
AH...

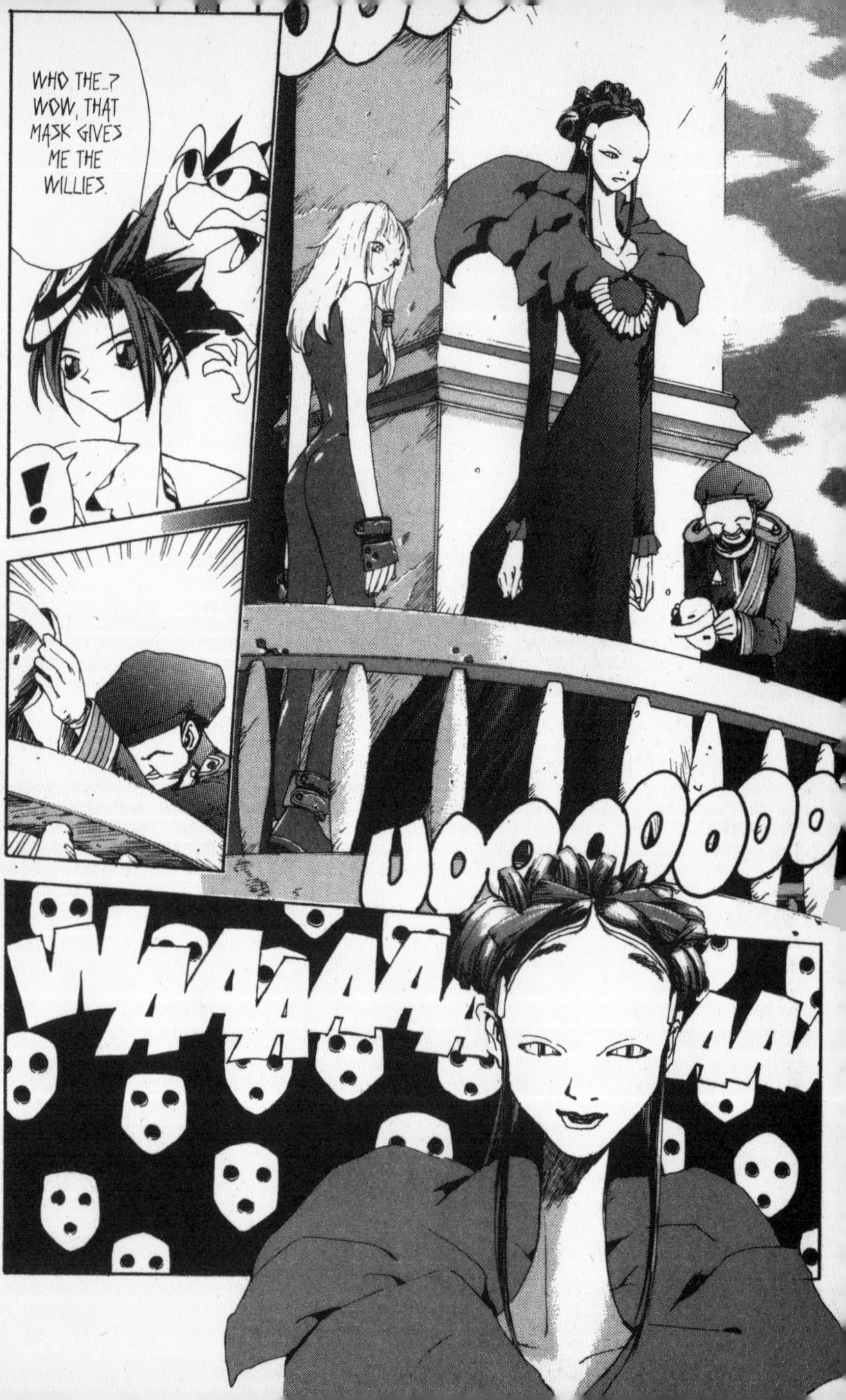
WHO THE...? WOW, THAT MASK GIVES ME THE WILLIES.
!
UOOOOOOO
WAAAAAAAA

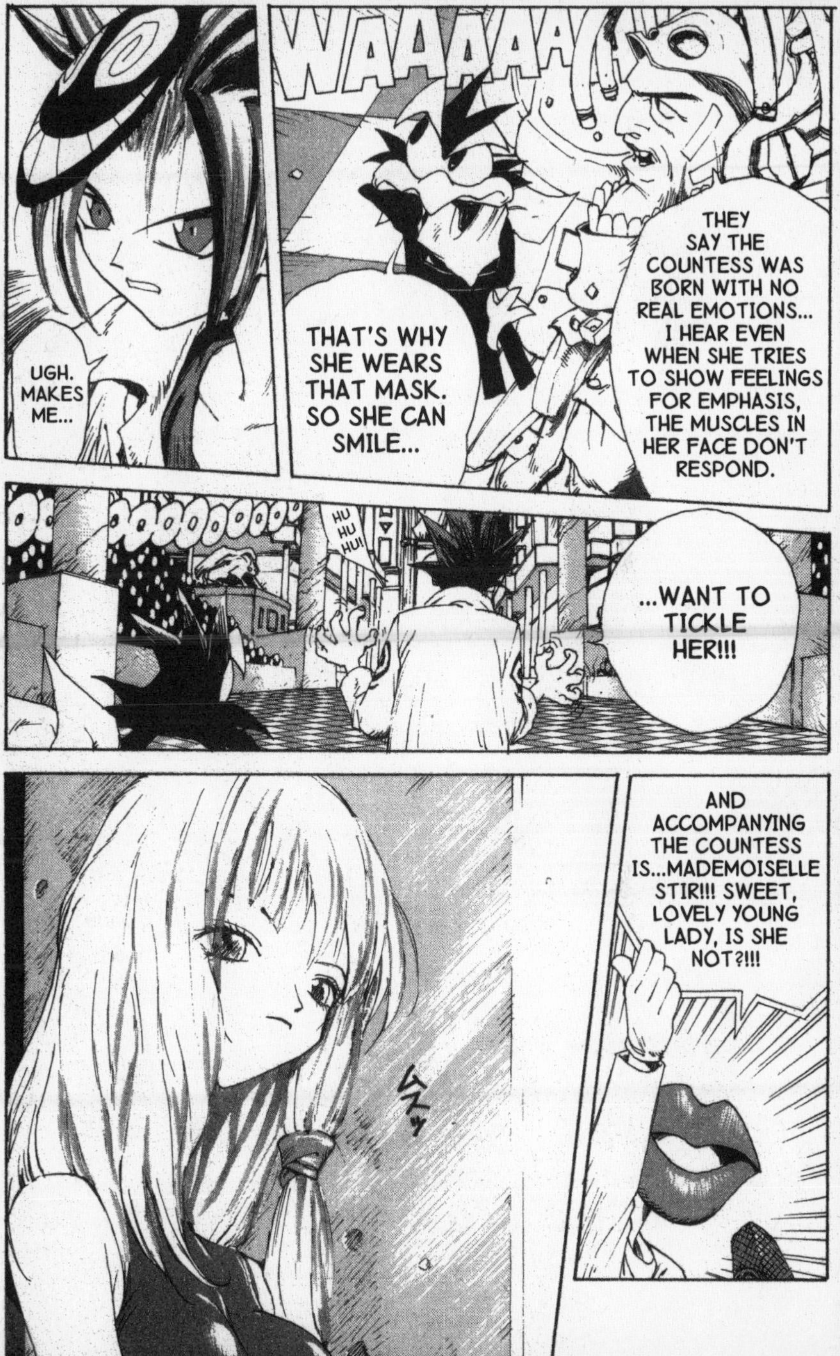

WAAAAA
THEY SAY THE COUNTESS WAS BORN WITH NO REAL EMOTIONS... I HEAR EVEN WHEN SHE TRIES TO SHOW FEELINGS FOR EMPHASIS, THE MUSCLES IN HER FACE DON'T RESPOND.
THAT'S WHY SHE WEARS THAT MASK. SO SHE CAN SMILE...
UGH. MAKES ME...
...WANT TO TICKLE HER!!!
HU HU HU!
AND ACCOMPANYING THE COUNTESS IS...MADEMOISELLE STIR!!! SWEET, LOVELY YOUNG LADY, IS SHE NOT?!!!

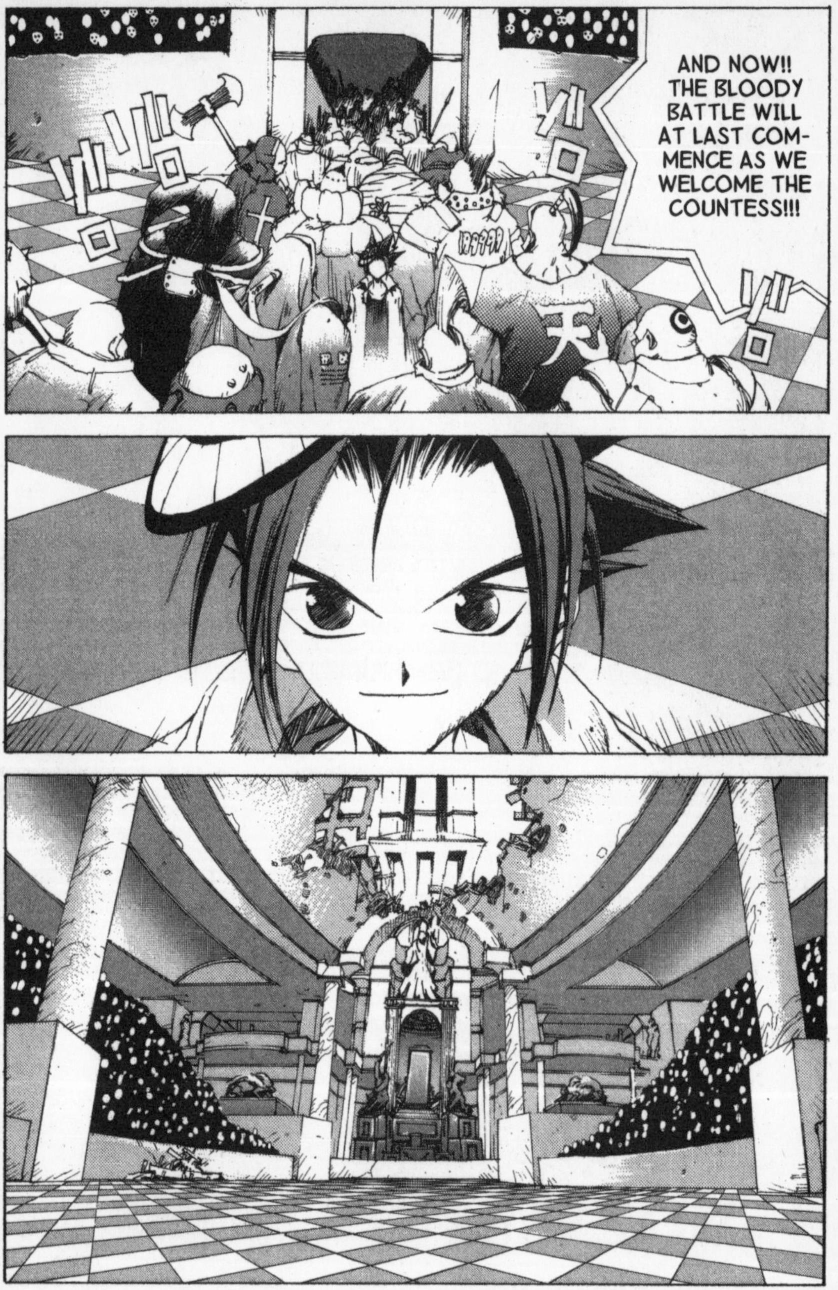
AND NOW!! THE BLOODY BATTLE WILL AT LAST COMMENCE AS WE WELCOME THE COUNTESS!!!

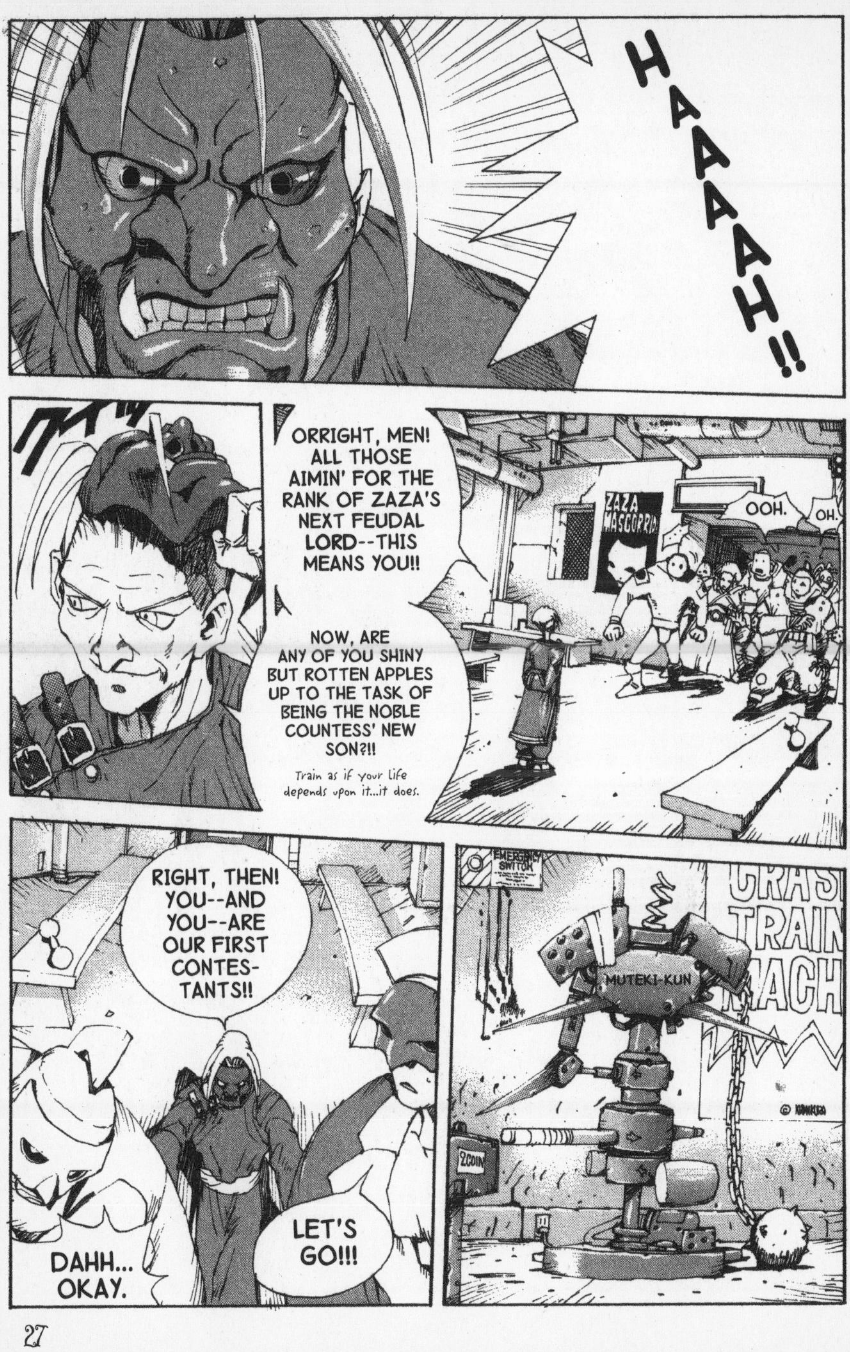
HAAAAAH!!
OH.
OOH.
ORRIGHT, MEN! ALL THOSE AIMIN' FOR THE RANK OF ZAZA'S NEXT FEUDAL LORD--THIS MEANS YOU!!
NOW, ARE ANY OF YOU SHINY BUT ROTTEN APPLES UP TO THE TASK OF BEING THE NOBLE COUNTESS' NEW SON?!!
Train as if your life depends upon it...it does.
ZAZA MASCORRID
EMERGENCY SWITCH
MUTEKI-KUN
2COIN
RIGHT, THEN! YOU--AND YOU--ARE OUR FIRST CONTES-TANTS!!
LET'S GO!!!
DAHH... OKAY.

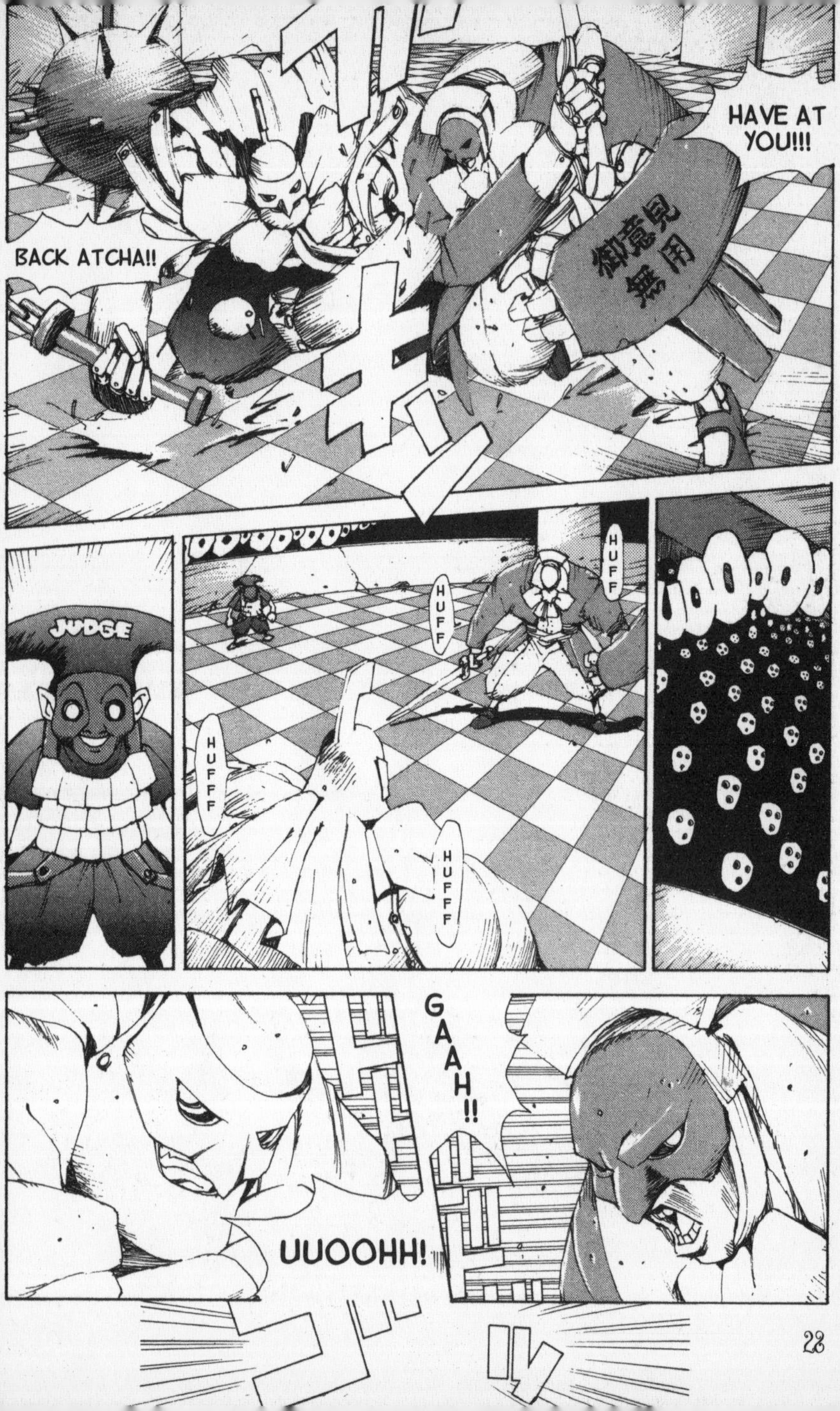
HAVE AT YOU!!!
御意見無用
BACK ATCHA!!
UOOOOO
HUFF
HUFF
HUFFF
HUFFF
JUDGE
GAAH!!
UUOOHH!

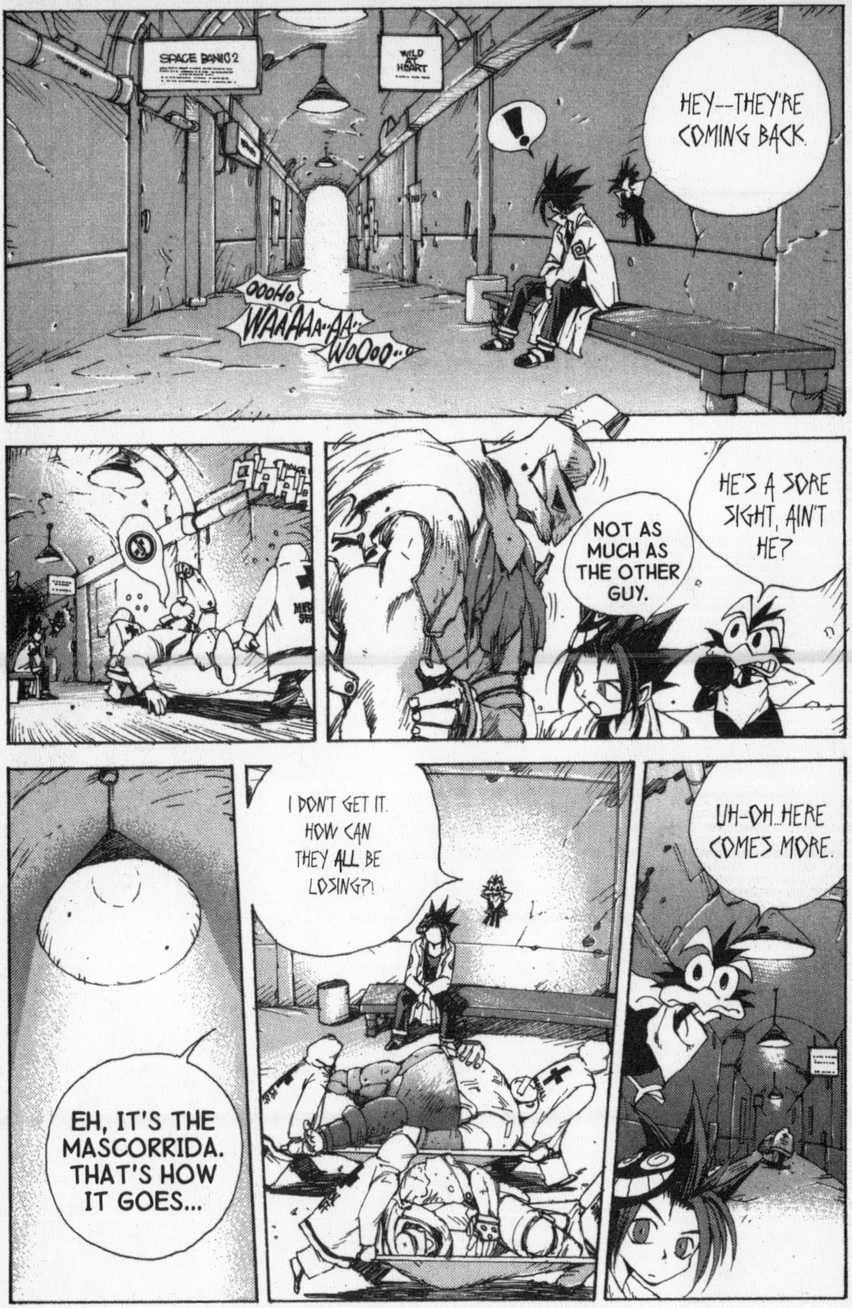
HEY--THEY'RE COMING BACK.
WILD AT HEART
SPACE BANIC 2
!
OOOHO
WAAAAA..AA..
WOOOO..
HE'S A SORE SIGHT, AIN'T HE?
NOT AS MUCH AS THE OTHER GUY.
UH-OH...HERE COMES MORE.
I DON'T GET IT. HOW CAN THEY ALL BE LOSING?!
EH, IT'S THE MASCORRIDA. THAT'S HOW IT GOES...

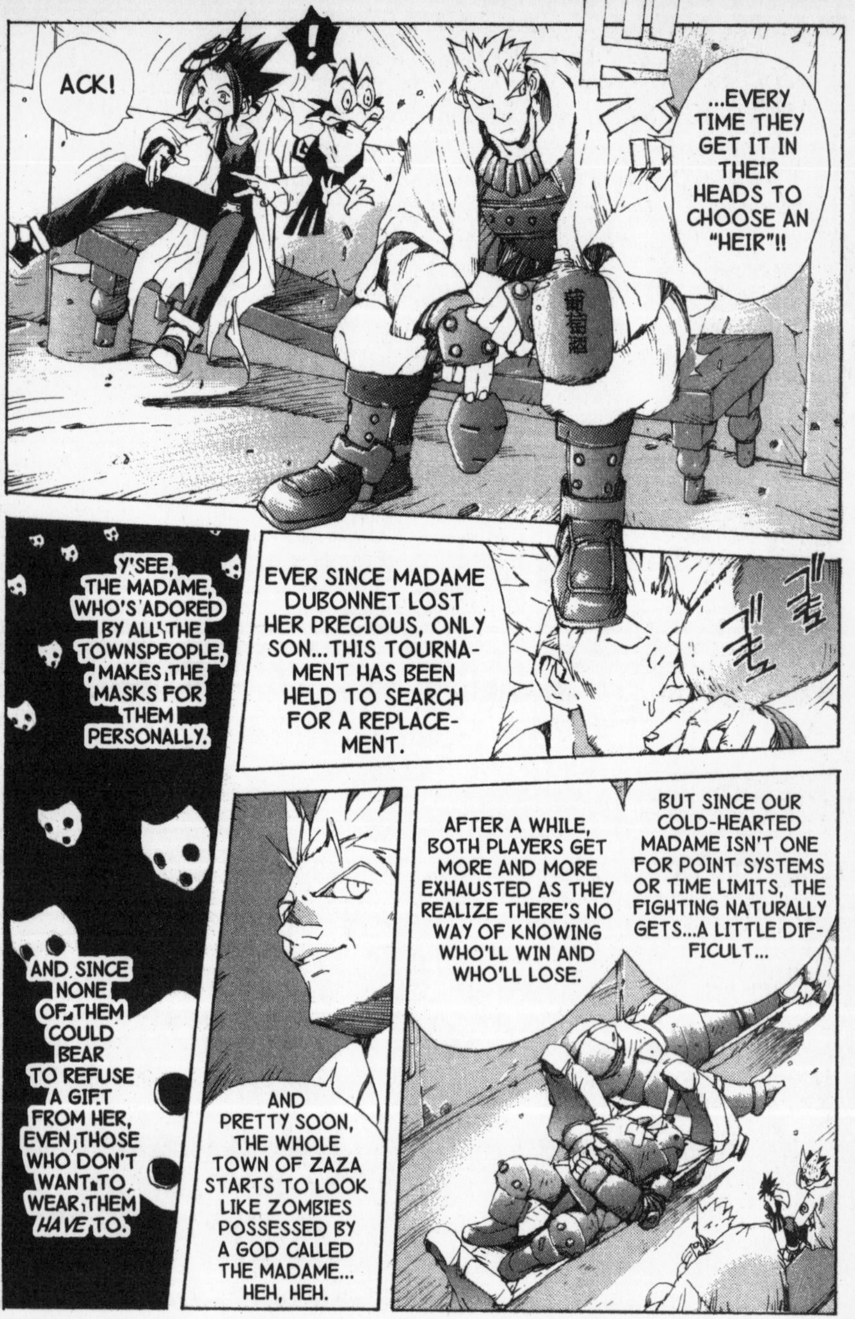
...EVERY TIME THEY GET IT IN THEIR HEADS TO CHOOSE AN "HEIR"!!
ACK!
EVER SINCE MADAME DUBONNET LOST HER PRECIOUS, ONLY SON...THIS TOURNAMENT HAS BEEN HELD TO SEARCH FOR A REPLACEMENT.
BUT SINCE OUR COLD-HEARTED MADAME ISN'T ONE FOR POINT SYSTEMS OR TIME LIMITS, THE FIGHTING NATURALLY GETS...A LITTLE DIFFICULT...
AFTER A WHILE, BOTH PLAYERS GET MORE AND MORE EXHAUSTED AS THEY REALIZE THERE'S NO WAY OF KNOWING WHO'LL WIN AND WHO'LL LOSE.
AND PRETTY SOON, THE WHOLE TOWN OF ZAZA STARTS TO LOOK LIKE ZOMBIES POSSESSED BY A GOD CALLED THE MADAME... HEH, HEH.
Y'SEE, THE MADAME, WHO'S ADORED BY ALL THE TOWNSPEOPLE, MAKES THE MASKS FOR THEM PERSONALLY.
AND SINCE NONE OF THEM COULD BEAR TO REFUSE A GIFT FROM HER, EVEN THOSE WHO DON'T WANT TO WEAR THEM *HAVE* TO.

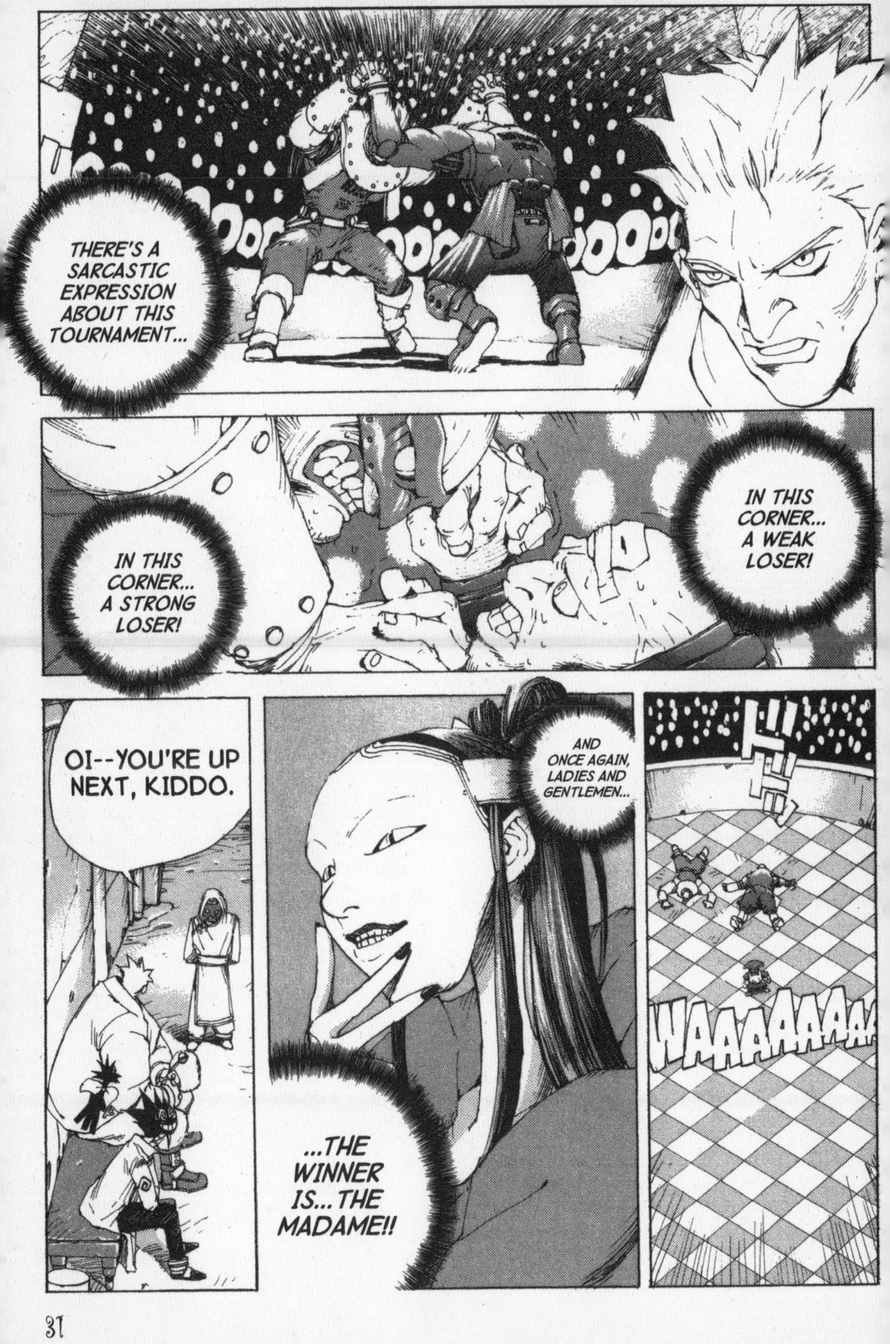
THERE'S A SARCASTIC EXPRESSION ABOUT THIS TOURNAMENT...
IN THIS CORNER... A WEAK LOSER!
IN THIS CORNER... A STRONG LOSER!
WAAAAAAA
AND ONCE AGAIN, LADIES AND GENTLEMEN...
...THE WINNER IS... THE MADAME!!
OI--YOU'RE UP NEXT, KIDDO.

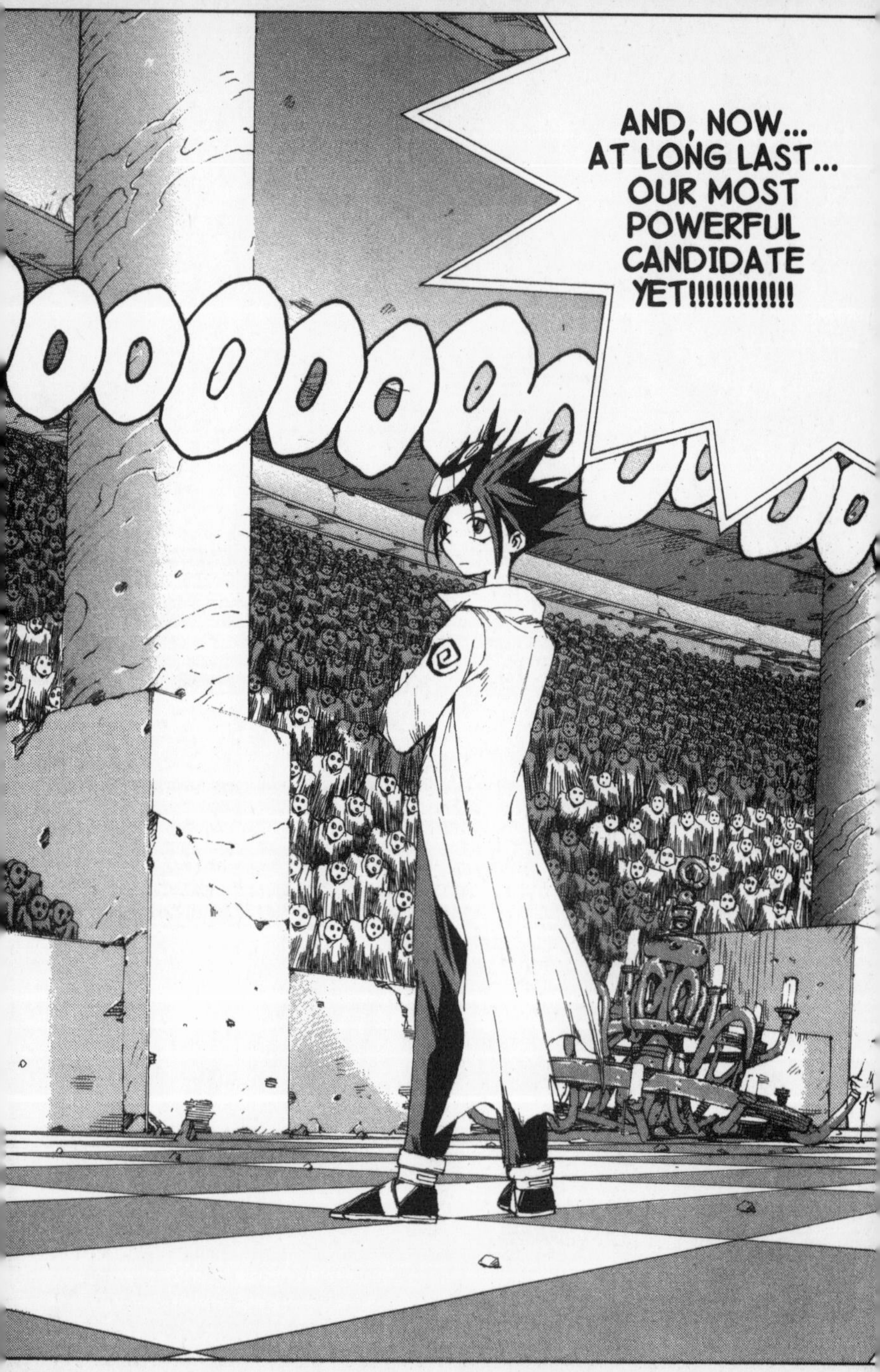
AND, NOW... AT LONG LAST... OUR MOST POWERFUL CANDIDATE YET!!!!!!!!!!!!
OOOOOOOOOOO

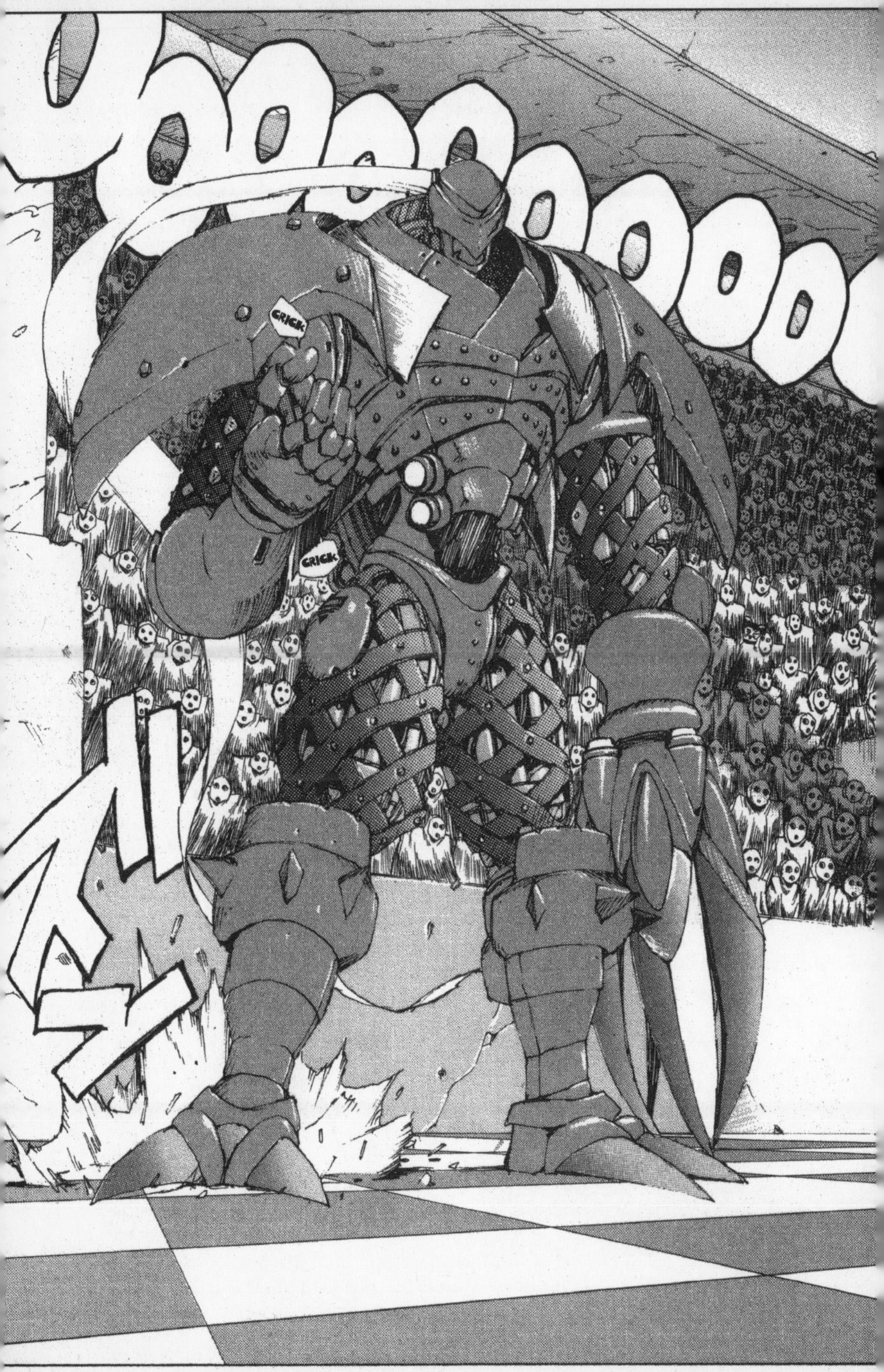
CRICK
CRICK

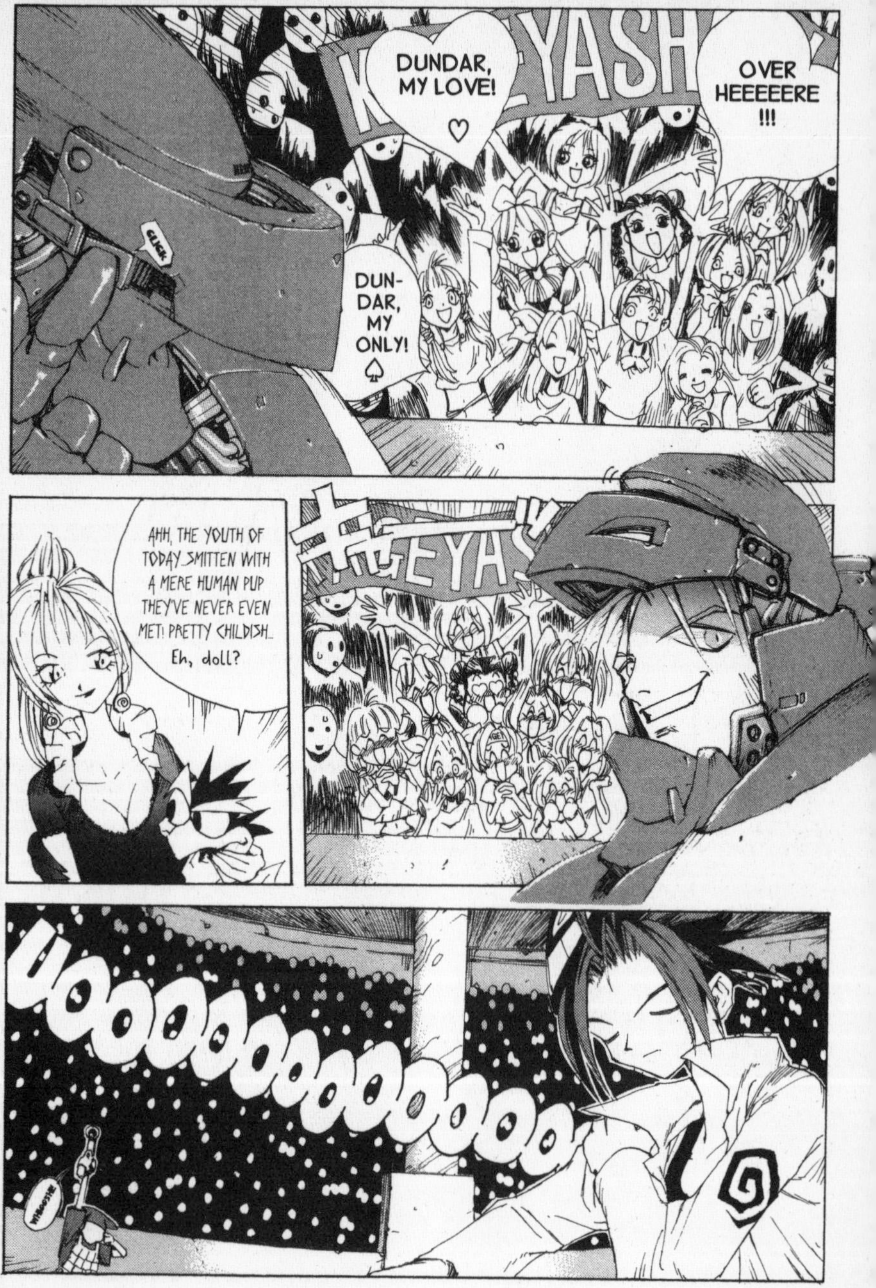
OVER HEEEEERE !!!
DUNDAR, MY LOVE! ♡
DUN-DAR, MY ONLY! ♠
CLICK
AHH, THE YOUTH OF TODAY SMITTEN WITH A MERE HUMAN PUP THEY'VE NEVER EVEN MET! PRETTY CHILDISH... Eh, doll?
UOOOOOOOOOOOOOOOO

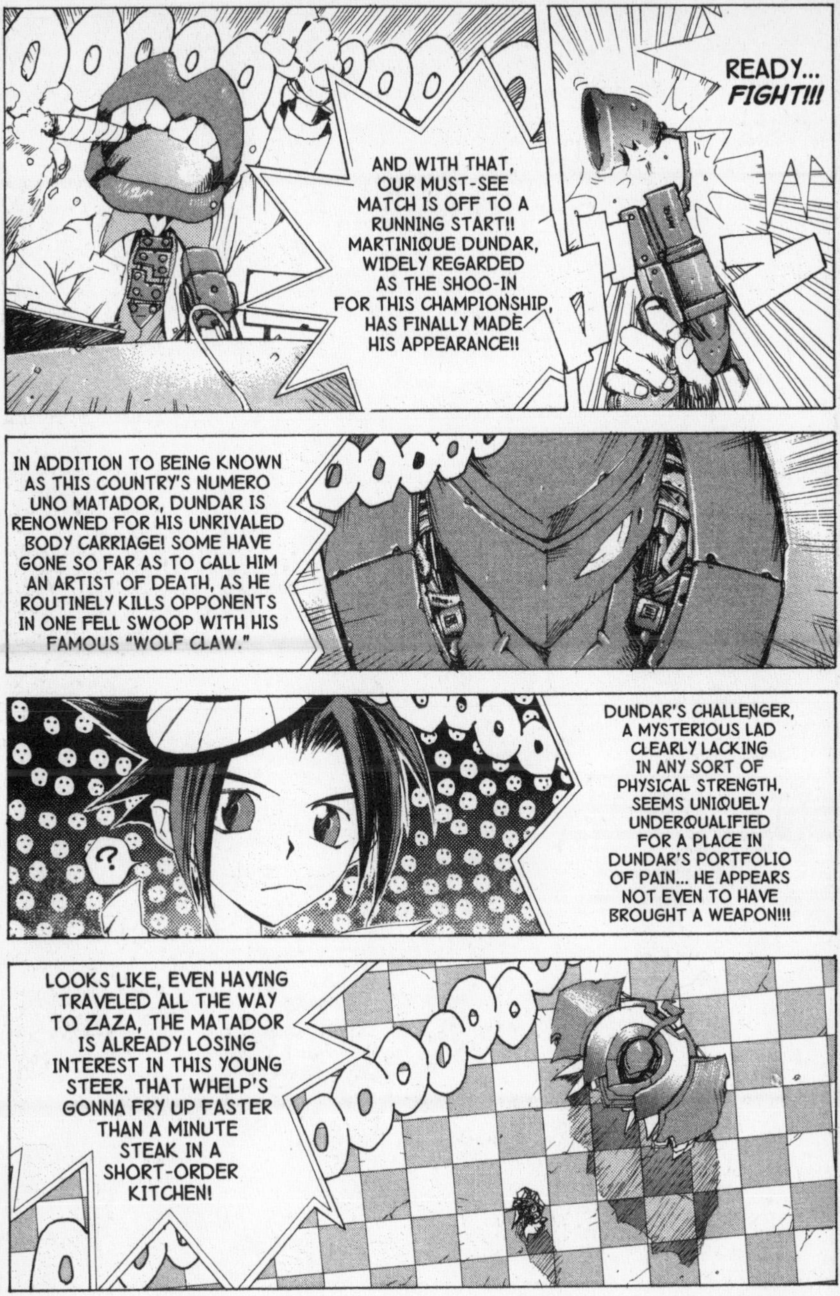
READY... FIGHT!!!
AND WITH THAT, OUR MUST-SEE MATCH IS OFF TO A RUNNING START!! MARTINIQUE DUNDAR, WIDELY REGARDED AS THE SHOO-IN FOR THIS CHAMPIONSHIP, HAS FINALLY MADE HIS APPEARANCE!!
IN ADDITION TO BEING KNOWN AS THIS COUNTRY'S NUMERO UNO MATADOR, DUNDAR IS RENOWNED FOR HIS UNRIVALED BODY CARRIAGE! SOME HAVE GONE SO FAR AS TO CALL HIM AN ARTIST OF DEATH, AS HE ROUTINELY KILLS OPPONENTS IN ONE FELL SWOOP WITH HIS FAMOUS "WOLF CLAW."
DUNDAR'S CHALLENGER, A MYSTERIOUS LAD CLEARLY LACKING IN ANY SORT OF PHYSICAL STRENGTH, SEEMS UNIQUELY UNDERQUALIFIED FOR A PLACE IN DUNDAR'S PORTFOLIO OF PAIN... HE APPEARS NOT EVEN TO HAVE BROUGHT A WEAPON!!!
?
LOOKS LIKE, EVEN HAVING TRAVELED ALL THE WAY TO ZAZA, THE MATADOR IS ALREADY LOSING INTEREST IN THIS YOUNG STEER. THAT WHELP'S GONNA FRY UP FASTER THAN A MINUTE STEAK IN A SHORT-ORDER KITCHEN!

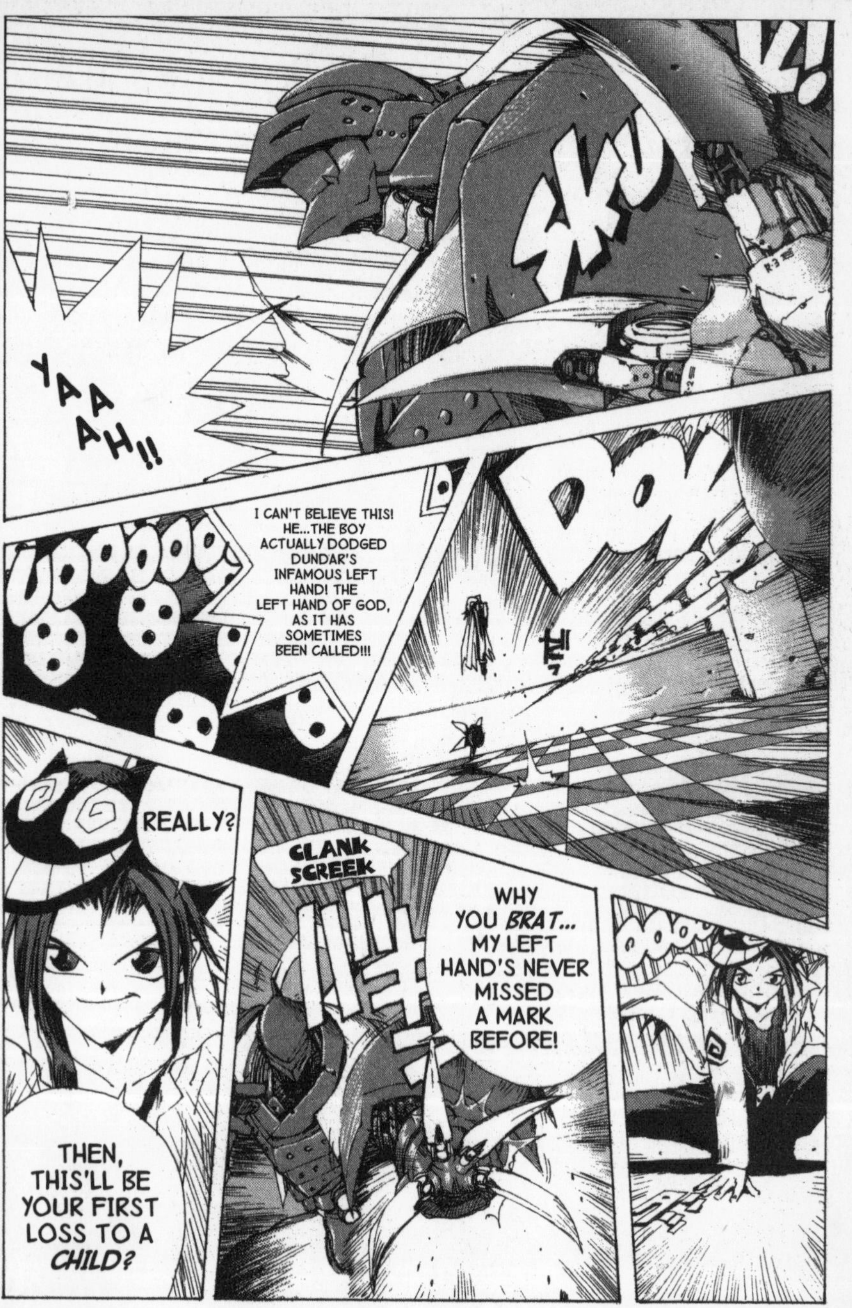

YAAAH!!
I CAN'T BELIEVE THIS! HE...THE BOY ACTUALLY DODGED DUNDAR'S INFAMOUS LEFT HAND! THE LEFT HAND OF GOD, AS IT HAS SOMETIMES BEEN CALLED!!!
CLANK SCREEK
WHY YOU *BRAT*... MY LEFT HAND'S NEVER MISSED A MARK BEFORE!
REALLY?
THEN, THIS'LL BE YOUR FIRST LOSS TO A *CHILD*?

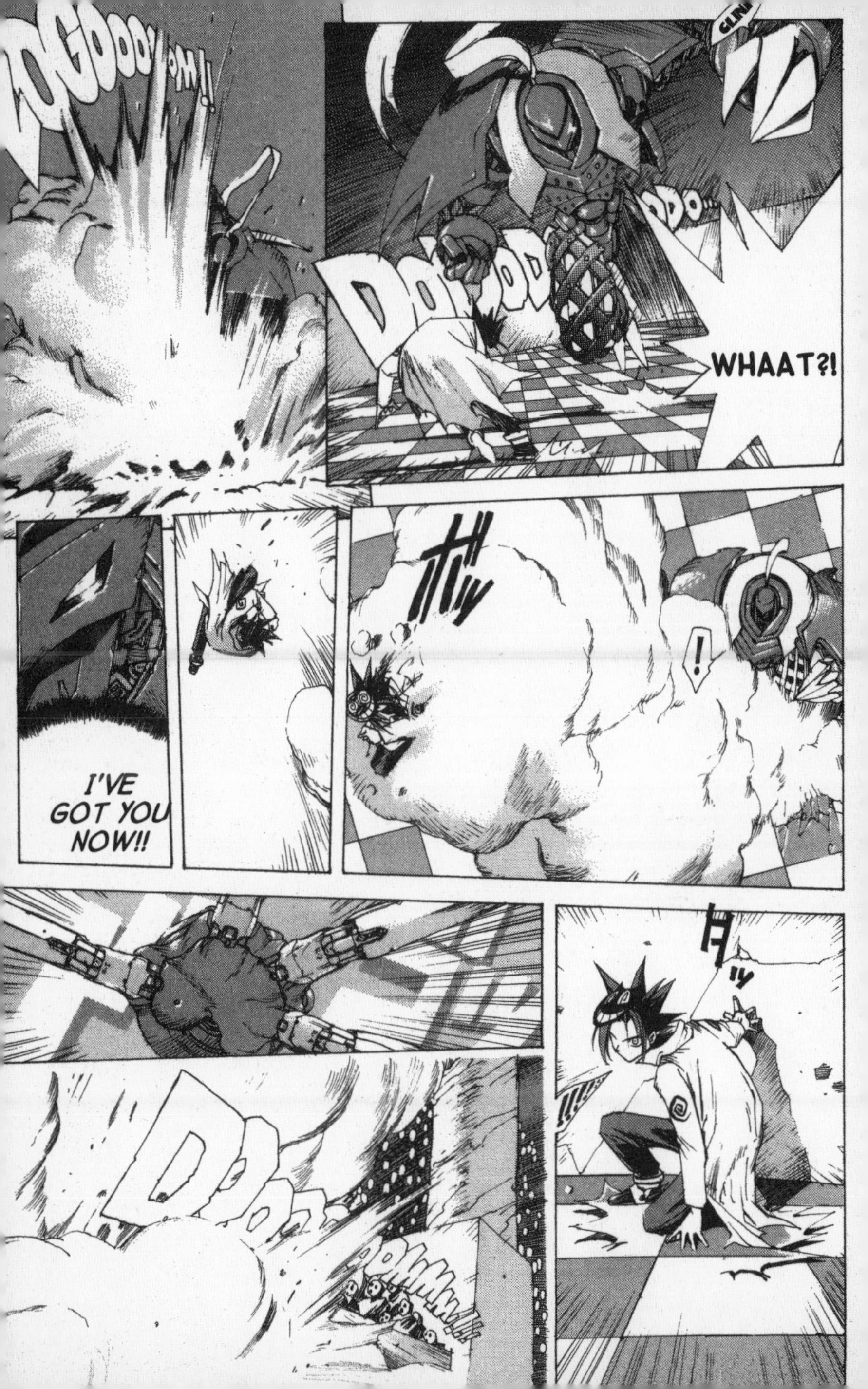
WHAAT?!
I'VE GOT YOU NOW!!
!

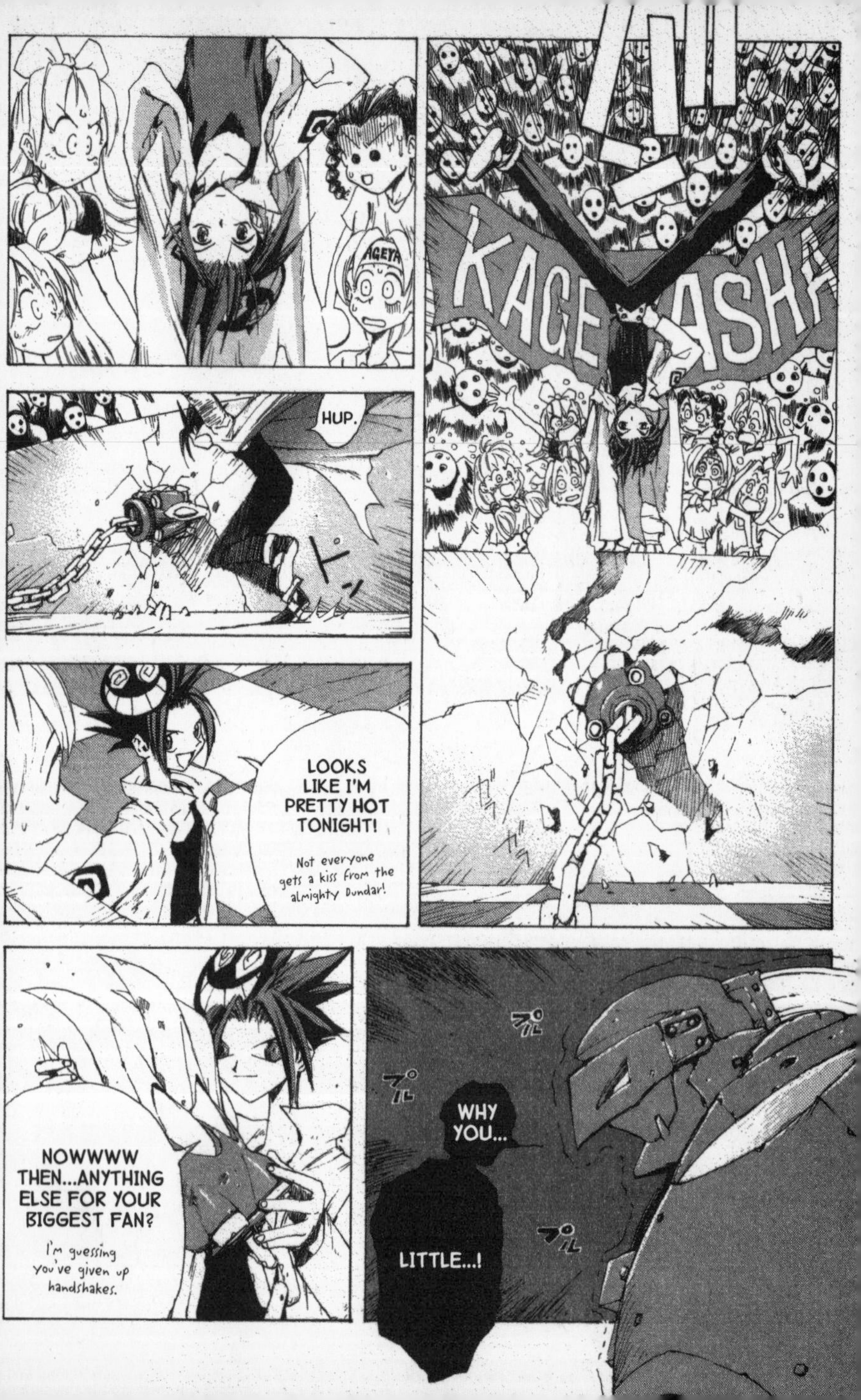
KAGE
ASHA
HUP.
LOOKS LIKE I'M PRETTY HOT TONIGHT!
Not everyone gets a kiss from the almighty Dundar!
WHY YOU...
LITTLE...!
NOWWWW THEN...ANYTHING ELSE FOR YOUR BIGGEST FAN?
I'm guessing you've given up handshakes.

OOH, QUITE AN UNEXPECTED TURN OF EVENTS!! LOOKS LIKE OUR YOUNG LAD HAS DUNDAR WRAPPED AROUND HIS LITTLE FINGER.

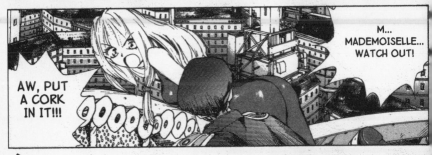

M... MADEMOISELLE... WATCH OUT!

AW, PUT A CORK IN IT!!!

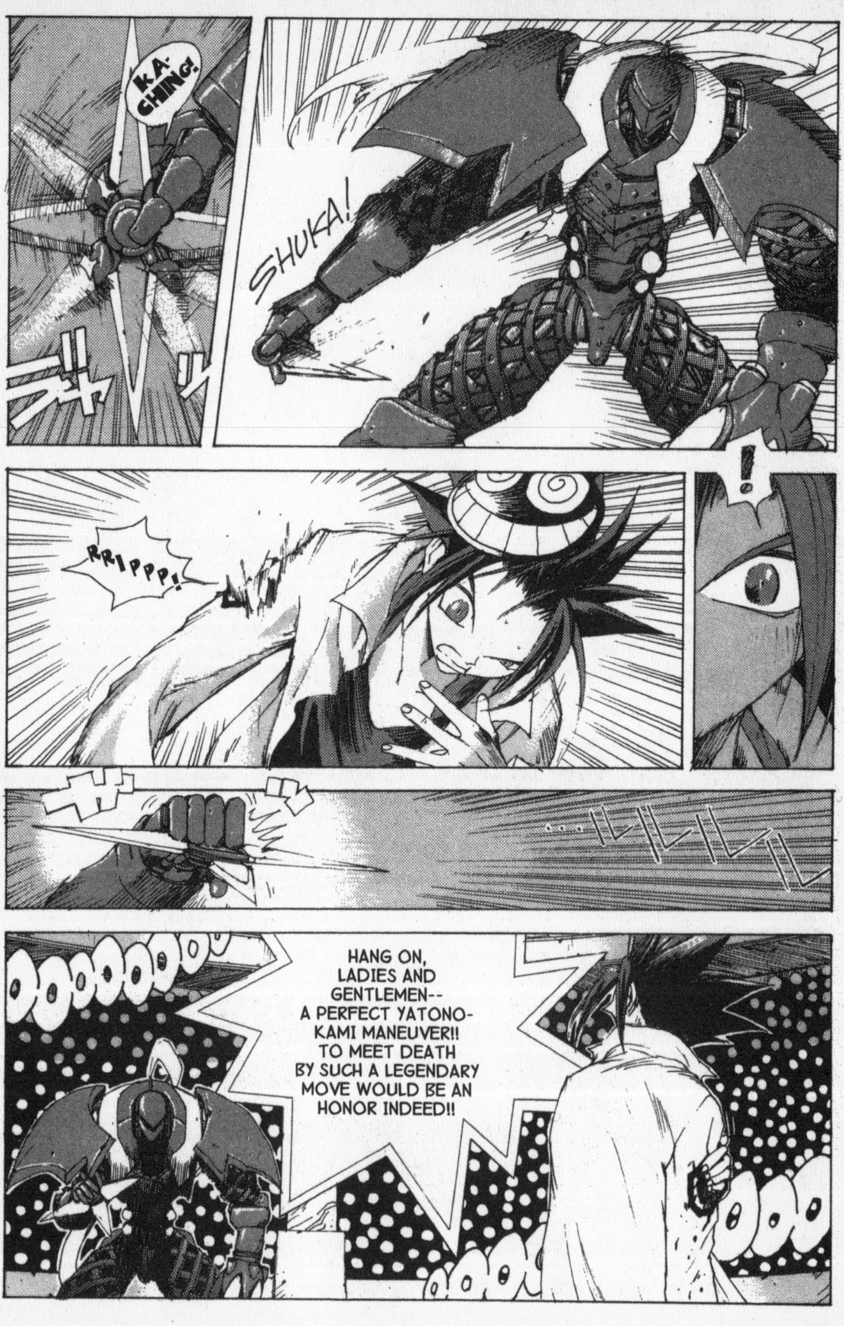
SHUKA!
KA-CHING!
!
RRIPPP!
...
HANG ON, LADIES AND GENTLEMEN-- A PERFECT YATONO-KAMI MANEUVER!! TO MEET DEATH BY SUCH A LEGENDARY MOVE WOULD BE AN HONOR INDEED!!
OOOOOOOOO
OOOOOOOOO

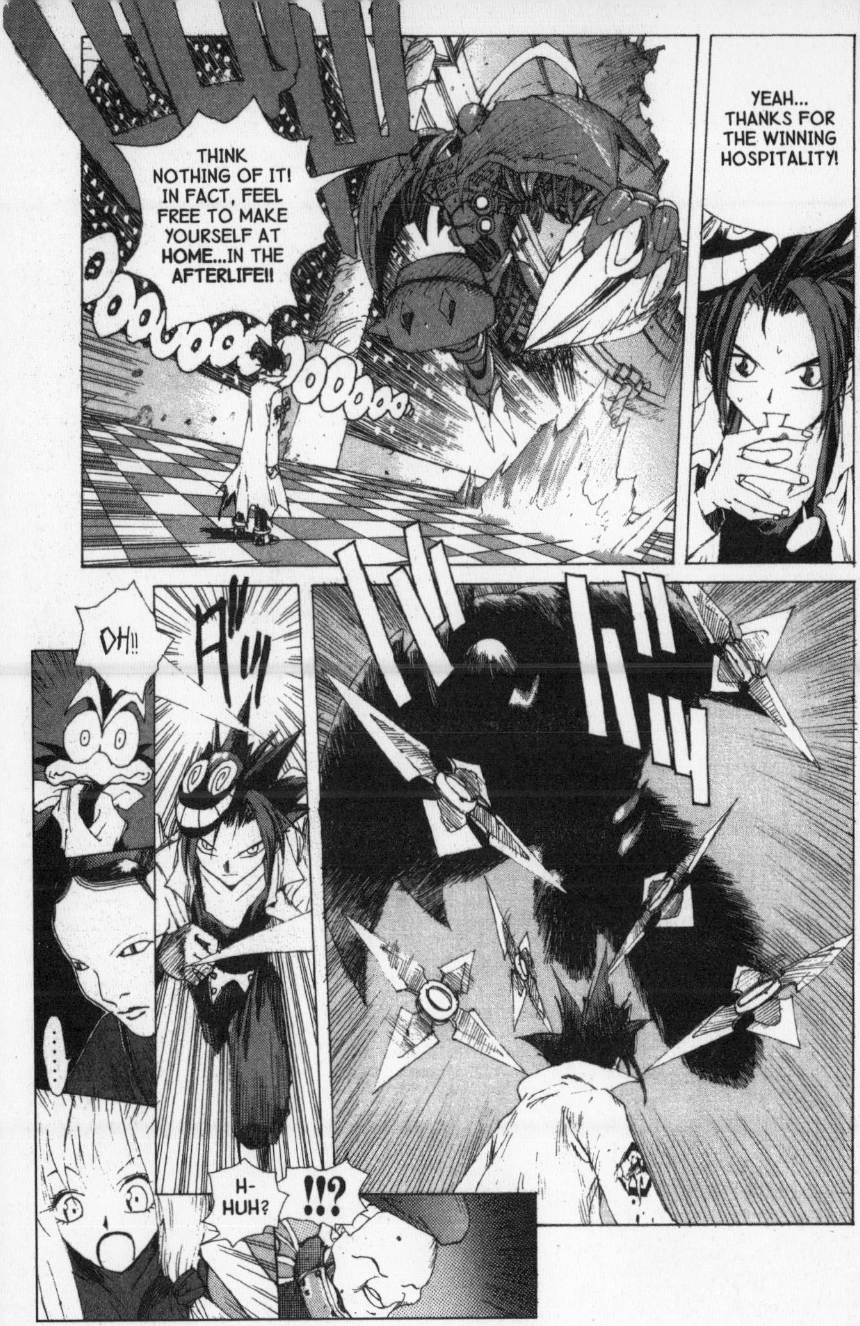
YEAH... THANKS FOR THE WINNING HOSPITALITY!
THINK NOTHING OF IT! IN FACT, FEEL FREE TO MAKE YOURSELF AT HOME...IN THE AFTERLIFE!!
OH!!
...
!!?
H-HUH?

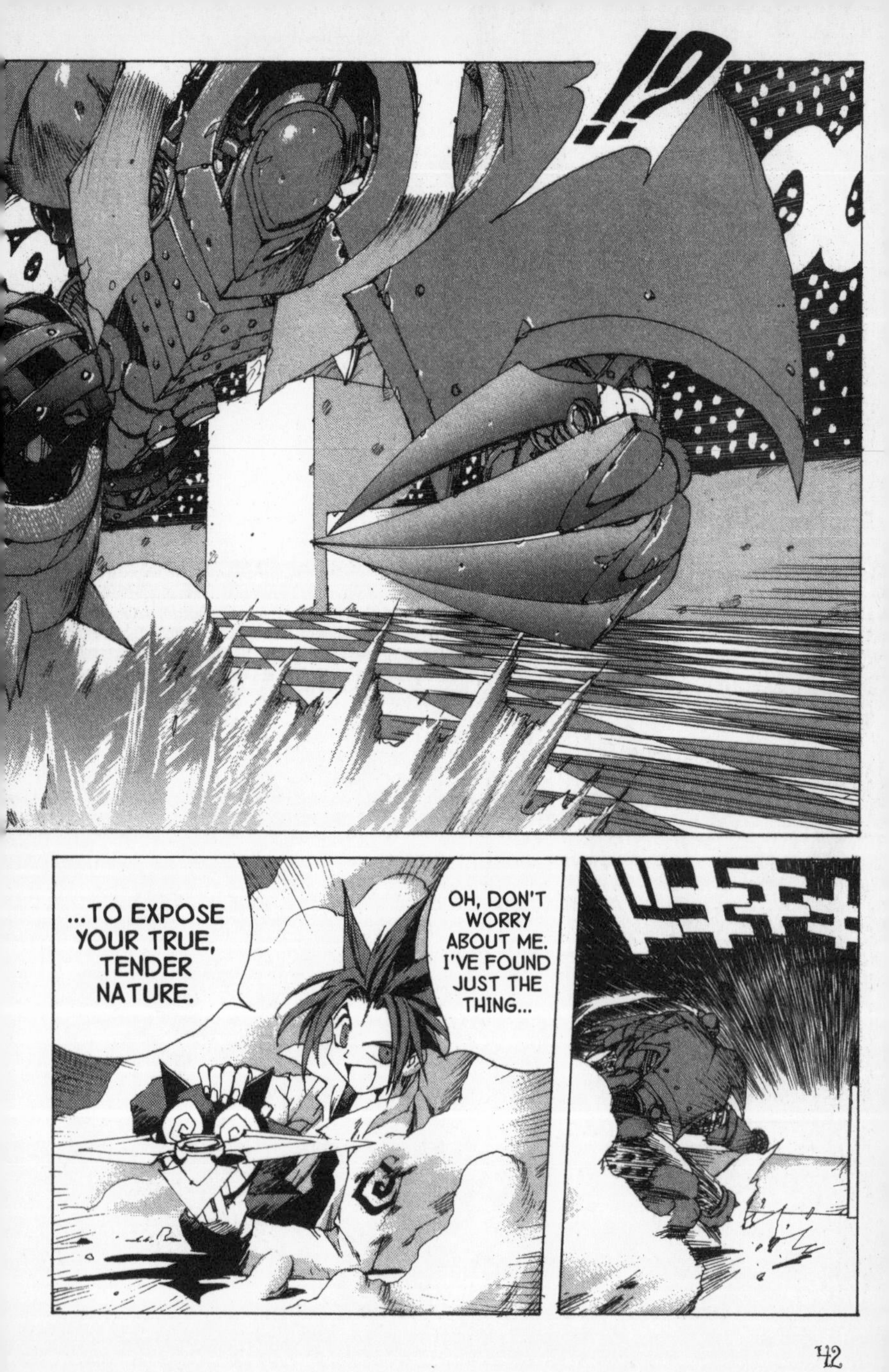
!?
OH, DON'T WORRY ABOUT ME. I'VE FOUND JUST THE THING...
...TO EXPOSE YOUR TRUE, TENDER NATURE.

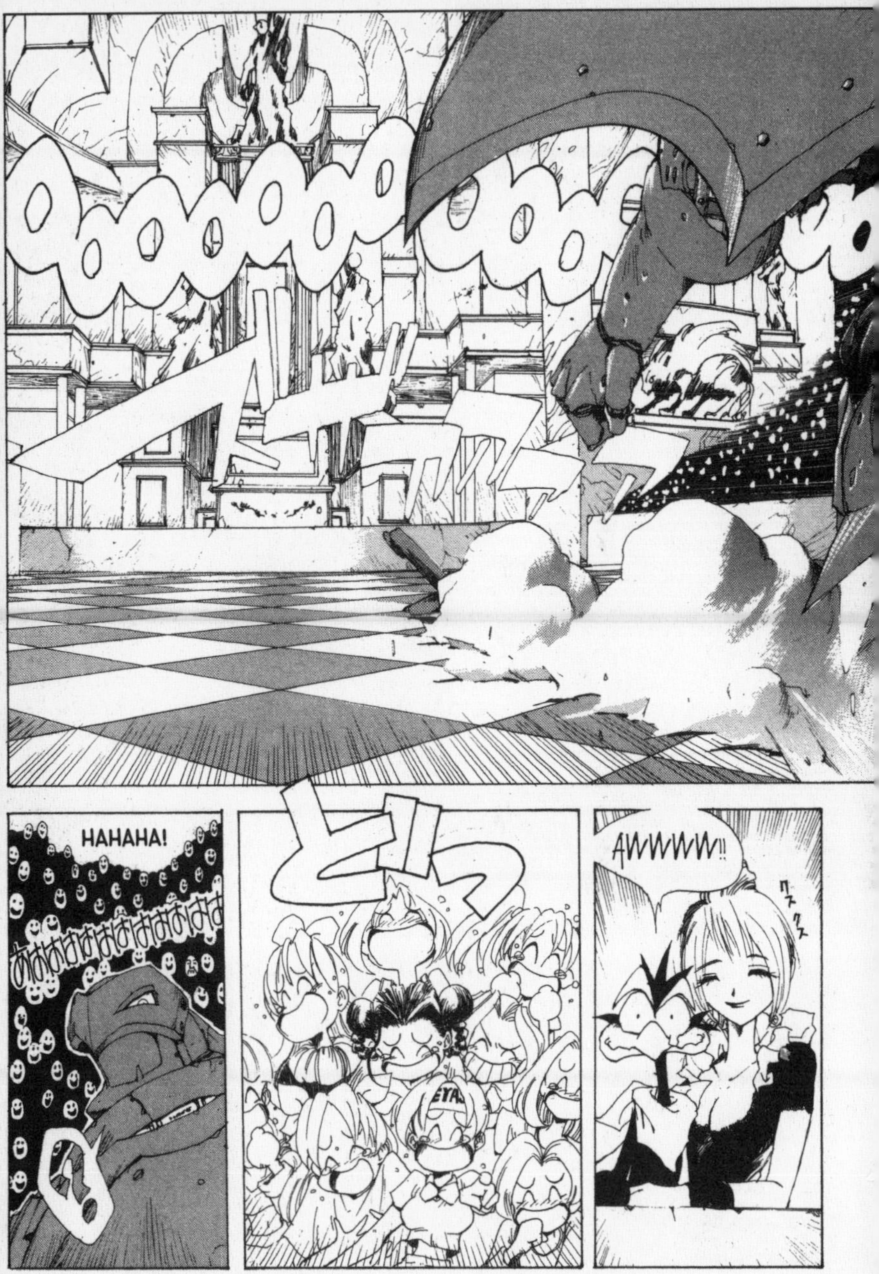
AWWWWW!!
HAHAHA!

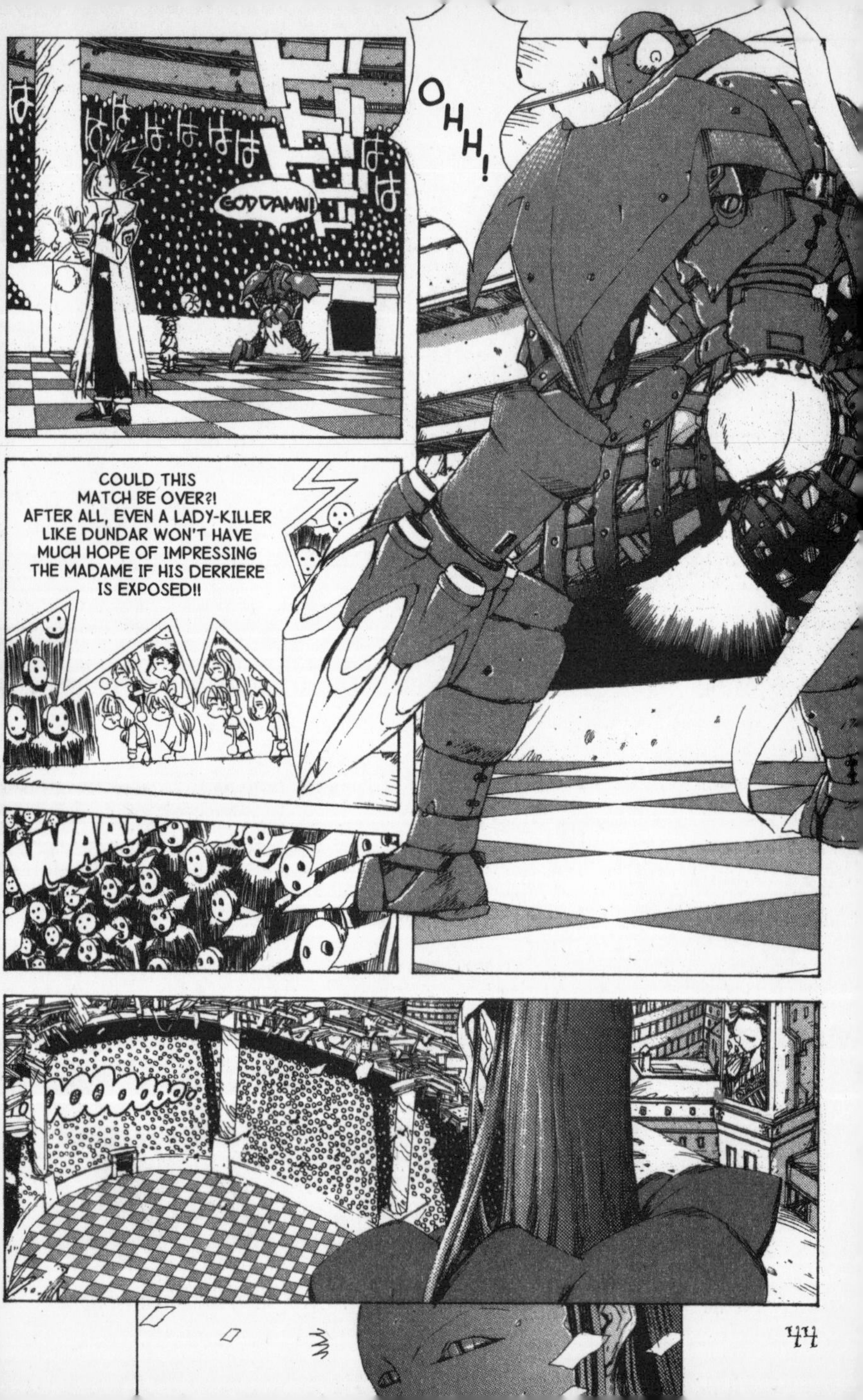
OHH!
GOD DAMN!
COULD THIS MATCH BE OVER?! AFTER ALL, EVEN A LADY-KILLER LIKE DUNDAR WON'T HAVE MUCH HOPE OF IMPRESSING THE MADAME IF HIS DERRIERE IS EXPOSED!!

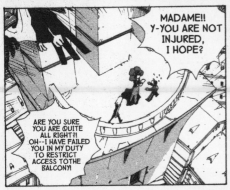

MADAME!!
Y-YOU ARE NOT INJURED, I HOPE?

ARE YOU SURE YOU ARE QUITE ALL RIGHT?! OH--I HAVE FAILED YOU IN MY DUTY TO RESTRICT ACCESS TO THE BALCONY!

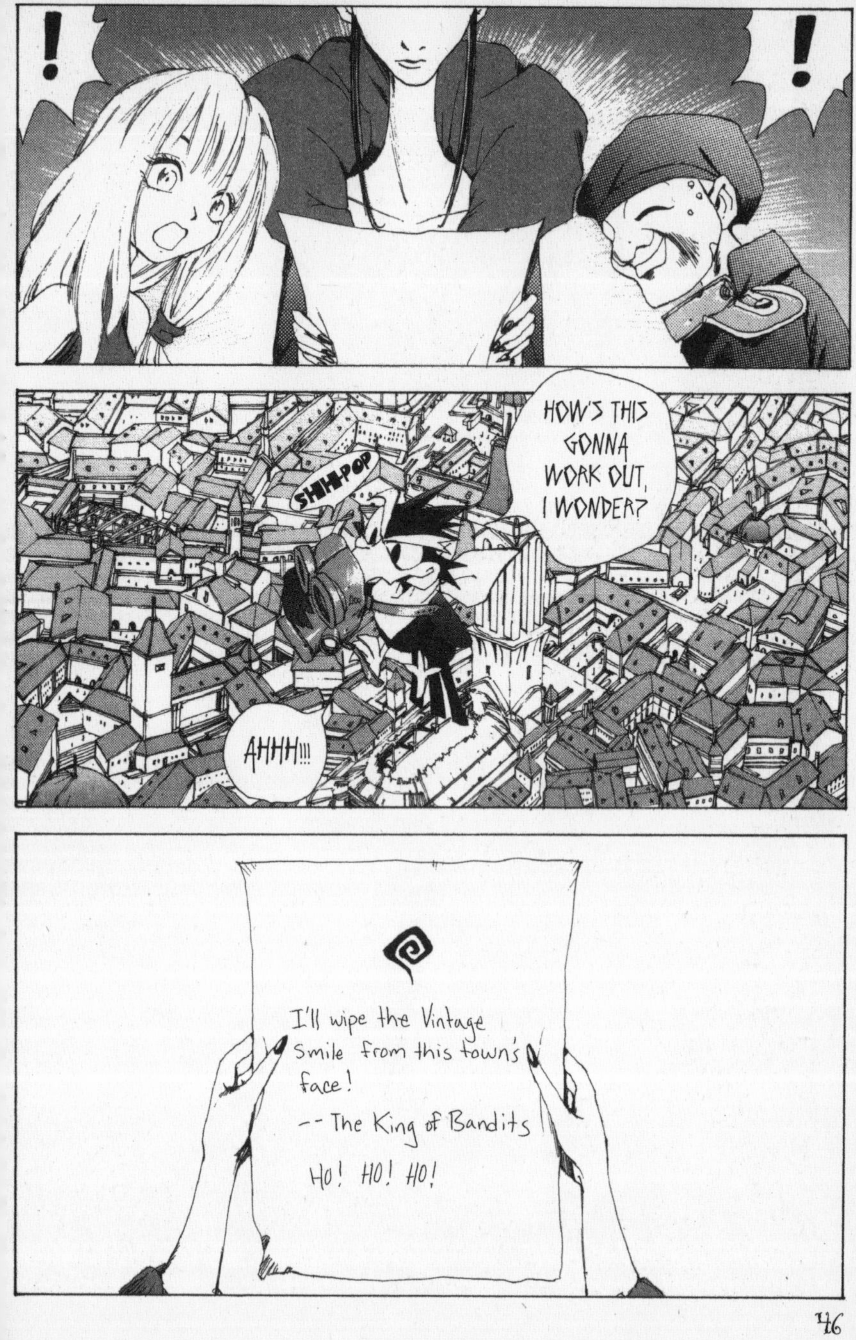
!
!
HOW'S THIS GONNA WORK OUT, I WONDER?
SHHH-POP
AHHH!!!
I'll wipe the Vintage Smile from this town's face!
-- The King of Bandits
HO! HO! HO!

20th SHOT - Vintage Smile

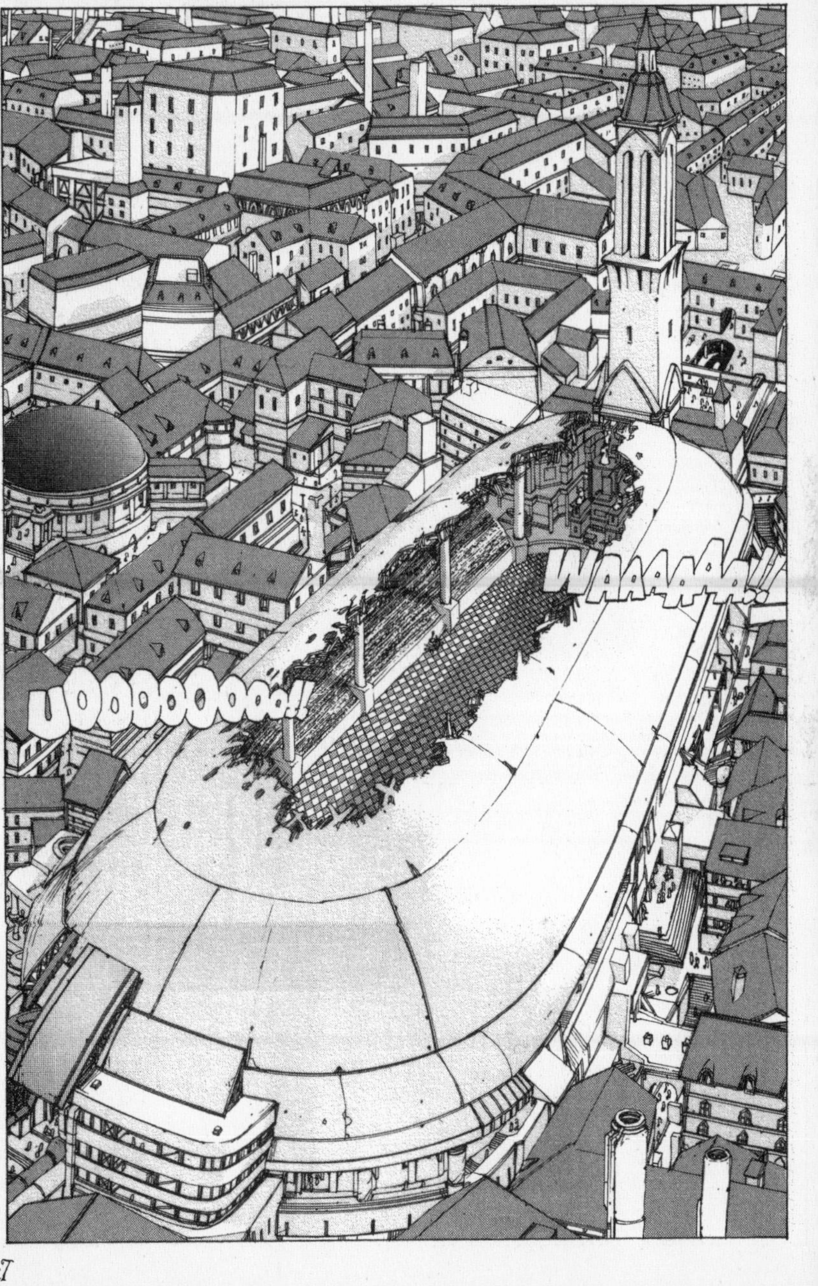
WAAAAAA!!
UOOOOOOoo!!

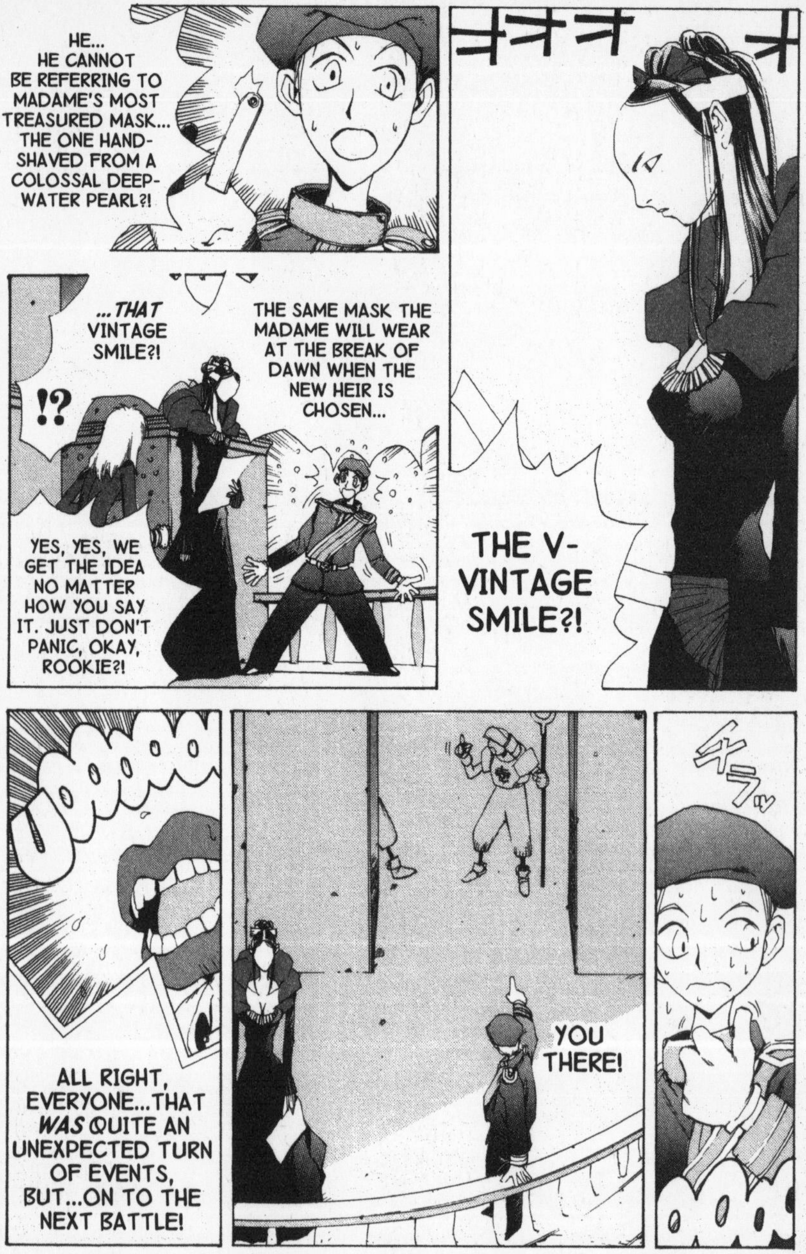

オオオ オ
THE V-VINTAGE SMILE?!
HE... HE CANNOT BE REFERRING TO MADAME'S MOST TREASURED MASK... THE ONE HAND-SHAVED FROM A COLOSSAL DEEP-WATER PEARL?!
THE SAME MASK THE MADAME WILL WEAR AT THE BREAK OF DAWN WHEN THE NEW HEIR IS CHOSEN...
...*THAT* VINTAGE SMILE?!
!?
YES, YES, WE GET THE IDEA NO MATTER HOW YOU SAY IT. JUST DON'T PANIC, OKAY, ROOKIE?!
チラッ
YOU THERE!
ALL RIGHT, EVERYONE...THAT *WAS* QUITE AN UNEXPECTED TURN OF EVENTS, BUT...ON TO THE NEXT BATTLE!

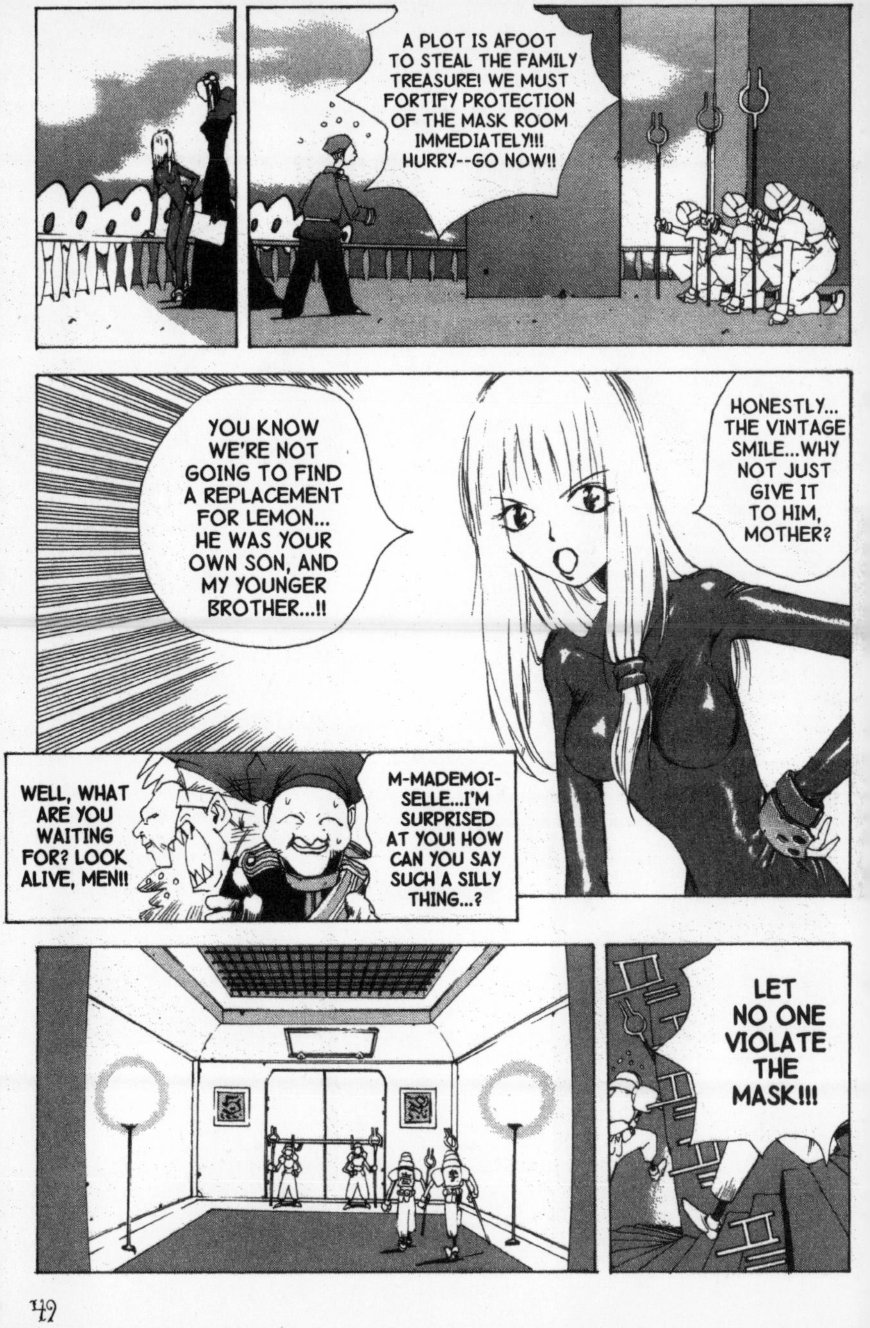
A PLOT IS AFOOT TO STEAL THE FAMILY TREASURE! WE MUST FORTIFY PROTECTION OF THE MASK ROOM IMMEDIATELY!!! HURRY--GO NOW!!
HONESTLY... THE VINTAGE SMILE...WHY NOT JUST GIVE IT TO HIM, MOTHER?
YOU KNOW WE'RE NOT GOING TO FIND A REPLACEMENT FOR LEMON... HE WAS YOUR OWN SON, AND MY YOUNGER BROTHER...!!
M-MADEMOISELLE...I'M SURPRISED AT YOU! HOW CAN YOU SAY SUCH A SILLY THING...?
WELL, WHAT ARE YOU WAITING FOR? LOOK ALIVE, MEN!!
LET NO ONE VIOLATE THE MASK!!!

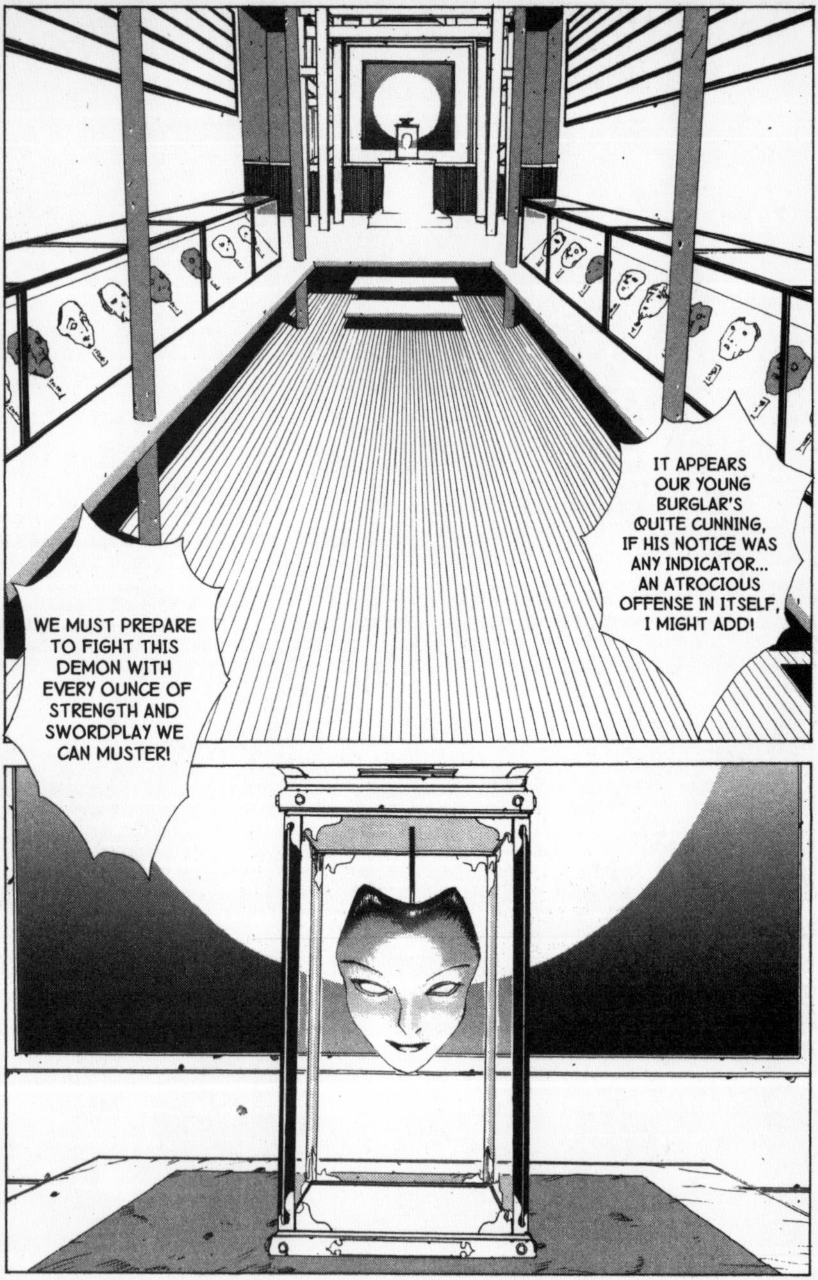
IT APPEARS OUR YOUNG BURGLAR'S QUITE CUNNING, IF HIS NOTICE WAS ANY INDICATOR... AN ATROCIOUS OFFENSE IN ITSELF, I MIGHT ADD!
WE MUST PREPARE TO FIGHT THIS DEMON WITH EVERY OUNCE OF STRENGTH AND SWORDPLAY WE CAN MUSTER!

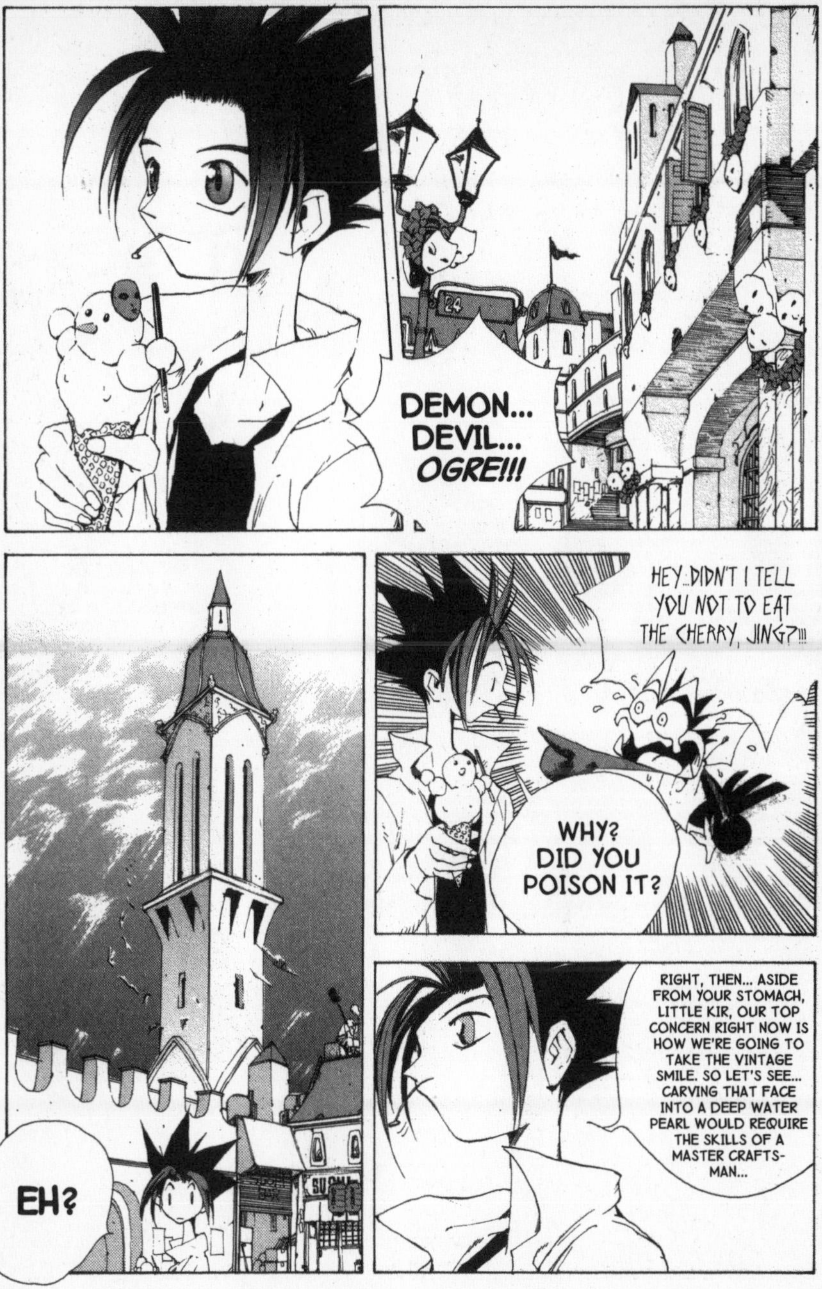
DEMON... DEVIL... OGRE!!!
HEY...DIDN'T I TELL YOU NOT TO EAT THE CHERRY, JING?!!!
WHY? DID YOU POISON IT?
RIGHT, THEN... ASIDE FROM YOUR STOMACH, LITTLE KIR, OUR TOP CONCERN RIGHT NOW IS HOW WE'RE GOING TO TAKE THE VINTAGE SMILE. SO LET'S SEE... CARVING THAT FACE INTO A DEEP WATER PEARL WOULD REQUIRE THE SKILLS OF A MASTER CRAFTS-MAN...
EH?

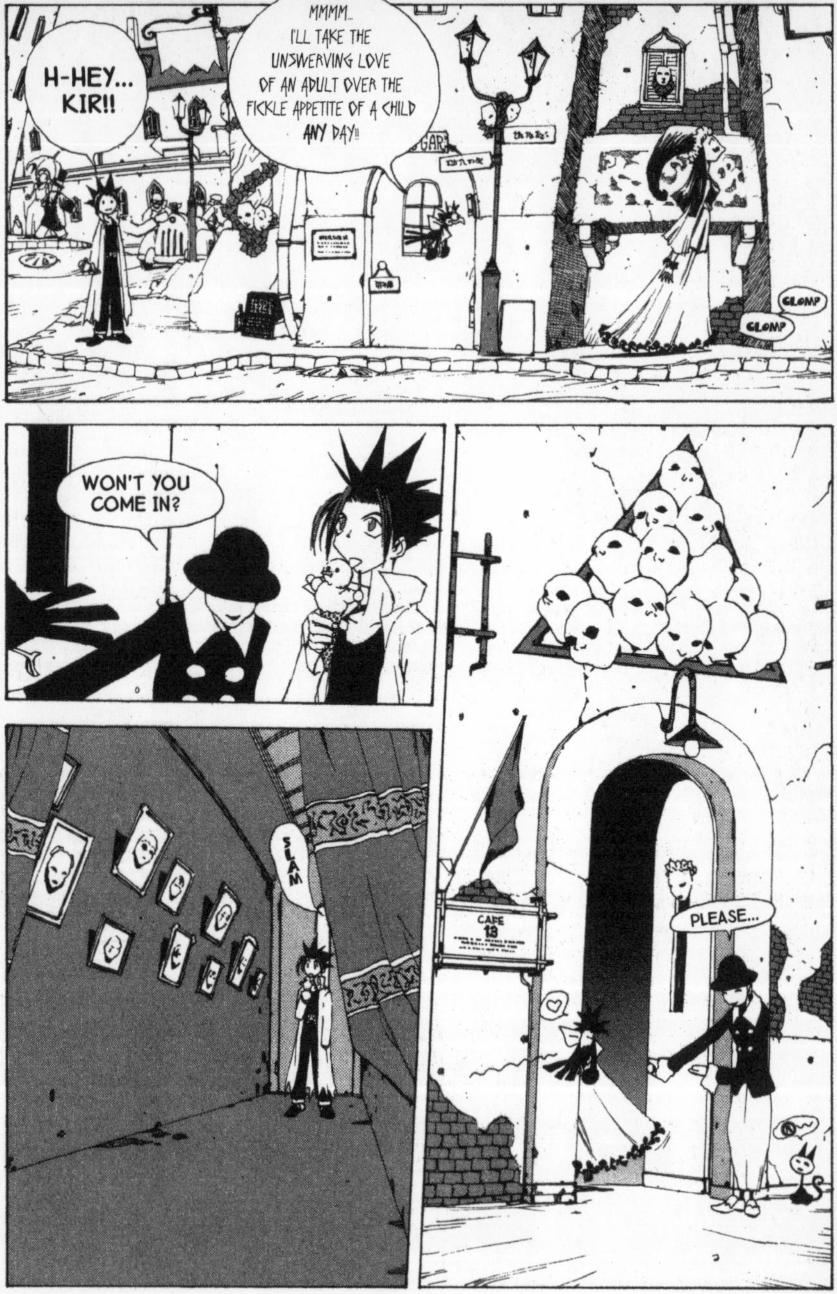
MMMM... I'LL TAKE THE UNSWERVING LOVE OF AN ADULT OVER THE FICKLE APPETITE OF A CHILD ANY DAY!!
H-HEY... KIR!!
GLOMP
GLOMP
CAFE 13
PLEASE...
WON'T YOU COME IN?
SLAM

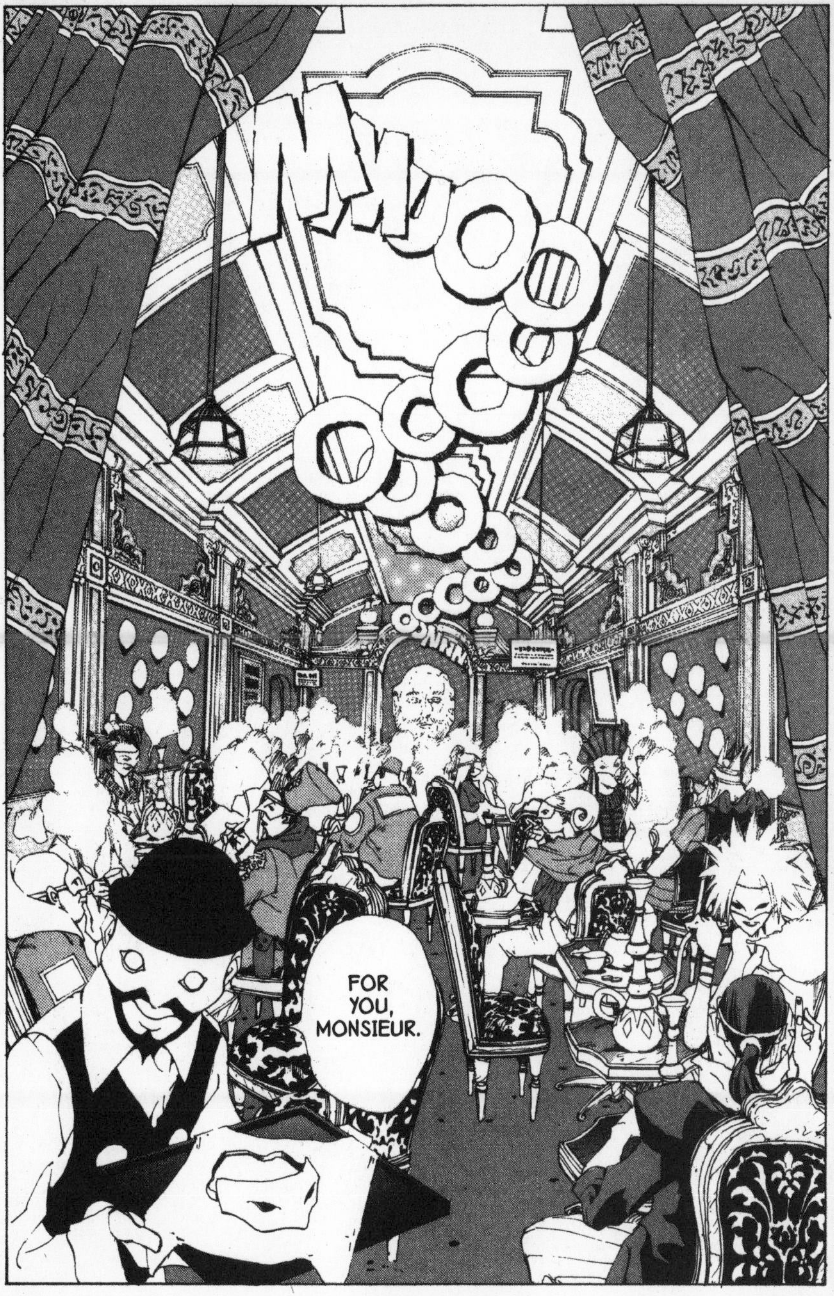
MMUOOOOOOOOOOOO
NNNN
FOR YOU, MONSIEUR.

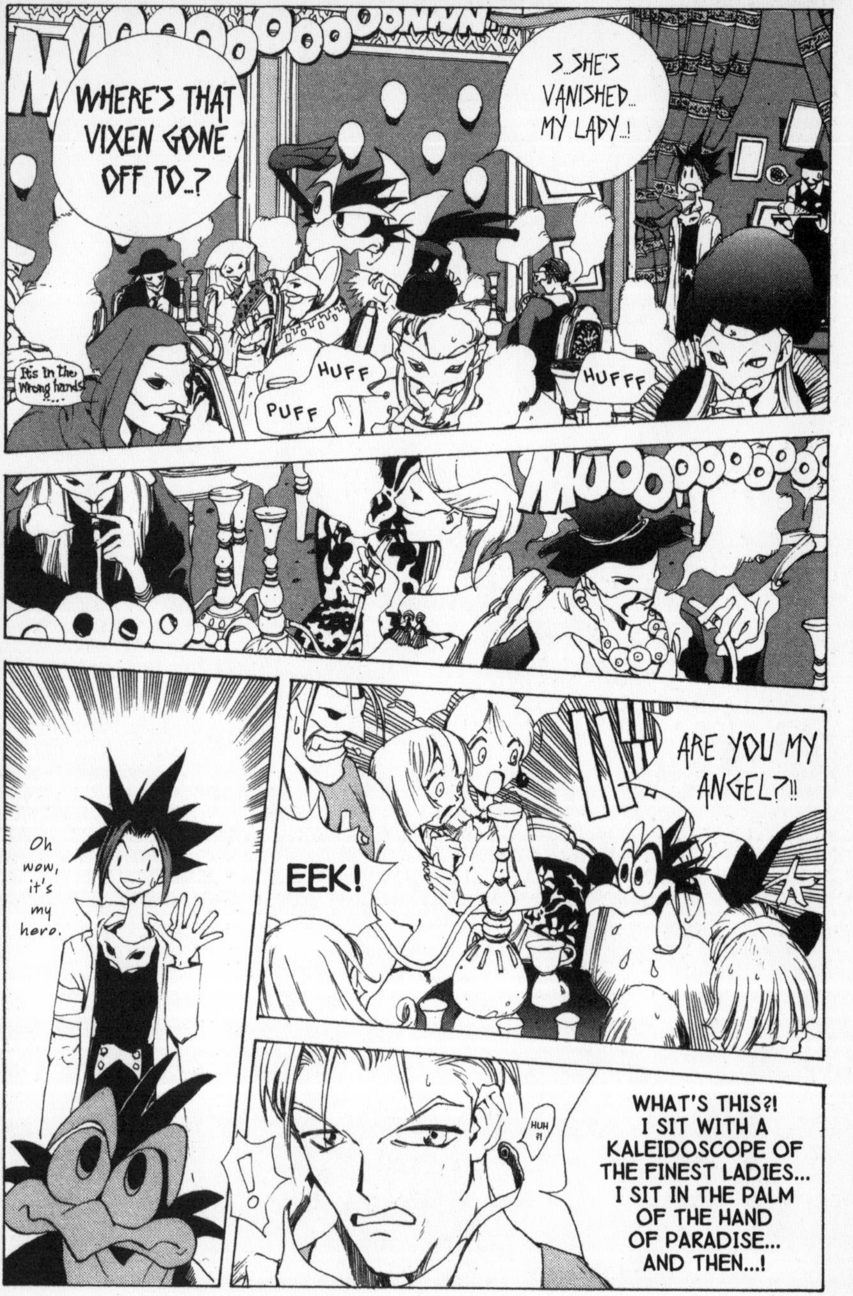
MUOOOOOOOOOONNN...
S...SHE'S VANISHED... MY LADY...!
WHERE'S THAT VIXEN GONE OFF TO...?
HUFFF
HUFF
PUFF
It's in the wrong hands!.....
MUOOOOOOOOO
OOOOO
ARE YOU MY ANGEL?!!
EEK!
WHAT'S THIS?! I SIT WITH A KALEIDOSCOPE OF THE FINEST LADIES... I SIT IN THE PALM OF THE HAND OF PARADISE... AND THEN...!
HUH ?!
Oh wow, it's my hero.

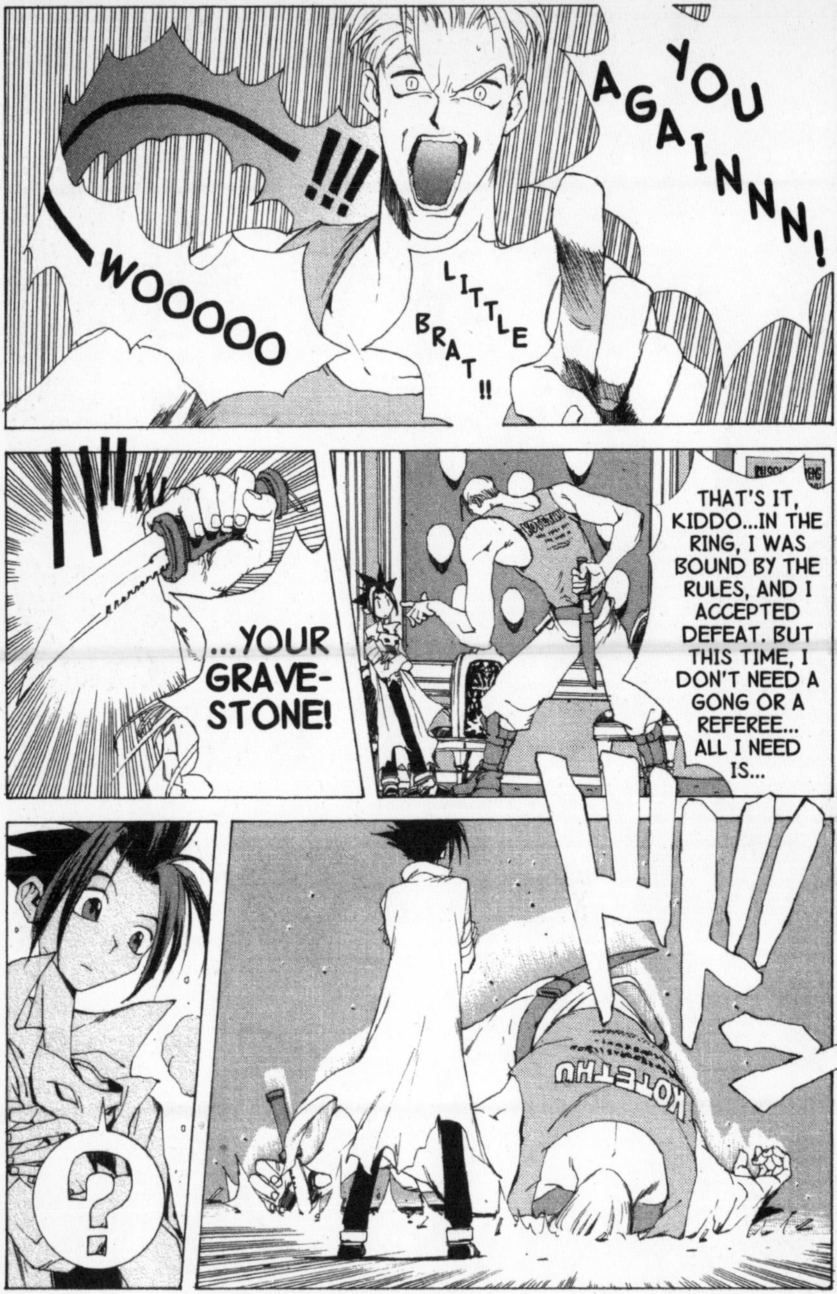
YOU AGAINNNN!
!!!
LITTLE BRAT!!
WOOOOO
THAT'S IT, KIDDO...IN THE RING, I WAS BOUND BY THE RULES, AND I ACCEPTED DEFEAT. BUT THIS TIME, I DON'T NEED A GONG OR A REFEREE... ALL I NEED IS...
...YOUR GRAVE-STONE!
?

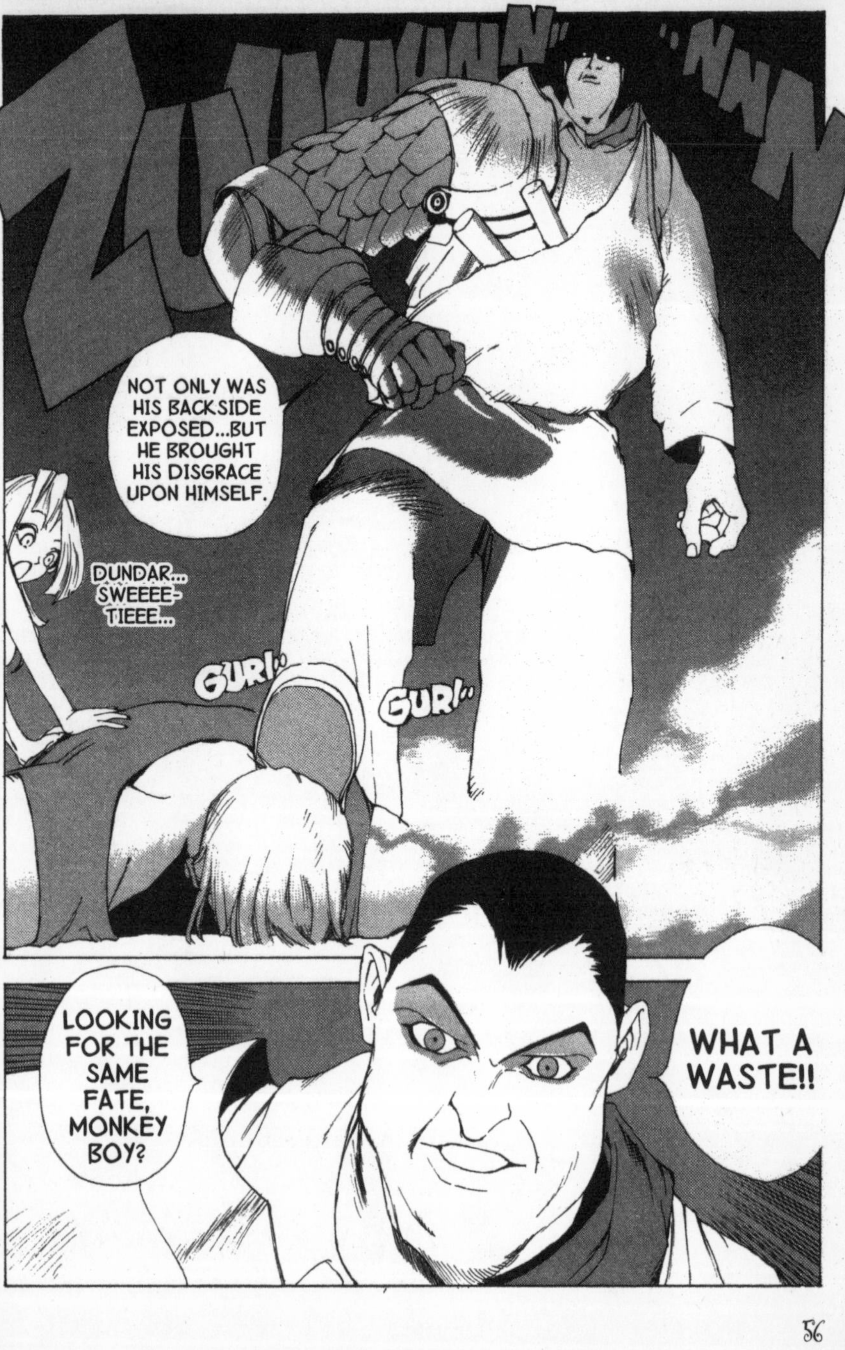

ZUWUUUNN''''NNN
NOT ONLY WAS HIS BACKSIDE EXPOSED...BUT HE BROUGHT HIS DISGRACE UPON HIMSELF.
DUNDAR... SWEEEE-TIEEE...
GURI!!
GURI!!
WHAT A WASTE!!
LOOKING FOR THE SAME FATE, MONKEY BOY?

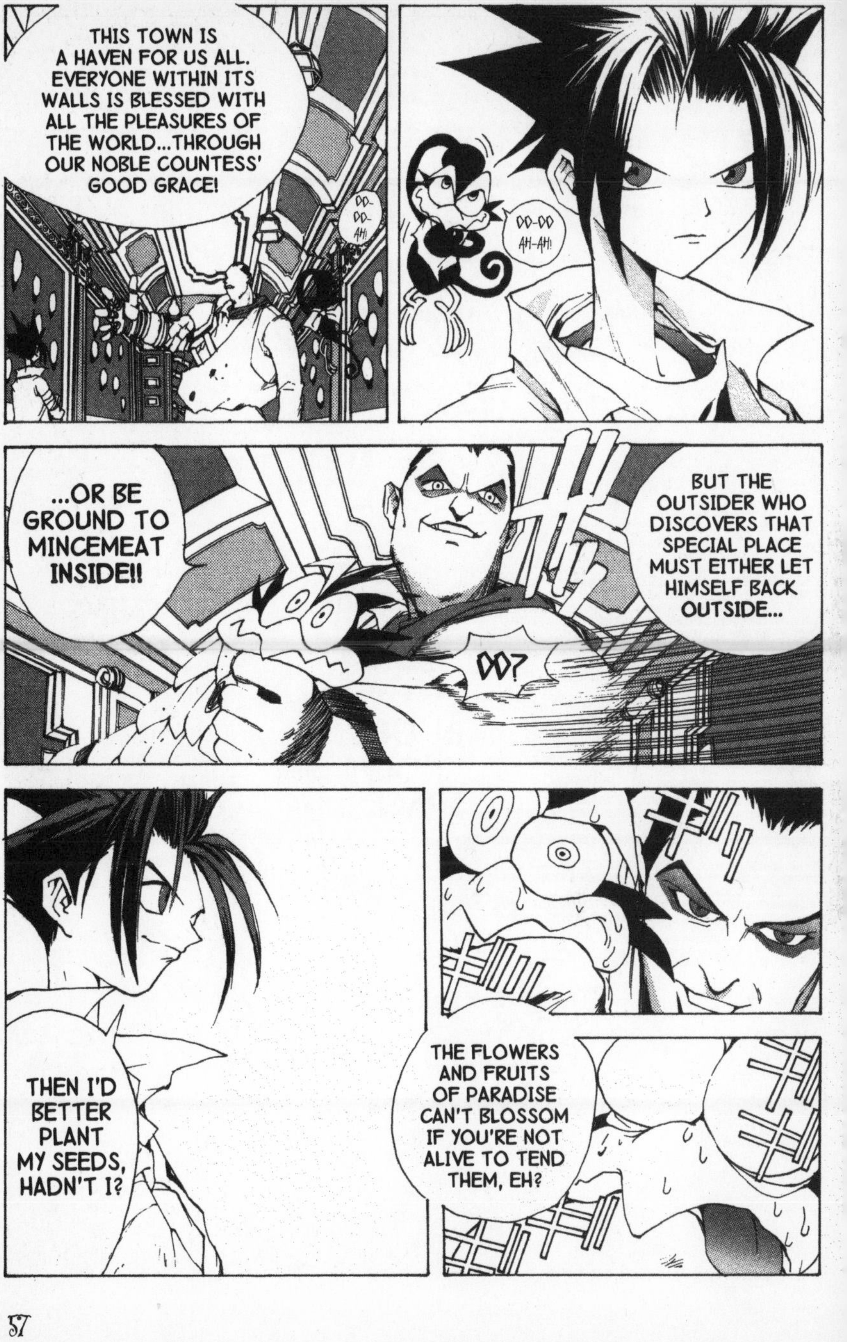
DO-DO AH-AH!
THIS TOWN IS A HAVEN FOR US ALL. EVERYONE WITHIN ITS WALLS IS BLESSED WITH ALL THE PLEASURES OF THE WORLD...THROUGH OUR NOBLE COUNTESS' GOOD GRACE!
DO-DO-AH!
BUT THE OUTSIDER WHO DISCOVERS THAT SPECIAL PLACE MUST EITHER LET HIMSELF BACK OUTSIDE...
...OR BE GROUND TO MINCEMEAT INSIDE!!
DO?
THE FLOWERS AND FRUITS OF PARADISE CAN'T BLOSSOM IF YOU'RE NOT ALIVE TO TEND THEM, EH?
THEN I'D BETTER PLANT MY SEEDS, HADN'T I?

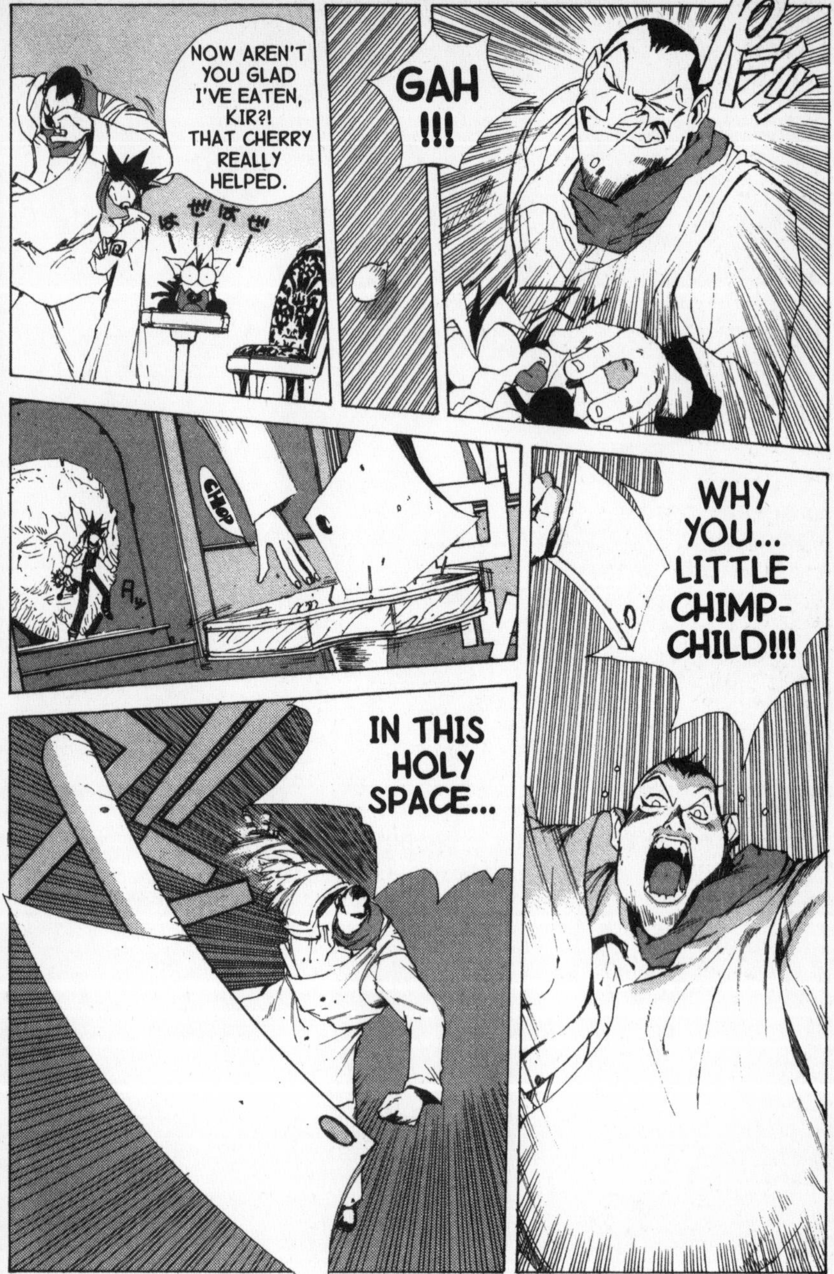
GAH !!!
NOW AREN'T YOU GLAD I'VE EATEN, KIR?! THAT CHERRY REALLY HELPED.
WHY YOU... LITTLE CHIMP-CHILD!!!
CHOP
IN THIS HOLY SPACE...

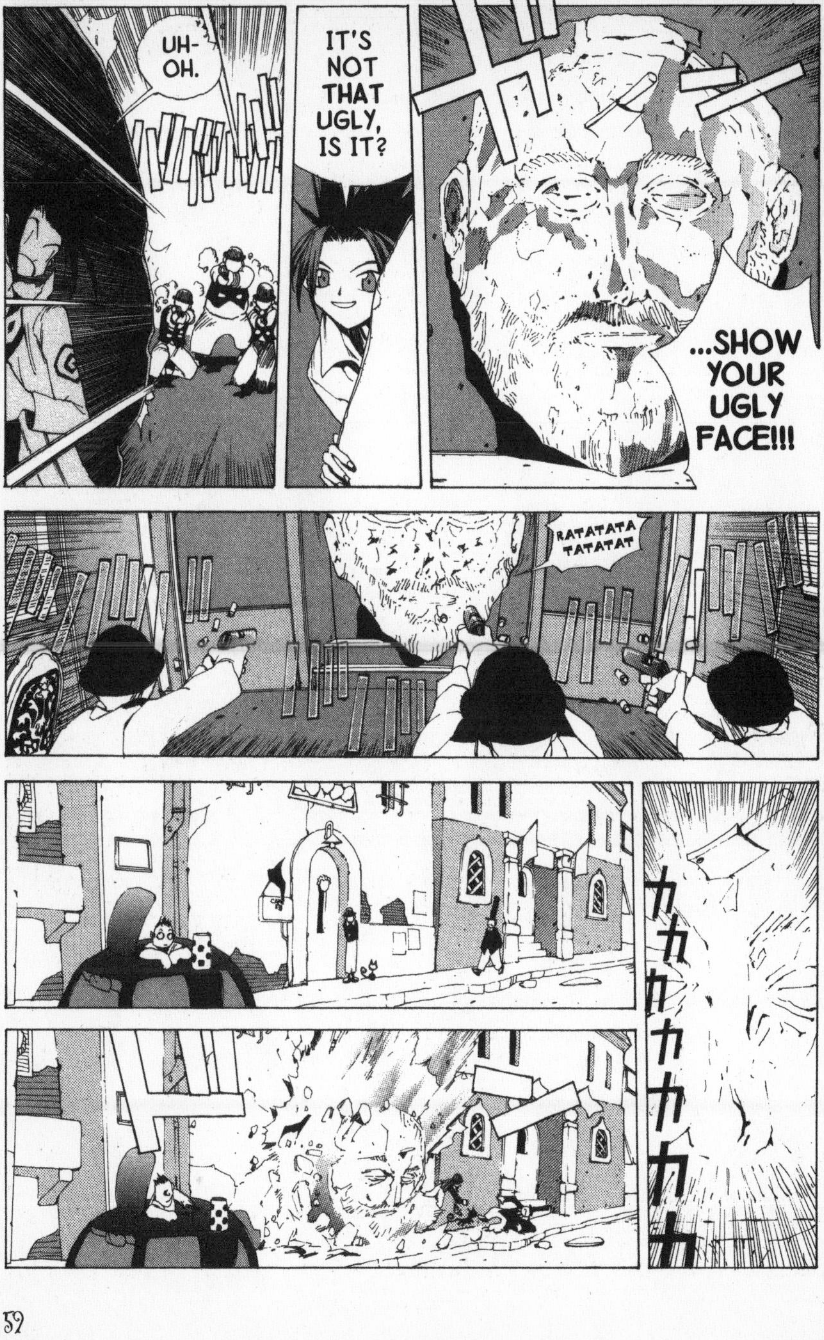

...SHOW YOUR UGLY FACE!!!
IT'S NOT THAT UGLY, IS IT?
UH-OH.
RATATATA TATATAT
カカカカカカ

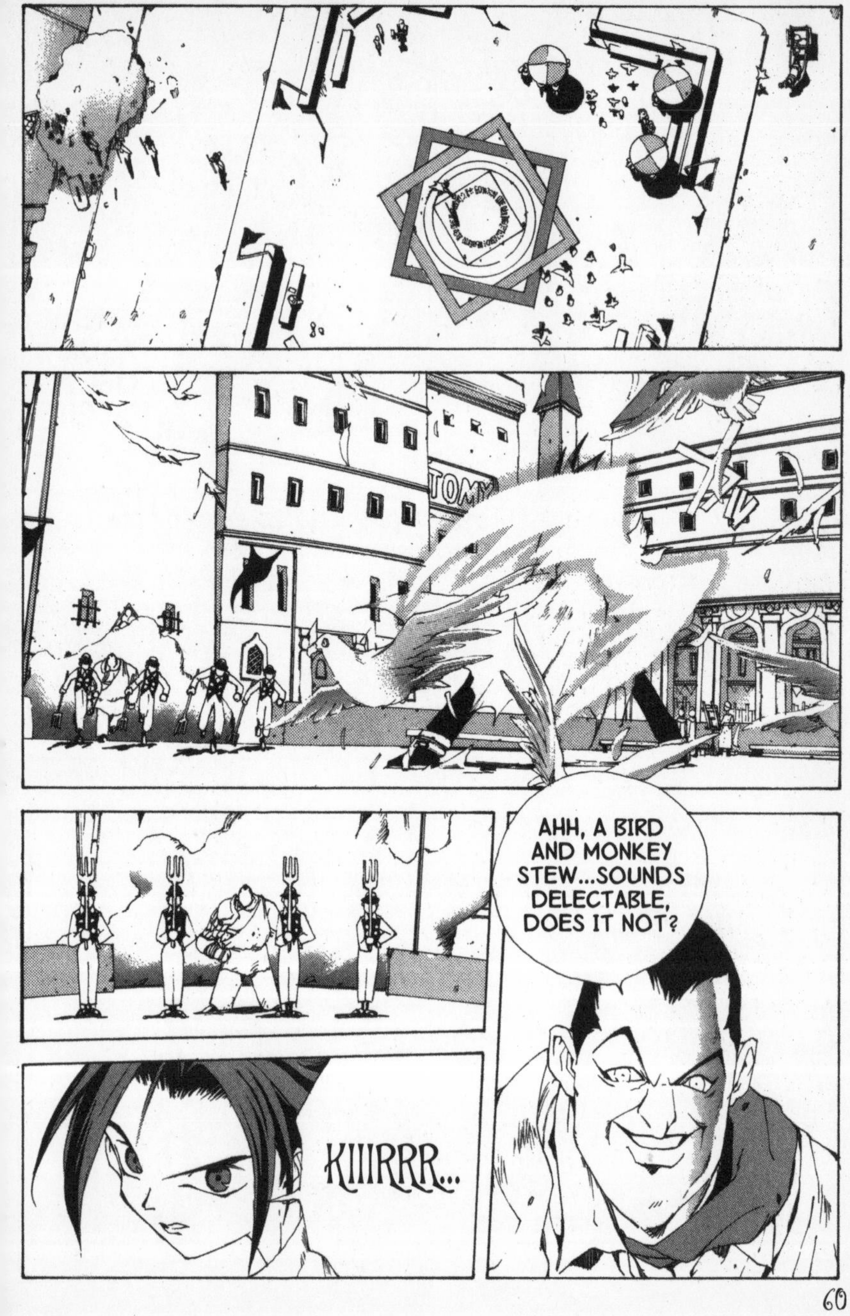
AHH, A BIRD AND MONKEY STEW...SOUNDS DELECTABLE, DOES IT NOT?
KIIIRRR...

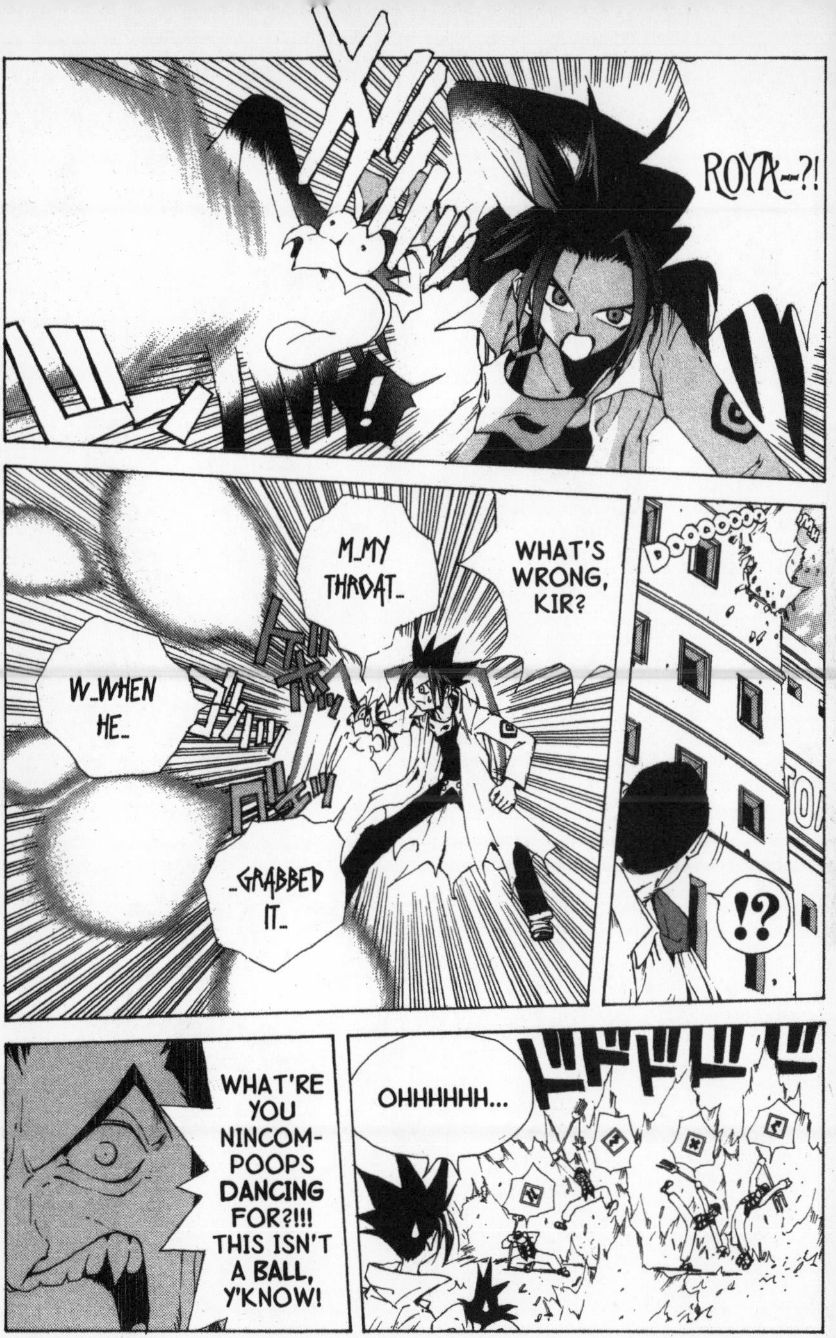
ROYA--?!
WHAT'S WRONG, KIR?
M..MY THROAT...
W..WHEN HE...
...GRABBED IT...
!?
OHHHHHH...
WHAT'RE YOU NINCOM-POOPS DANCING FOR?!!! THIS ISN'T A BALL, Y'KNOW!

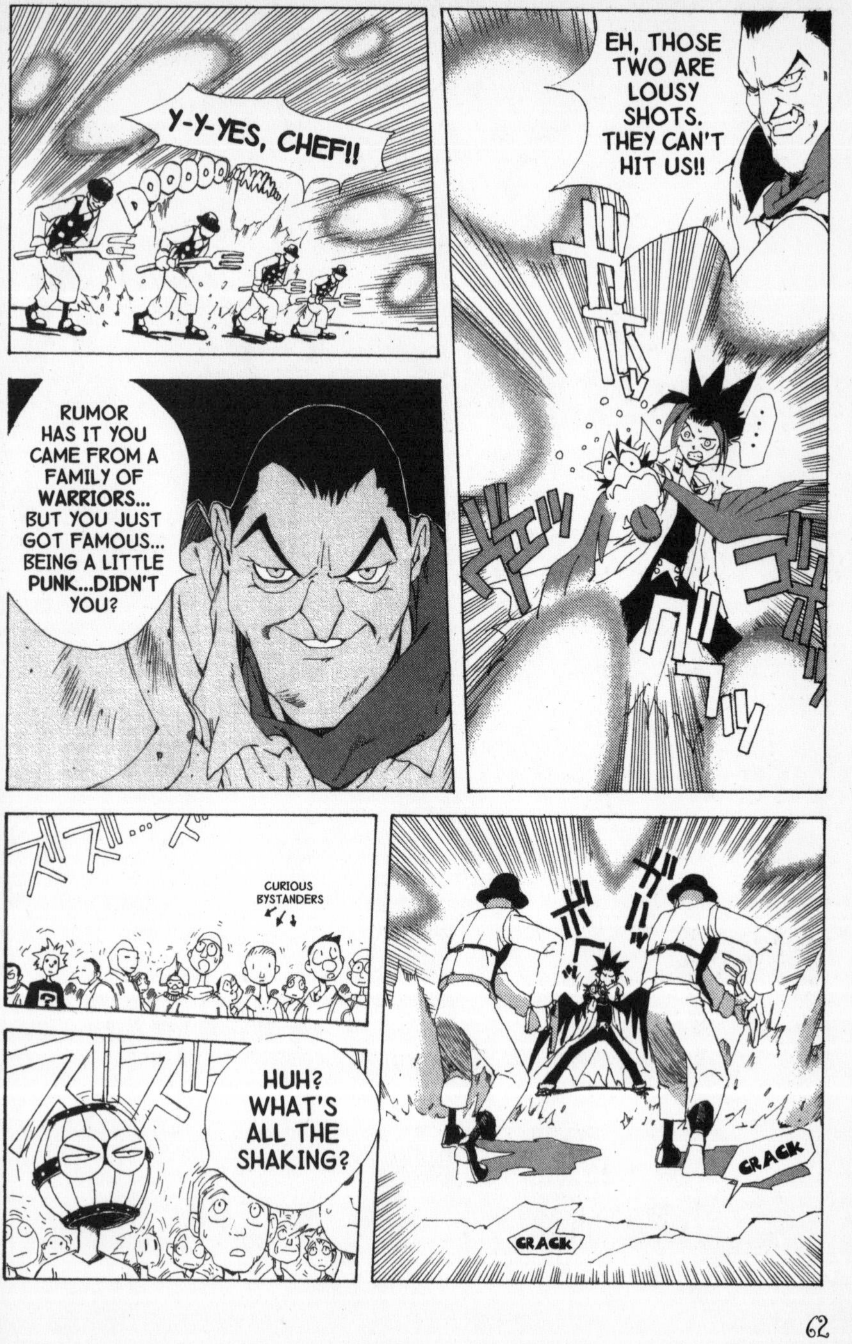

EH, THOSE TWO ARE LOUSY SHOTS. THEY CAN'T HIT US!!
...
Y-Y-YES, CHEF!!
RUMOR HAS IT YOU CAME FROM A FAMILY OF WARRIORS... BUT YOU JUST GOT FAMOUS... BEING A LITTLE PUNK...DIDN'T YOU?
CRACK
CRACK
CURIOUS BYSTANDERS
HUH? WHAT'S ALL THE SHAKING?

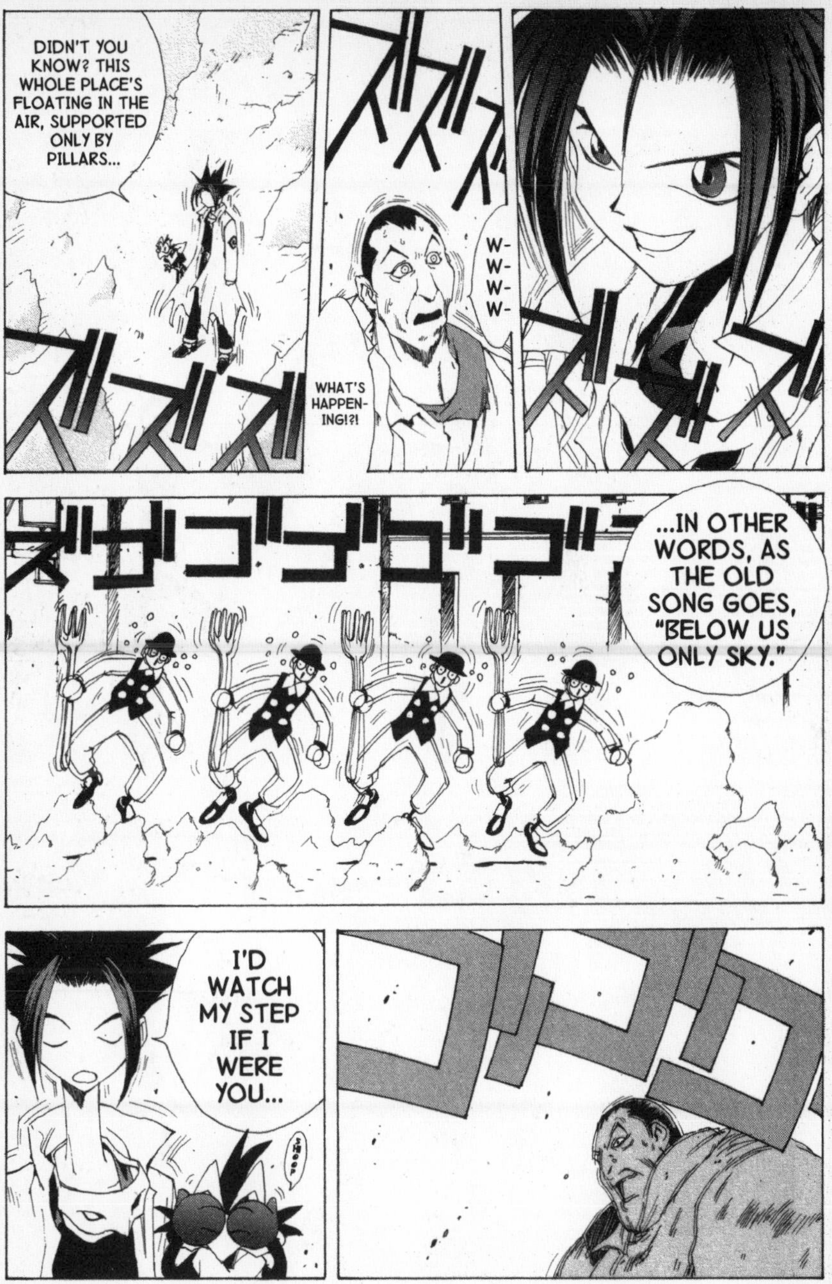
W- W- W- W-
WHAT'S HAPPENING!?!
DIDN'T YOU KNOW? THIS WHOLE PLACE'S FLOATING IN THE AIR, SUPPORTED ONLY BY PILLARS...
...IN OTHER WORDS, AS THE OLD SONG GOES, "BELOW US ONLY SKY."
I'D WATCH MY STEP IF I WERE YOU...

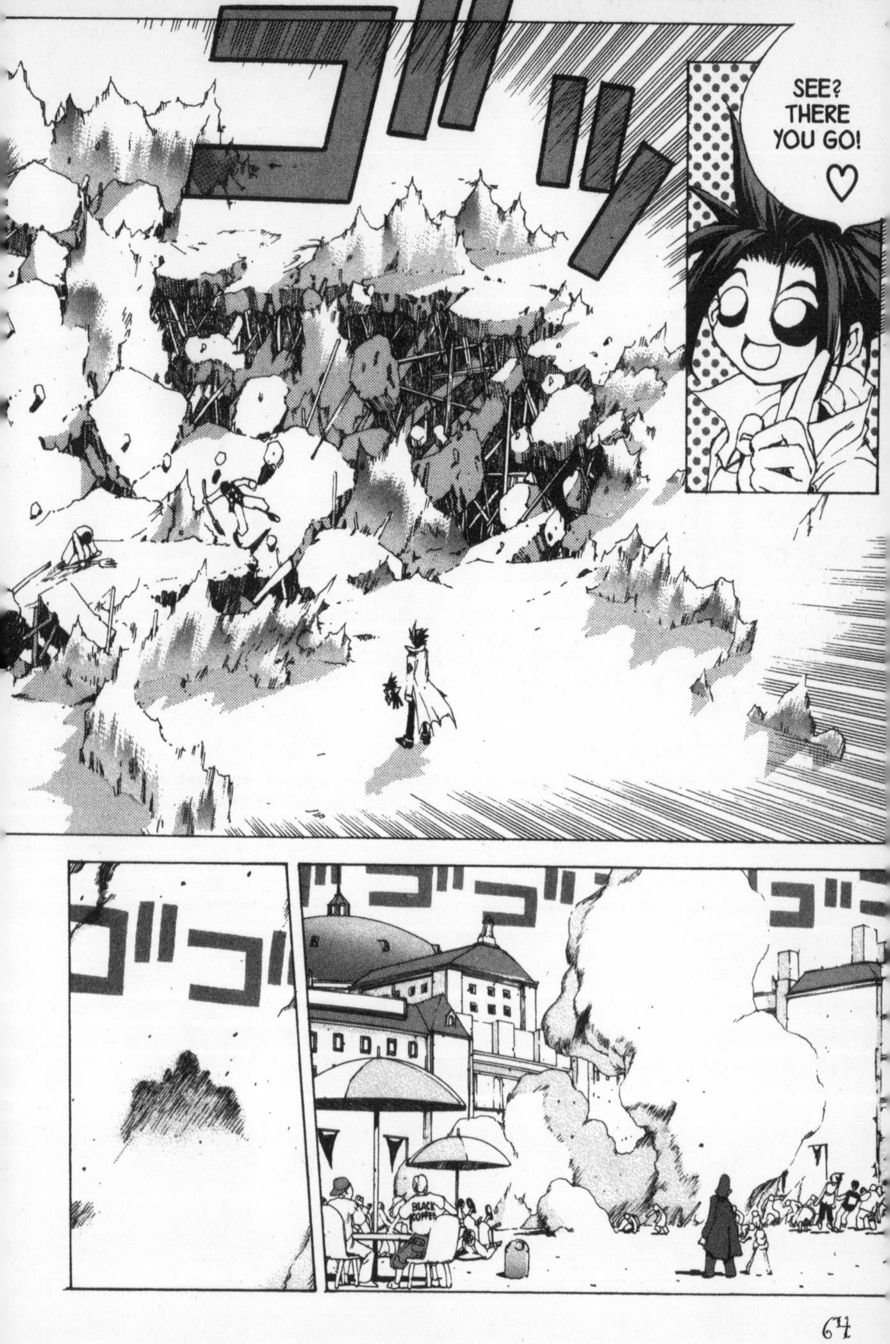
SEE? THERE YOU GO! ♡

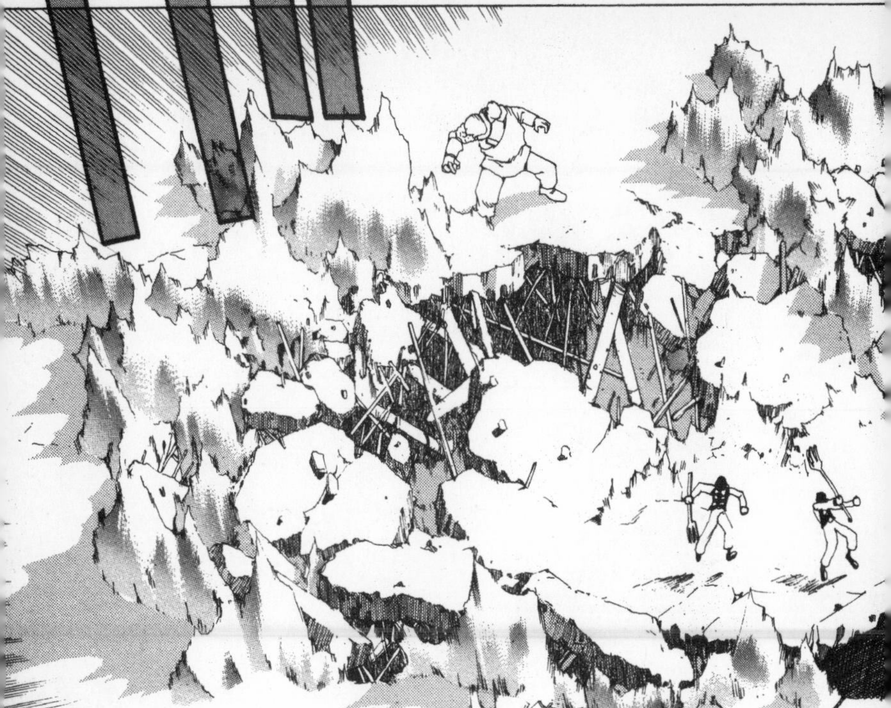

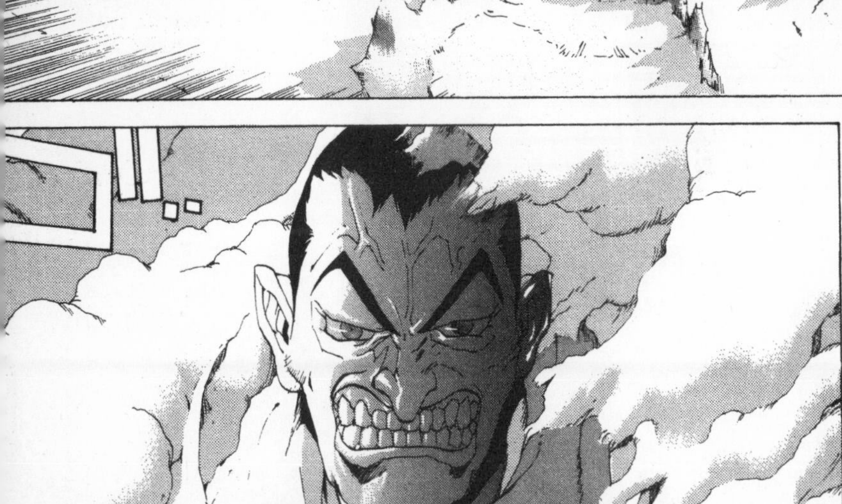

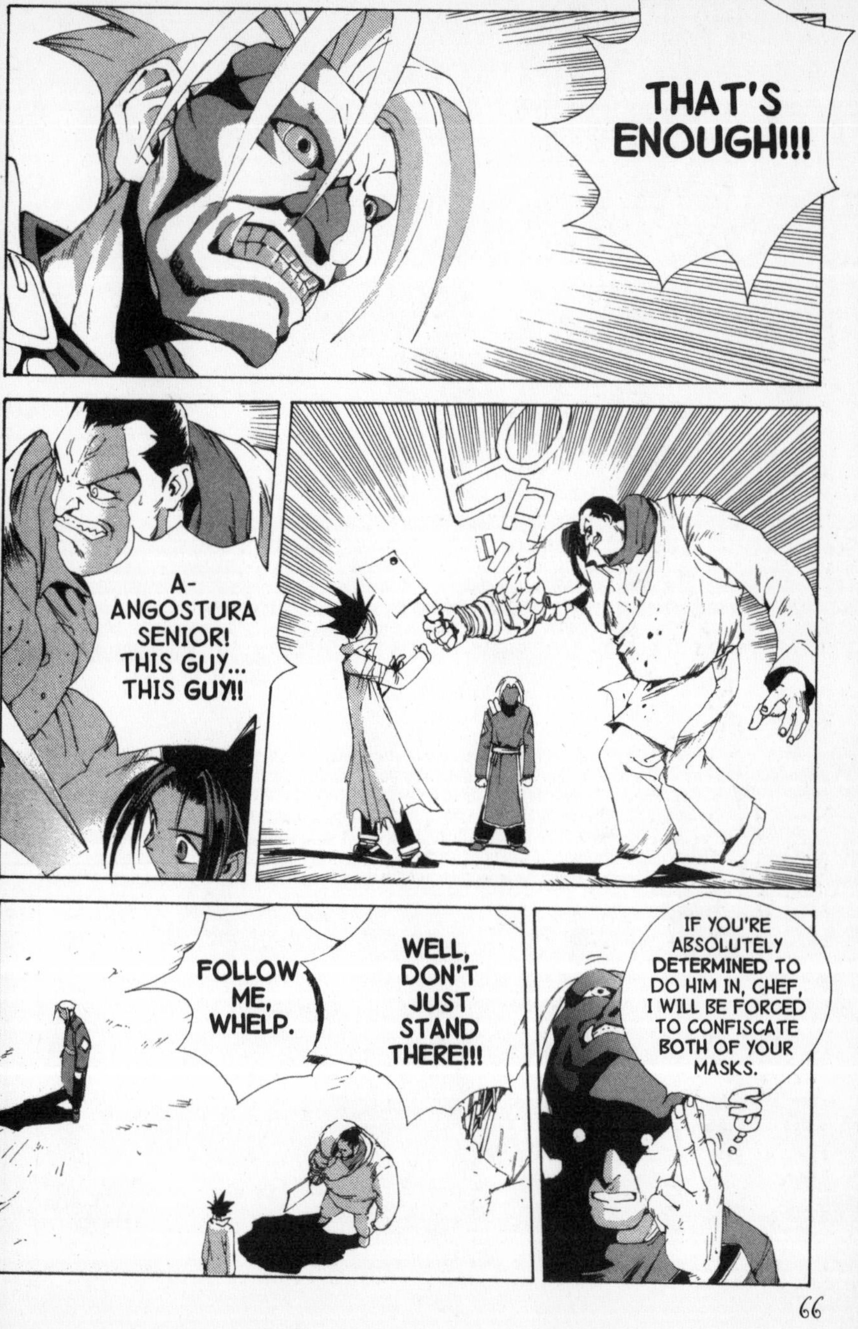
THAT'S ENOUGH!!!
A- ANGOSTURA SENIOR! THIS GUY... THIS GUY!!
IF YOU'RE ABSOLUTELY DETERMINED TO DO HIM IN, CHEF, I WILL BE FORCED TO CONFISCATE BOTH OF YOUR MASKS.
WELL, DON'T JUST STAND THERE!!!
FOLLOW ME, WHELP.

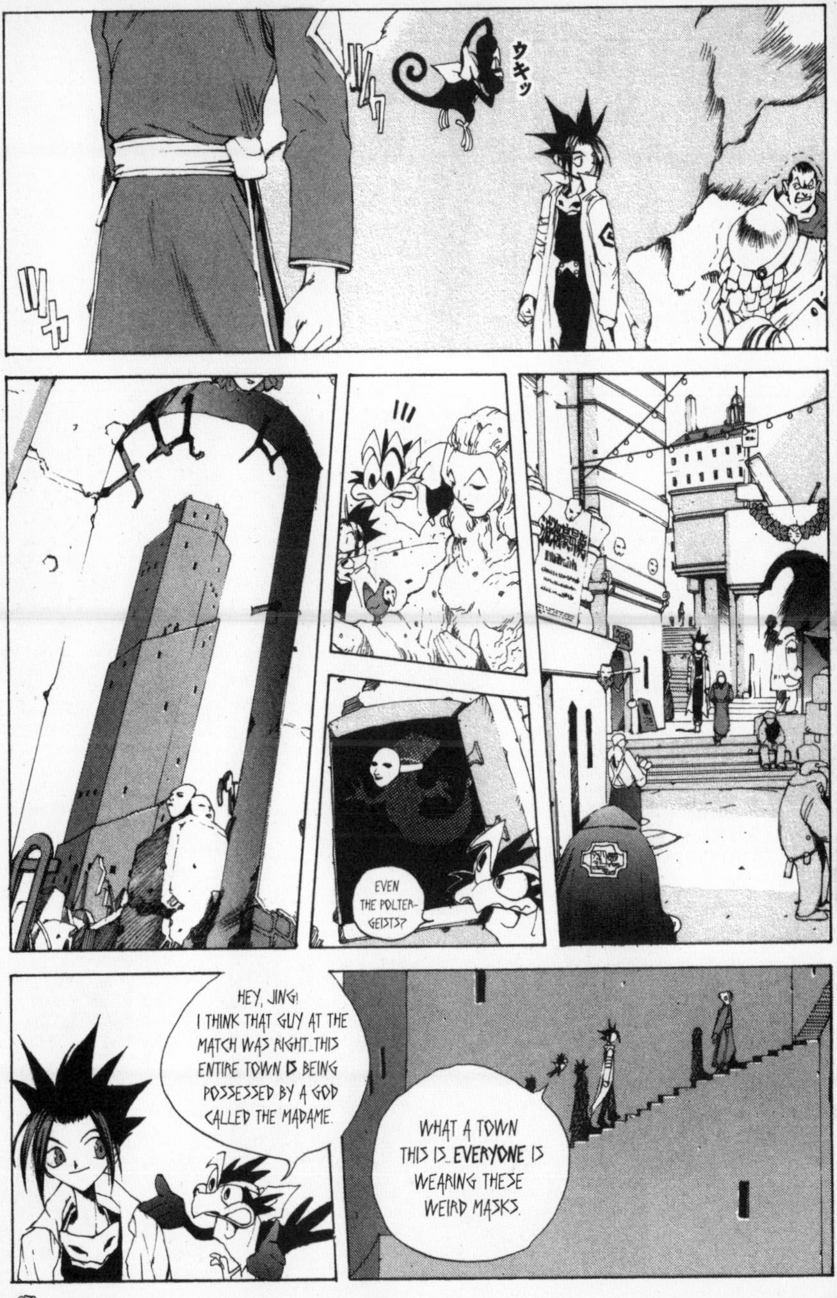
ウキッ
EVEN THE POLTER-GEISTS?
WHAT A TOWN THIS IS... EVERYONE IS WEARING THESE WEIRD MASKS.
HEY, JING! I THINK THAT GUY AT THE MATCH WAS RIGHT... THIS ENTIRE TOWN IS BEING POSSESSED BY A GOD CALLED THE MADAME.

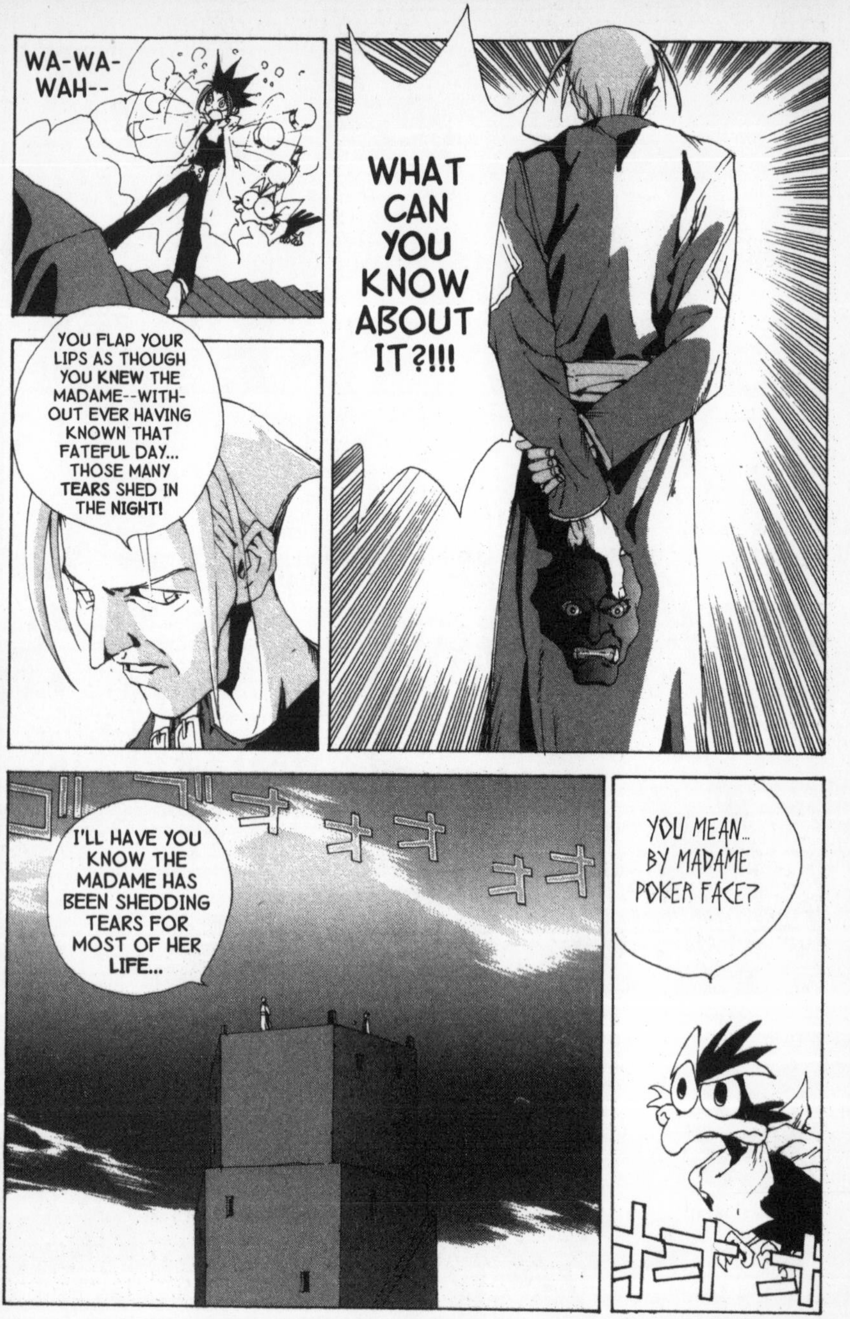
WHAT CAN YOU KNOW ABOUT IT?!!!
WA-WA-WAH--
YOU FLAP YOUR LIPS AS THOUGH YOU KNEW THE MADAME--WITH-OUT EVER HAVING KNOWN THAT FATEFUL DAY... THOSE MANY TEARS SHED IN THE NIGHT!
YOU MEAN... BY MADAME POKER FACE?
I'LL HAVE YOU KNOW THE MADAME HAS BEEN SHEDDING TEARS FOR MOST OF HER LIFE...

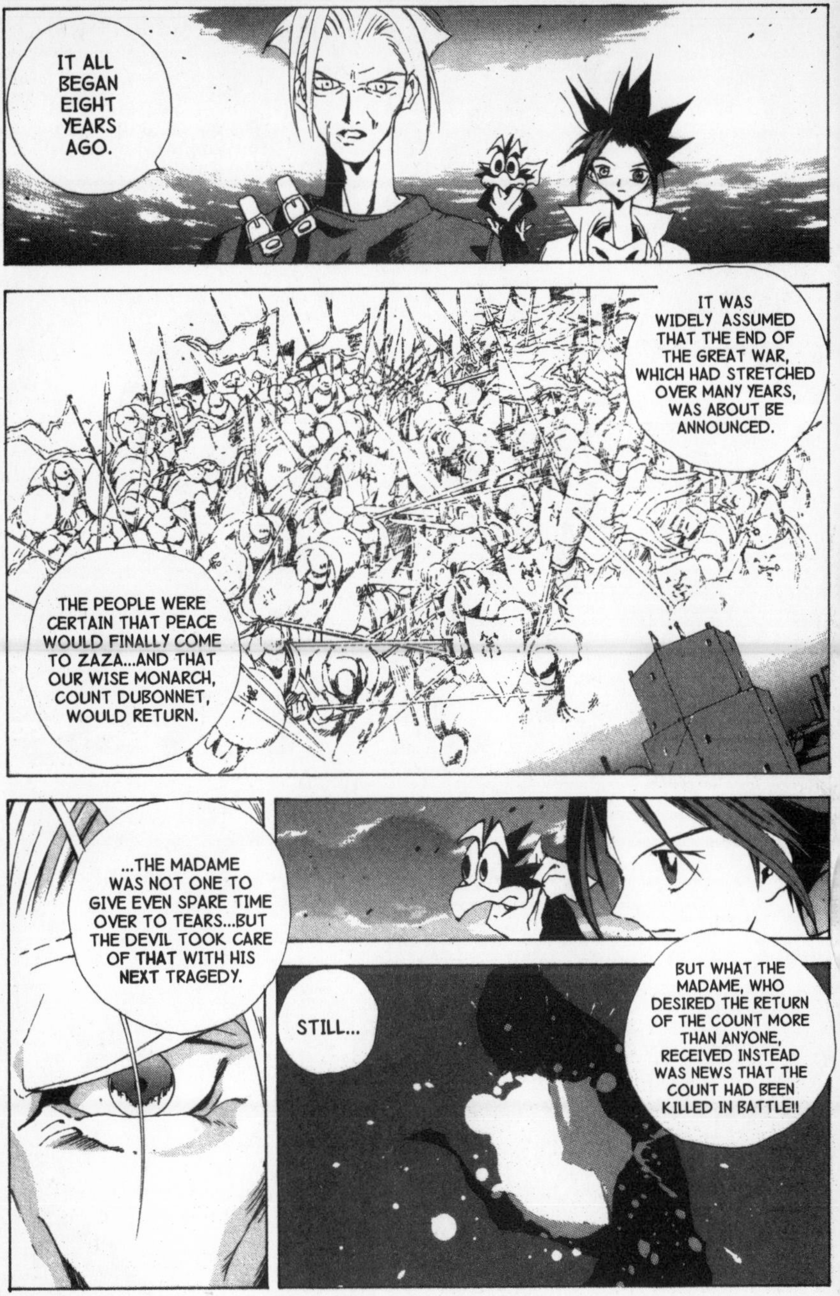
IT ALL BEGAN EIGHT YEARS AGO.
IT WAS WIDELY ASSUMED THAT THE END OF THE GREAT WAR, WHICH HAD STRETCHED OVER MANY YEARS, WAS ABOUT BE ANNOUNCED.
THE PEOPLE WERE CERTAIN THAT PEACE WOULD FINALLY COME TO ZAZA...AND THAT OUR WISE MONARCH, COUNT DUBONNET, WOULD RETURN.
BUT WHAT THE MADAME, WHO DESIRED THE RETURN OF THE COUNT MORE THAN ANYONE, RECEIVED INSTEAD WAS NEWS THAT THE COUNT HAD BEEN KILLED IN BATTLE!!
STILL...
...THE MADAME WAS NOT ONE TO GIVE EVEN SPARE TIME OVER TO TEARS...BUT THE DEVIL TOOK CARE OF THAT WITH HIS NEXT TRAGEDY.

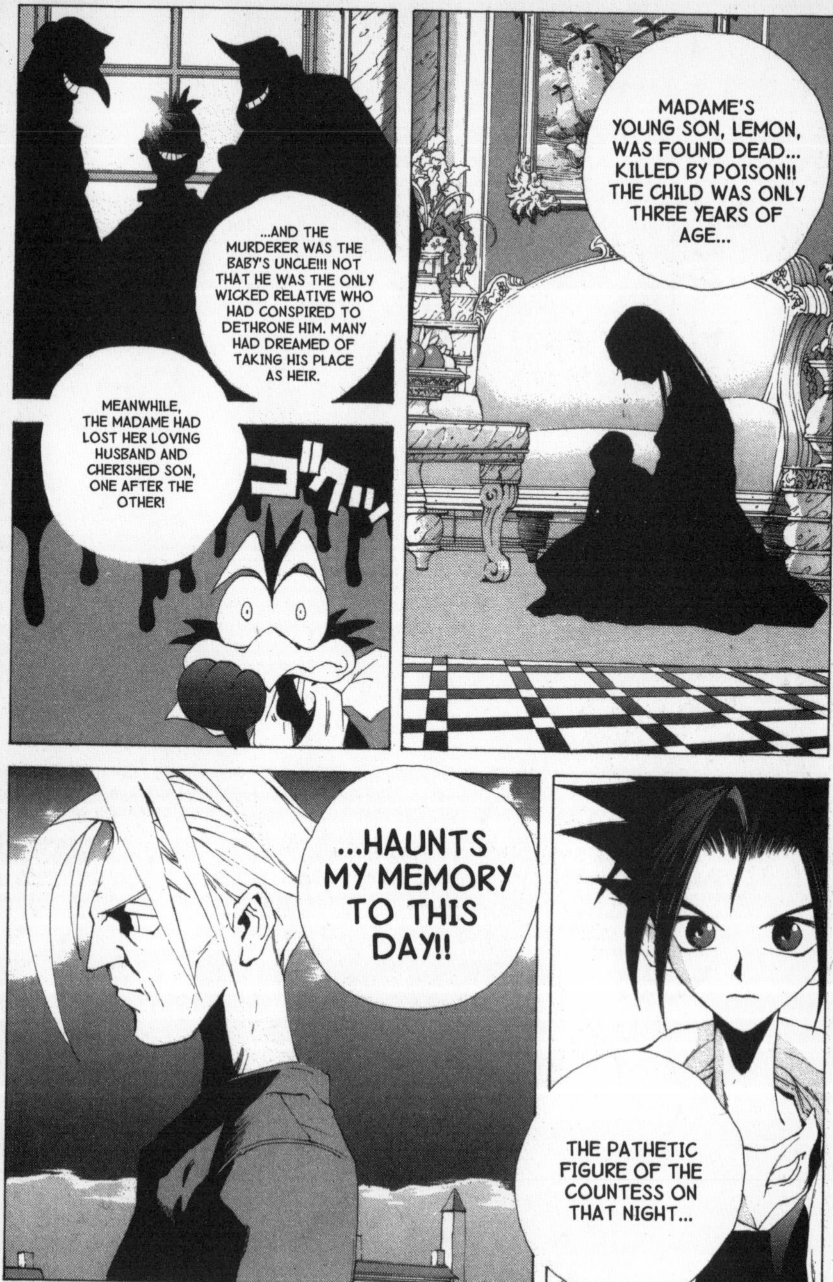
MADAME'S YOUNG SON, LEMON, WAS FOUND DEAD... KILLED BY POISON!! THE CHILD WAS ONLY THREE YEARS OF AGE...
...AND THE MURDERER WAS THE BABY'S UNCLE!!! NOT THAT HE WAS THE ONLY WICKED RELATIVE WHO HAD CONSPIRED TO DETHRONE HIM. MANY HAD DREAMED OF TAKING HIS PLACE AS HEIR.
MEANWHILE, THE MADAME HAD LOST HER LOVING HUSBAND AND CHERISHED SON, ONE AFTER THE OTHER!
ゴクッ
THE PATHETIC FIGURE OF THE COUNTESS ON THAT NIGHT...
...HAUNTS MY MEMORY TO THIS DAY!!

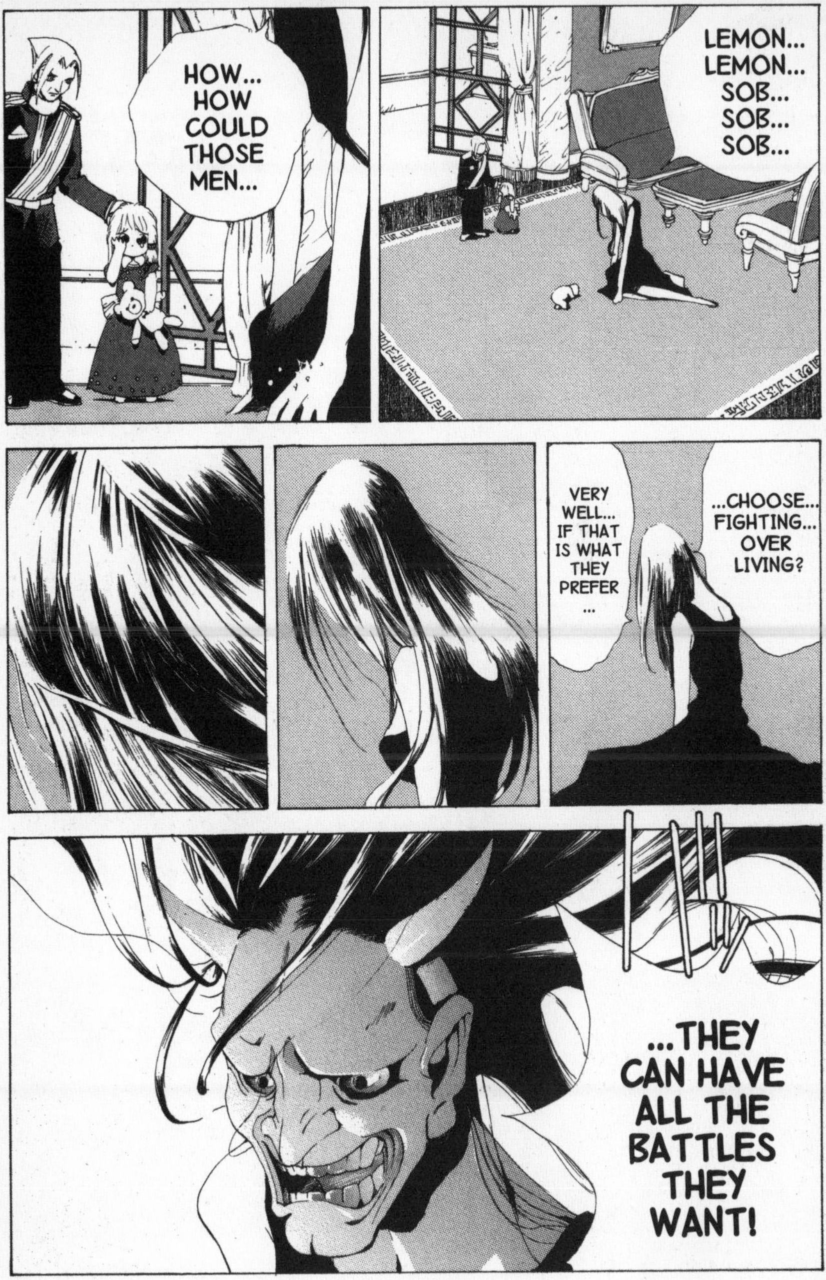
LEMON... LEMON... SOB... SOB... SOB...
HOW... HOW COULD THOSE MEN...
...CHOOSE... FIGHTING... OVER LIVING?
VERY WELL... IF THAT IS WHAT THEY PREFER ...
...THEY CAN HAVE ALL THE BATTLES THEY WANT!

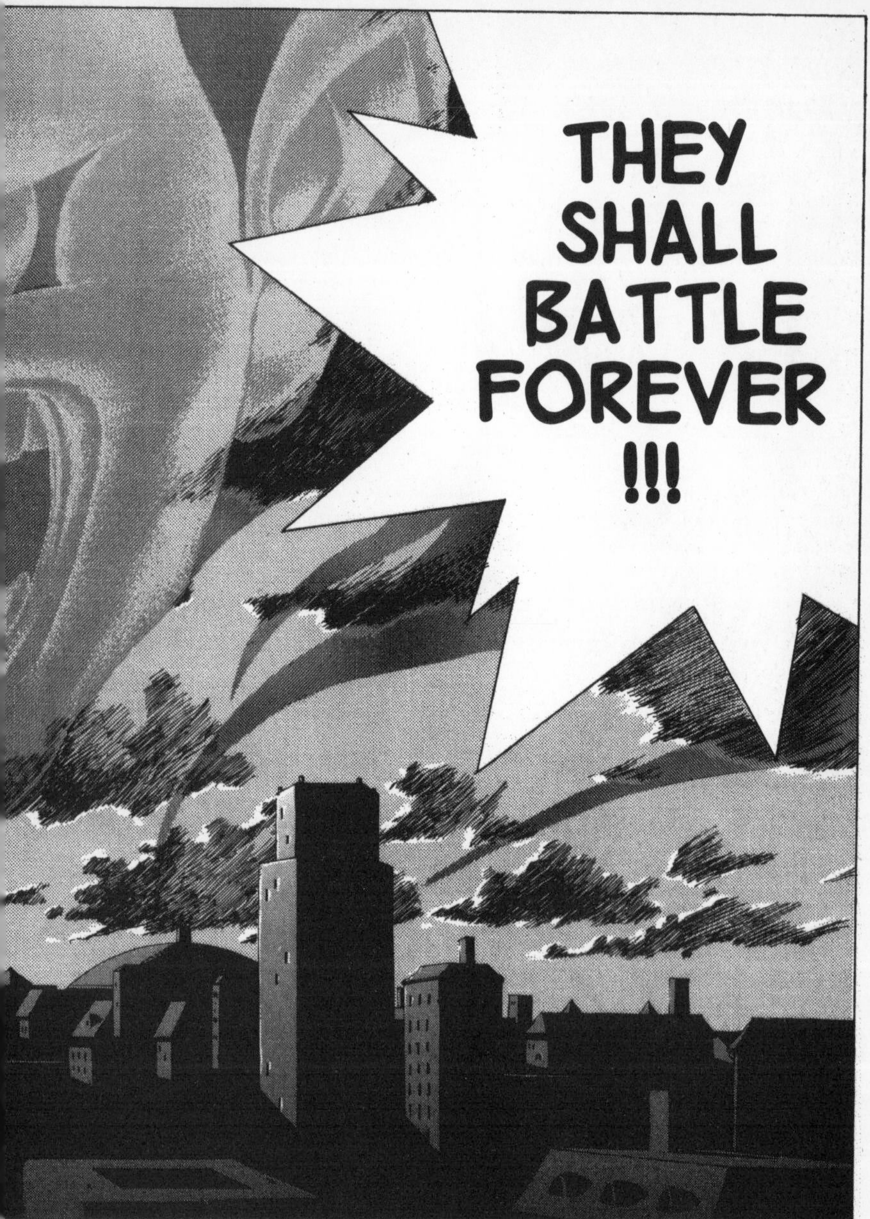
THEY SHALL BATTLE FOREVER !!!

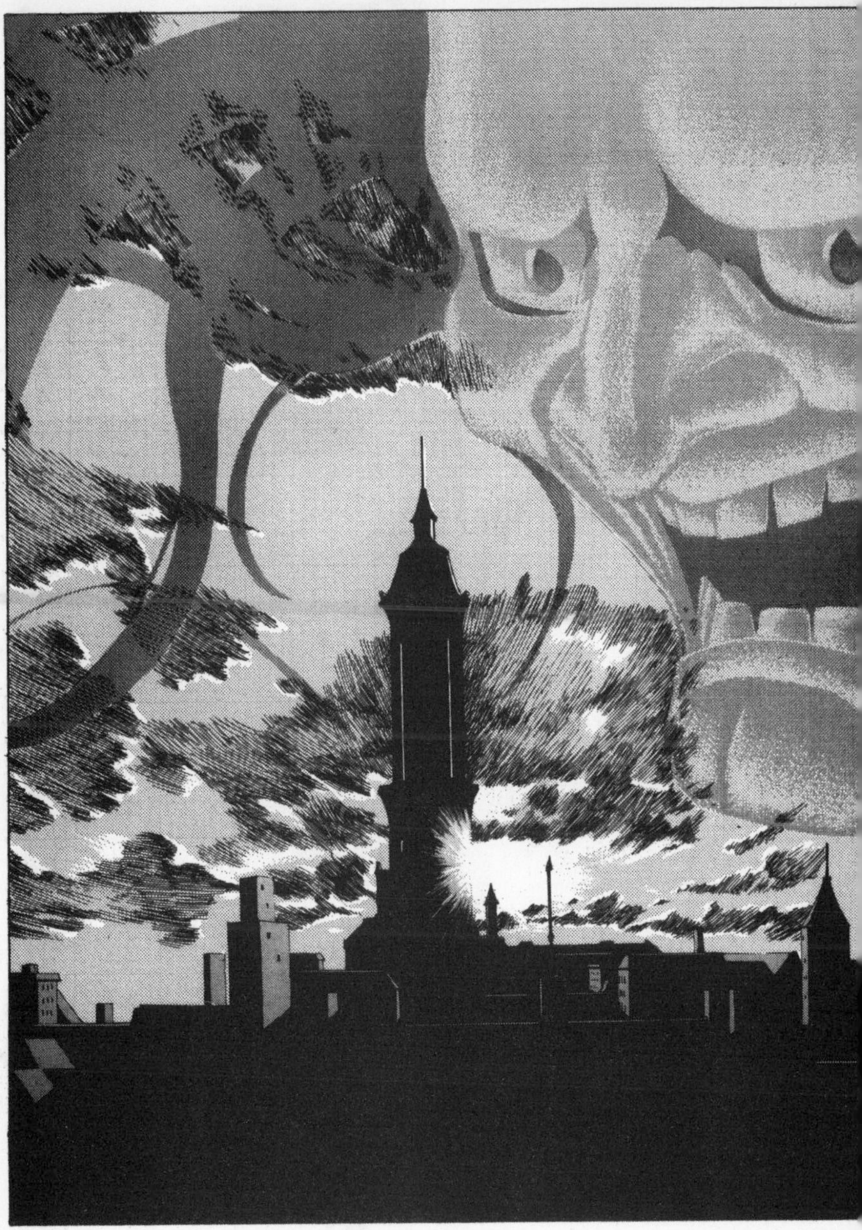

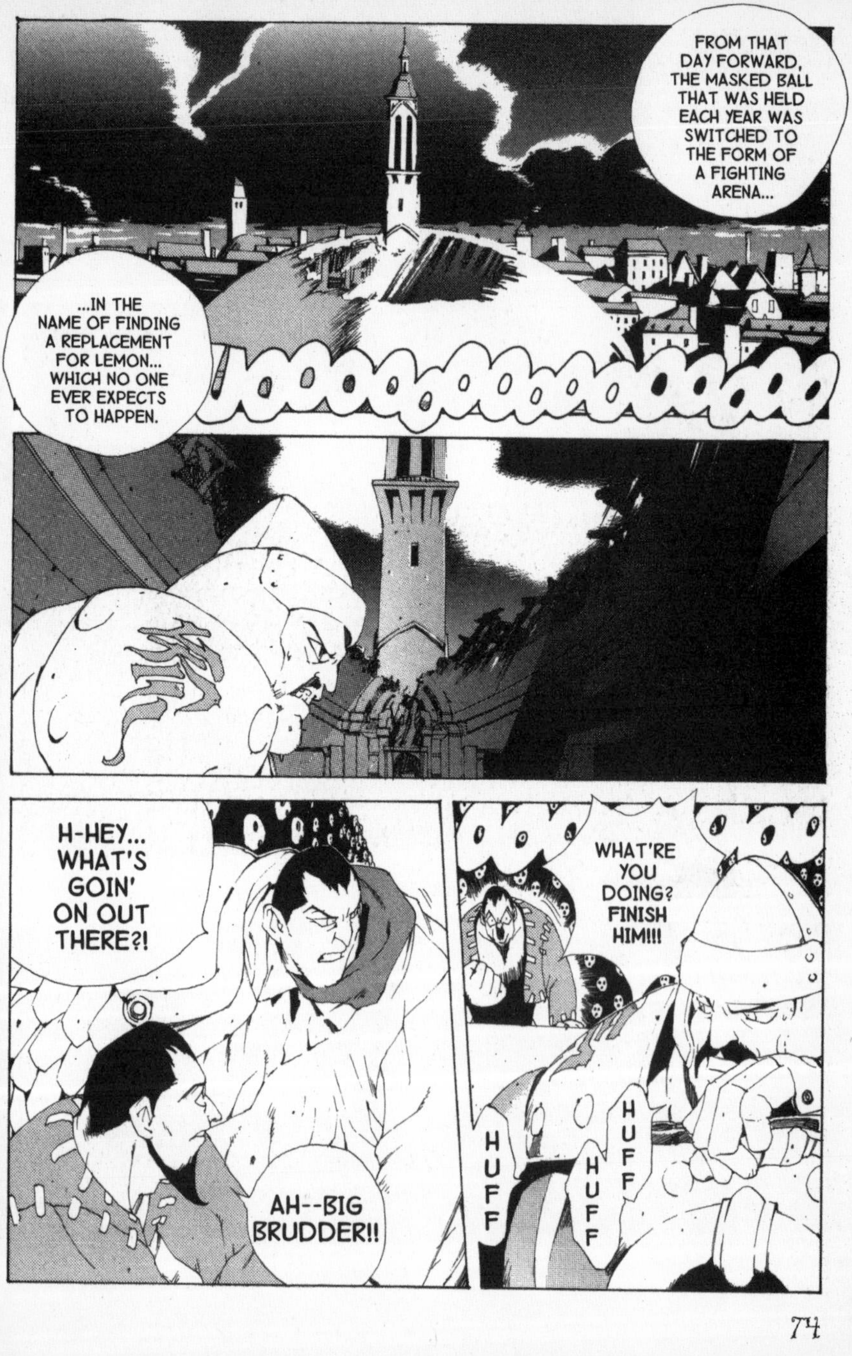
FROM THAT DAY FORWARD, THE MASKED BALL THAT WAS HELD EACH YEAR WAS SWITCHED TO THE FORM OF A FIGHTING ARENA...
...IN THE NAME OF FINDING A REPLACEMENT FOR LEMON... WHICH NO ONE EVER EXPECTS TO HAPPEN.
WHAT'RE YOU DOING? FINISH HIM!!!
HUFF
HUFF
HUFF
HUFF
H-HEY... WHAT'S GOIN' ON OUT THERE?!
AH--BIG BRUDDER!!

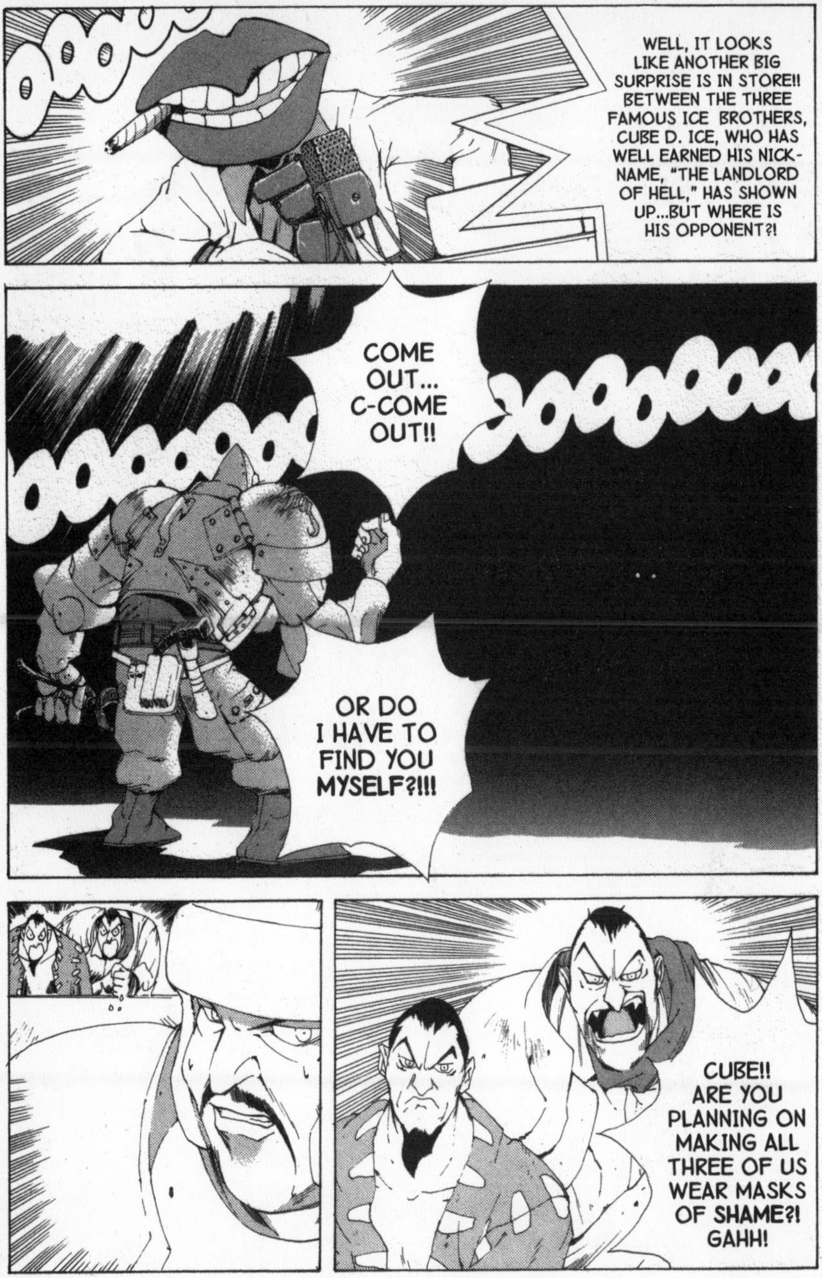
WELL, IT LOOKS LIKE ANOTHER BIG SURPRISE IS IN STORE!! BETWEEN THE THREE FAMOUS ICE BROTHERS, CUBE D. ICE, WHO HAS WELL EARNED HIS NICK-NAME, "THE LANDLORD OF HELL," HAS SHOWN UP...BUT WHERE IS HIS OPPONENT?!
COME OUT... C-COME OUT!!
OR DO I HAVE TO FIND YOU MYSELF?!!!
CUBE!! ARE YOU PLANNING ON MAKING ALL THREE OF US WEAR MASKS OF SHAME?! GAHH!

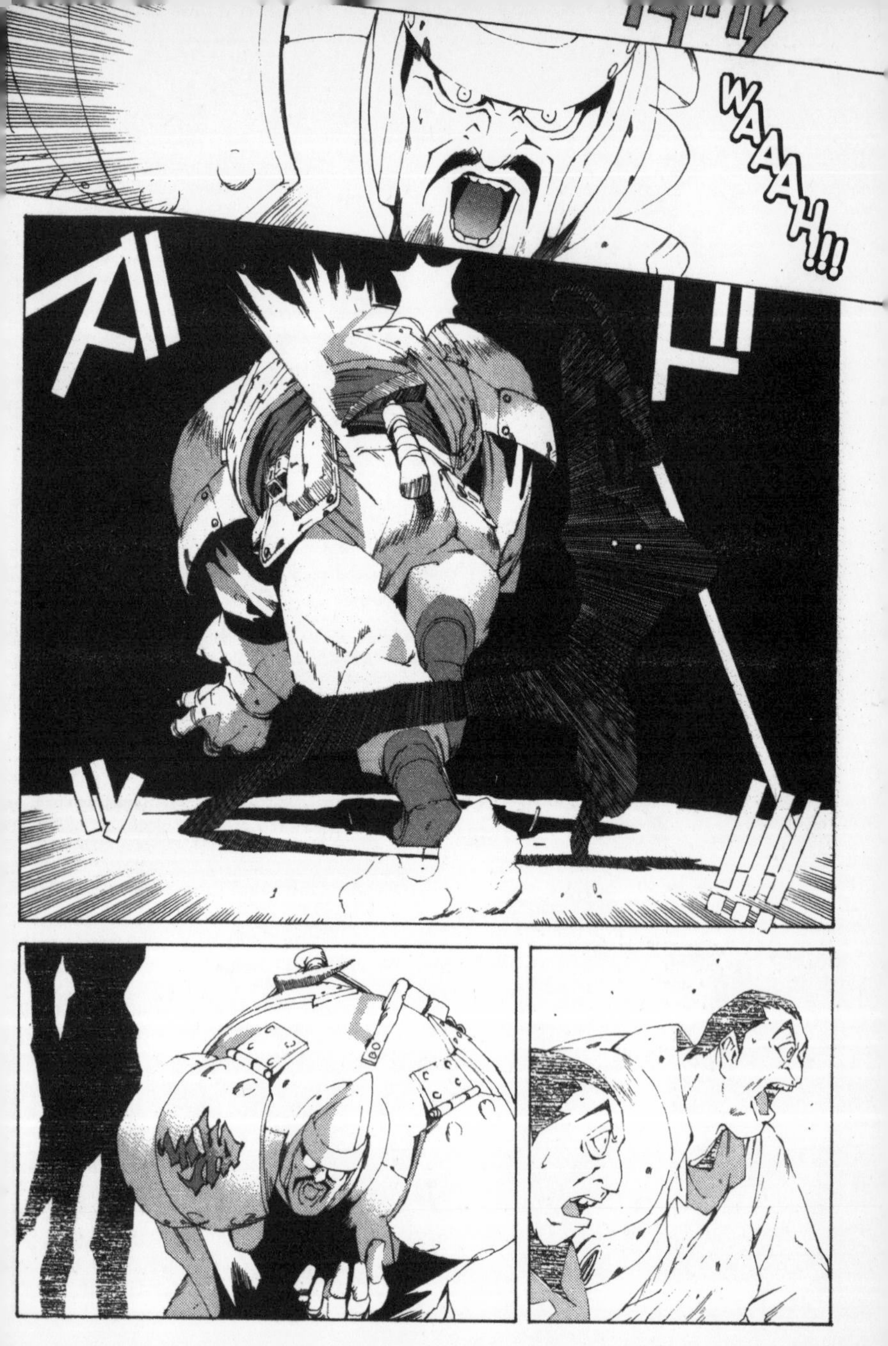
WAAAAH!!!

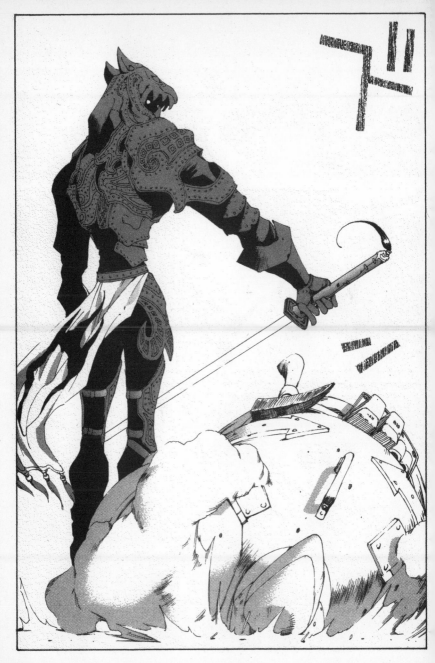

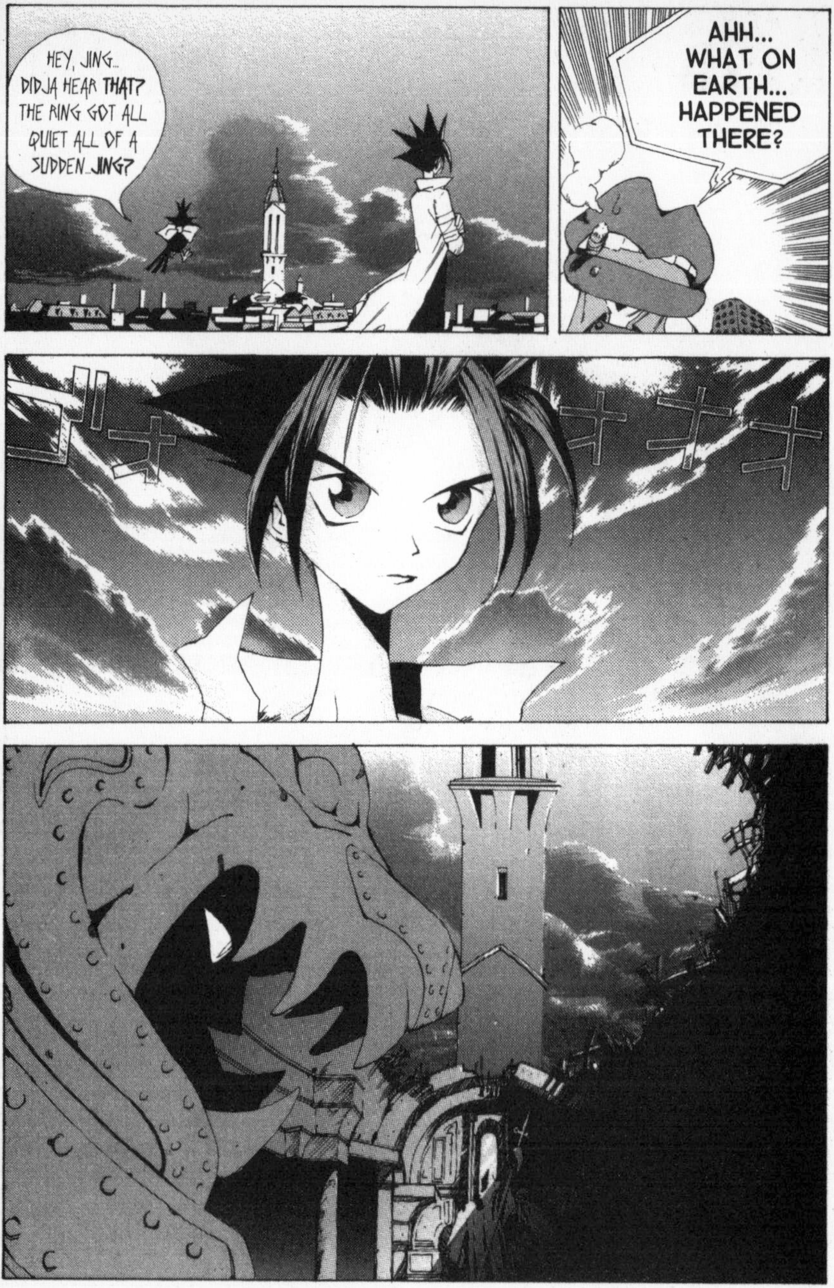
AHH... WHAT ON EARTH... HAPPENED THERE?
HEY, JING... DIDJA HEAR THAT? THE RING GOT ALL QUIET ALL OF A SUDDEN...JING?

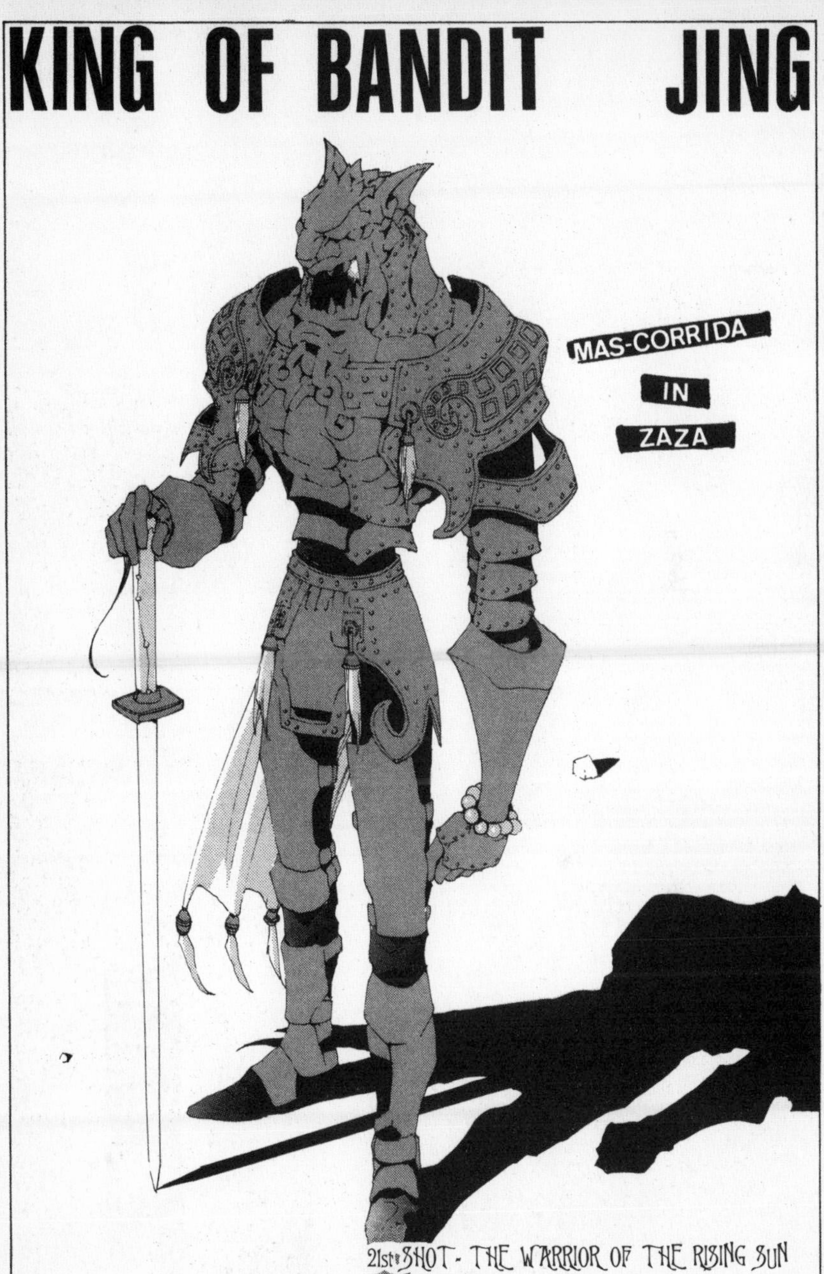
KING OF BANDIT JING
MAS-CORRIDA
IN
ZAZA
21st SHOT - THE WARRIOR OF THE RISING SUN

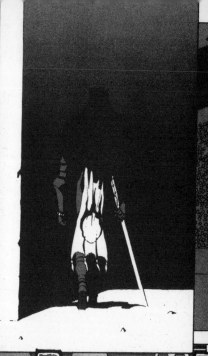

AAAAAAAAAAAAAAAA

WHERE ON EARTH DID HE COME FROM?

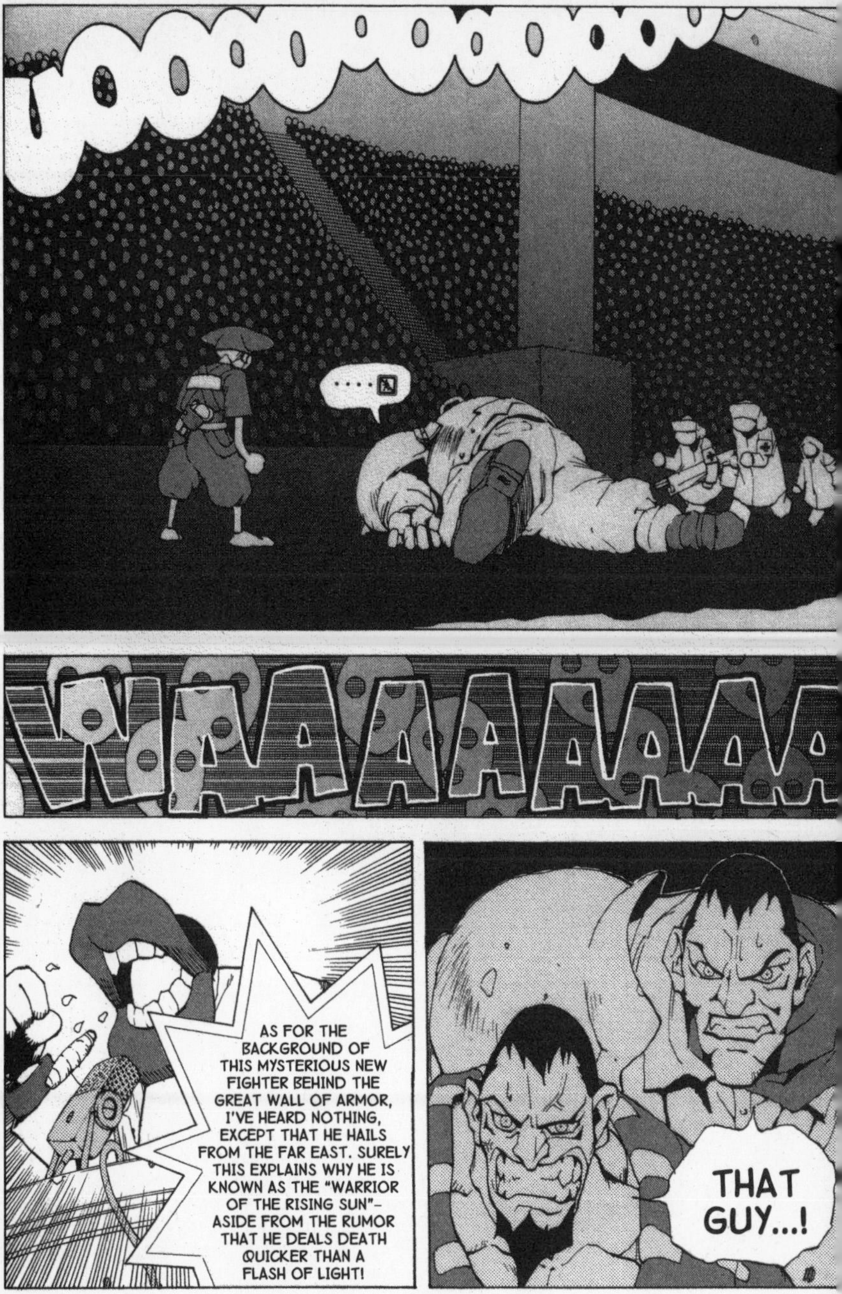
OOOOOOOOOO
....
WAAAAAAAAA
THAT GUY...!
AS FOR THE BACKGROUND OF THIS MYSTERIOUS NEW FIGHTER BEHIND THE GREAT WALL OF ARMOR, I'VE HEARD NOTHING, EXCEPT THAT HE HAILS FROM THE FAR EAST. SURELY THIS EXPLAINS WHY HE IS KNOWN AS THE "WARRIOR OF THE RISING SUN"– ASIDE FROM THE RUMOR THAT HE DEALS DEATH QUICKER THAN A FLASH OF LIGHT!

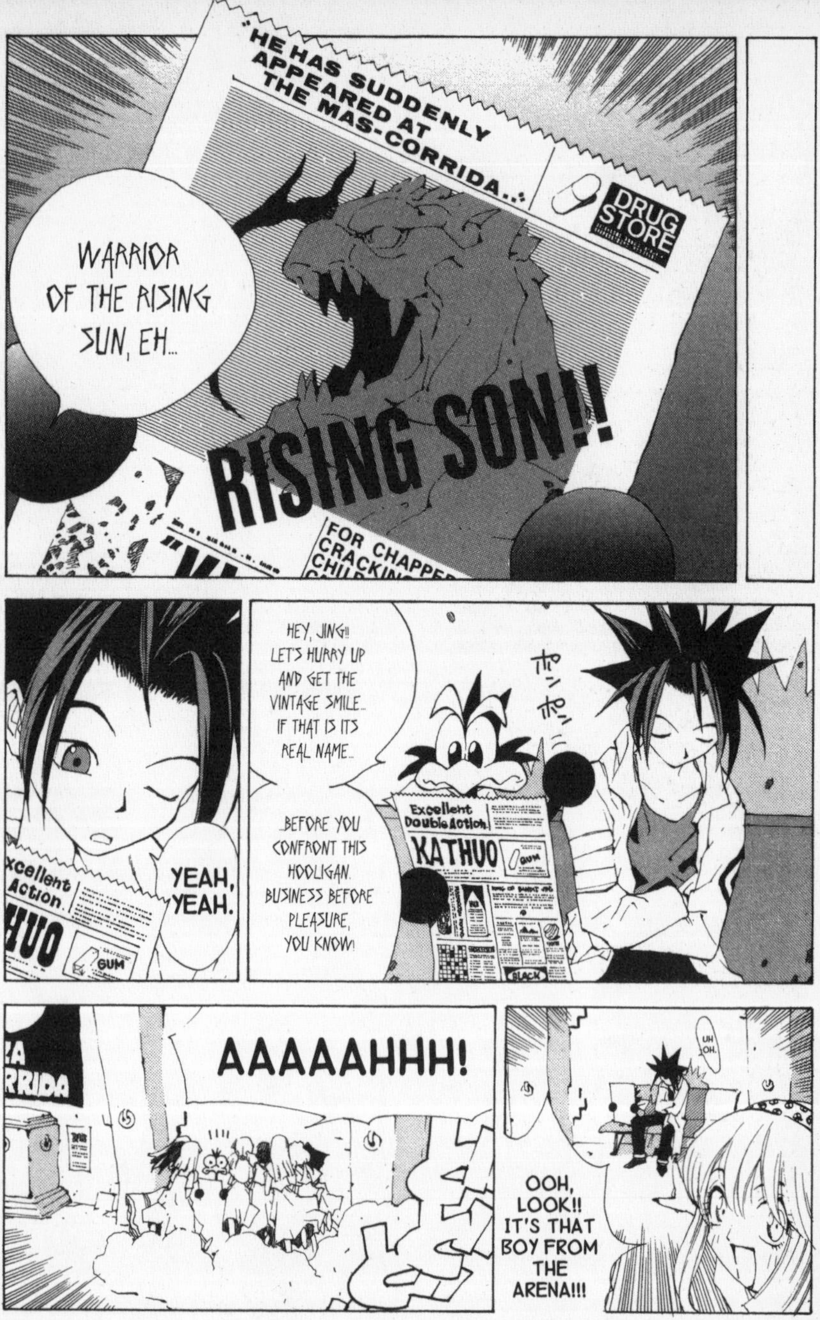
"HE HAS SUDDENLY APPEARED AT THE MAS-CORRIDA..!
DRUG STORE
WARRIOR OF THE RISING SUN, EH...
RISING SON!!
HEY, JING!! LET'S HURRY UP AND GET THE VINTAGE SMILE... IF THAT IS ITS REAL NAME...
...BEFORE YOU CONFRONT THIS HOOLIGAN. BUSINESS BEFORE PLEASURE, YOU KNOW!
ポンポン
Excellent Double Action
KATHUO
GUM
BLACK
YEAH, YEAH.
UH OH.
OOH, LOOK!! IT'S THAT BOY FROM THE ARENA!!!
AAAAAHHH!

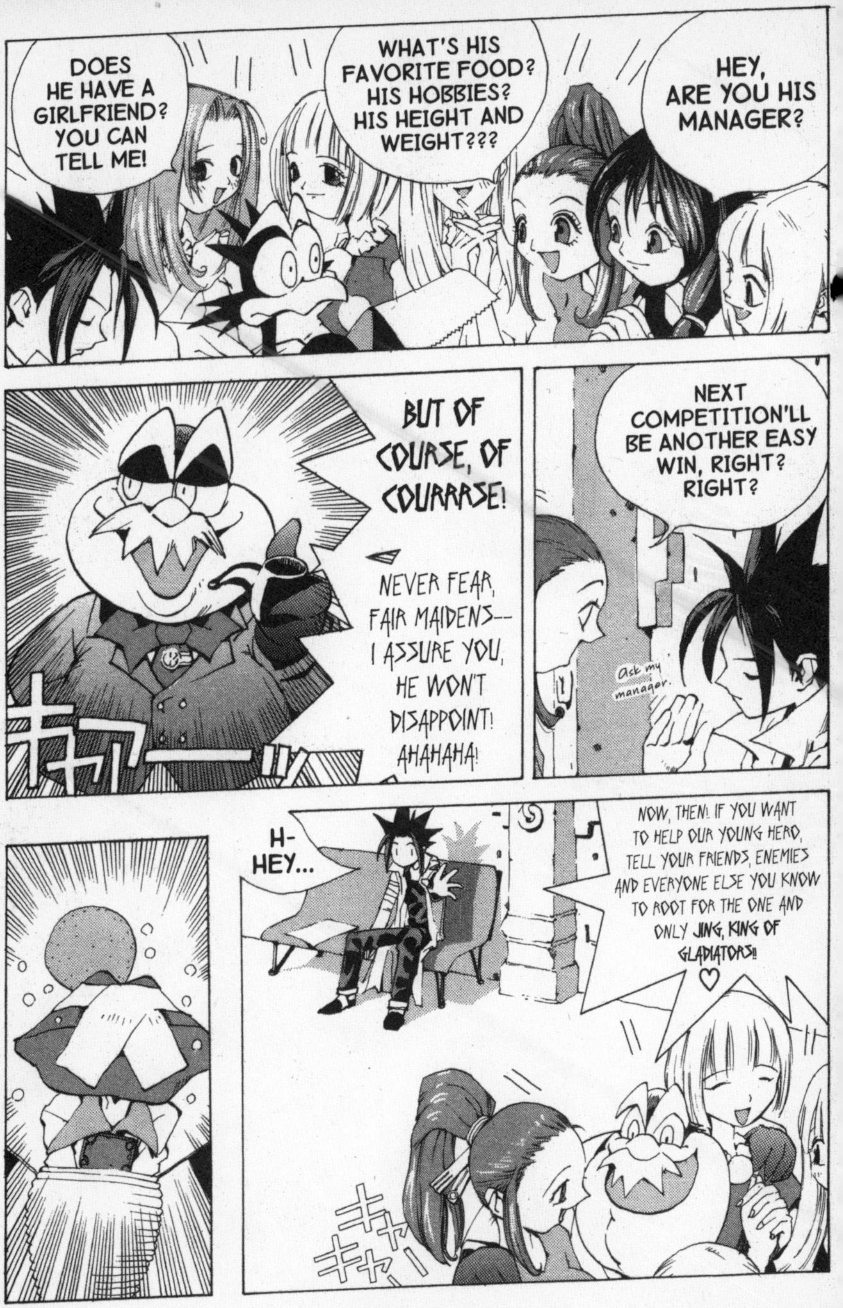
HEY, ARE YOU HIS MANAGER?
WHAT'S HIS FAVORITE FOOD? HIS HOBBIES? HIS HEIGHT AND WEIGHT???
DOES HE HAVE A GIRLFRIEND? YOU CAN TELL ME!
NEXT COMPETITION'LL BE ANOTHER EASY WIN, RIGHT? RIGHT?
Ask my manager.
BUT OF COURSE, OF COURRRSE!
NEVER FEAR, FAIR MAIDENS-- I ASSURE YOU, HE WON'T DISAPPOINT! AHAHAHA!
キャアーーッ
NOW, THEN! IF YOU WANT TO HELP OUR YOUNG HERO, TELL YOUR FRIENDS, ENEMIES AND EVERYONE ELSE YOU KNOW TO ROOT FOR THE ONE AND ONLY JING, KING OF GLADIATORS!! ♡
H- HEY...
キャ キャ!

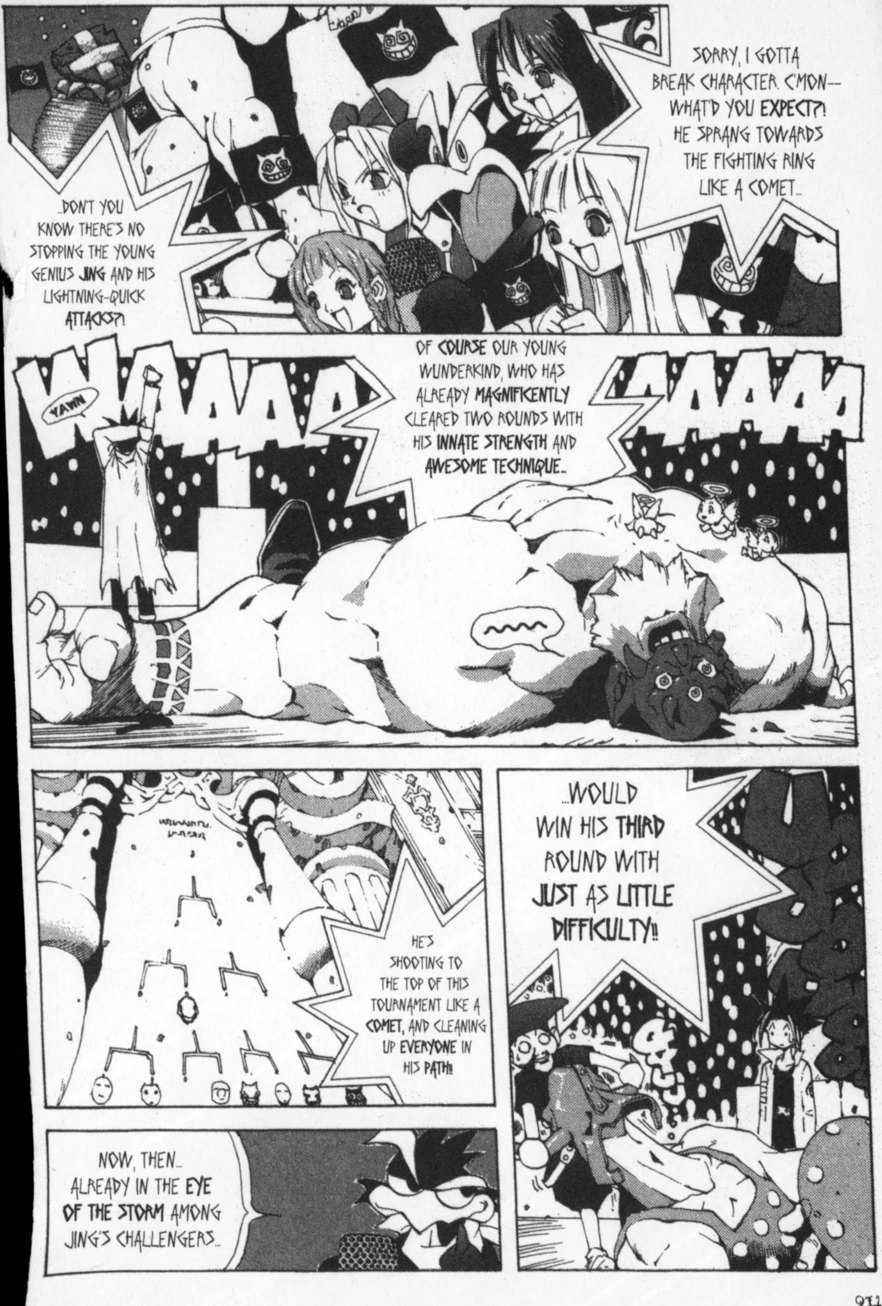

SORRY, I GOTTA BREAK CHARACTER. C'MON-- WHAT'D YOU EXPECT?! HE SPRANG TOWARDS THE FIGHTING RING LIKE A COMET...
...DON'T YOU KNOW THERE'S NO STOPPING THE YOUNG GENIUS JING AND HIS LIGHTNING-QUICK ATTACKS?!
WAAAAAAAA
YAWN
OF COURSE OUR YOUNG WUNDERKIND, WHO HAS ALREADY MAGNIFICENTLY CLEARED TWO ROUNDS WITH HIS INNATE STRENGTH AND AWESOME TECHNIQUE...
~~~
...WOULD WIN HIS THIRD ROUND WITH JUST AS LITTLE DIFFICULTY!!
HE'S SHOOTING TO THE TOP OF THIS TOURNAMENT LIKE A COMET, AND CLEANING UP EVERYONE IN HIS PATH!!
NOW, THEN... ALREADY IN THE EYE OF THE STORM AMONG JING'S CHALLENGERS...
~~~

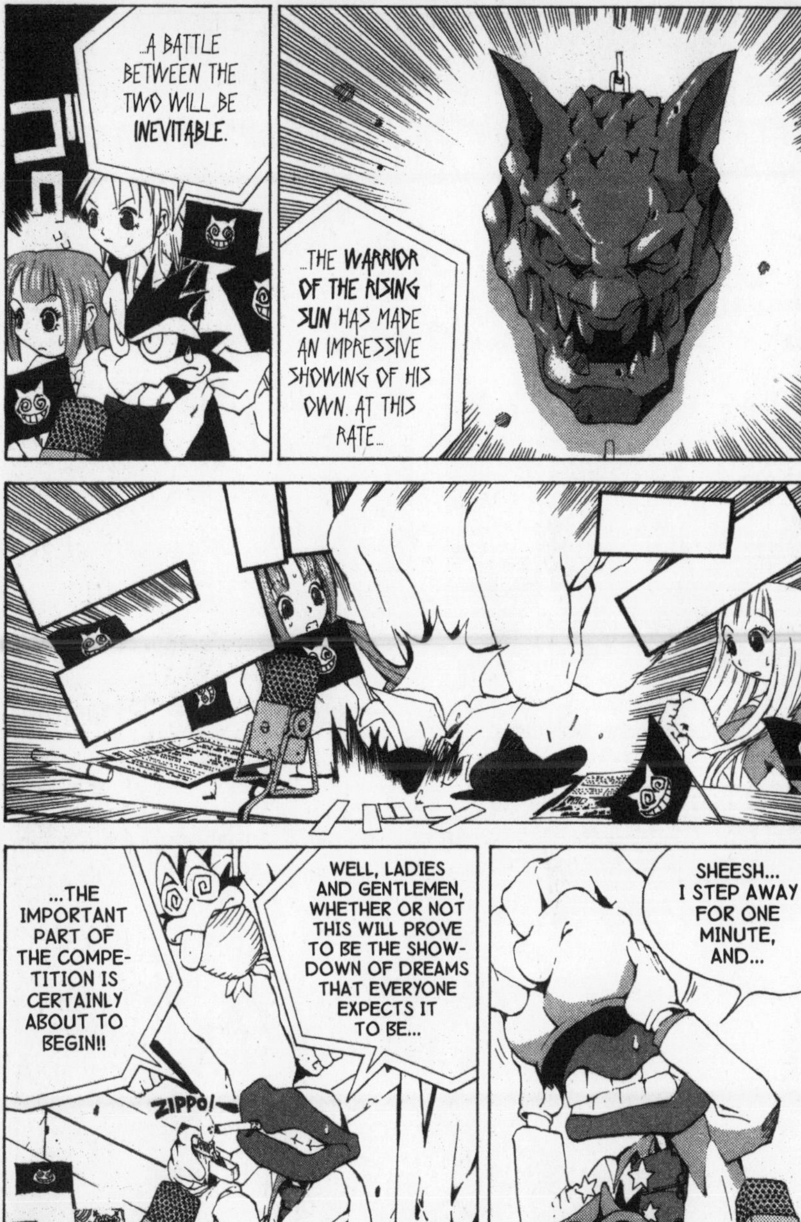
...THE WARRIOR OF THE RISING SUN HAS MADE AN IMPRESSIVE SHOWING OF HIS OWN. AT THIS RATE...
...A BATTLE BETWEEN THE TWO WILL BE INEVITABLE.
SHEESH... I STEP AWAY FOR ONE MINUTE, AND...
WELL, LADIES AND GENTLEMEN, WHETHER OR NOT THIS WILL PROVE TO BE THE SHOW-DOWN OF DREAMS THAT EVERYONE EXPECTS IT TO BE...
...THE IMPORTANT PART OF THE COMPE-TITION IS CERTAINLY ABOUT TO BEGIN!!
ZIPPO!

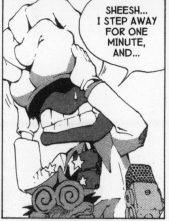

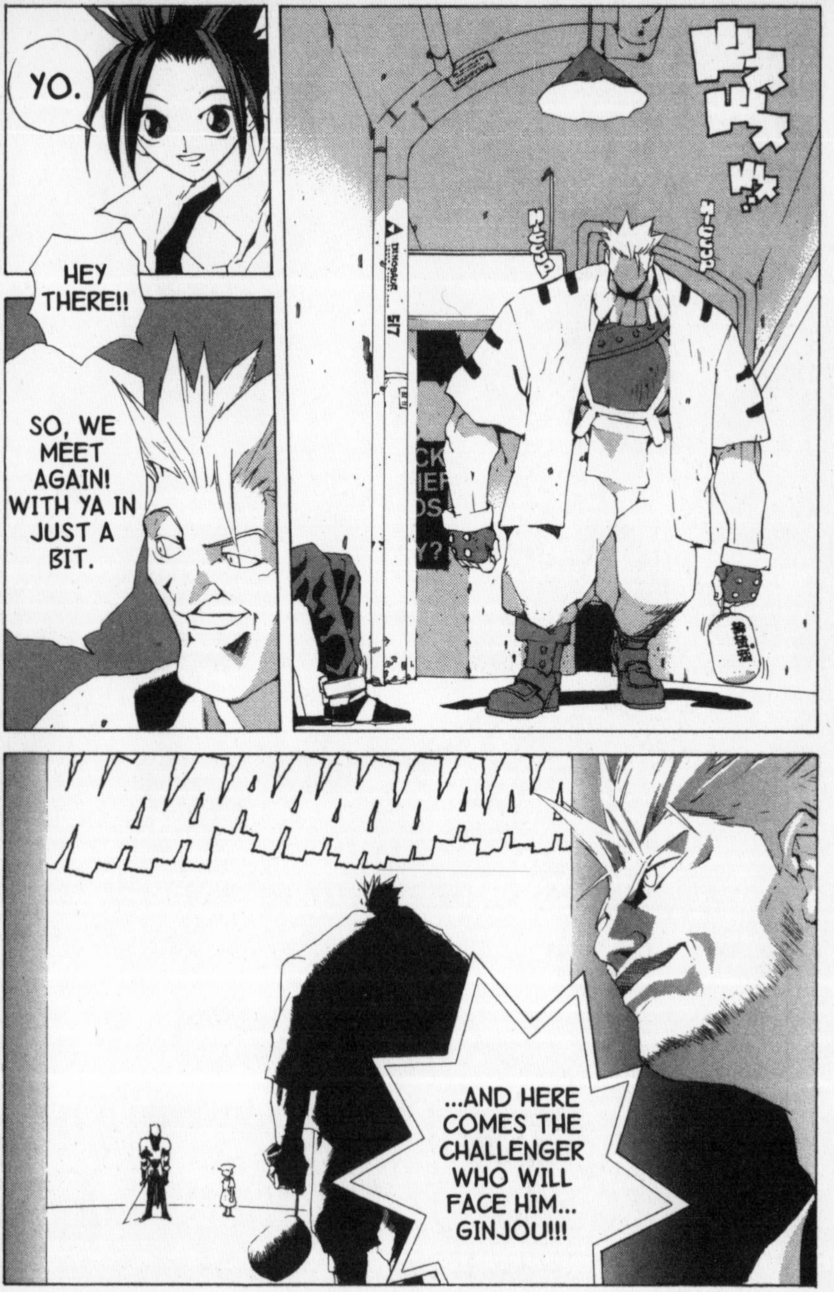
YO.
HEY THERE!!
SO, WE MEET AGAIN! WITH YA IN JUST A BIT.
...AND HERE COMES THE CHALLENGER WHO WILL FACE HIM... GINJOU!!!

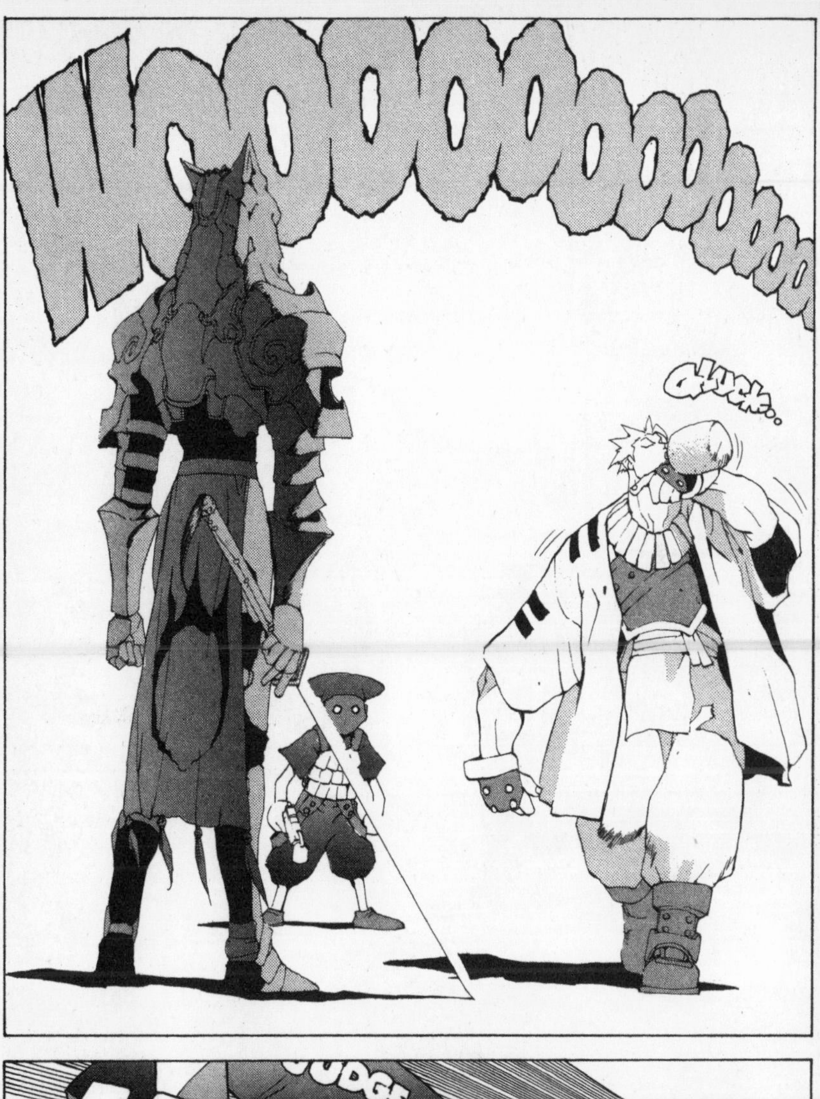
WHOOOOOOOOOOOOOOO
CHUCK...

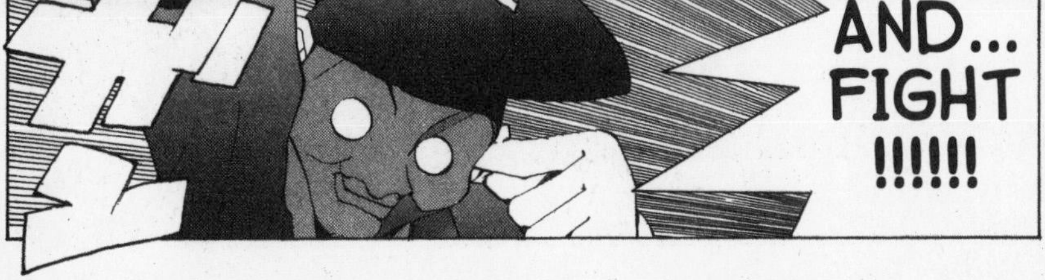
JUDGE
AND... FIGHT !!!!!!

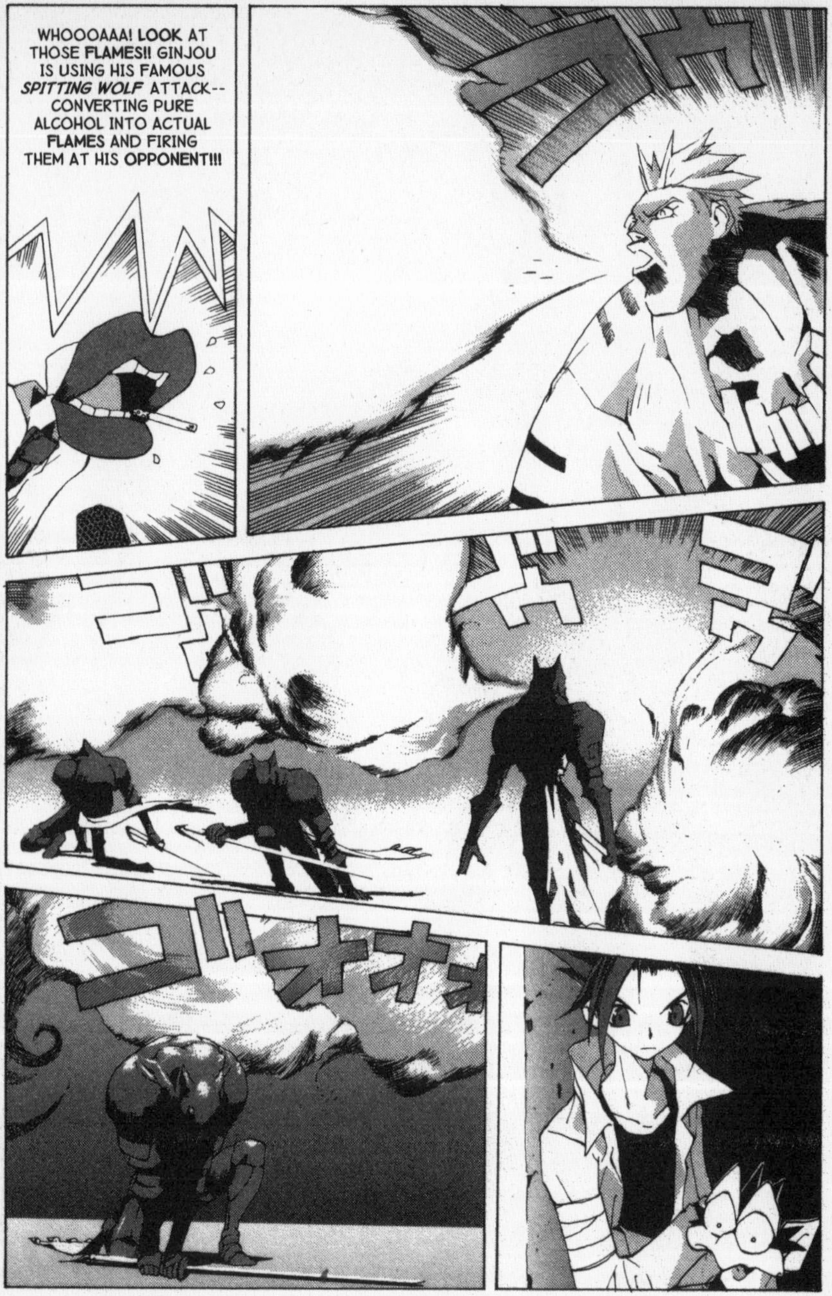
WHOOOAAA! **LOOK** AT THOSE **FLAMES!!** GINJOU IS USING HIS FAMOUS ***SPITTING WOLF*** ATTACK-- CONVERTING PURE ALCOHOL INTO ACTUAL **FLAMES** AND FIRING THEM AT HIS **OPPONENT!!!**

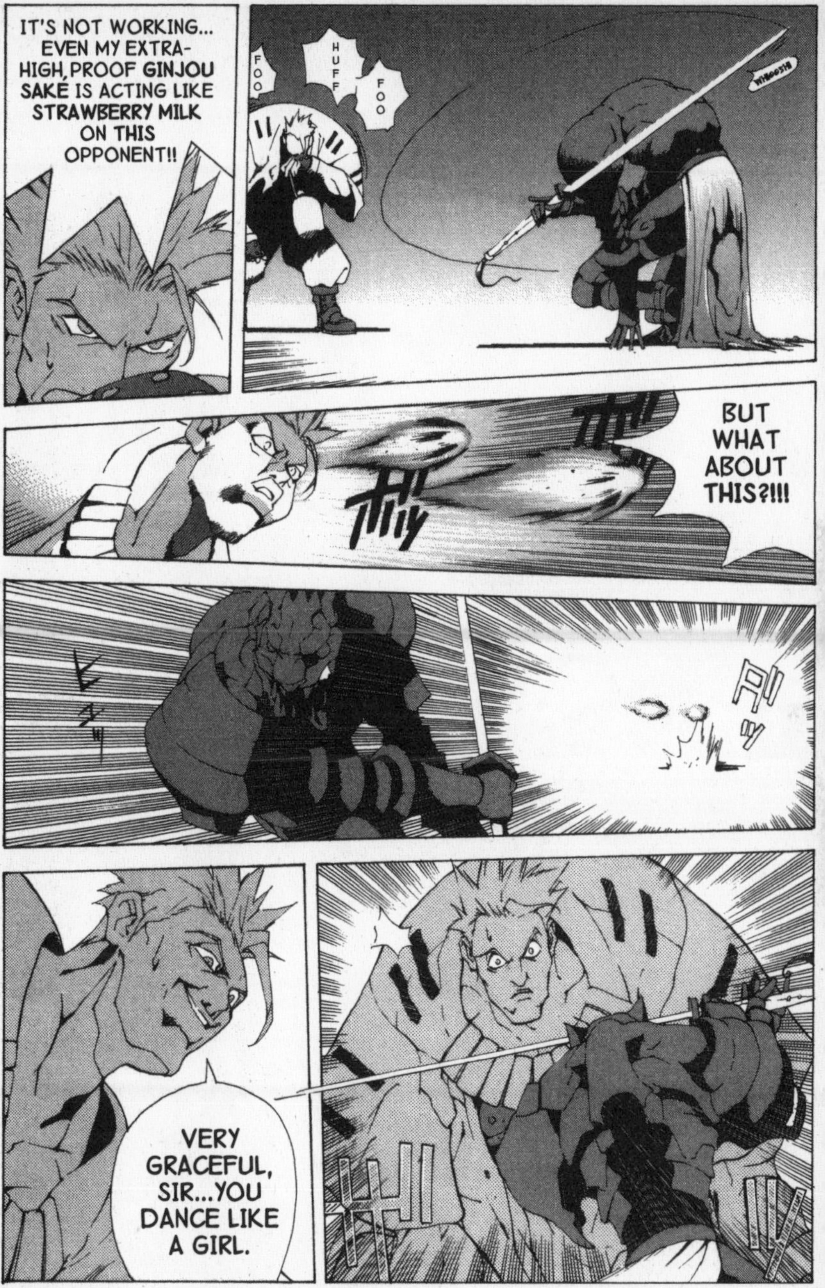
WHOOSH
FOO
HUFF
FOO
IT'S NOT WORKING... EVEN MY EXTRA-HIGH, PROOF GINJOU SAKÉ IS ACTING LIKE STRAWBERRY MILK ON THIS OPPONENT!!
BUT WHAT ABOUT THIS?!!!
VERY GRACEFUL, SIR...YOU DANCE LIKE A GIRL.

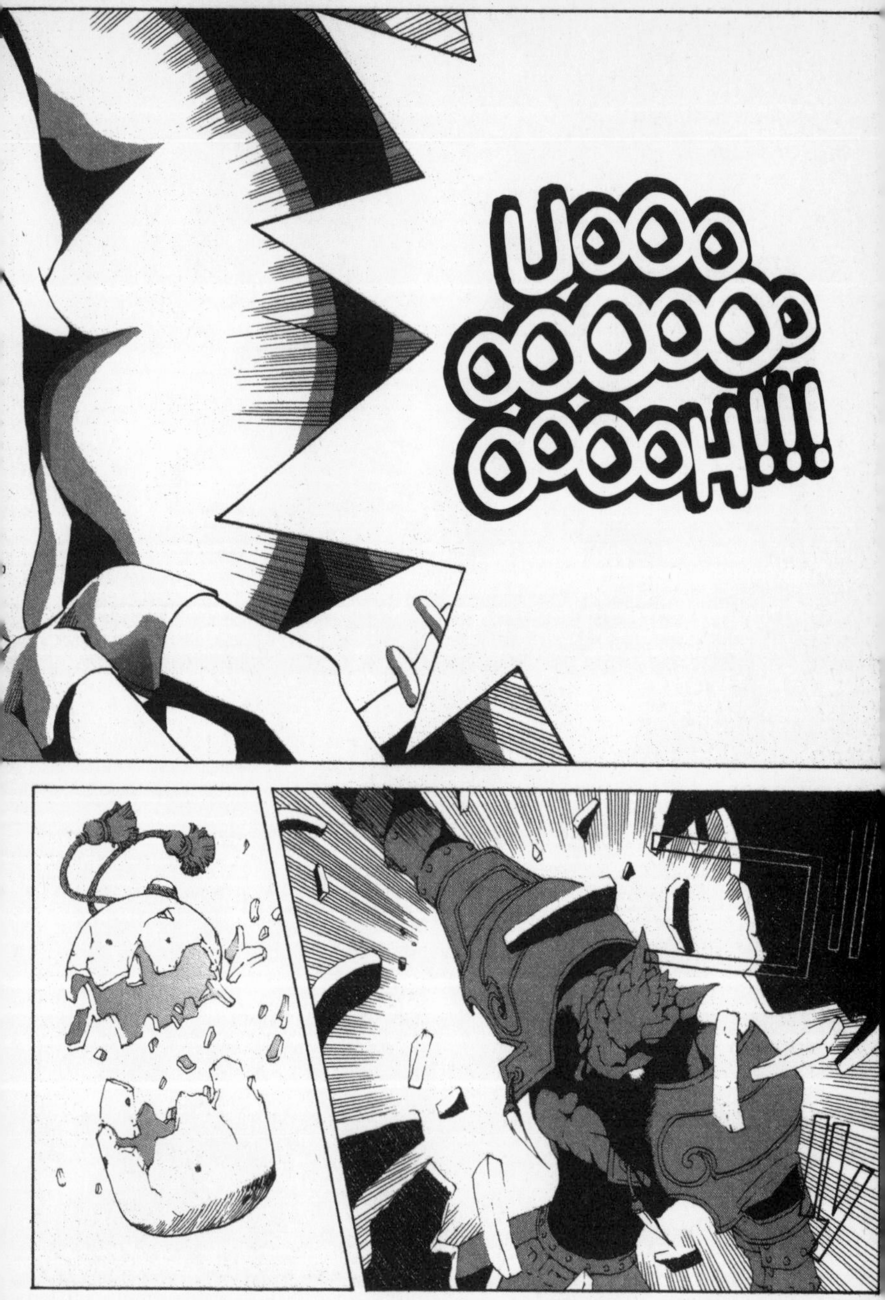
UOOOOOOOOOOOOOH!!!

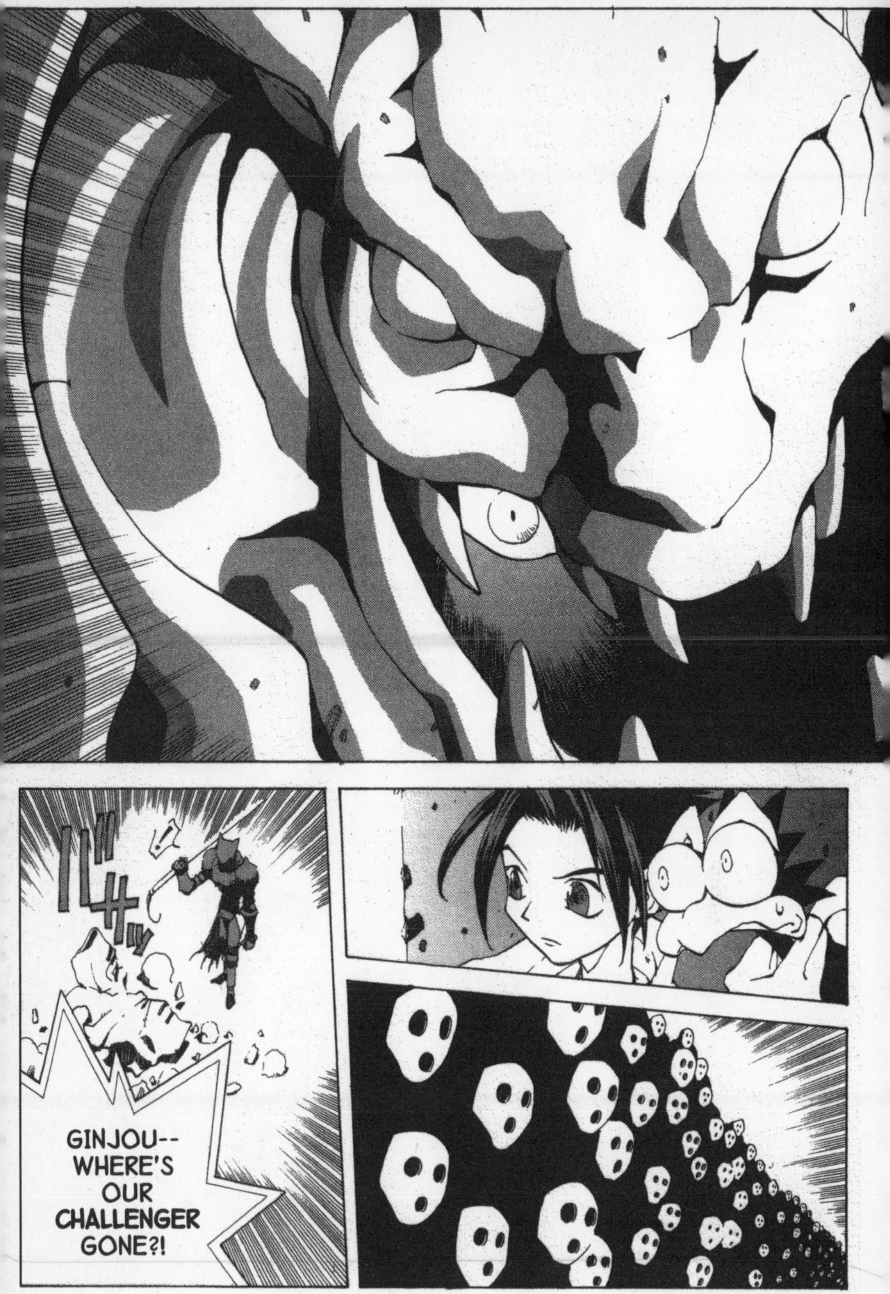
GINJOU-- WHERE'S OUR CHALLENGER GONE?!

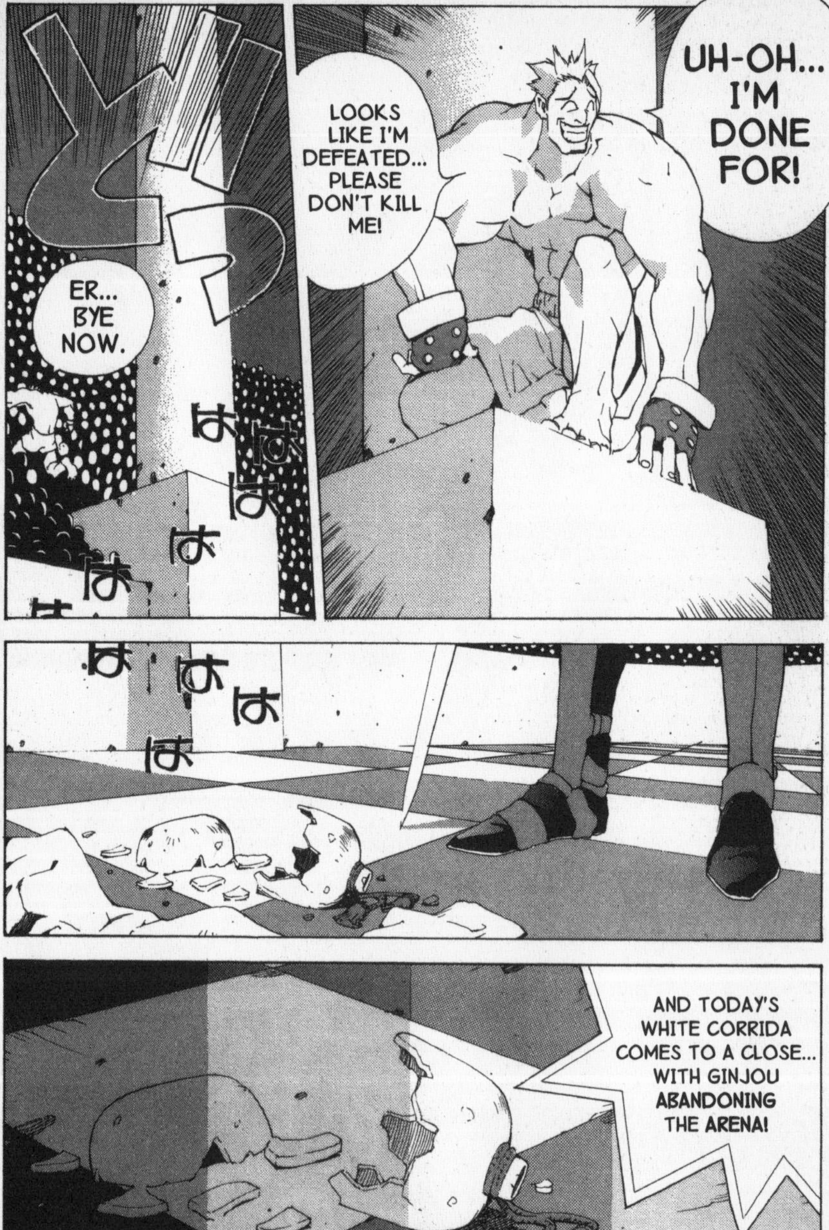
UH-OH... I'M DONE FOR!
LOOKS LIKE I'M DEFEATED... PLEASE DON'T KILL ME!
ER... BYE NOW.
AND TODAY'S WHITE CORRIDA COMES TO A CLOSE... WITH GINJOU ABANDONING THE ARENA!

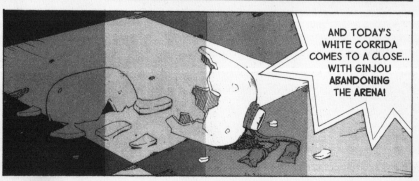

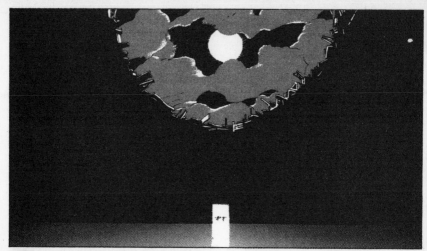

WOO WOO WOO WOO WOO WOO WOO

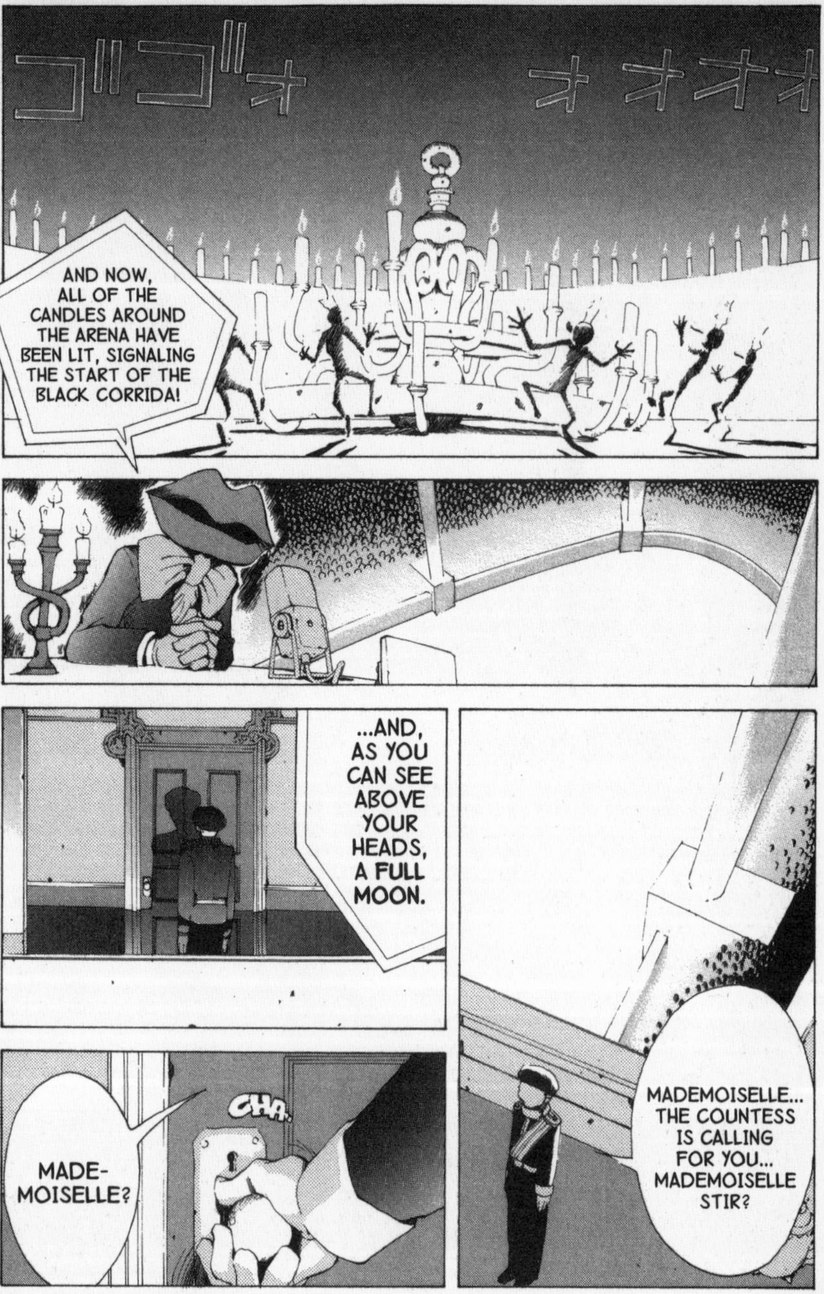
ゴゴォ
オオオオ
AND NOW, ALL OF THE CANDLES AROUND THE ARENA HAVE BEEN LIT, SIGNALING THE START OF THE BLACK CORRIDA!
MADEMOISELLE... THE COUNTESS IS CALLING FOR YOU... MADEMOISELLE STIR?
...AND, AS YOU CAN SEE ABOVE YOUR HEADS, A FULL MOON.
CHA.
MADE-MOISELLE?

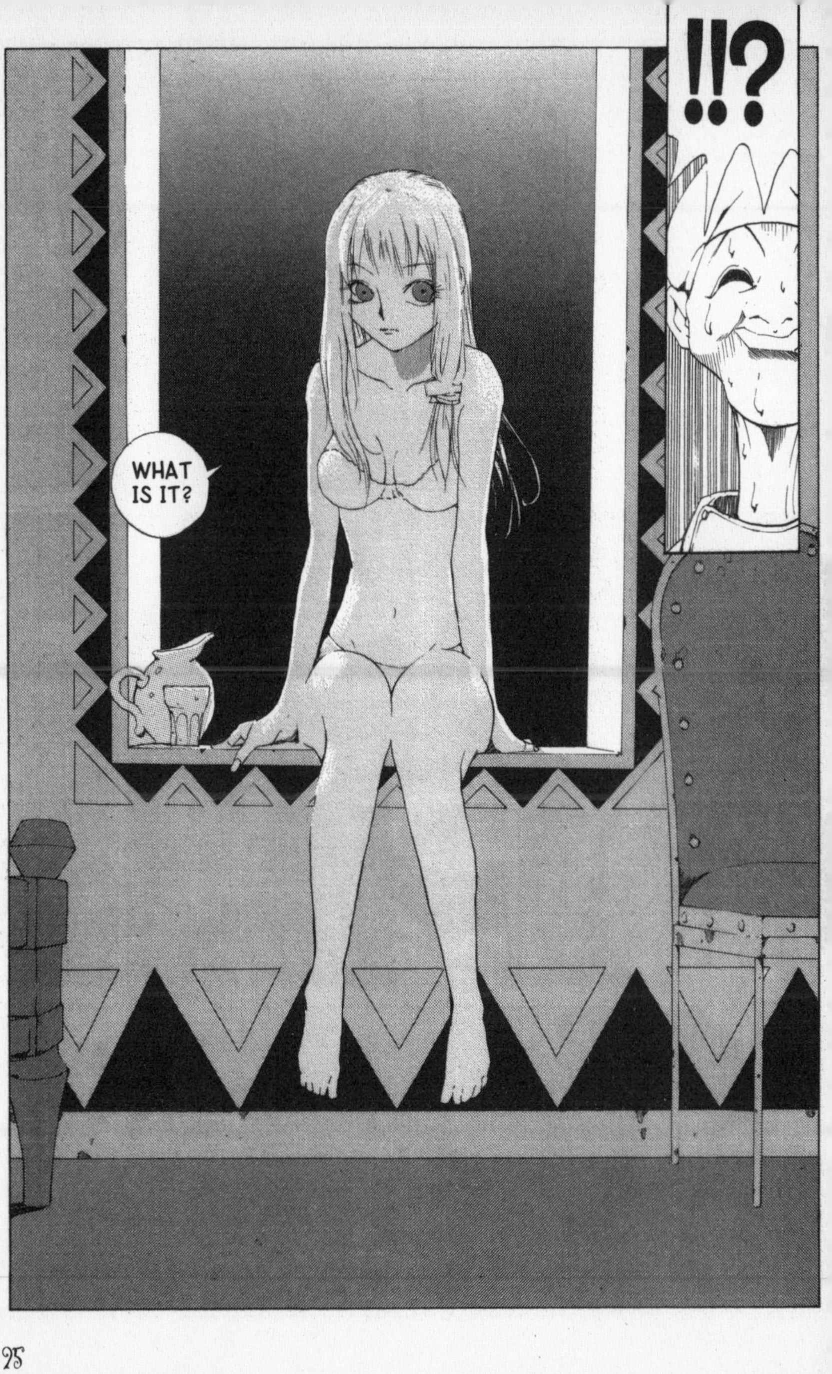
!!?
WHAT IS IT?

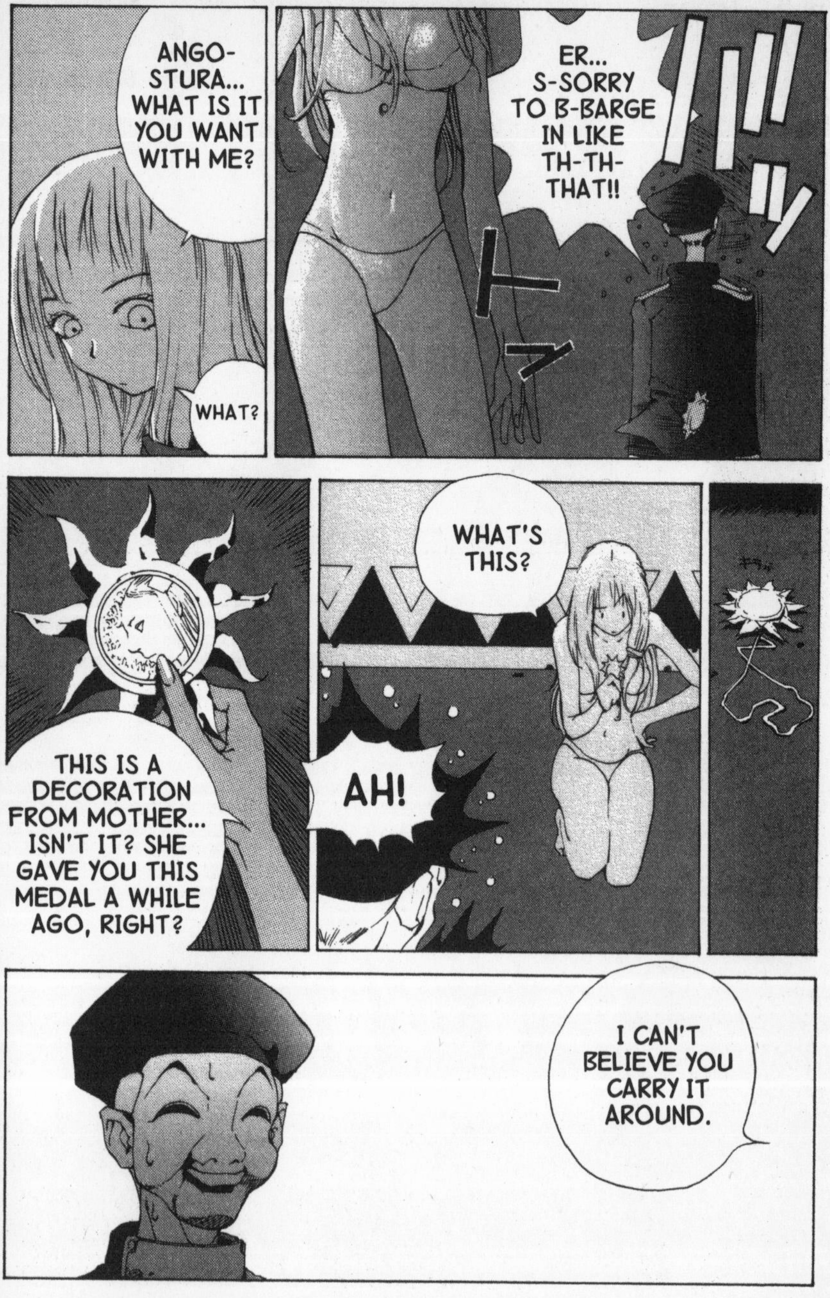
ER... S-SORRY TO B-BARGE IN LIKE TH-TH-THAT!!
ANGO-STURA... WHAT IS IT YOU WANT WITH ME?
WHAT?
WHAT'S THIS?
AH!
THIS IS A DECORATION FROM MOTHER... ISN'T IT? SHE GAVE YOU THIS MEDAL A WHILE AGO, RIGHT?
I CAN'T BELIEVE YOU CARRY IT AROUND.

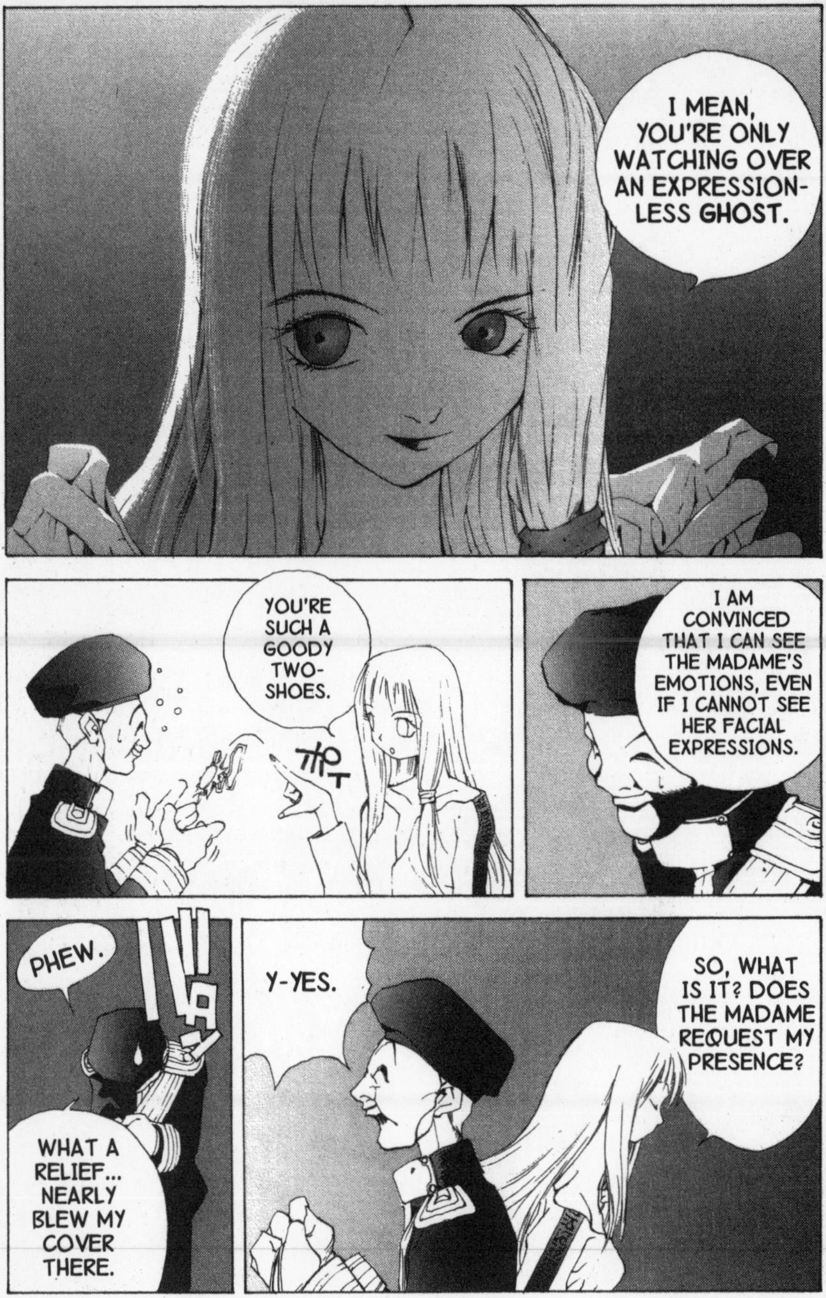
I MEAN, YOU'RE ONLY WATCHING OVER AN EXPRESSION-LESS GHOST.
I AM CONVINCED THAT I CAN SEE THE MADAME'S EMOTIONS, EVEN IF I CANNOT SEE HER FACIAL EXPRESSIONS.
YOU'RE SUCH A GOODY TWO-SHOES.
SO, WHAT IS IT? DOES THE MADAME REQUEST MY PRESENCE?
Y-YES.
PHEW.
WHAT A RELIEF... NEARLY BLEW MY COVER THERE.

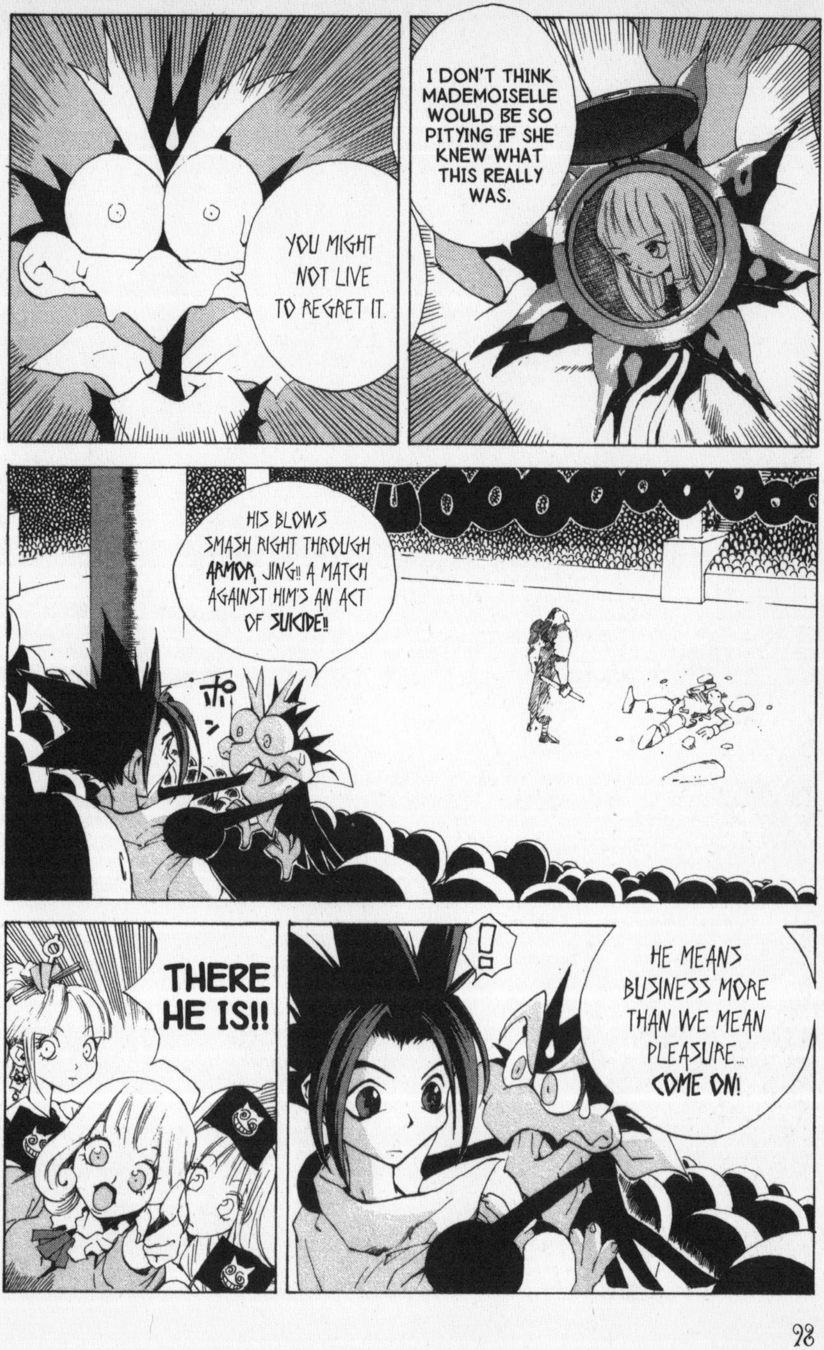
I DON'T THINK MADEMOISELLE WOULD BE SO PITYING IF SHE KNEW WHAT THIS REALLY WAS.
YOU MIGHT NOT LIVE TO REGRET IT.
HIS BLOWS SMASH RIGHT THROUGH ARMOR, JING!! A MATCH AGAINST HIM'S AN ACT OF SUICIDE!!
HE MEANS BUSINESS MORE THAN WE MEAN PLEASURE... COME ON!
!
THERE HE IS!!

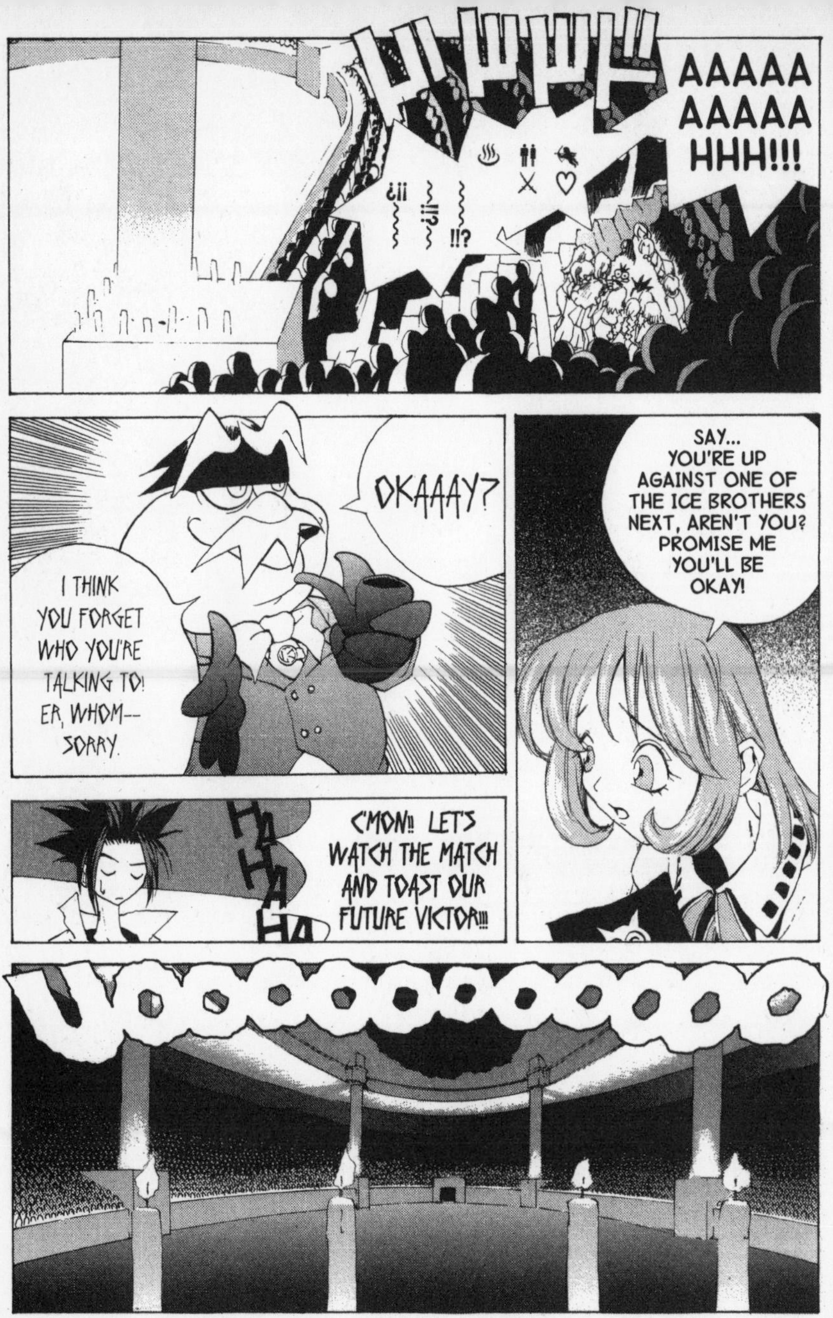
AAAAA AAAAA HHH!!!
¿¡¡ ~~ ¿¡!! ~~ !!?
SAY... YOU'RE UP AGAINST ONE OF THE ICE BROTHERS NEXT, AREN'T YOU? PROMISE ME YOU'LL BE OKAY!
OKAAAY?
I THINK YOU FORGET WHO YOU'RE TALKING TO! ER, WHOM-- SORRY.
C'MON!! LET'S WATCH THE MATCH AND TOAST OUR FUTURE VICTOR!!!
HA HA HA HA
UOOOOOOOOOO

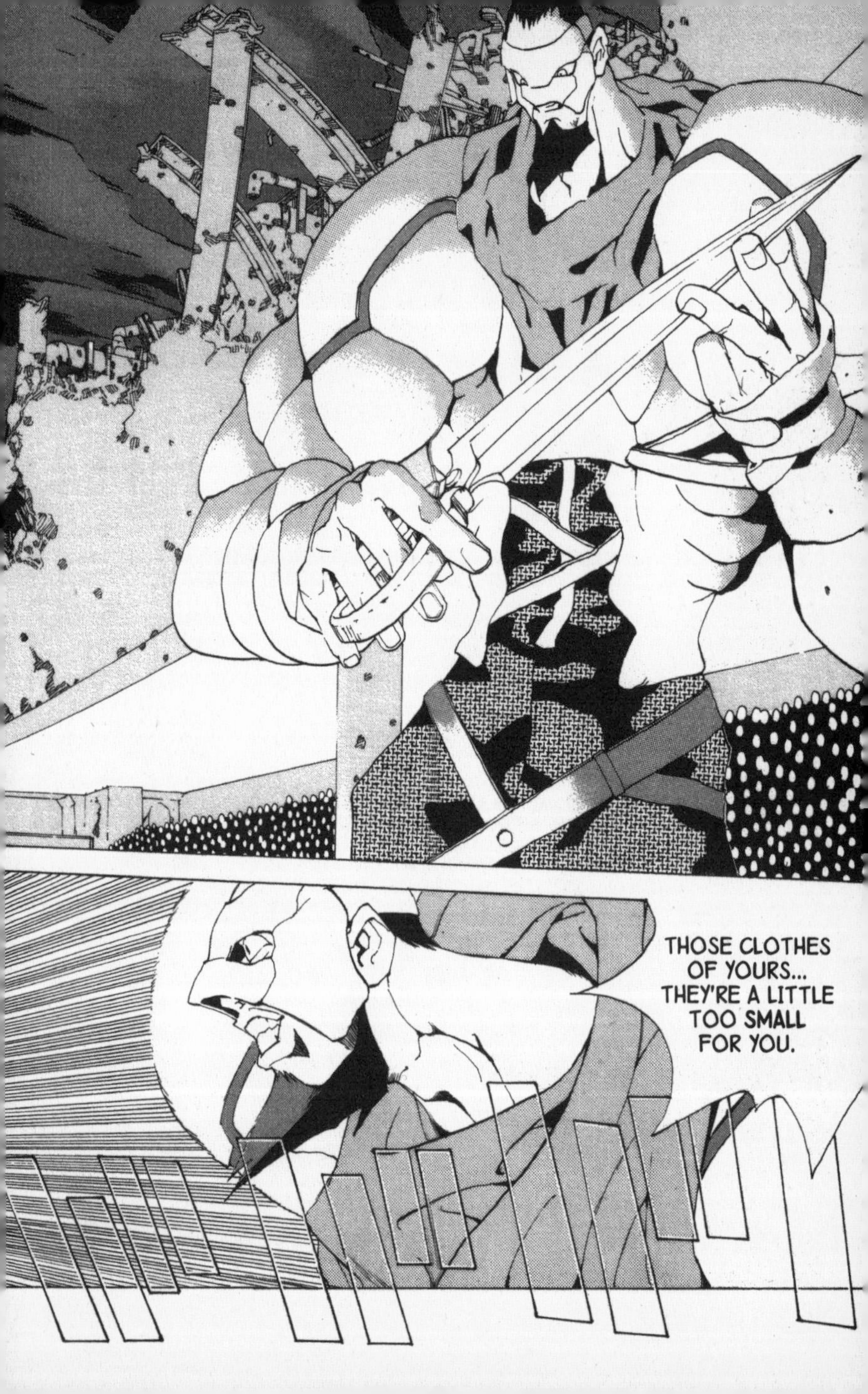
THOSE CLOTHES OF YOURS... THEY'RE A LITTLE TOO SMALL FOR YOU.

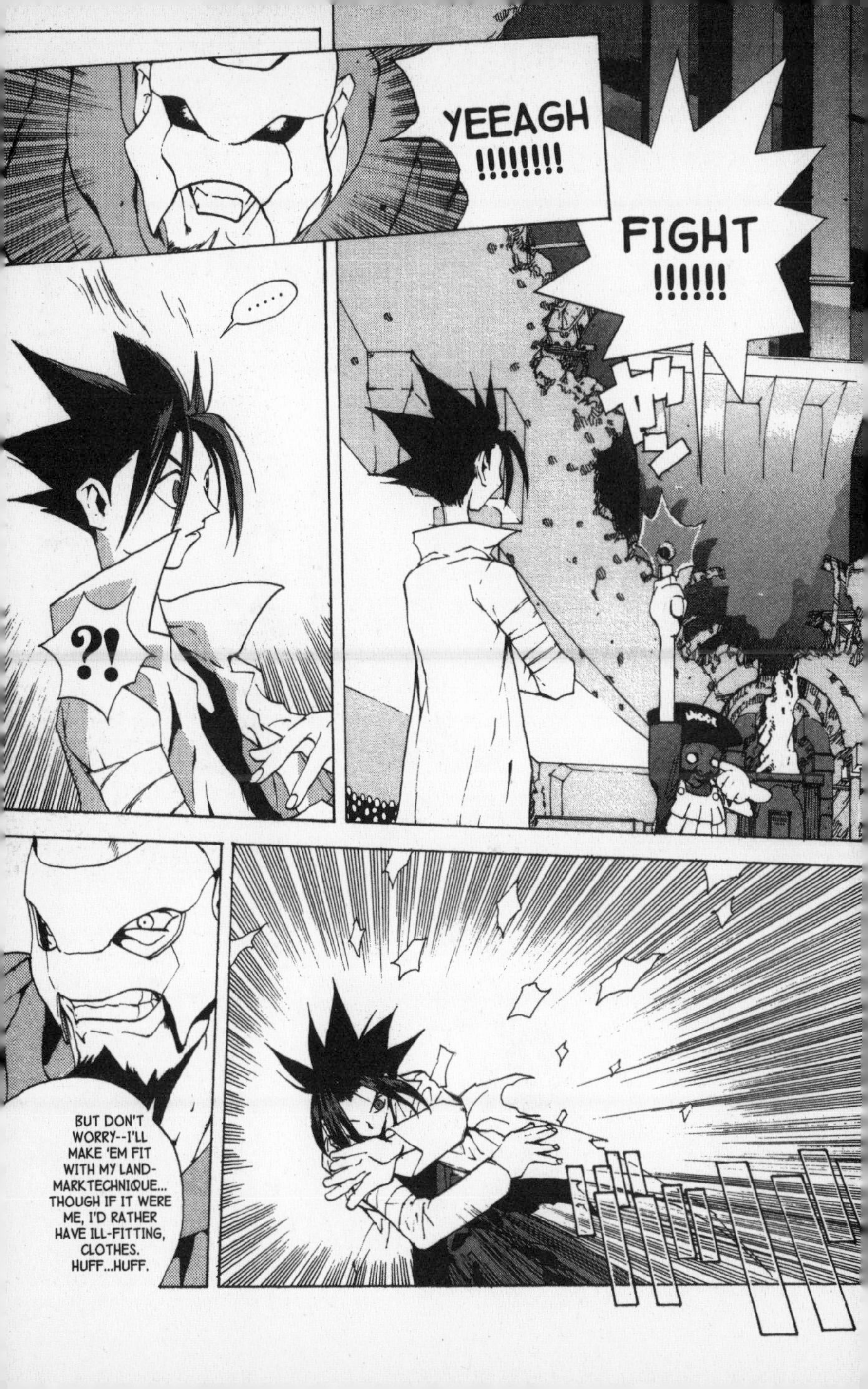
YEEAGH !!!!!!!!
FIGHT !!!!!!
やッ
.....
?!
BUT DON'T WORRY--I'LL MAKE 'EM FIT WITH MY LAND-MARKTECHNIQUE... THOUGH IF IT WERE ME, I'D RATHER HAVE ILL-FITTING, CLOTHES. HUFF...HUFF.

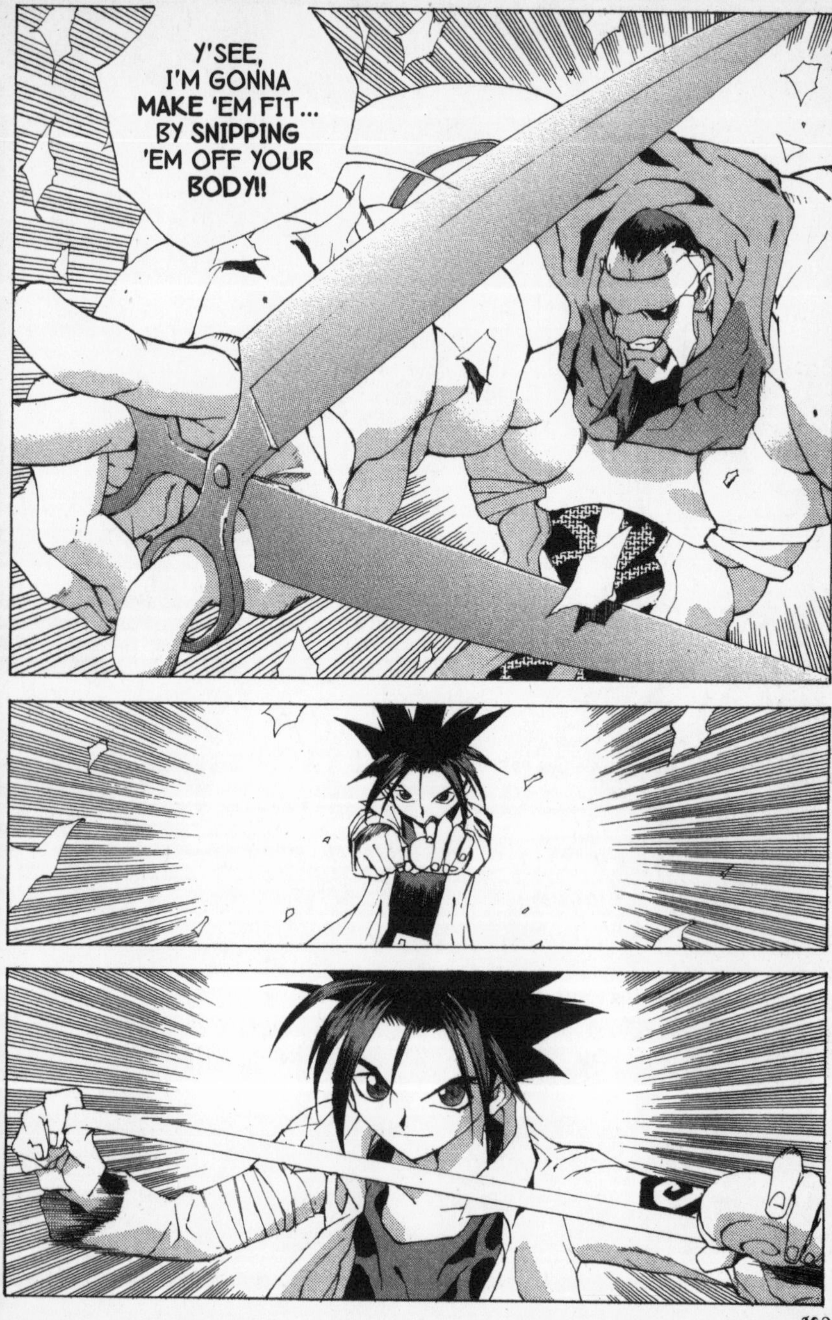
Y'SEE, I'M GONNA MAKE 'EM FIT... BY SNIPPING 'EM OFF YOUR BODY!!

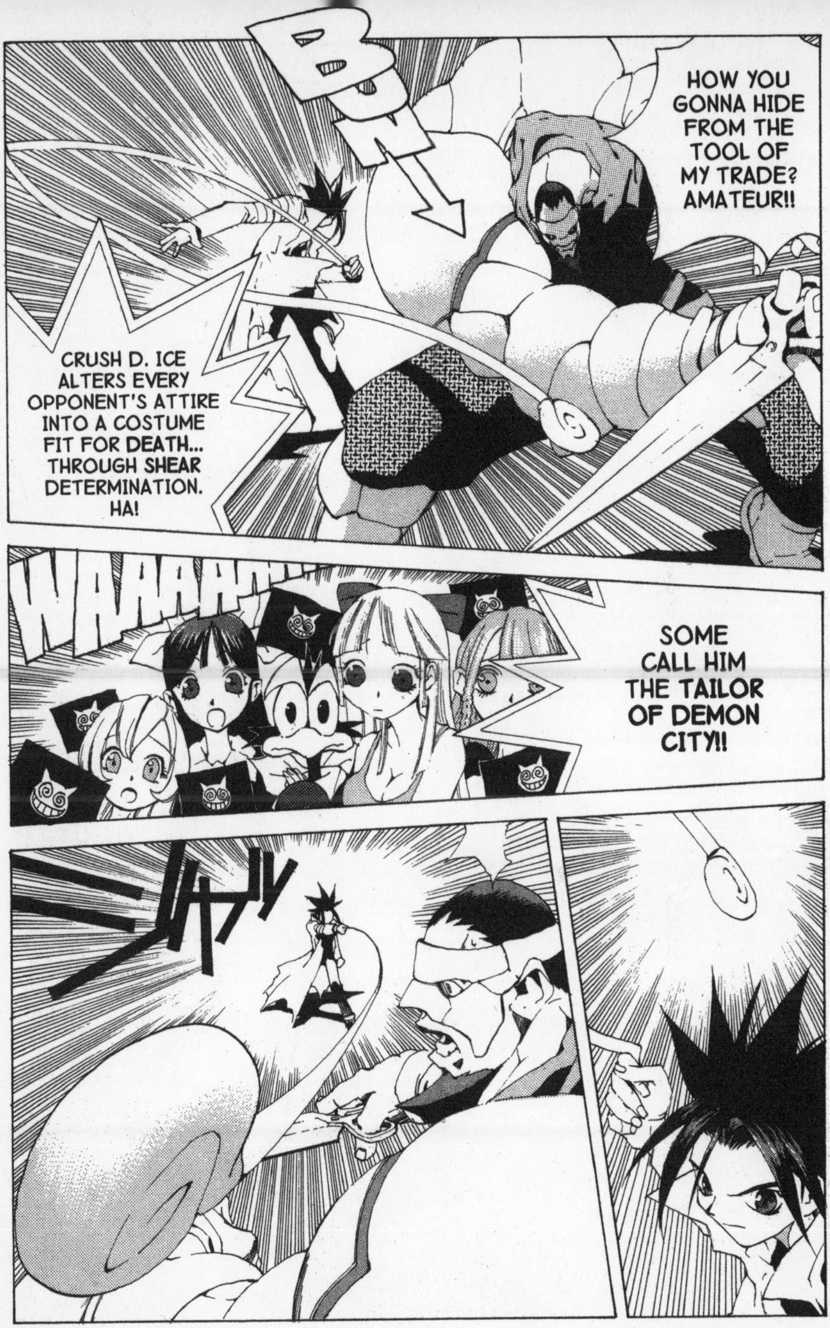
HOW YOU GONNA HIDE FROM THE TOOL OF MY TRADE? AMATEUR!!
CRUSH D. ICE ALTERS EVERY OPPONENT'S ATTIRE INTO A COSTUME FIT FOR DEATH... THROUGH SHEAR DETERMINATION. HA!
SOME CALL HIM THE TAILOR OF DEMON CITY!!

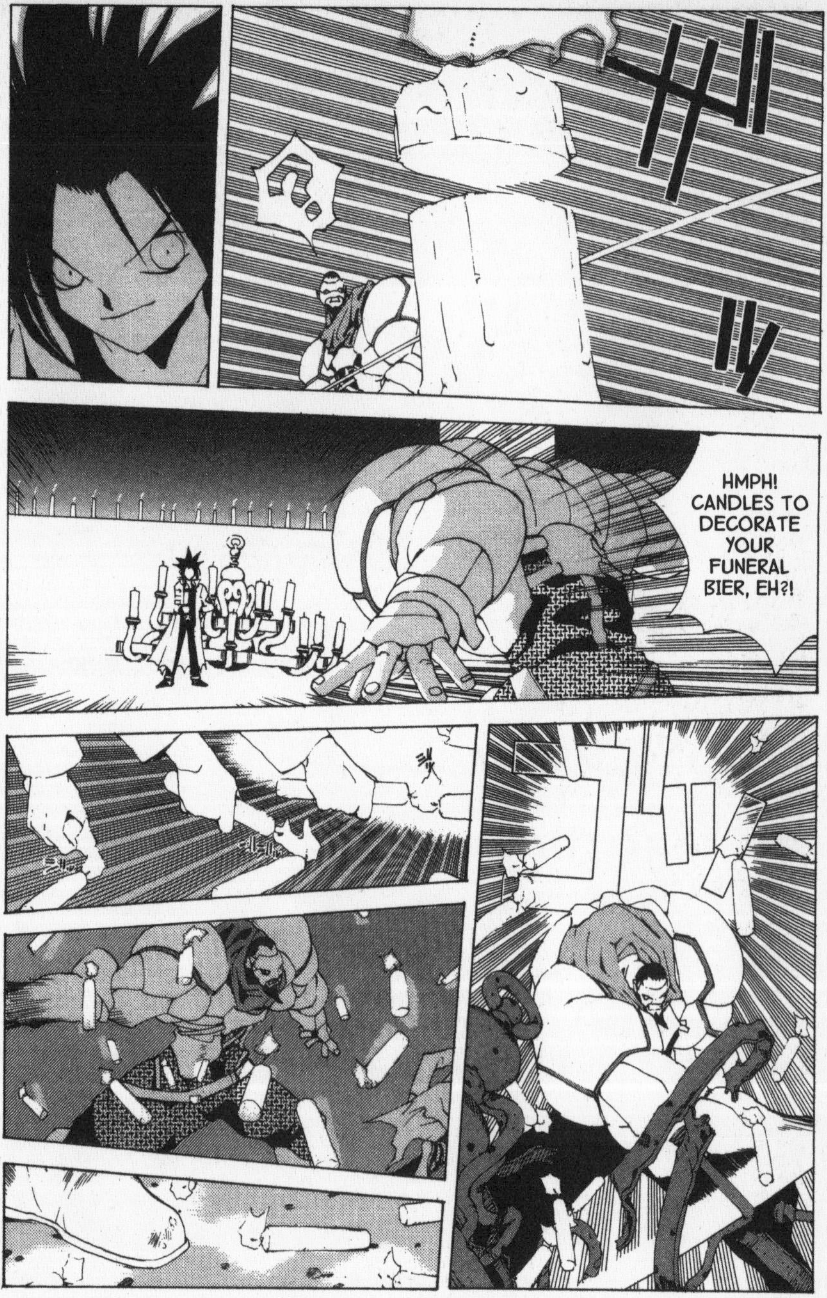
HMPH! CANDLES TO DECORATE YOUR FUNERAL BIER, EH?!

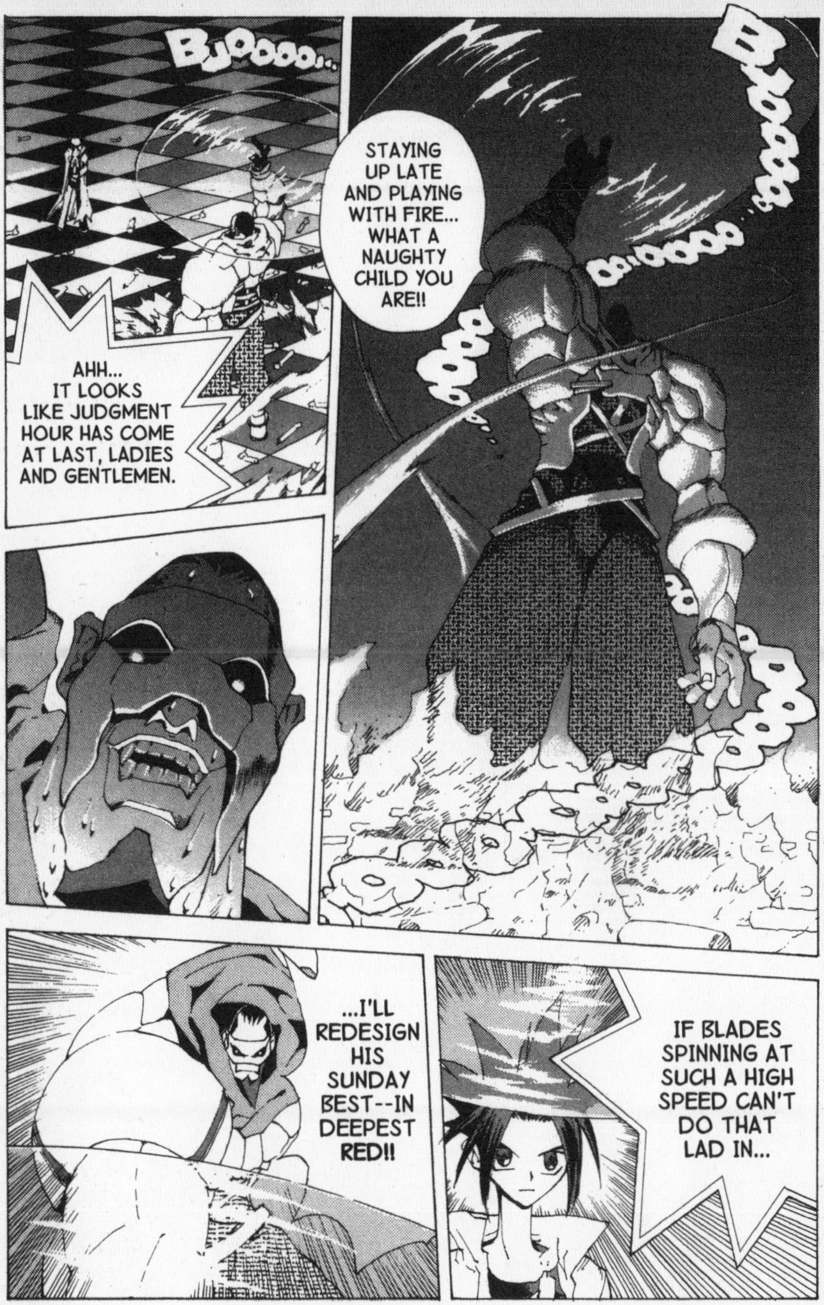
STAYING UP LATE AND PLAYING WITH FIRE... WHAT A NAUGHTY CHILD YOU ARE!!
BJOOOOO..
AHH... IT LOOKS LIKE JUDGMENT HOUR HAS COME AT LAST, LADIES AND GENTLEMEN.
IF BLADES SPINNING AT SUCH A HIGH SPEED CAN'T DO THAT LAD IN...
...I'LL REDESIGN HIS SUNDAY BEST--IN DEEPEST RED!!

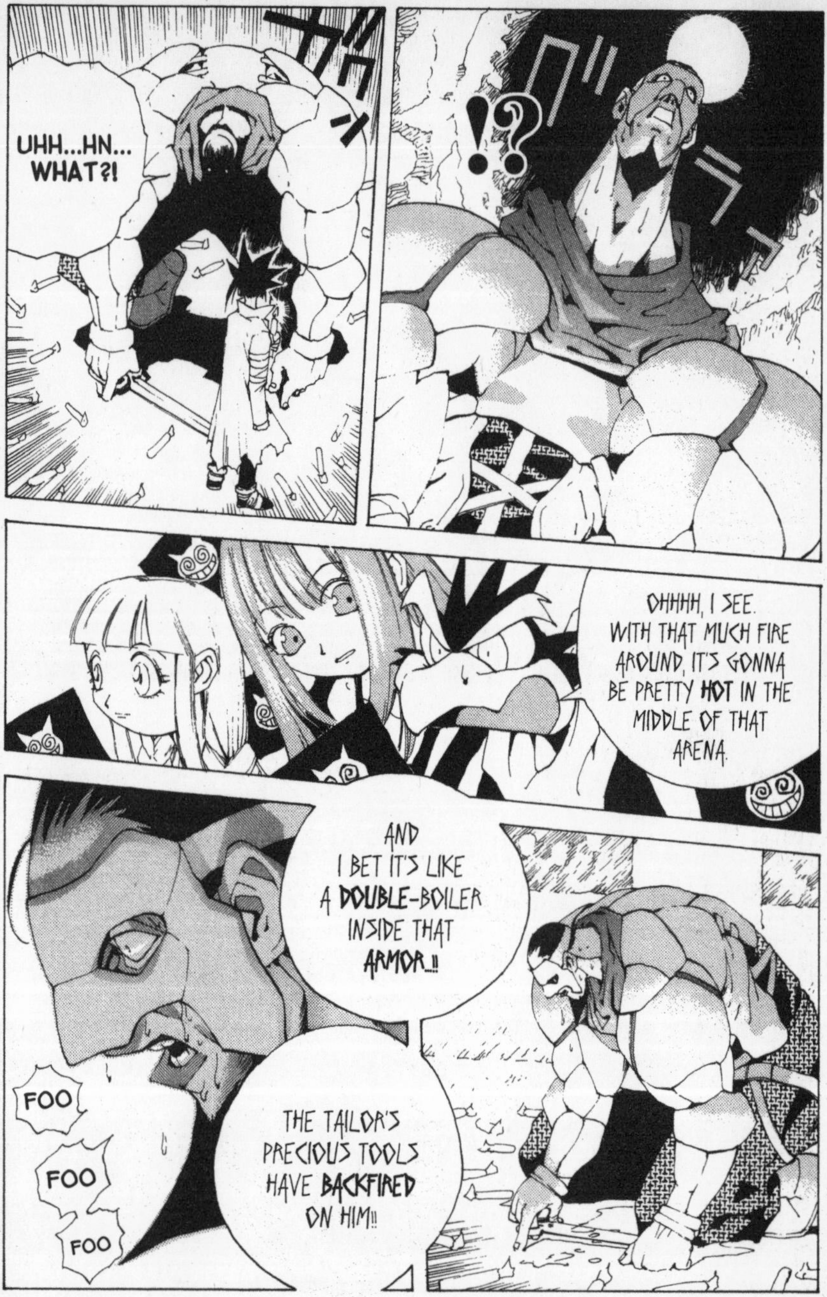
!?
UHH...HN... WHAT?!
OHHHH, I SEE. WITH THAT MUCH FIRE AROUND, IT'S GONNA BE PRETTY **HOT** IN THE MIDDLE OF THAT ARENA.
AND I BET IT'S LIKE A **DOUBLE**-BOILER INSIDE THAT **ARMOR**!!
THE TAILOR'S PRECIOUS TOOLS HAVE **BACKFIRED** ON HIM!!
FOO
FOO
FOO

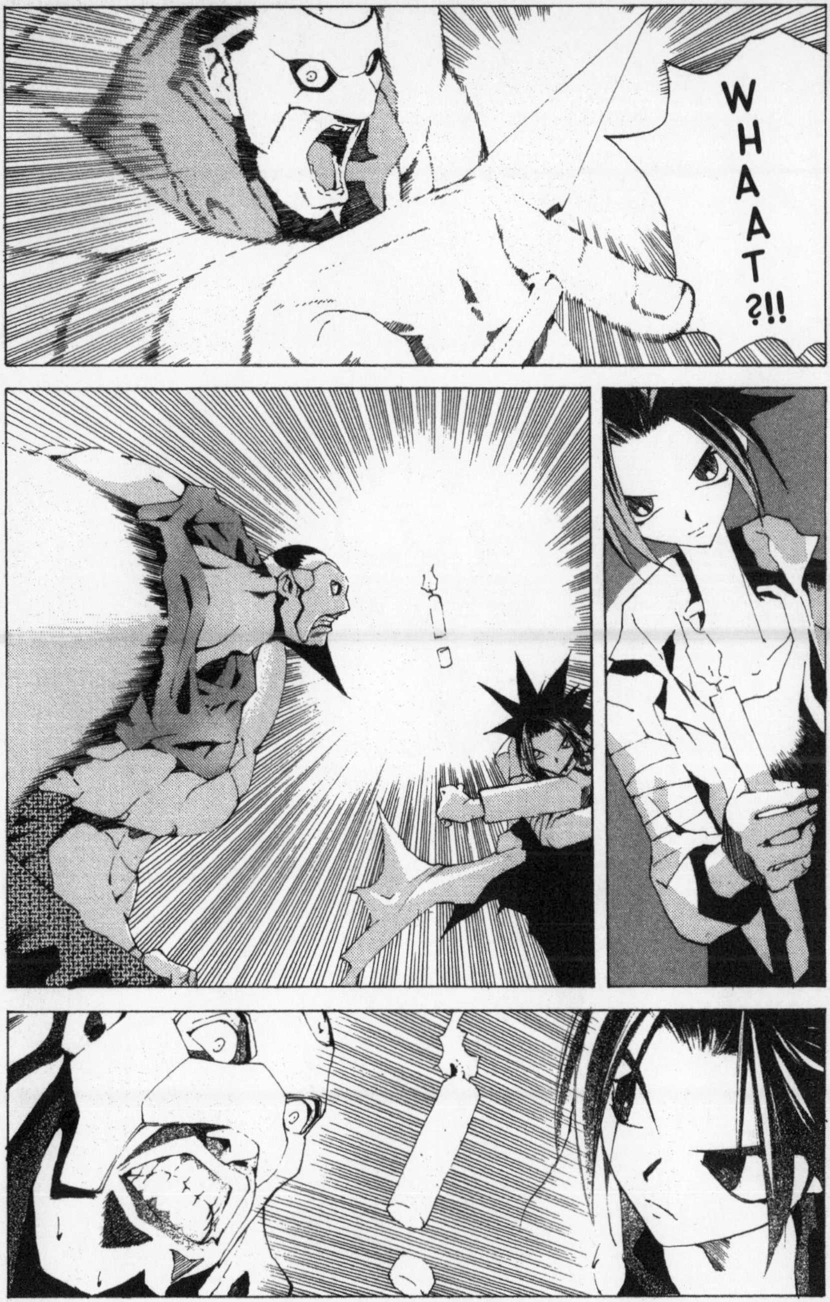
WHAAT?!!

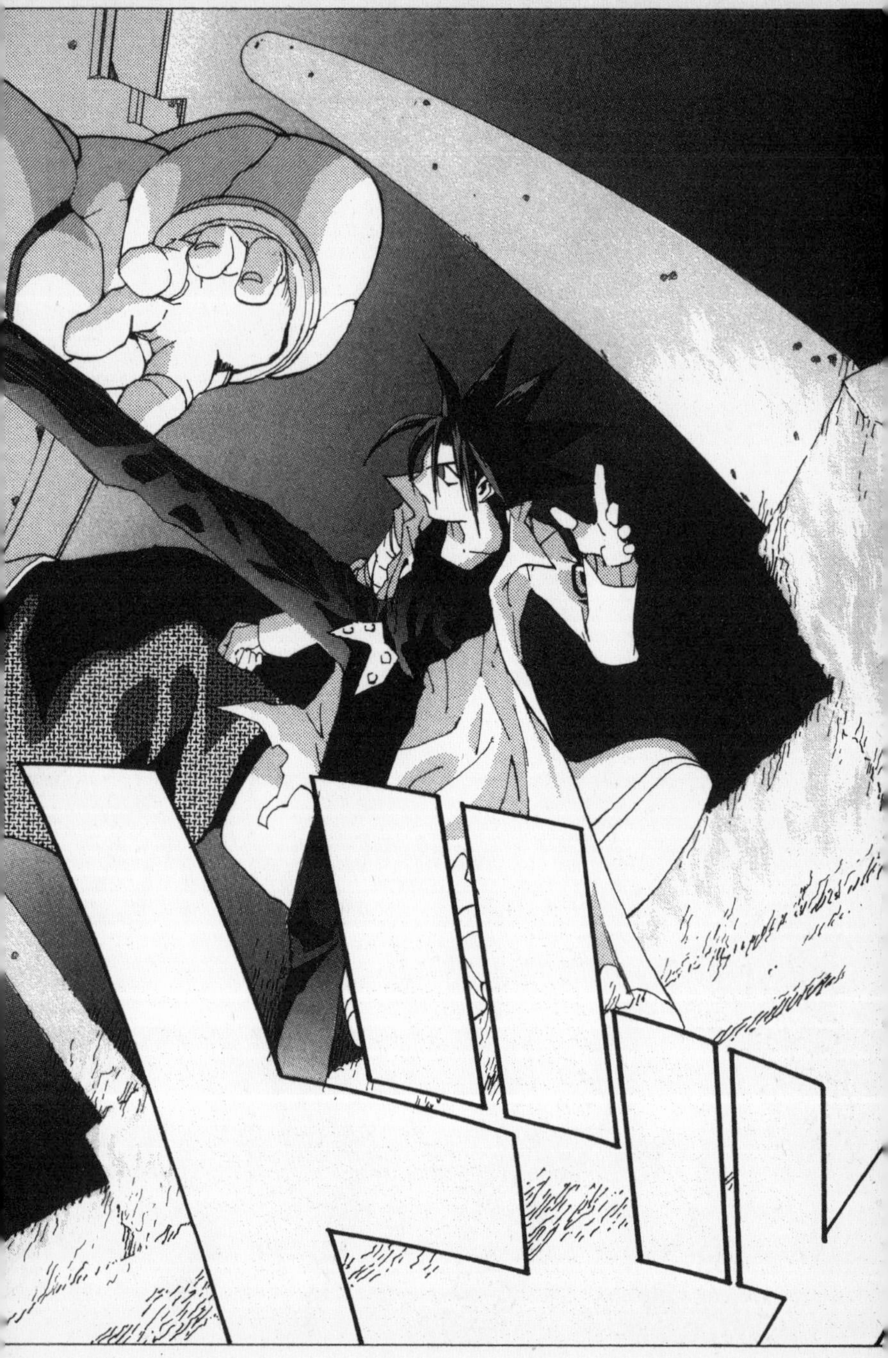

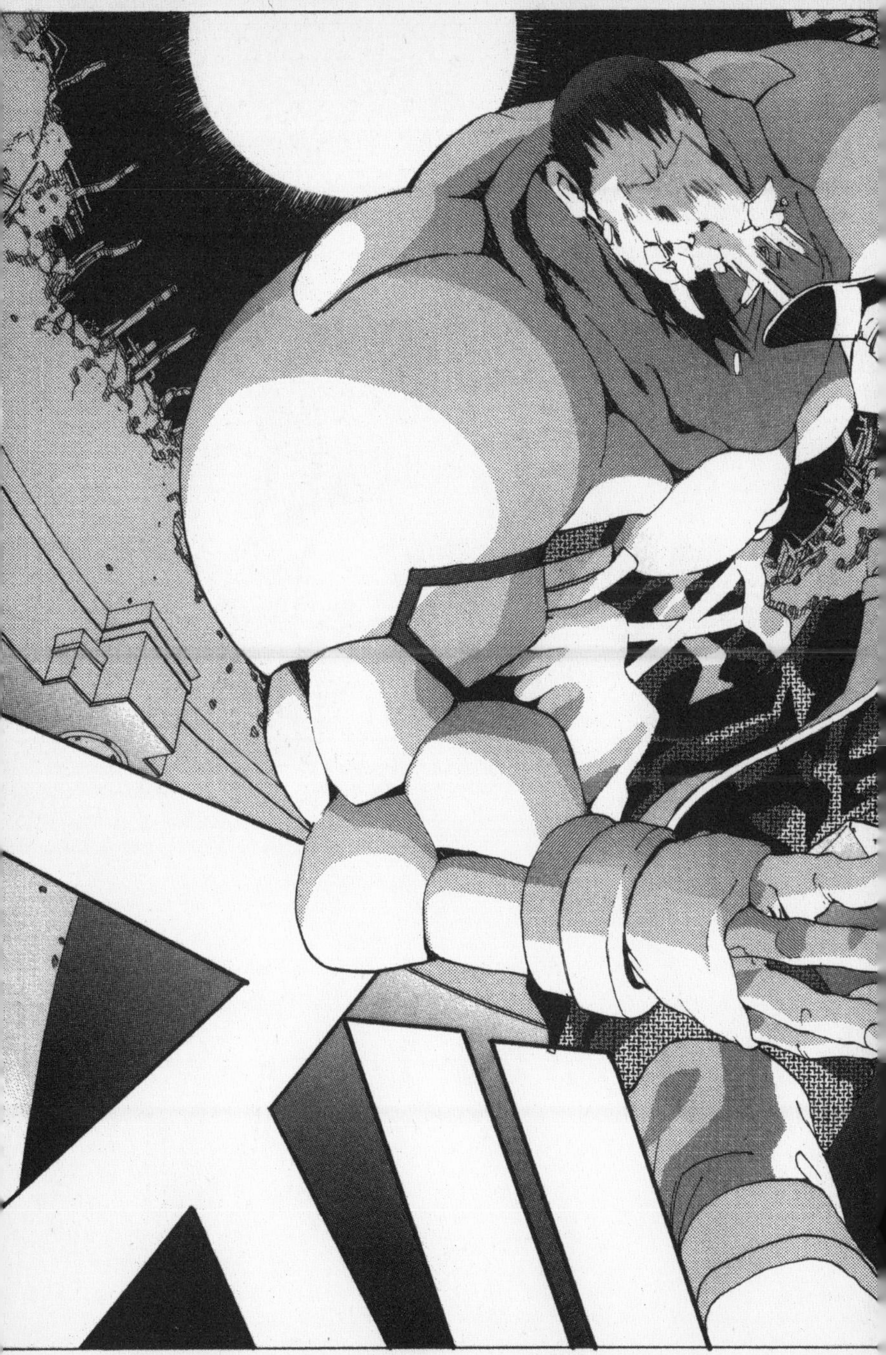

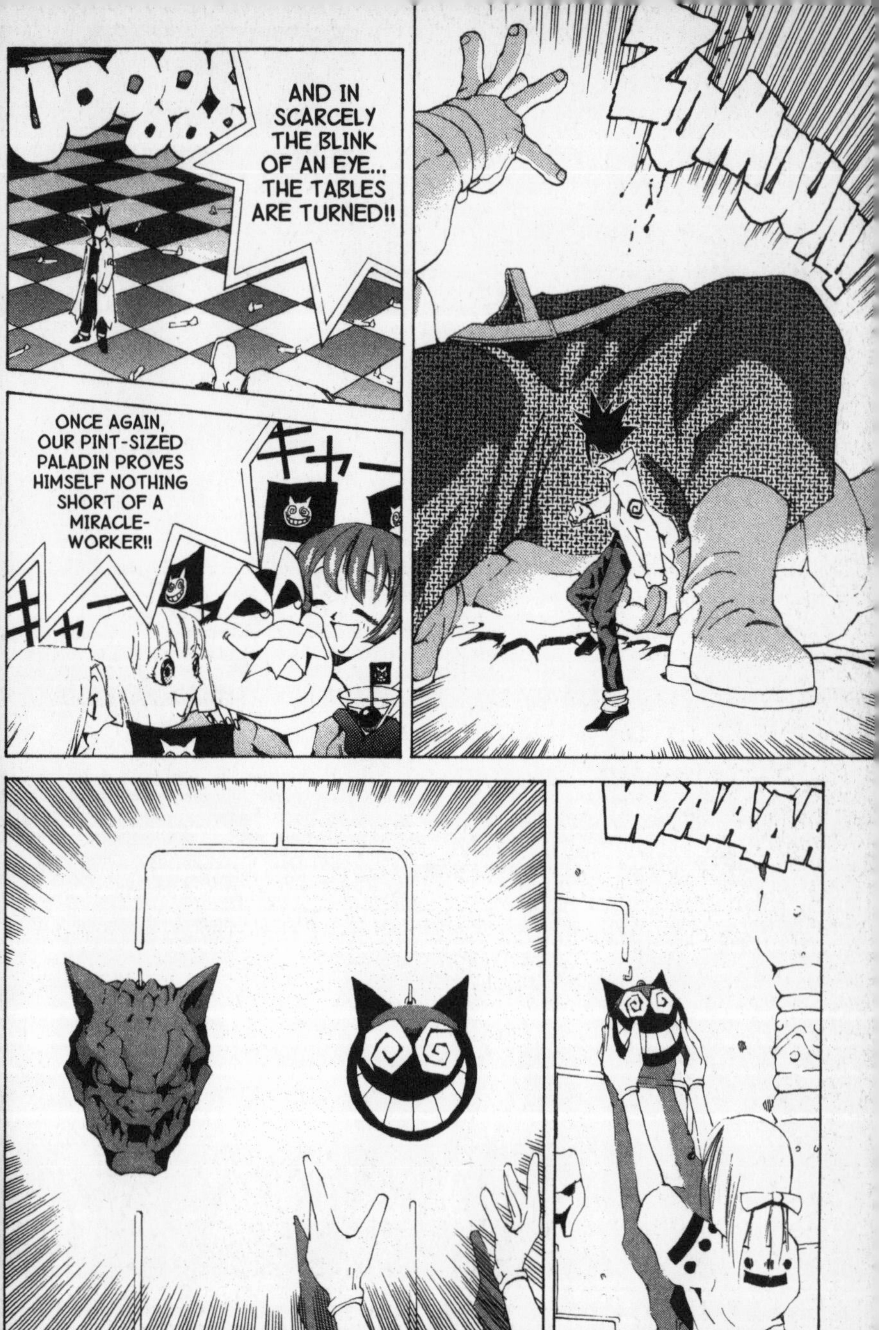
AND IN SCARCELY THE BLINK OF AN EYE... THE TABLES ARE TURNED!!
ONCE AGAIN, OUR PINT-SIZED PALADIN PROVES HIMSELF NOTHING SHORT OF A MIRACLE-WORKER!!
キャー
キャー

As Intense as the Rising Sun!!

Will Mystery Contestant be Zaza's Next Heir?

A strange assassin appeared at Sunday's Mascorrida,
the likes of which the tournament had never seen. The mysterious
gladiator, enshrouded in armor so dark that it appeared his entire
body was made of steel, left a most unusual and foreboding
impression upon the crowd. The origins of this warrior, who just barely
made the deadline for this year's match, are completely unknown.
If we are to believe the few words the warrior has spoken of himself,
his most recent living was as a mercenary in the East. Since the candidate's
face is well-hidden inside that strongly built armor, it is impossible to read
his expressions. Still, this somehow only intensifies the impression of sheer
determination that radiates from his entire body. What is certain is that no
other contestant has been able to withstand his advance in the rankings,
and currently, no other candidate will face him willingly.
Certainly, he has taken the city of Zaza by storm.
This man seems as sure to rise as champion
as the sun is sure to rise in the East.

It is easy to see how one of his
caliber would become known as
the Warrior of the Rising Sun.

(From a local Zaza Newspaper)

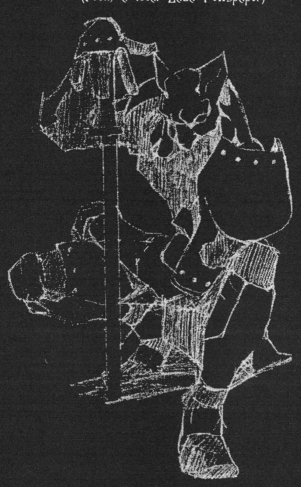

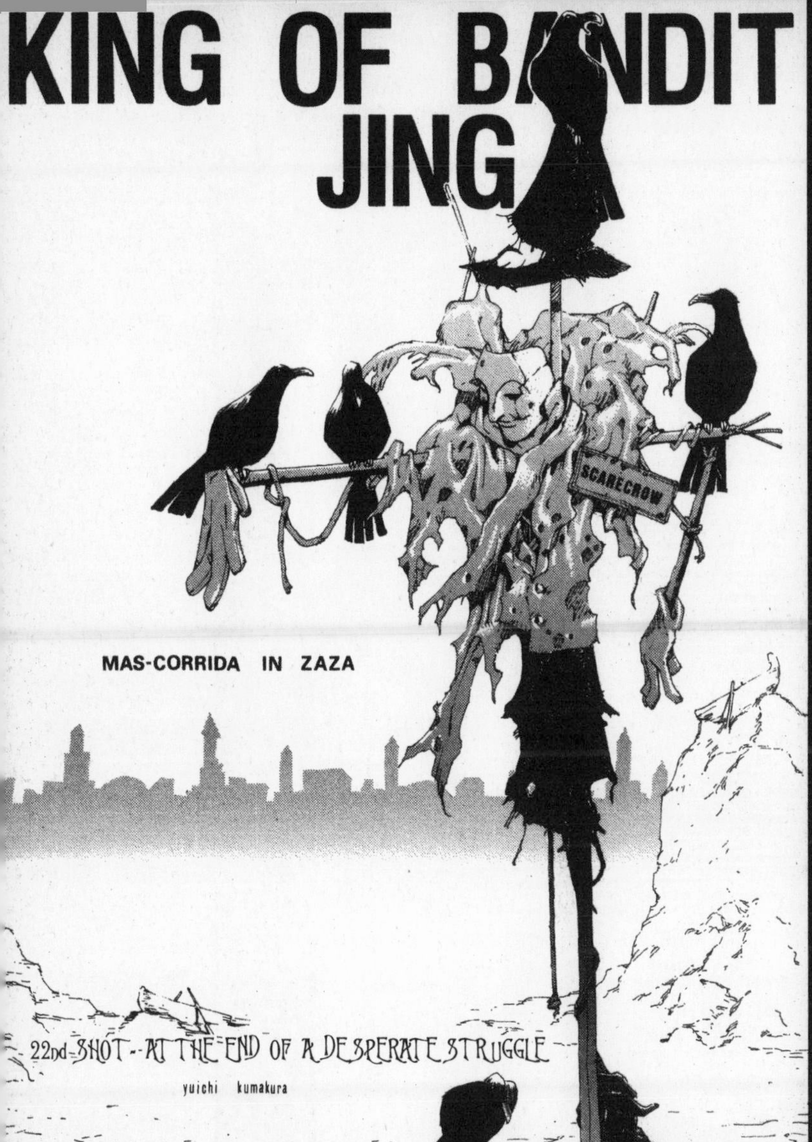
KING OF BANDIT
JING
SCARECROW
MAS-CORRIDA IN ZAZA
22nd SHOT - AT THE END OF A DESPERATE STRUGGLE
yuichi kumakura

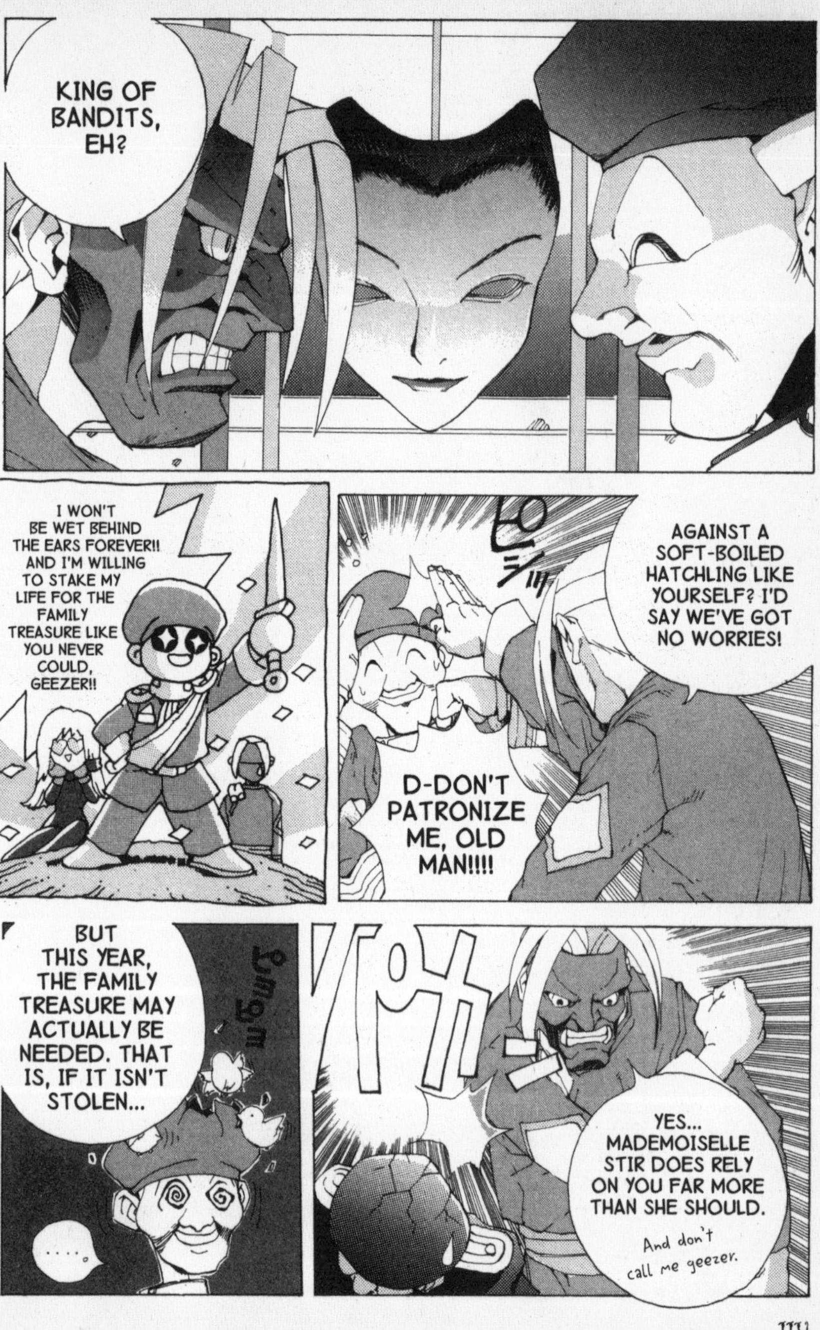
KING OF BANDITS, EH?
AGAINST A SOFT-BOILED HATCHLING LIKE YOURSELF? I'D SAY WE'VE GOT NO WORRIES!
D-DON'T PATRONIZE ME, OLD MAN!!!!
I WON'T BE WET BEHIND THE EARS FOREVER!! AND I'M WILLING TO STAKE MY LIFE FOR THE FAMILY TREASURE LIKE YOU NEVER COULD, GEEZER!!
YES... MADEMOISELLE STIR DOES RELY ON YOU FAR MORE THAN SHE SHOULD.
And don't call me geezer.
BUT THIS YEAR, THE FAMILY TREASURE MAY ACTUALLY BE NEEDED. THAT IS, IF IT ISN'T STOLEN...
.....

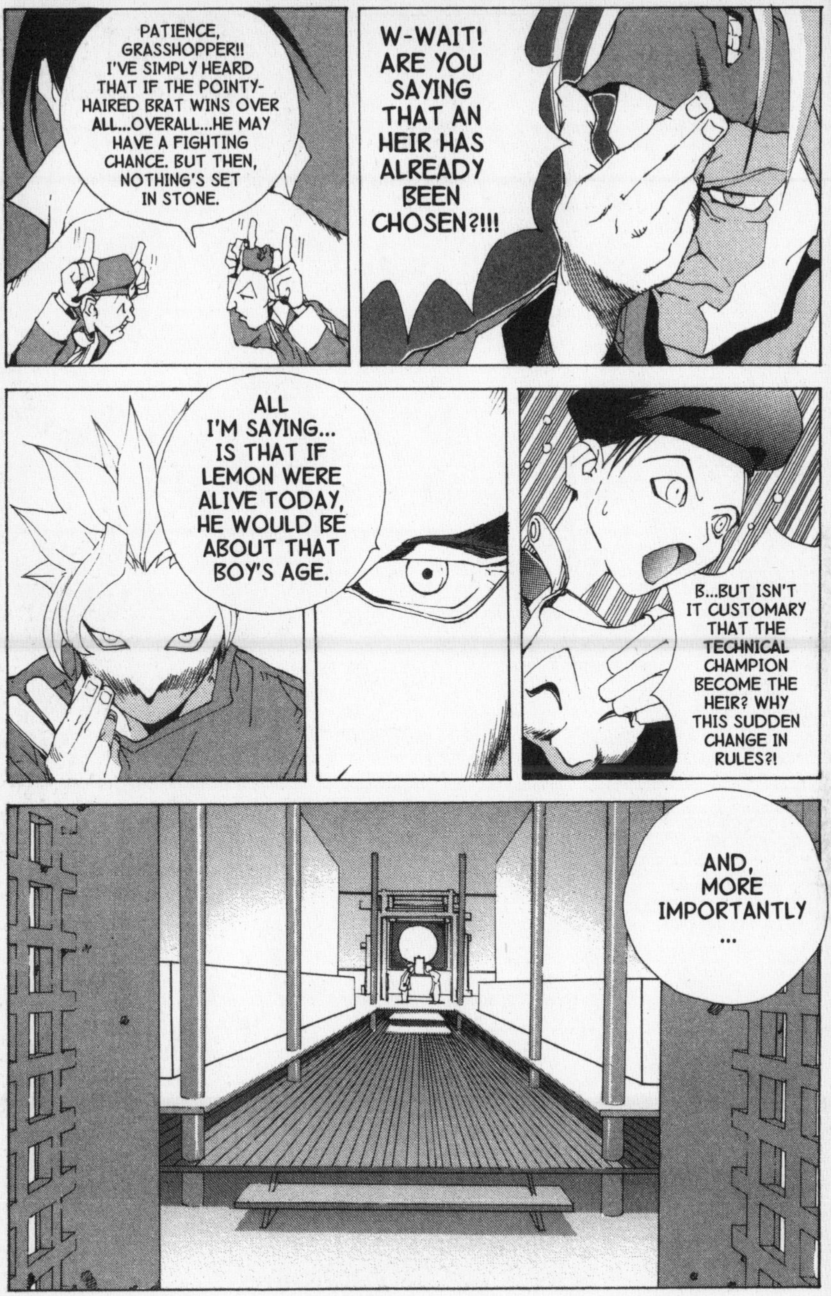
W-WAIT! ARE YOU SAYING THAT AN HEIR HAS ALREADY BEEN CHOSEN?!!!
PATIENCE, GRASSHOPPER!! I'VE SIMPLY HEARD THAT IF THE POINTY-HAIRED BRAT WINS OVER ALL...OVERALL...HE MAY HAVE A FIGHTING CHANCE. BUT THEN, NOTHING'S SET IN STONE.
B...BUT ISN'T IT CUSTOMARY THAT THE TECHNICAL CHAMPION BECOME THE HEIR? WHY THIS SUDDEN CHANGE IN RULES?!
ALL I'M SAYING... IS THAT IF LEMON WERE ALIVE TODAY, HE WOULD BE ABOUT THAT BOY'S AGE.
AND, MORE IMPORTANTLY ...

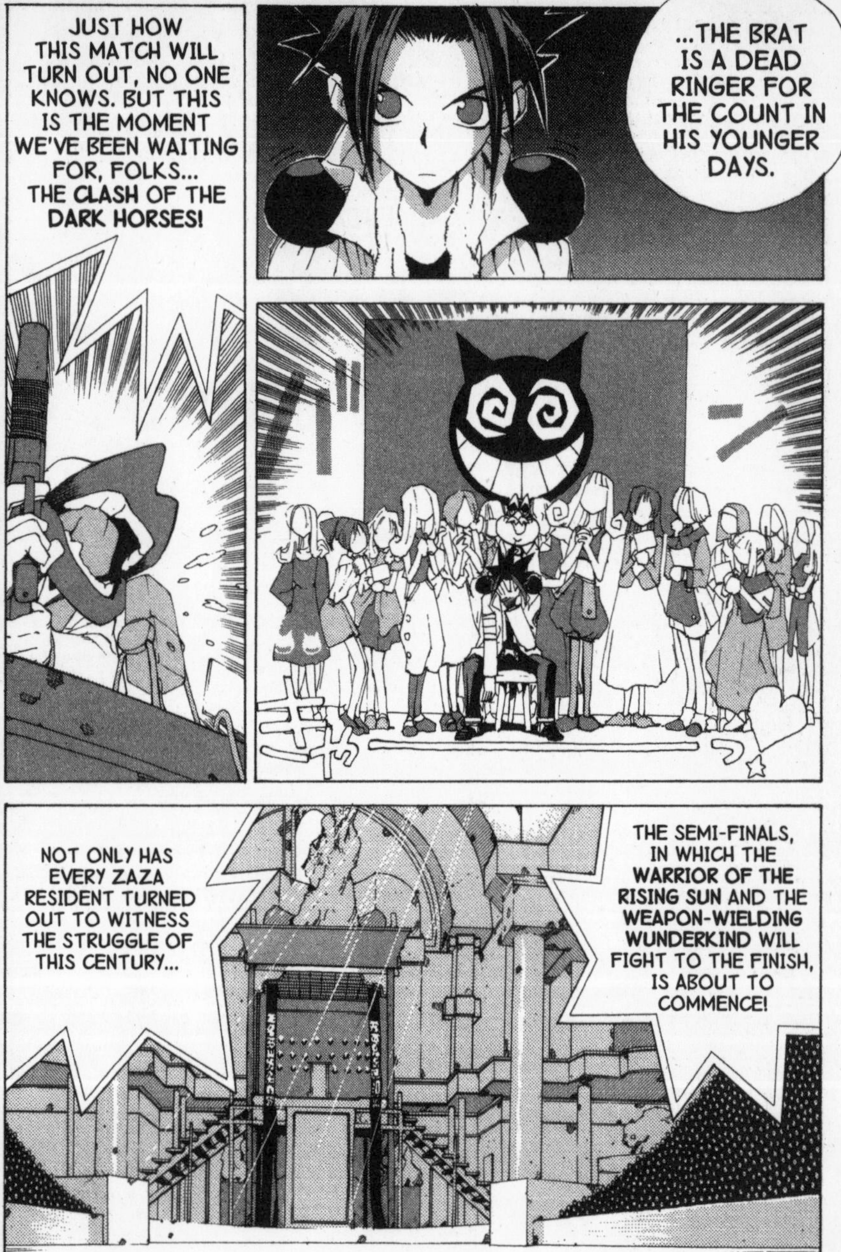
...THE BRAT IS A DEAD RINGER FOR THE COUNT IN HIS YOUNGER DAYS.
JUST HOW THIS MATCH WILL TURN OUT, NO ONE KNOWS. BUT THIS IS THE MOMENT WE'VE BEEN WAITING FOR, FOLKS... THE CLASH OF THE DARK HORSES!
THE SEMI-FINALS, IN WHICH THE WARRIOR OF THE RISING SUN AND THE WEAPON-WIELDING WUNDERKIND WILL FIGHT TO THE FINISH, IS ABOUT TO COMMENCE!
NOT ONLY HAS EVERY ZAZA RESIDENT TURNED OUT TO WITNESS THE STRUGGLE OF THIS CENTURY...

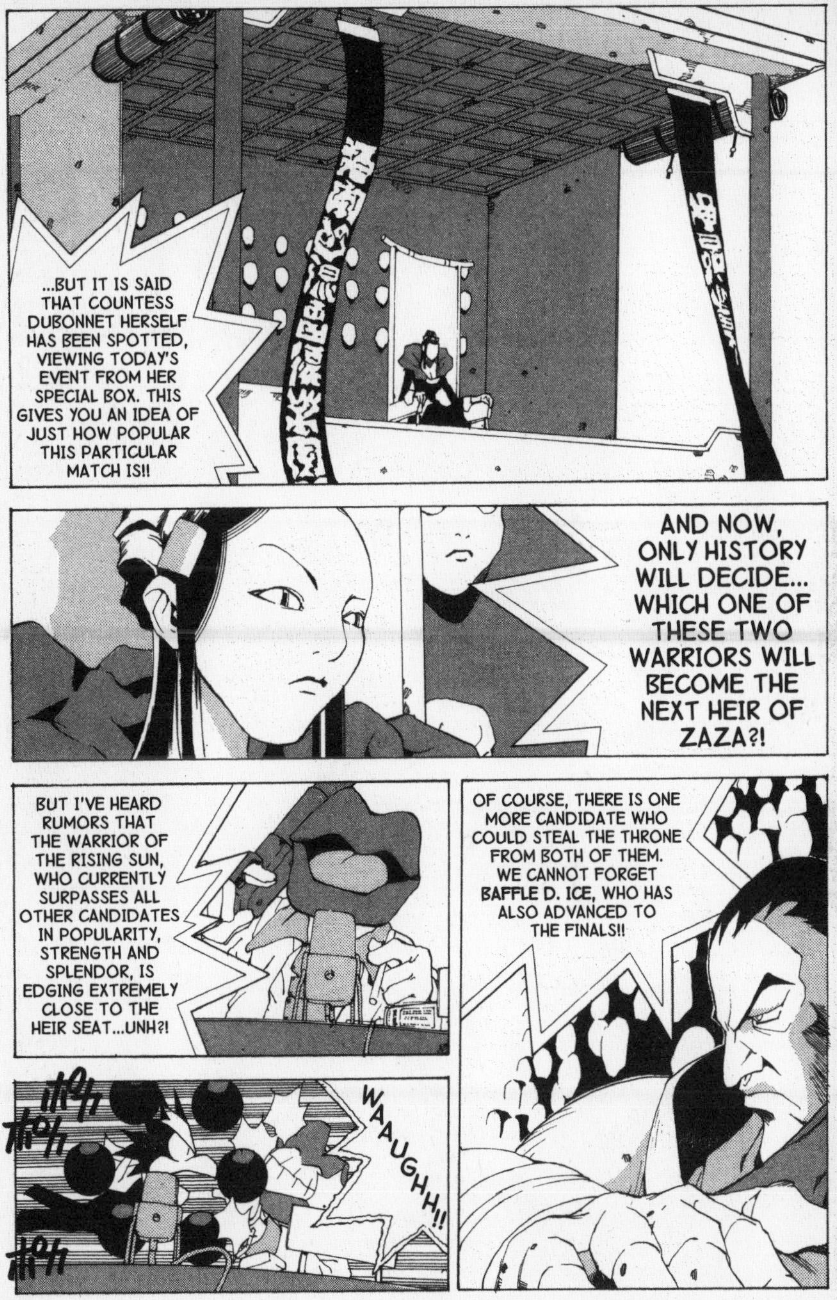
...BUT IT IS SAID THAT COUNTESS DUBONNET HERSELF HAS BEEN SPOTTED, VIEWING TODAY'S EVENT FROM HER SPECIAL BOX. THIS GIVES YOU AN IDEA OF JUST HOW POPULAR THIS PARTICULAR MATCH IS!!
AND NOW, ONLY HISTORY WILL DECIDE... WHICH ONE OF THESE TWO WARRIORS WILL BECOME THE NEXT HEIR OF ZAZA?!
OF COURSE, THERE IS ONE MORE CANDIDATE WHO COULD STEAL THE THRONE FROM BOTH OF THEM. WE CANNOT FORGET BAFFLE D. ICE, WHO HAS ALSO ADVANCED TO THE FINALS!!
BUT I'VE HEARD RUMORS THAT THE WARRIOR OF THE RISING SUN, WHO CURRENTLY SURPASSES ALL OTHER CANDIDATES IN POPULARITY, STRENGTH AND SPLENDOR, IS EDGING EXTREMELY CLOSE TO THE HEIR SEAT...UNH?!
WAAUGHH!!

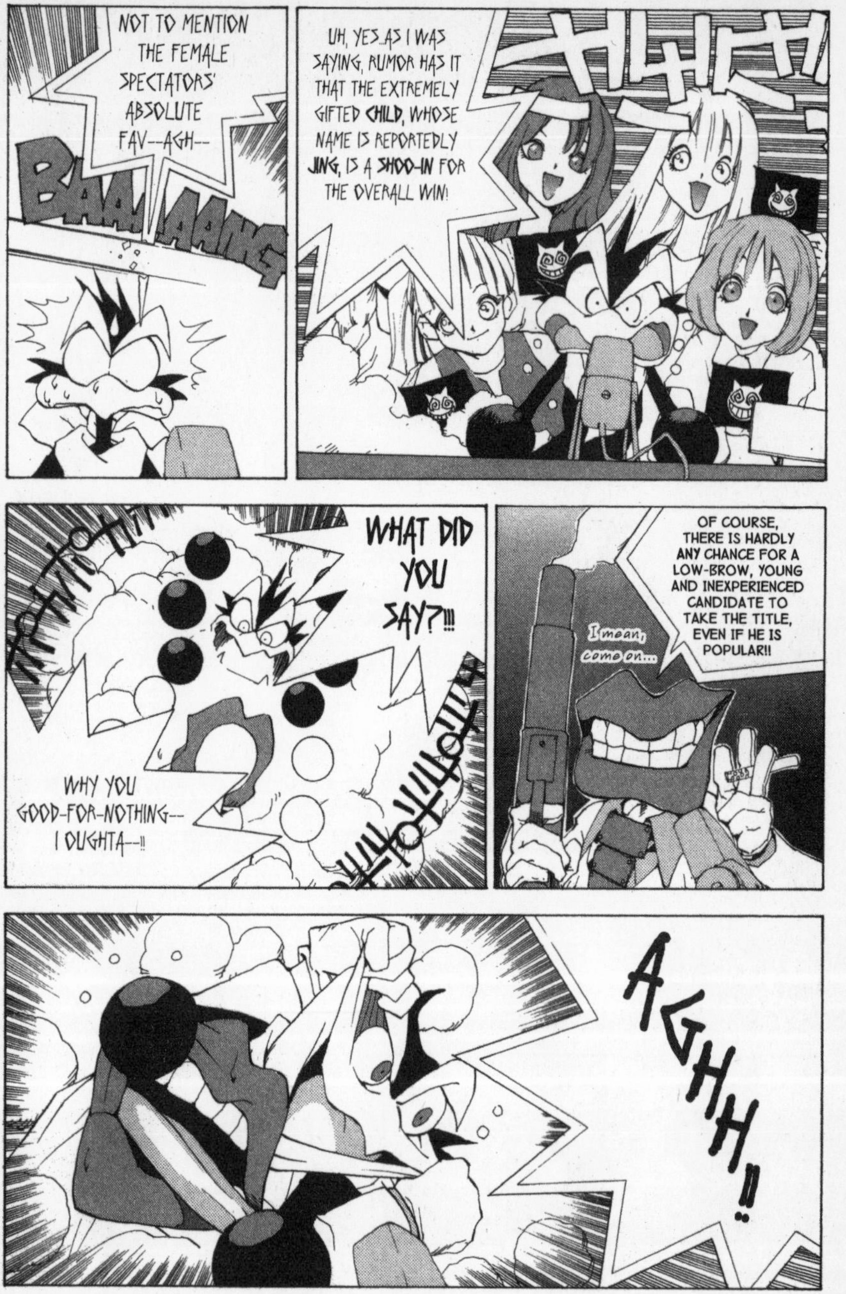
UH, YES...AS I WAS SAYING, RUMOR HAS IT THAT THE EXTREMELY GIFTED **CHILD**, WHOSE NAME IS REPORTEDLY **JING**, IS A **SHOO-IN** FOR THE OVERALL WIN!
NOT TO MENTION THE FEMALE SPECTATORS' ABSOLUTE FAV--AGH--
BAAAAANG
OF COURSE, THERE IS HARDLY ANY CHANCE FOR A LOW-BROW, YOUNG AND INEXPERIENCED CANDIDATE TO TAKE THE TITLE, EVEN IF HE IS POPULAR!!
I mean, come on...
WHAT DID YOU SAY?!!!
WHY YOU GOOD-FOR-NOTHING--- I OUGHTA--!!
AGHH!!

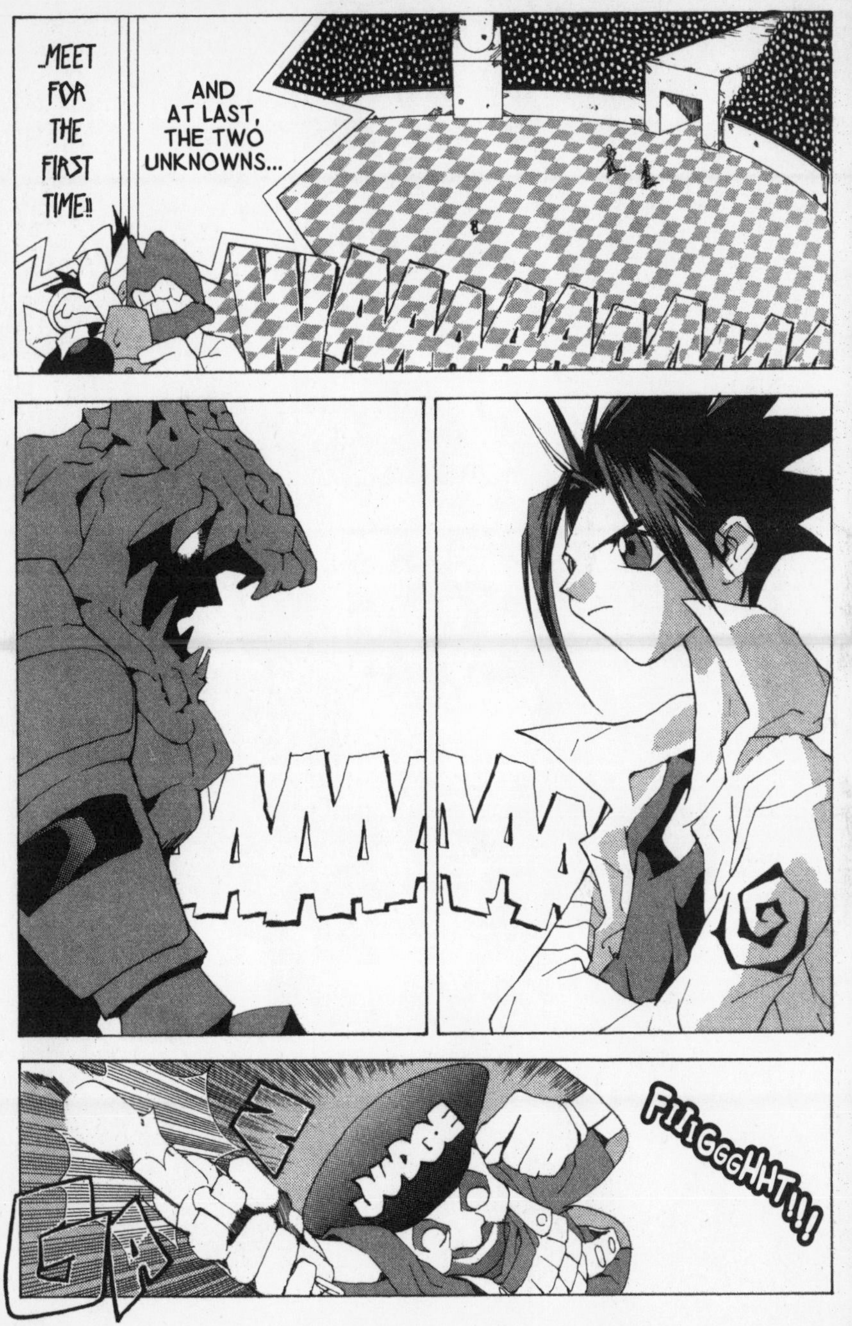
AND AT LAST, THE TWO UNKNOWNS...
...MEET FOR THE FIRST TIME!!
FIIIGGGHHT!!!
JUDGE
GA

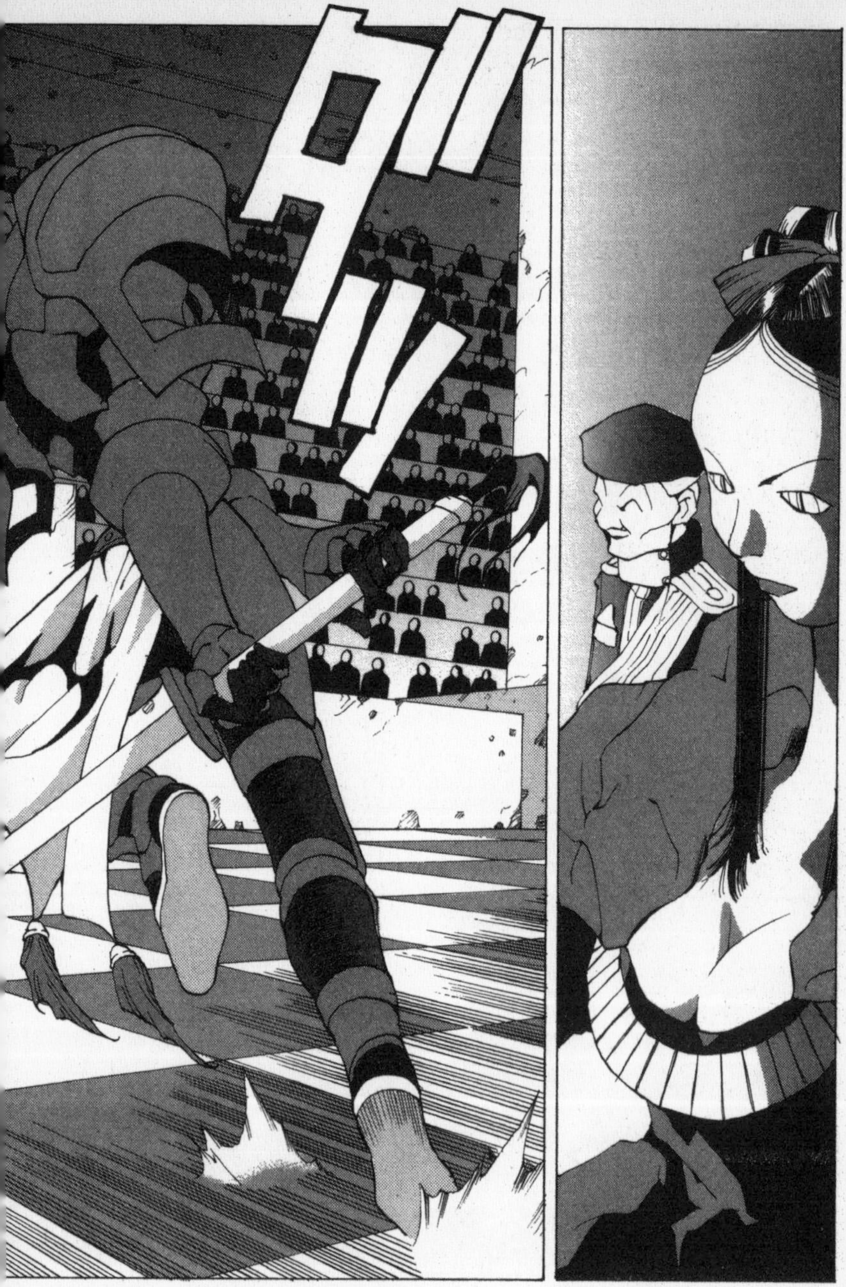
ダッ

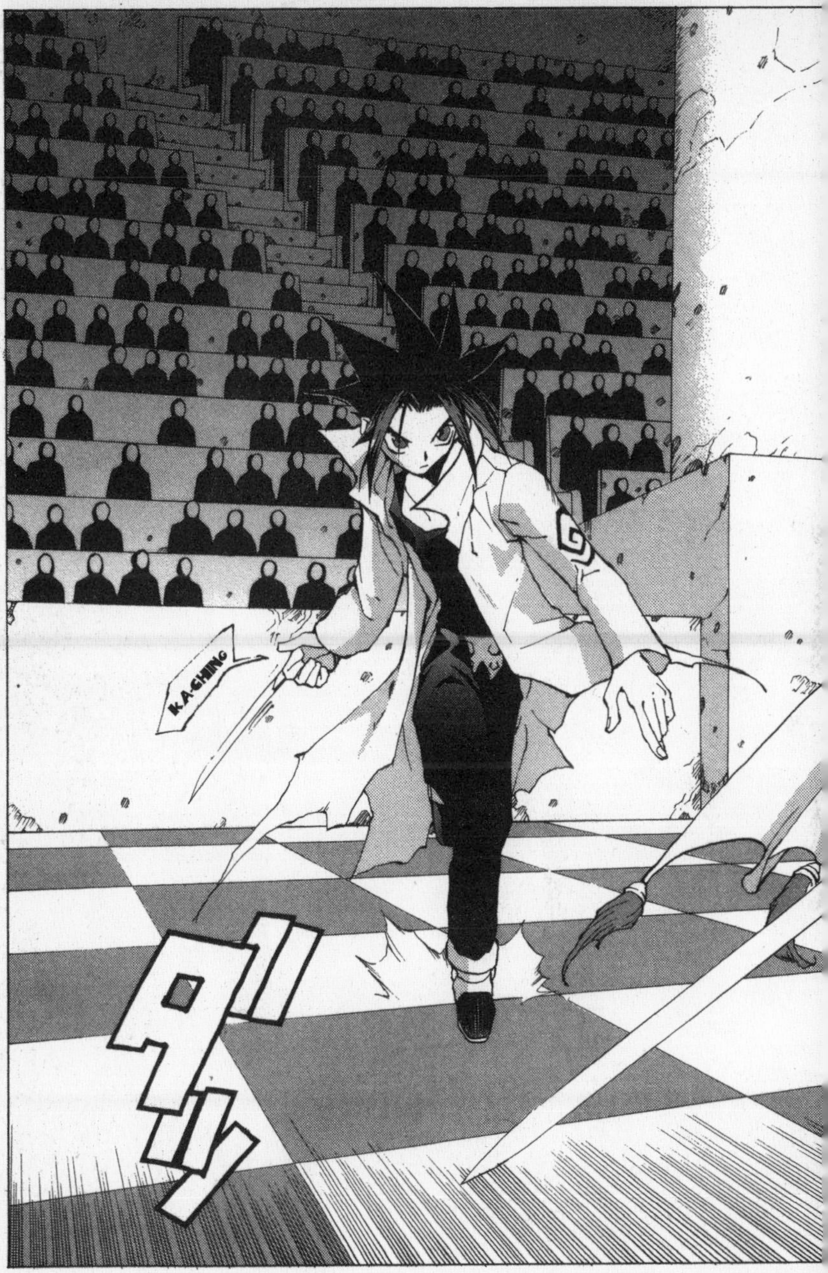
KA-CHING

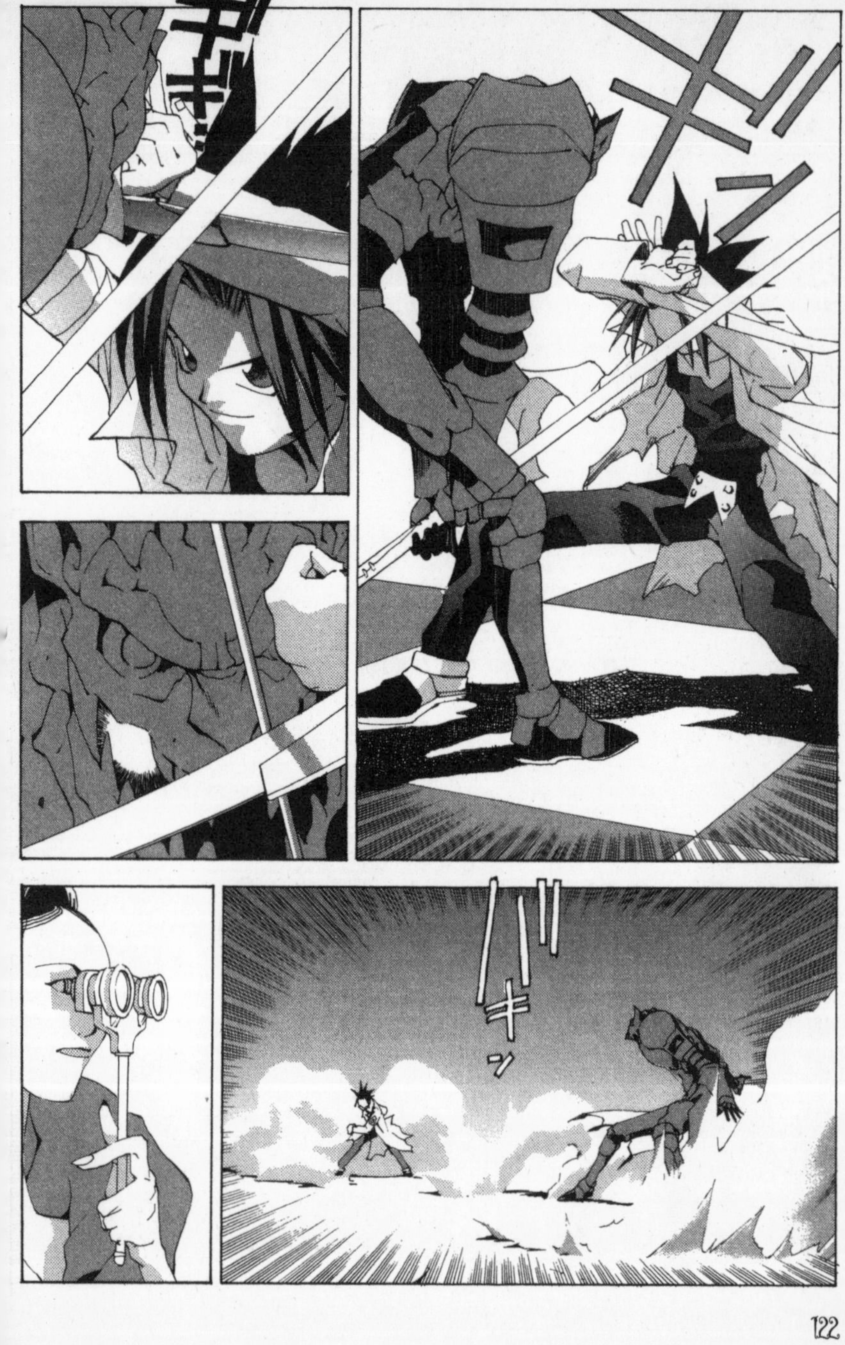
ギン
ギギ…
バキン

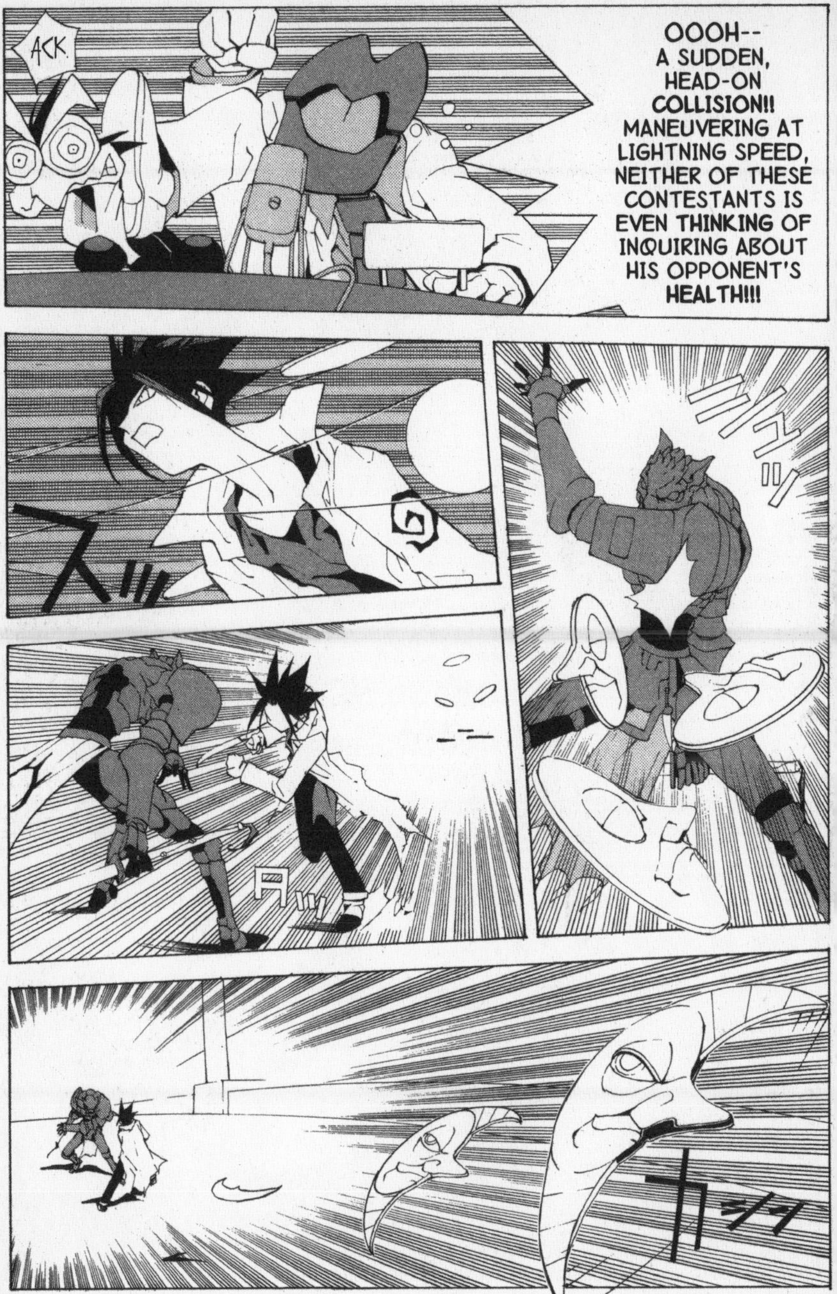
OOOH-- A SUDDEN, HEAD-ON COLLISION!! MANEUVERING AT LIGHTNING SPEED, NEITHER OF THESE CONTESTANTS IS EVEN THINKING OF INQUIRING ABOUT HIS OPPONENT'S HEALTH!!!
ACK.

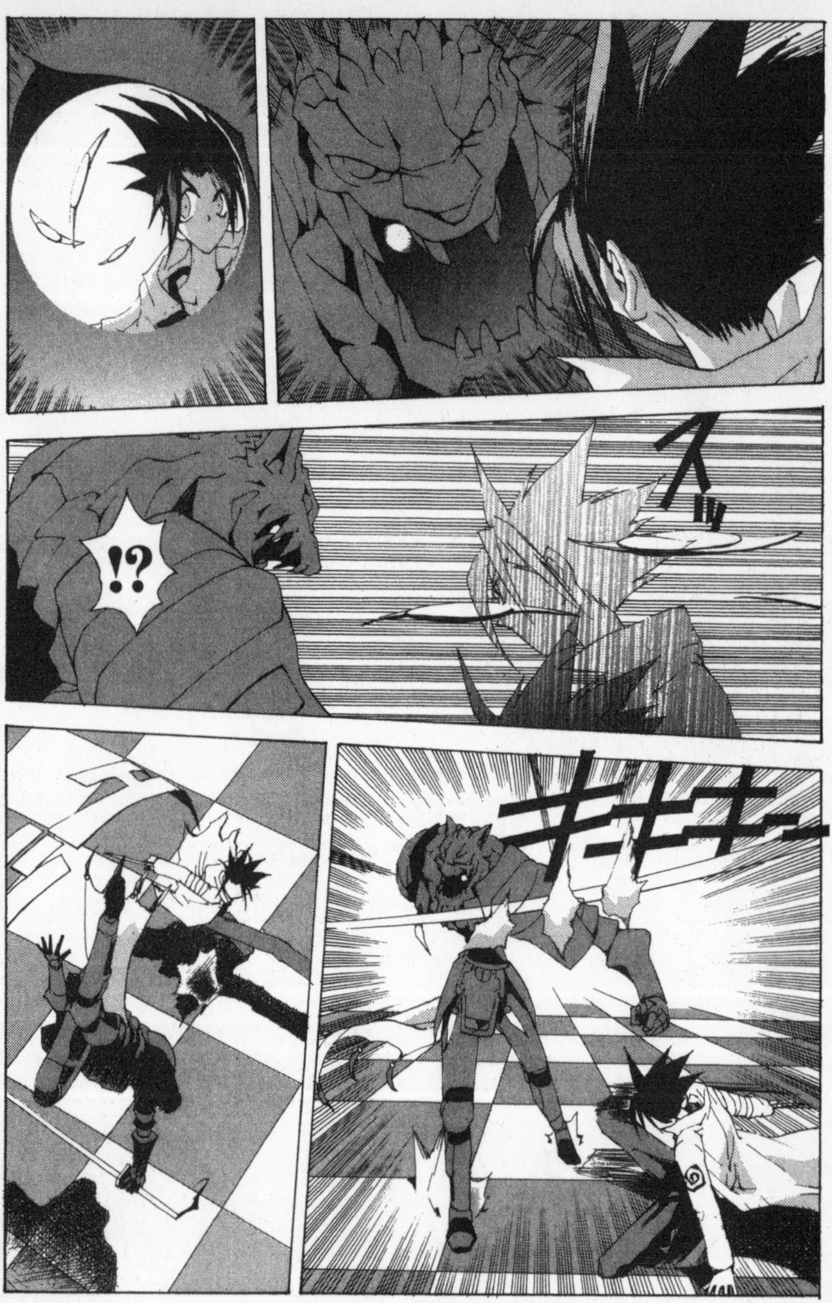
スッ
!?
キキキー

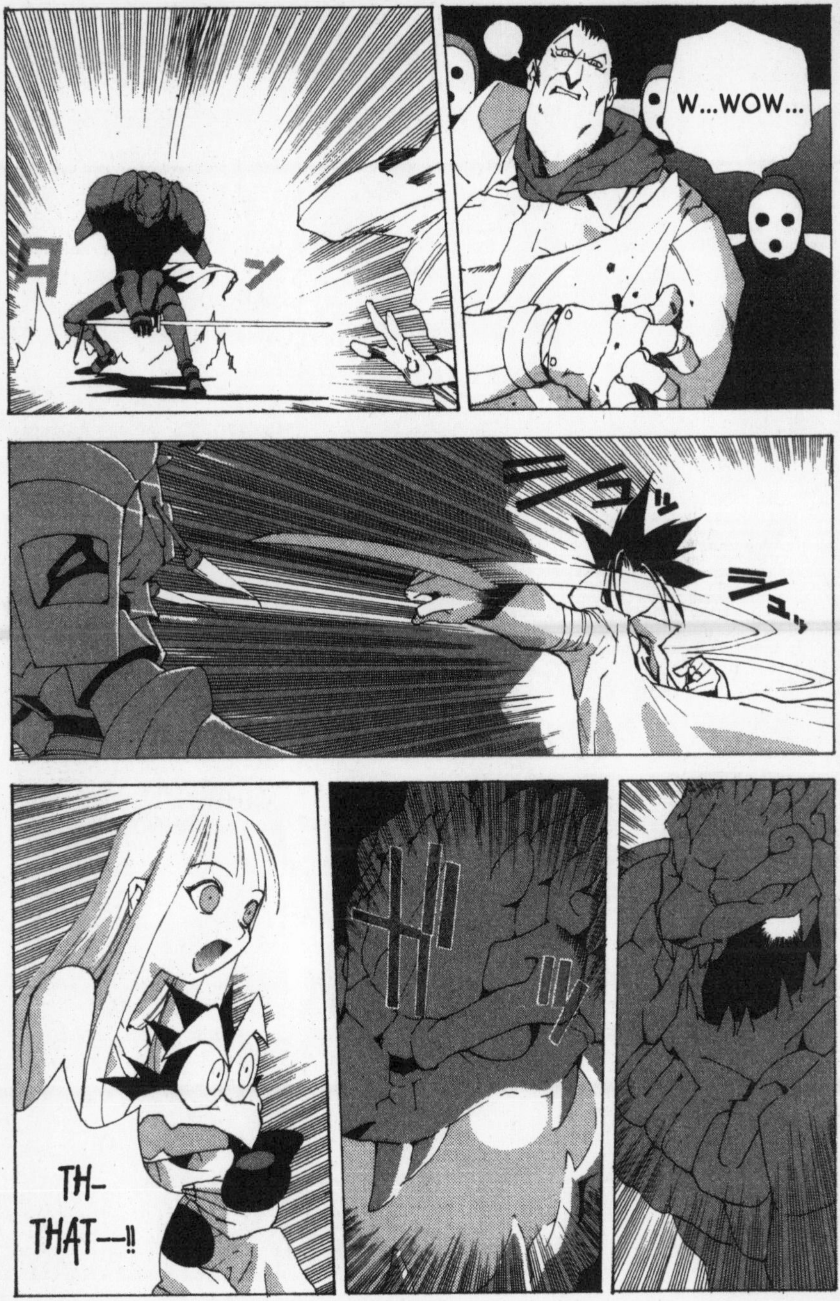
W...WOW...
TH-
THAT--!!

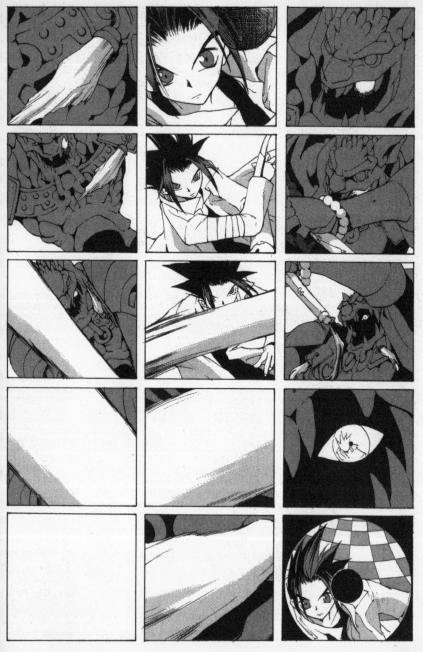

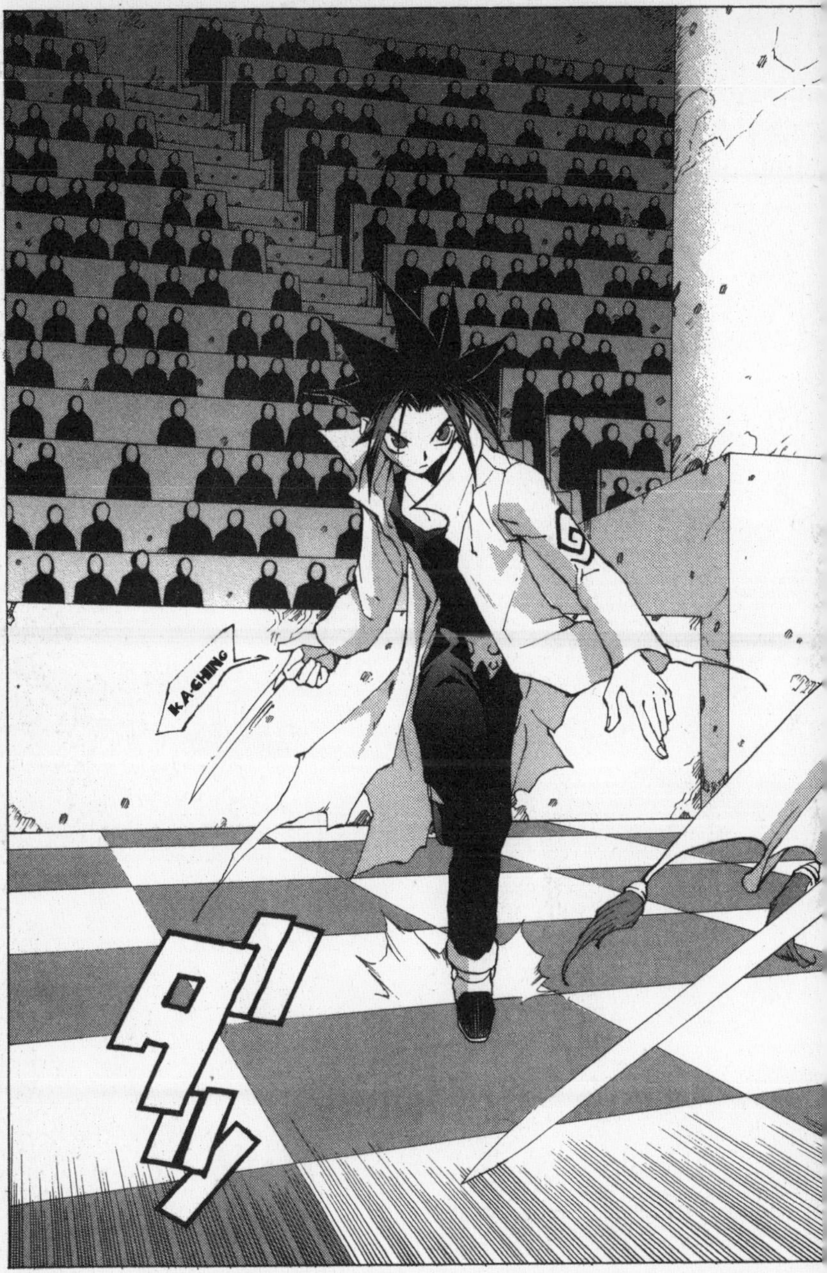
KA-CHING

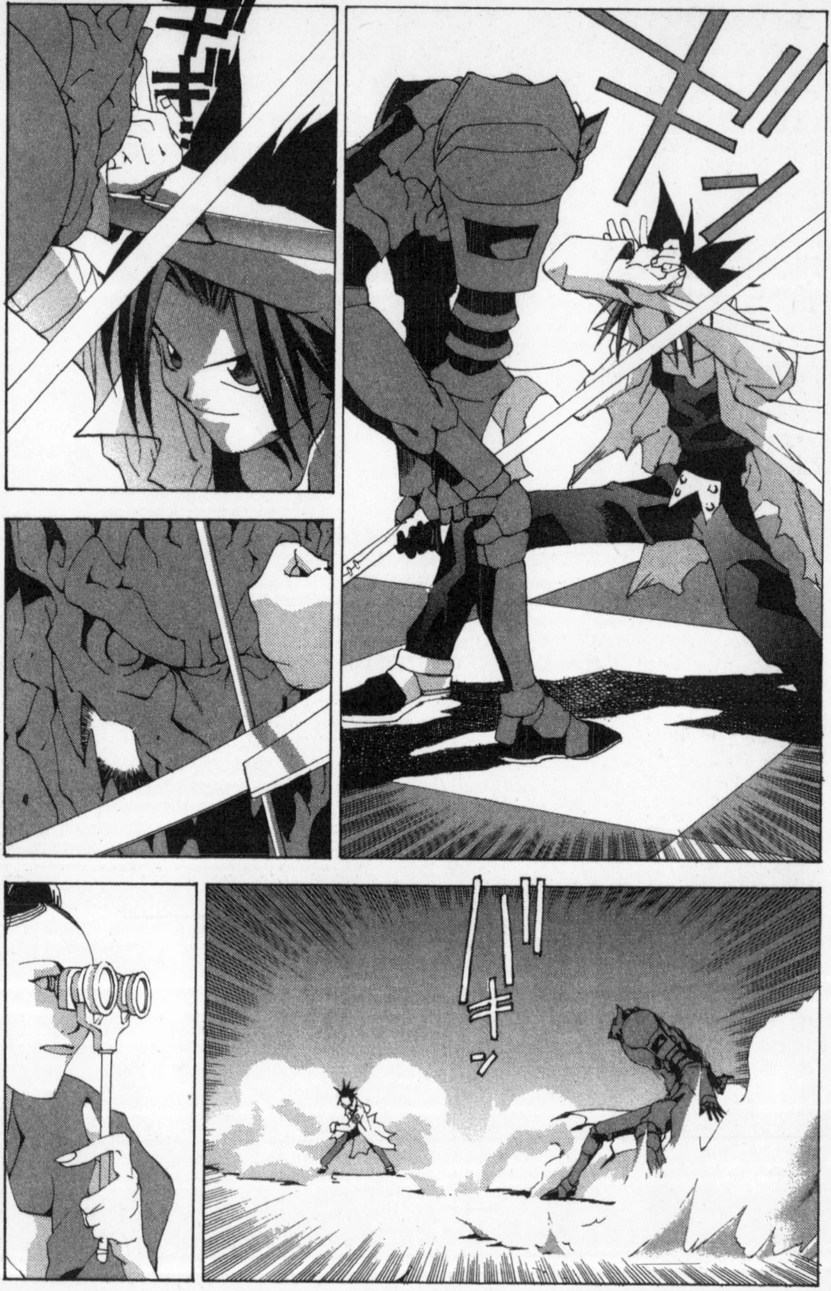
ギン
ガギッ
バキン

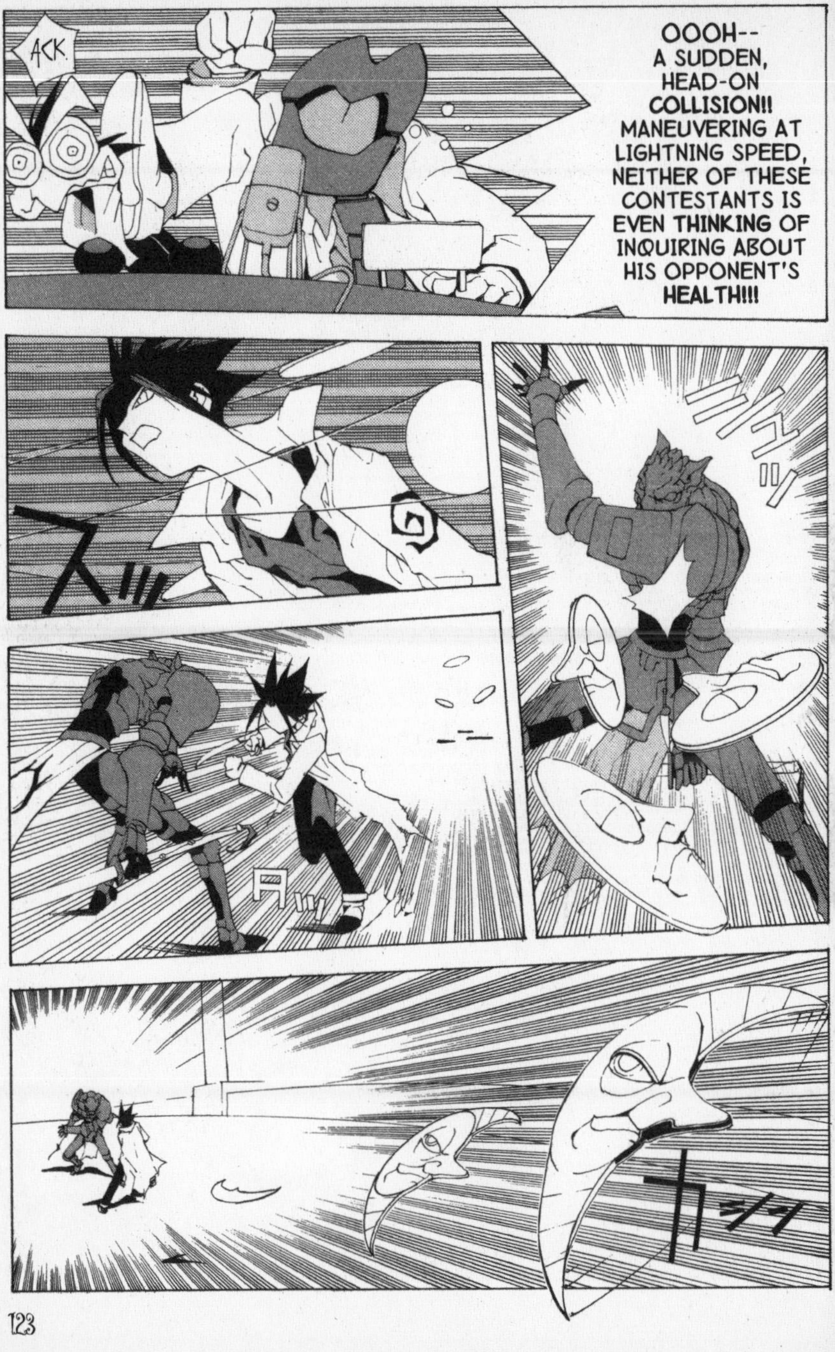
OOOH-- A SUDDEN, HEAD-ON COLLISION!! MANEUVERING AT LIGHTNING SPEED, NEITHER OF THESE CONTESTANTS IS EVEN THINKING OF INQUIRING ABOUT HIS OPPONENT'S HEALTH!!!
ACK.

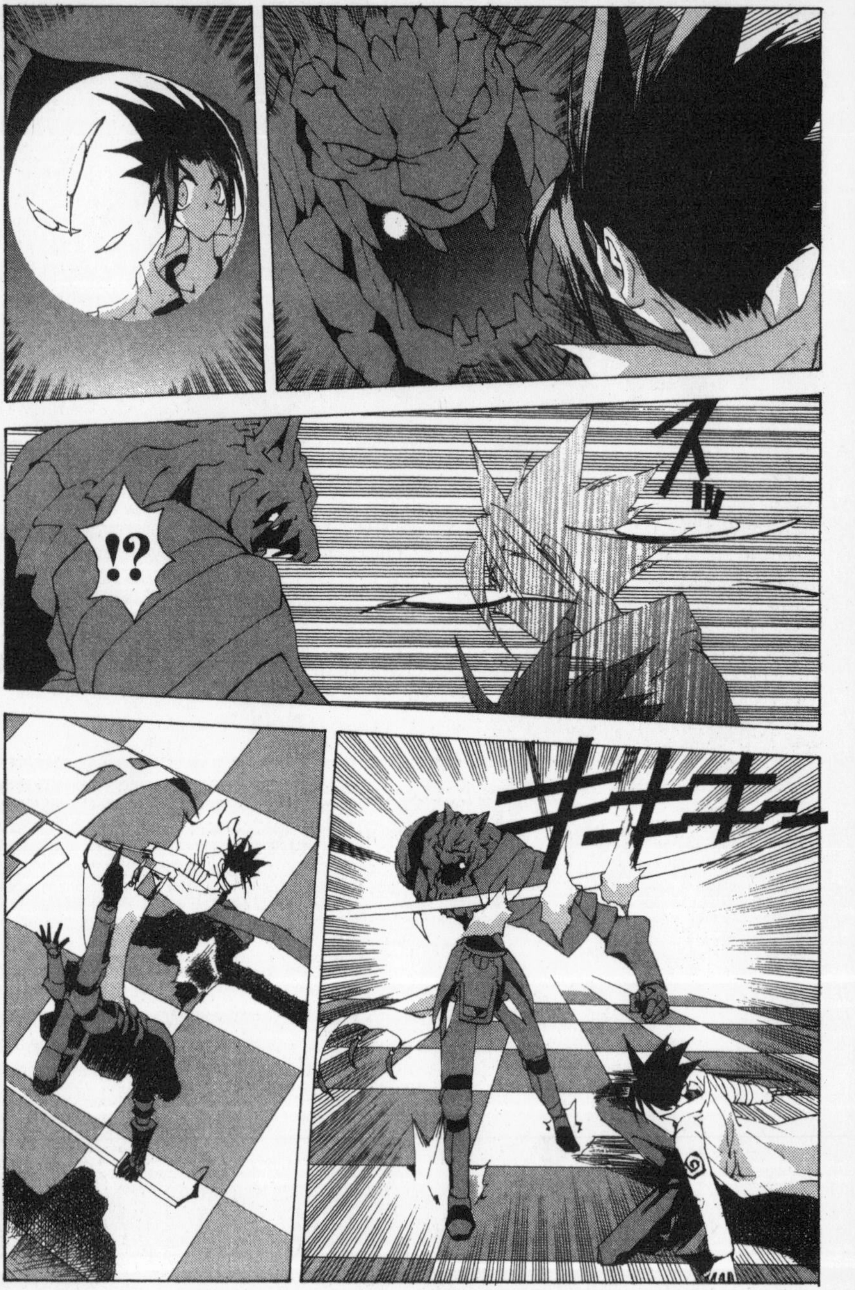
スッ
!?
キキキー

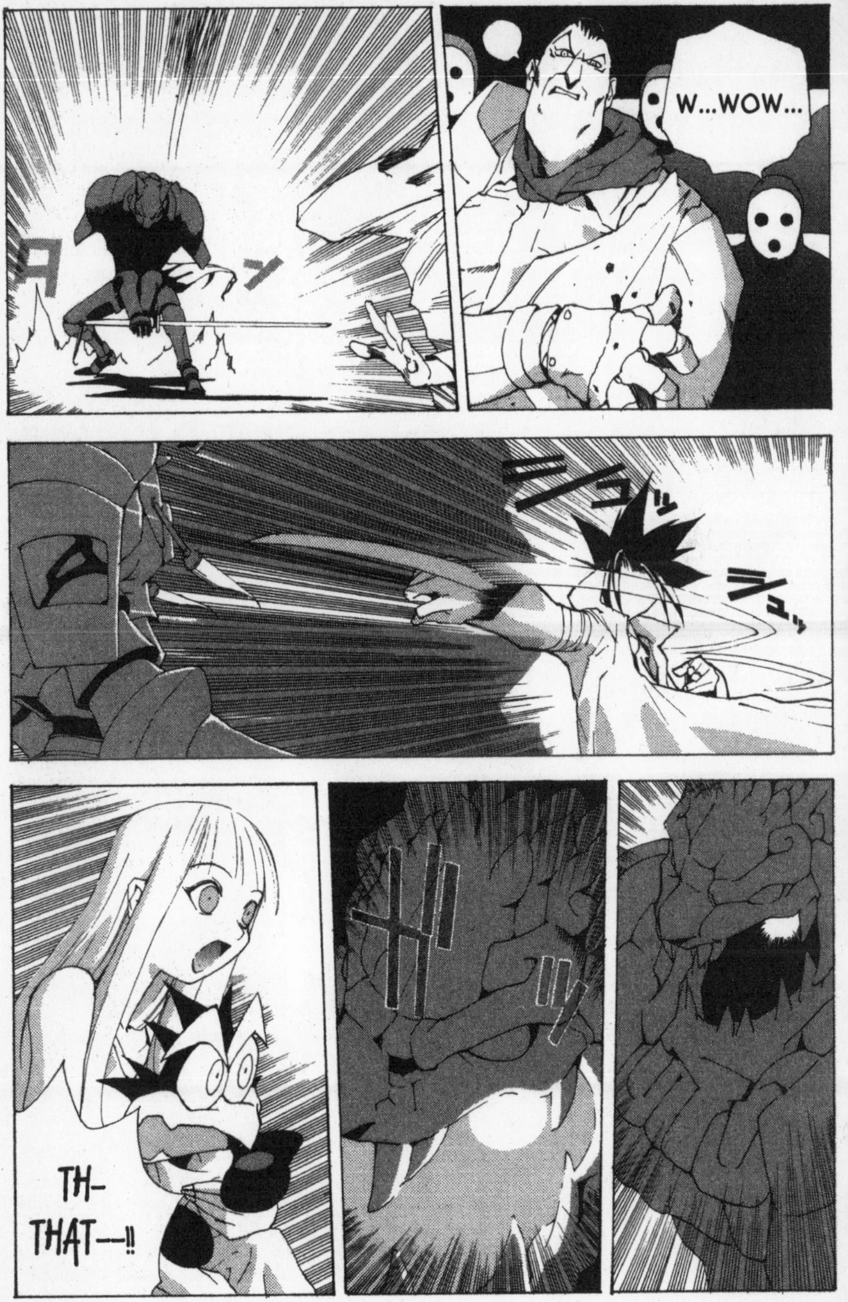
W...WOW...
TH-
THAT--!!

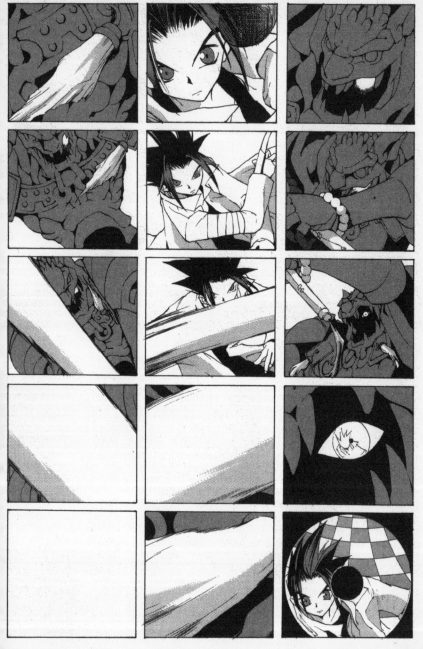

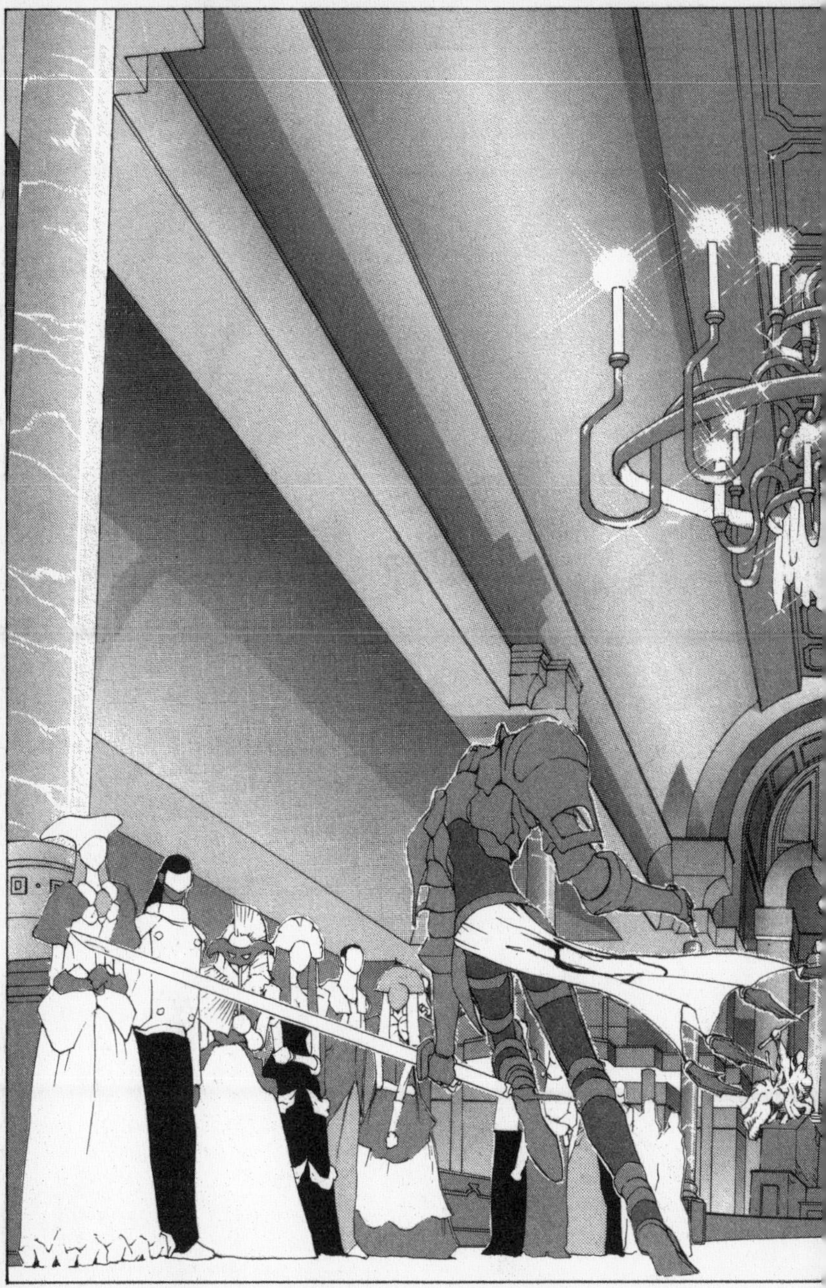

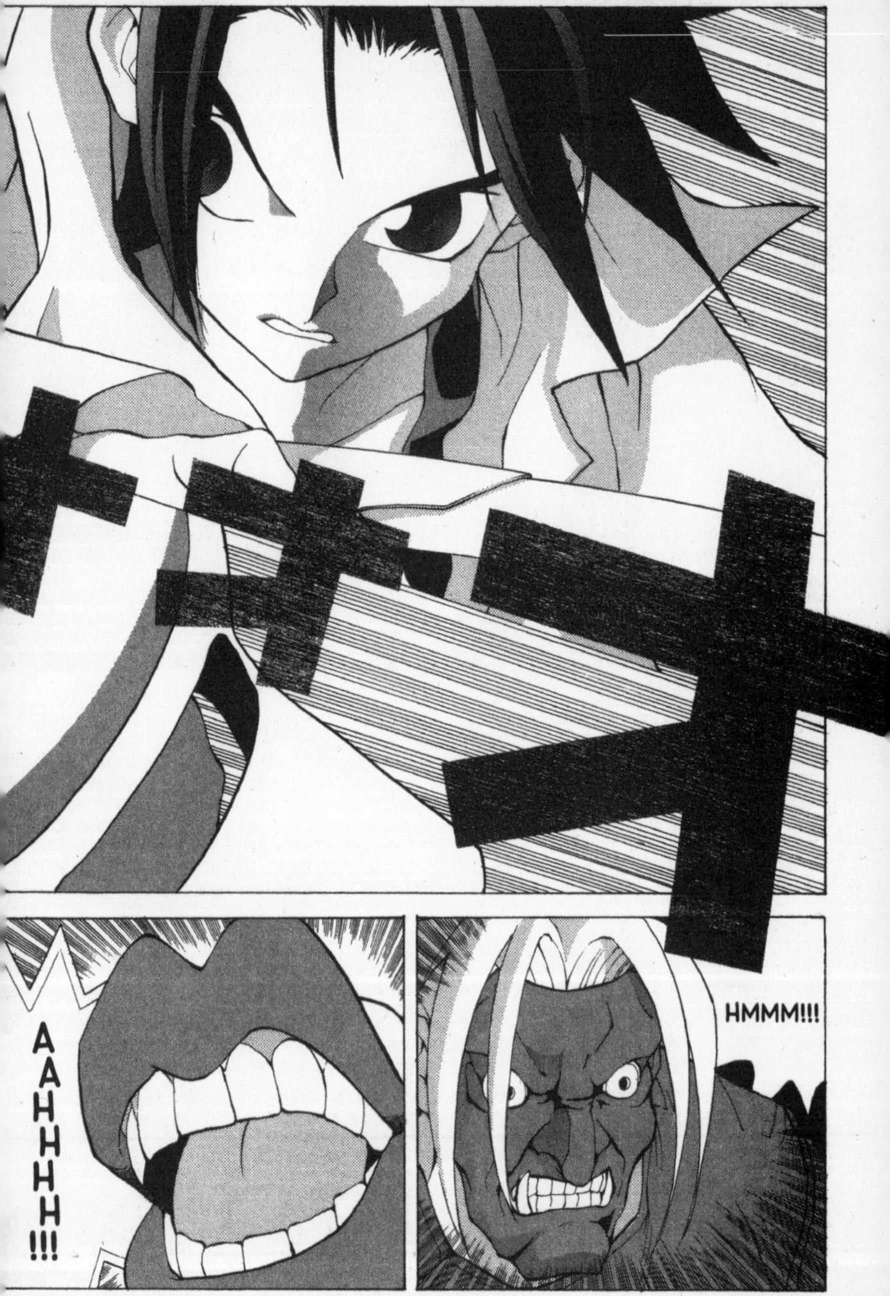
HMMM!!!
AAHHHH!!!

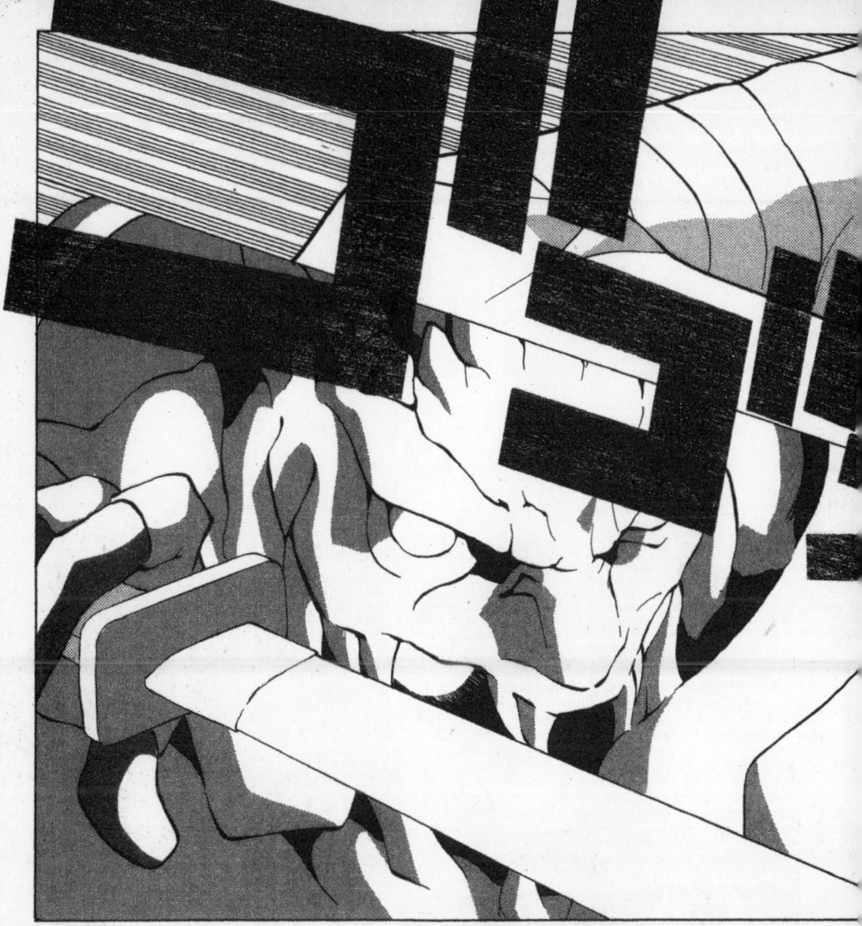

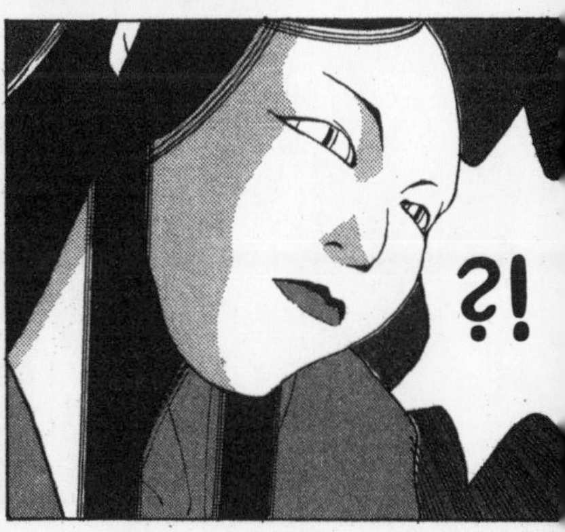
?!

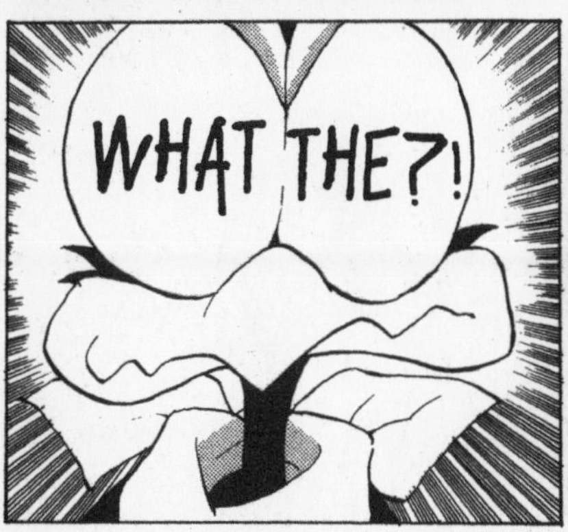
WHAT THE?!

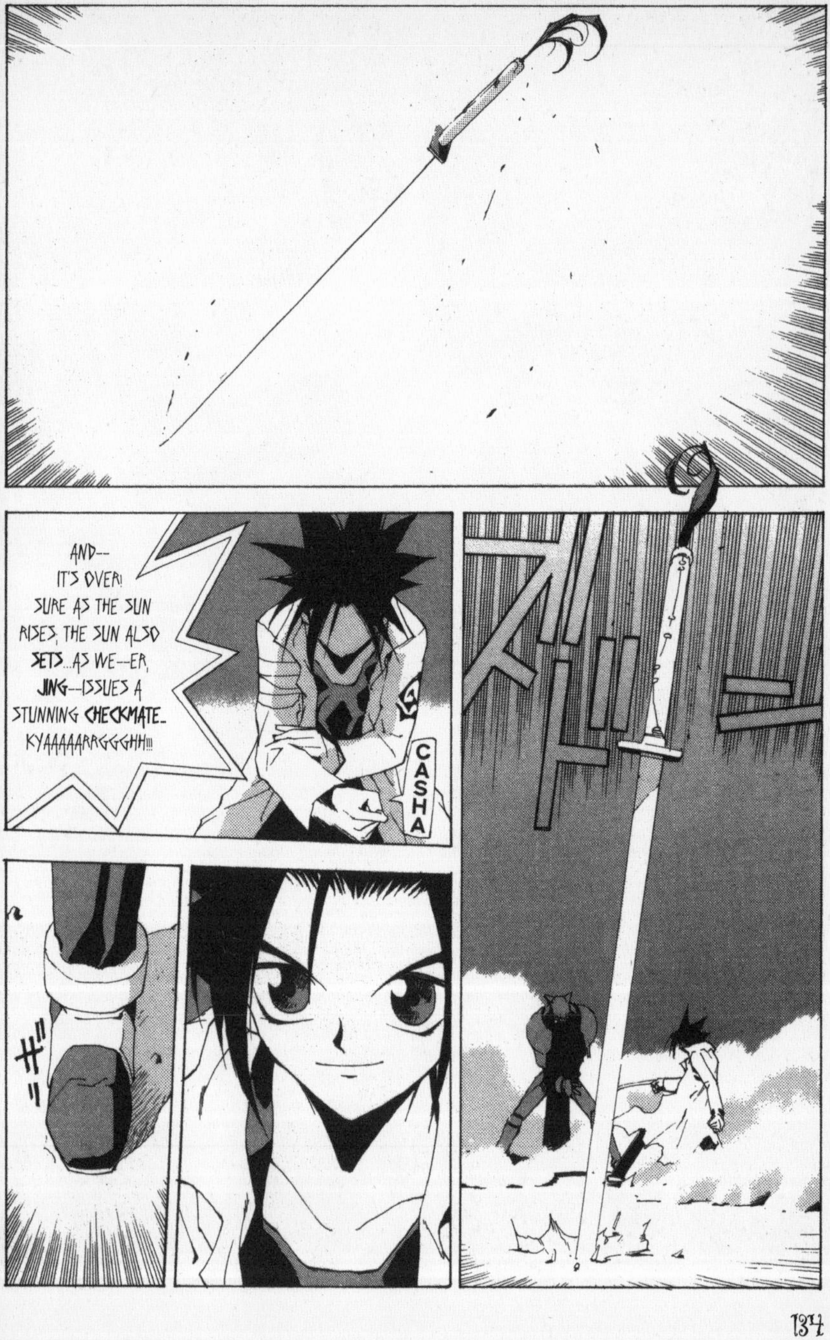
CASHA
AND-- IT'S OVER! SURE AS THE SUN RISES, THE SUN ALSO SETS...AS WE--ER, JING--ISSUES A STUNNING CHECKMATE... KYAAAAARRGGGHH!!!

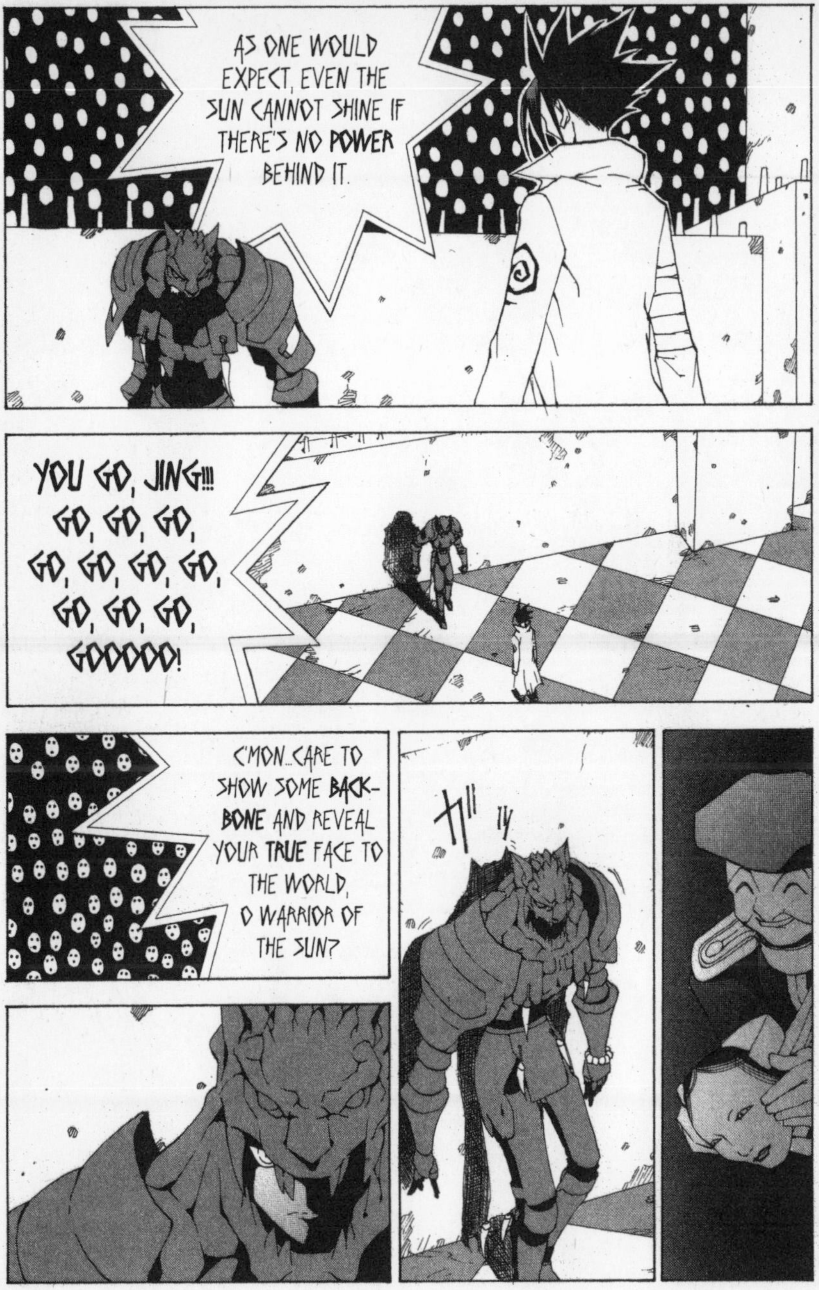
AS ONE WOULD EXPECT, EVEN THE SUN CANNOT SHINE IF THERE'S NO POWER BEHIND IT.
YOU GO, JING!!! GO, GO, GO, GO, GO, GO, GO, GO, GO, GO, GOOOOO!
C'MON...CARE TO SHOW SOME BACK-BONE AND REVEAL YOUR TRUE FACE TO THE WORLD, O WARRIOR OF THE SUN?

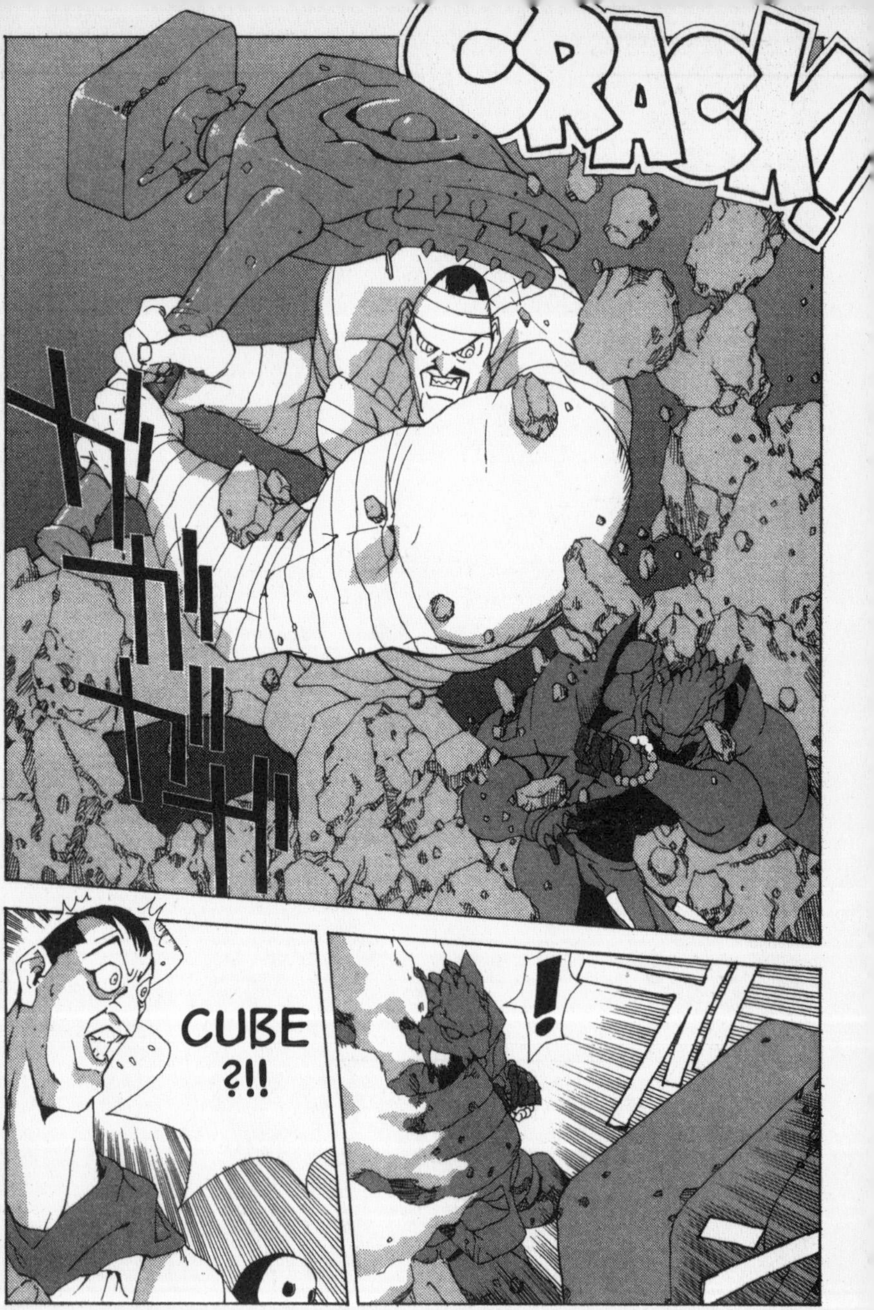
CRACK!!
!
CUBE ?!!

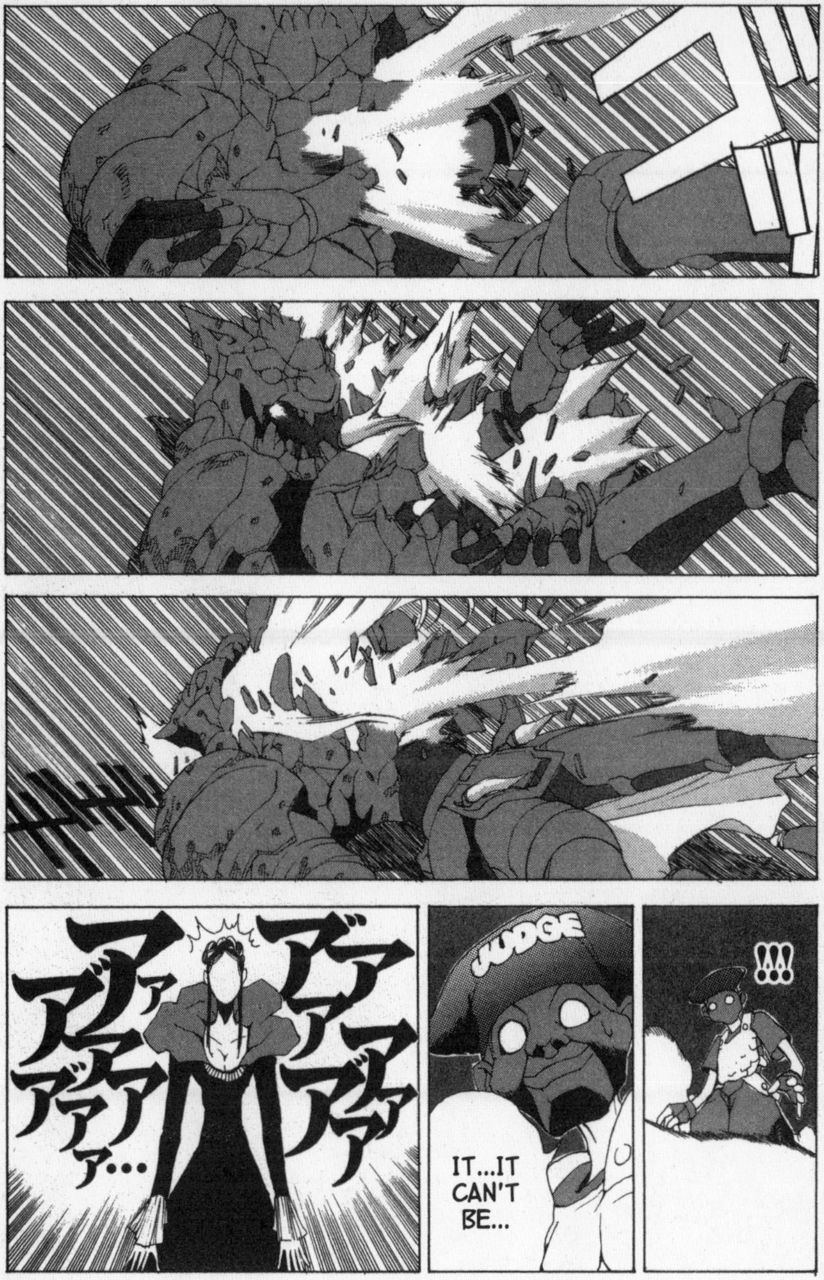
!!!
IT...IT CAN'T BE...

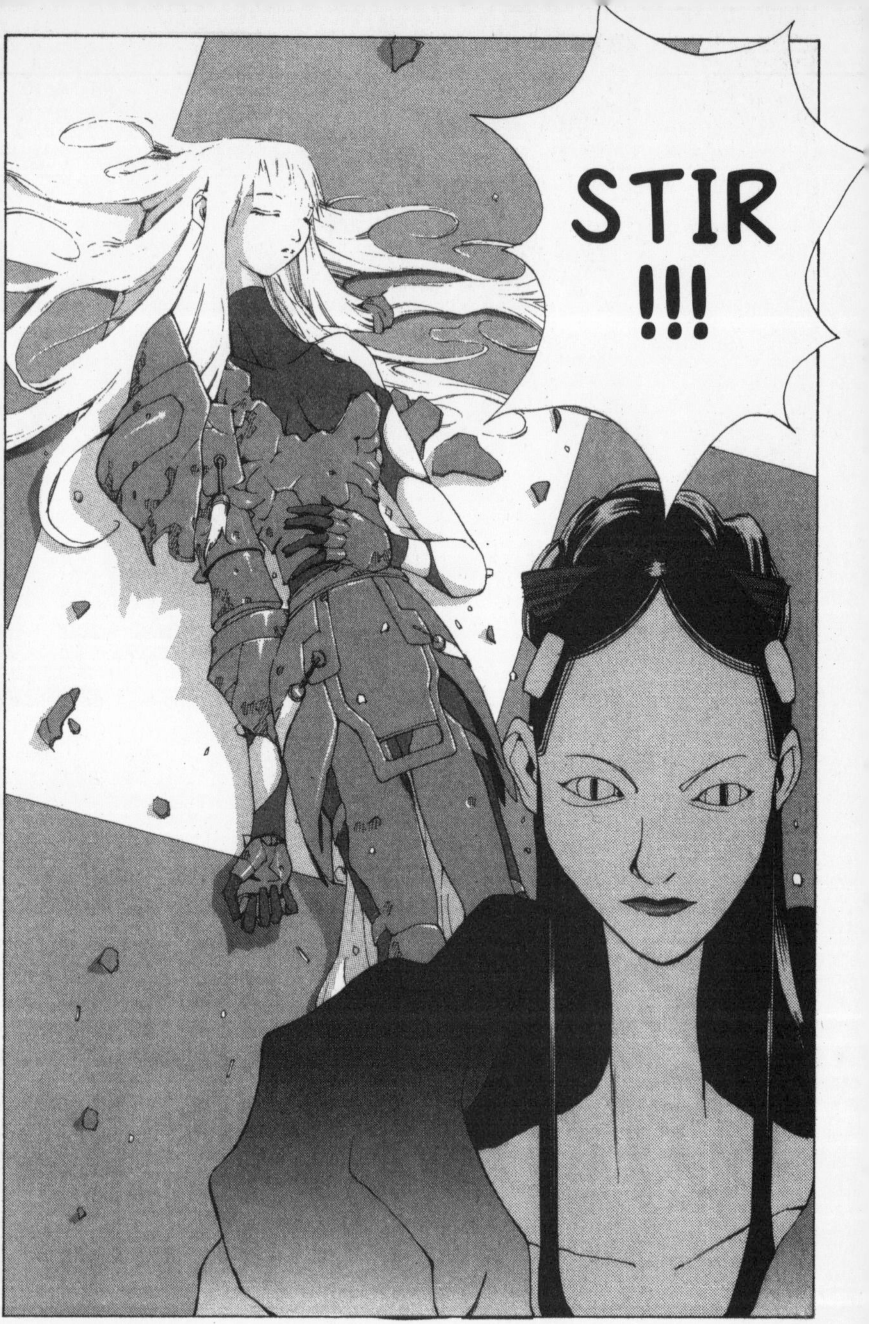
STIR
!!!

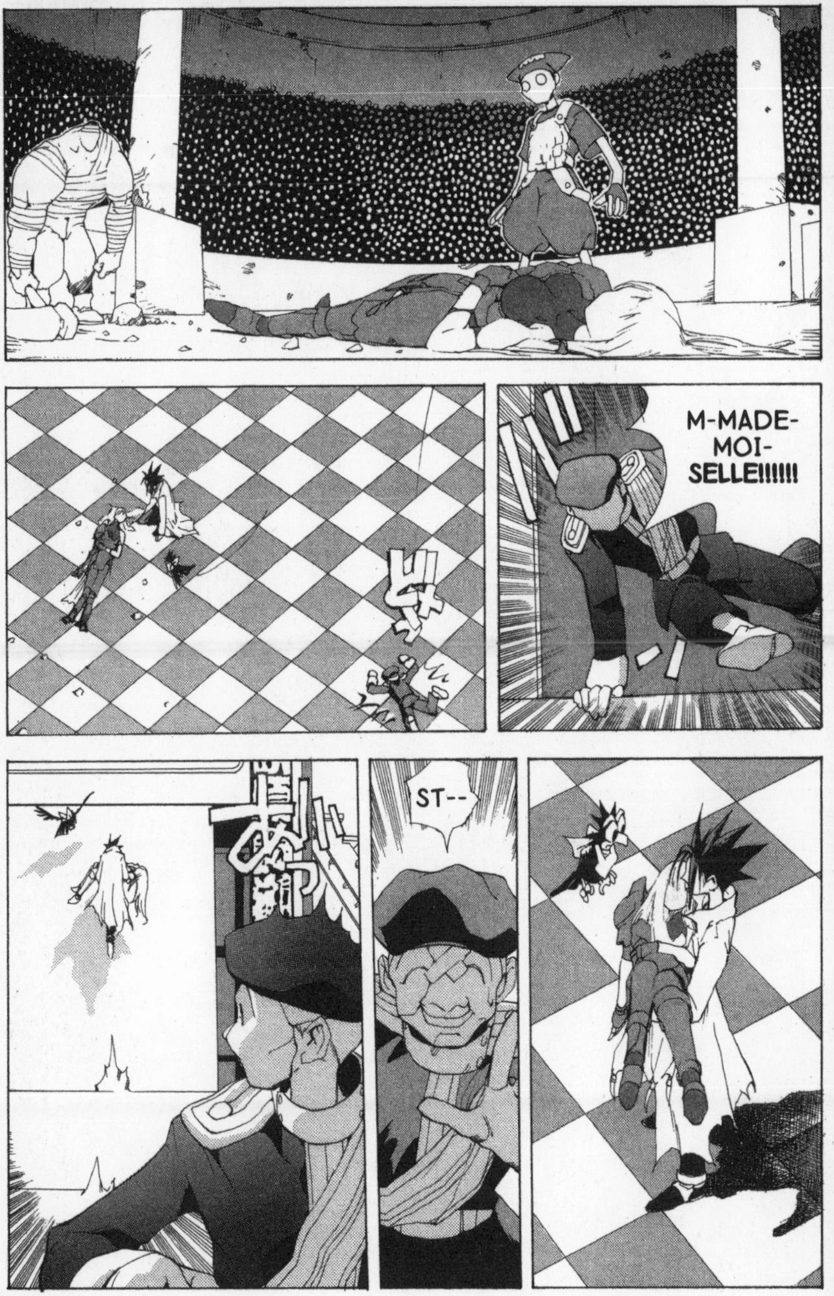
M-MADE-MOI-SELLE!!!!!!
ST--

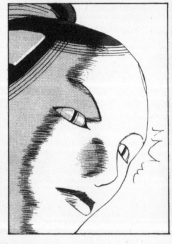

STOP
HIM!!!

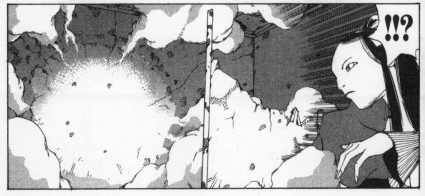

!!!?

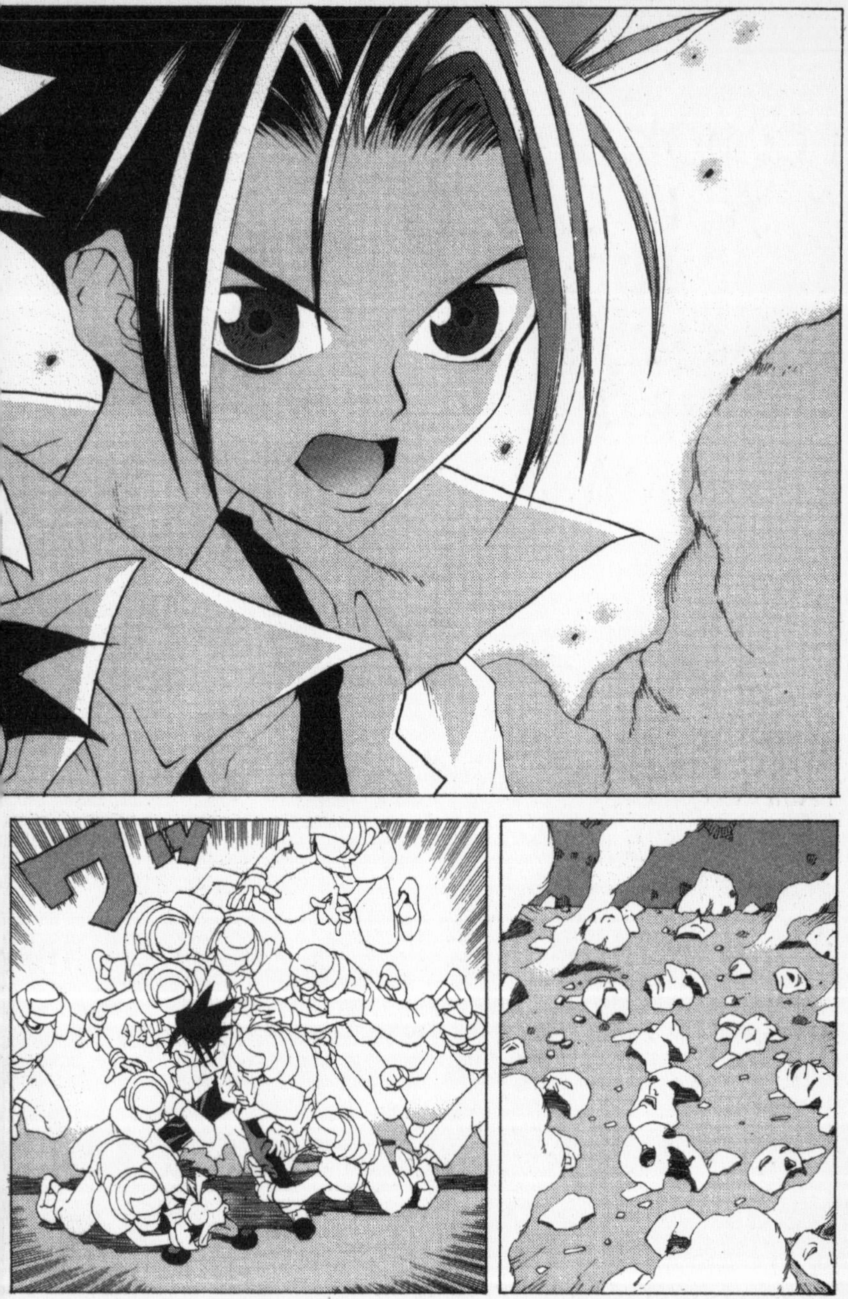

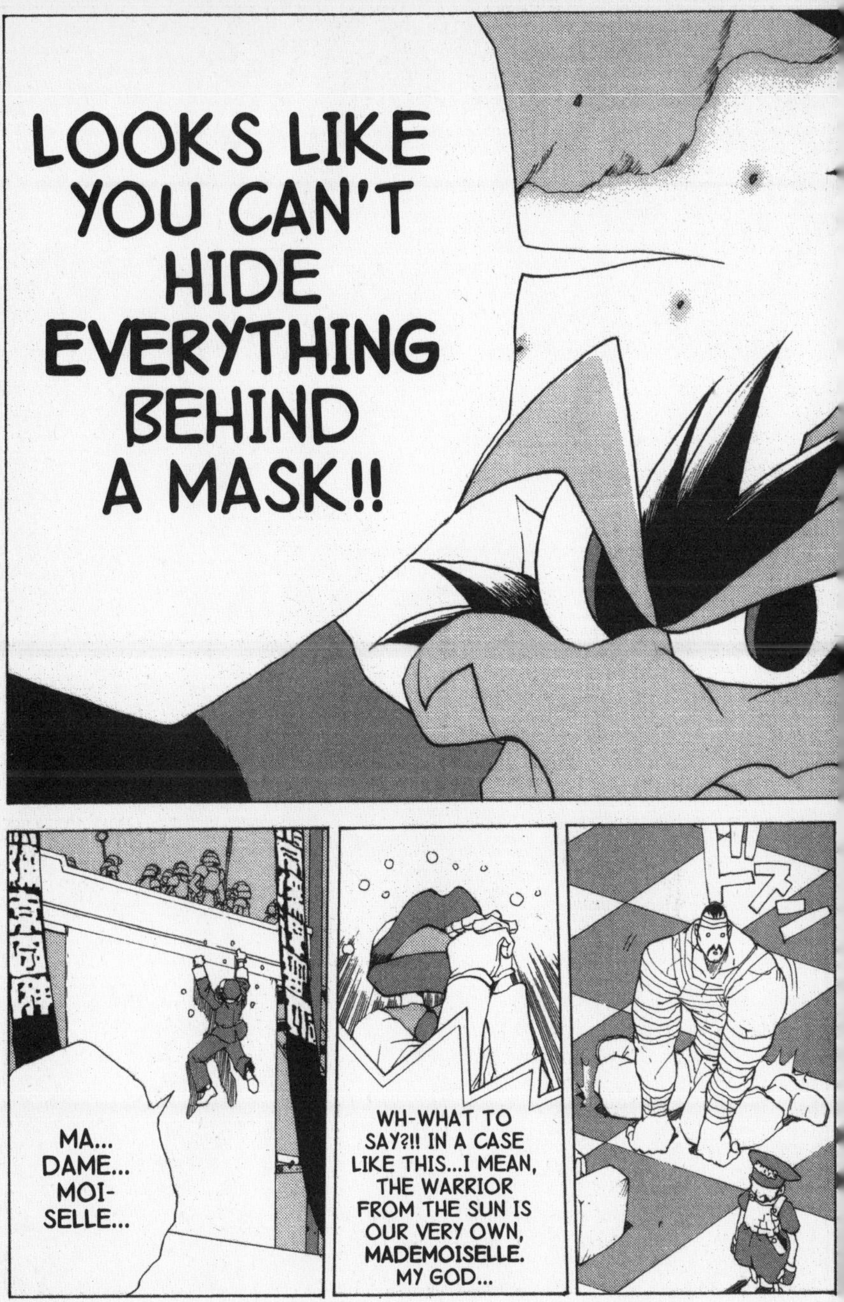
LOOKS LIKE YOU CAN'T HIDE EVERYTHING BEHIND A MASK!!
WH-WHAT TO SAY?!! IN A CASE LIKE THIS...I MEAN, THE WARRIOR FROM THE SUN IS OUR VERY OWN, MADEMOISELLE. MY GOD...
MA... DAME... MOI- SELLE...

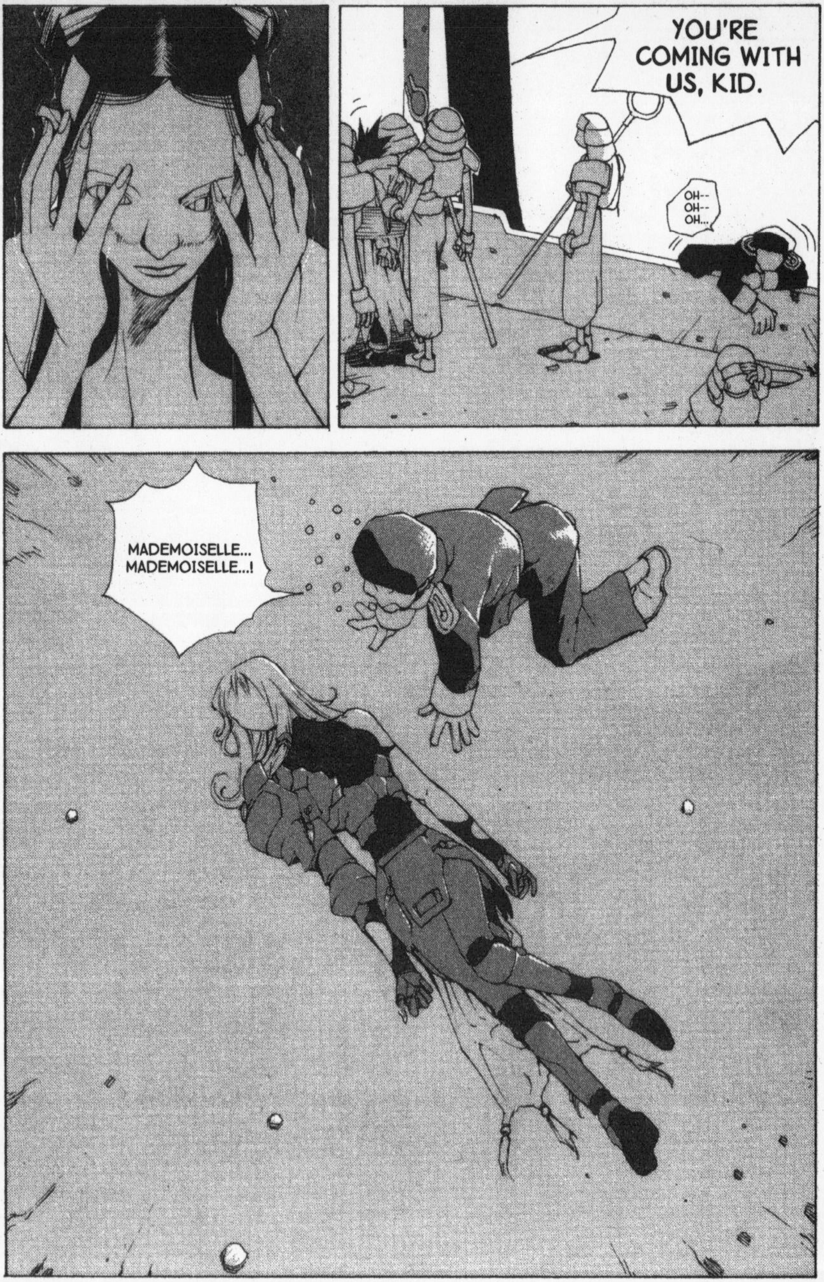
YOU'RE COMING WITH US, KID.
OH-- OH-- OH...
MADEMOISELLE... MADEMOISELLE...!

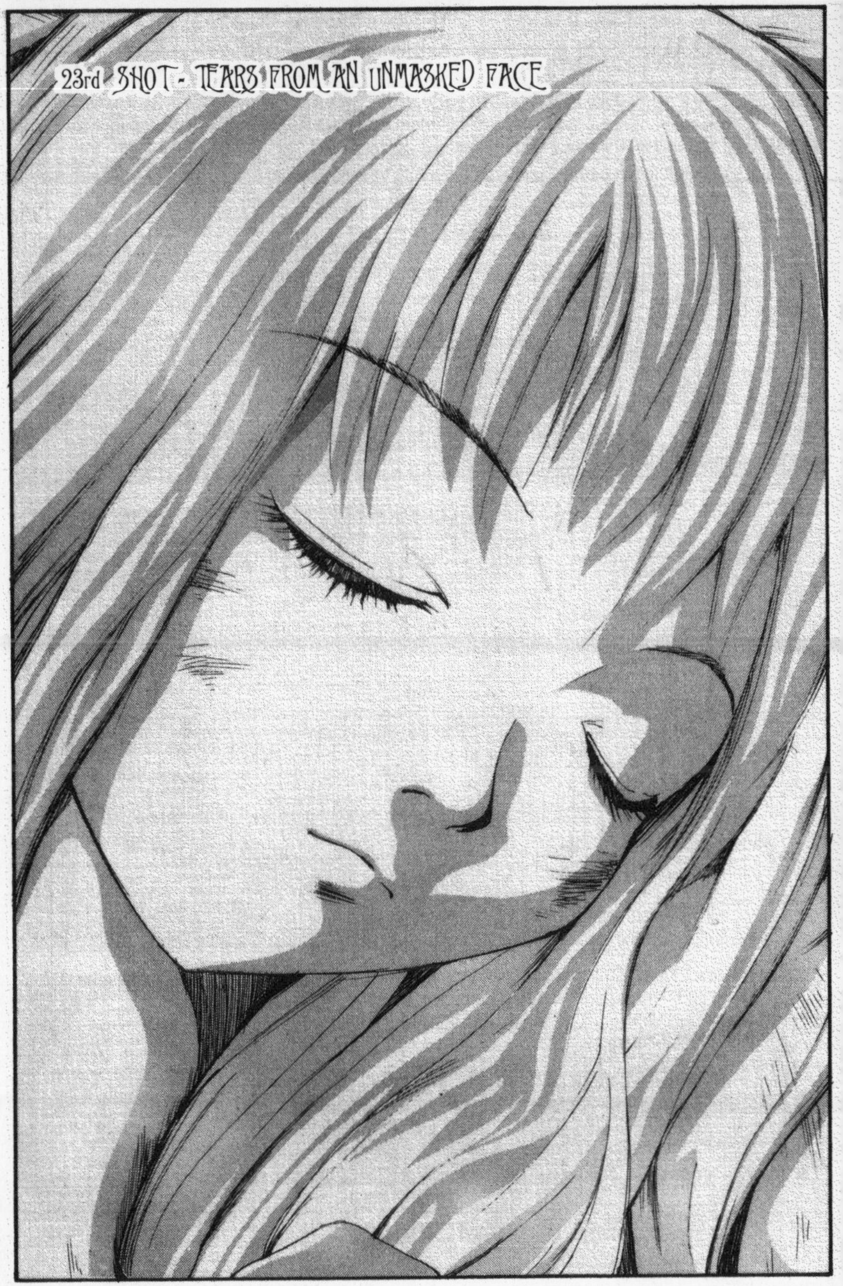
23rd SHOT - TEARS FROM AN UNMASKED FACE

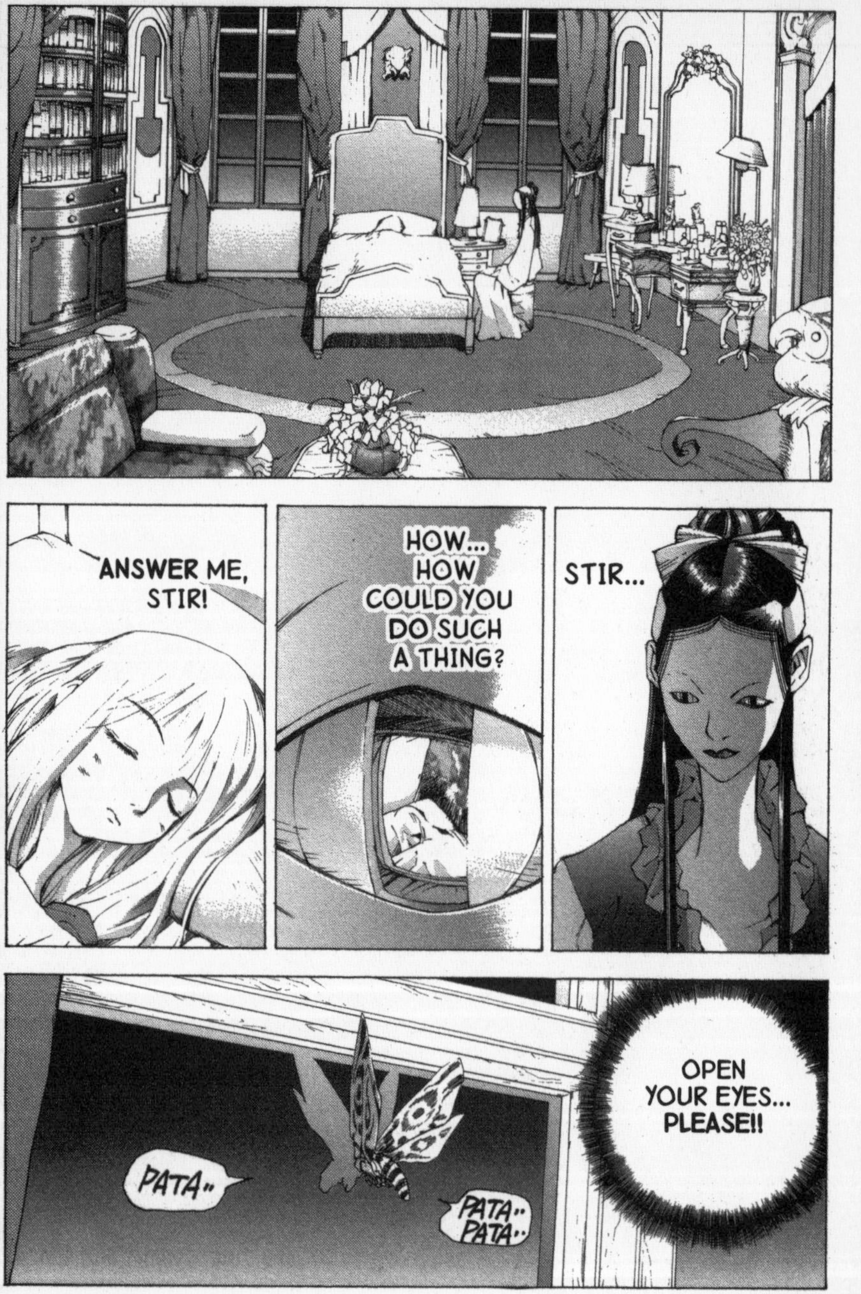
STIR...
HOW... HOW COULD YOU DO SUCH A THING?
ANSWER ME, STIR!
OPEN YOUR EYES... PLEASE!!
PATA.. PATA..
PATA..

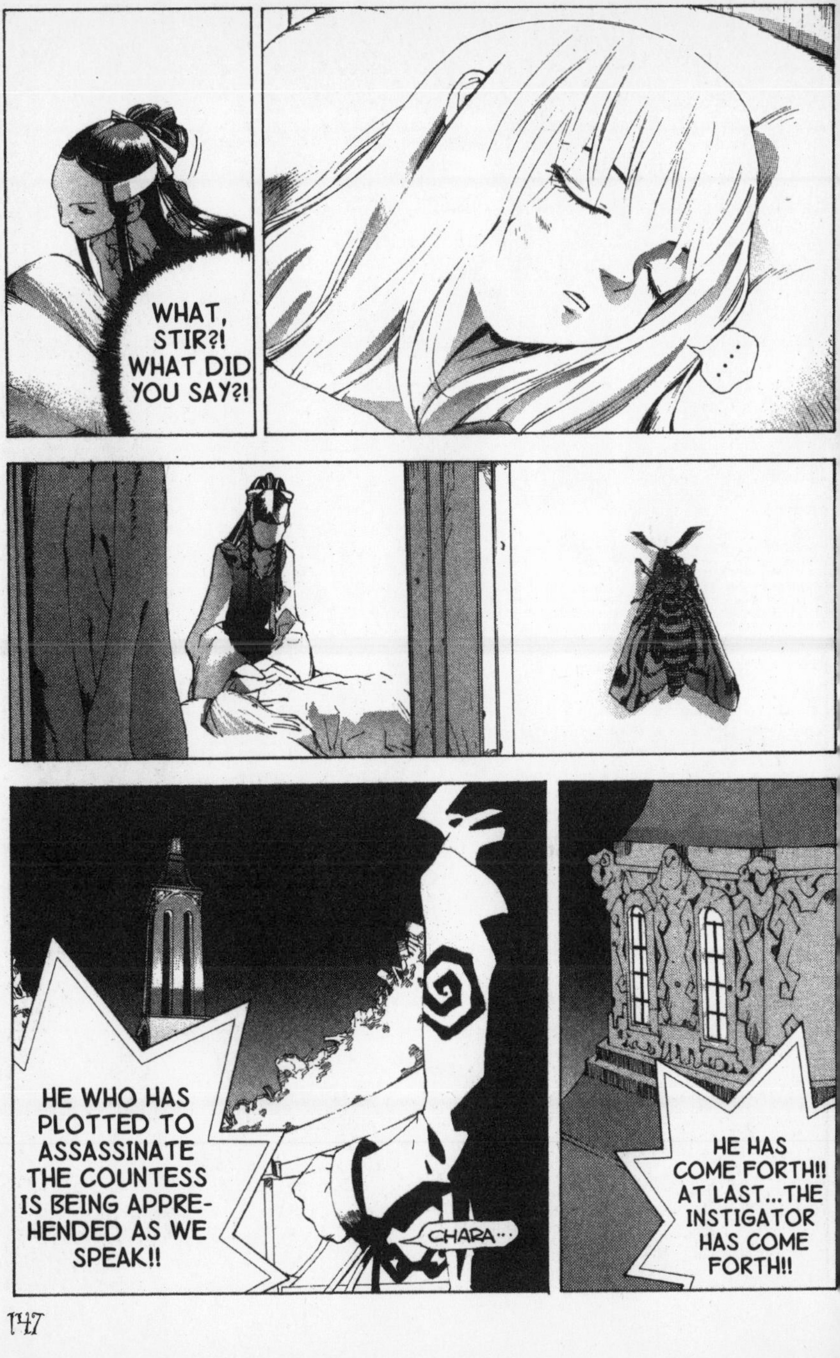
...
WHAT, STIR?! WHAT DID YOU SAY?!
HE HAS COME FORTH!! AT LAST...THE INSTIGATOR HAS COME FORTH!!
HE WHO HAS PLOTTED TO ASSASSINATE THE COUNTESS IS BEING APPREHENDED AS WE SPEAK!!
CHARA...

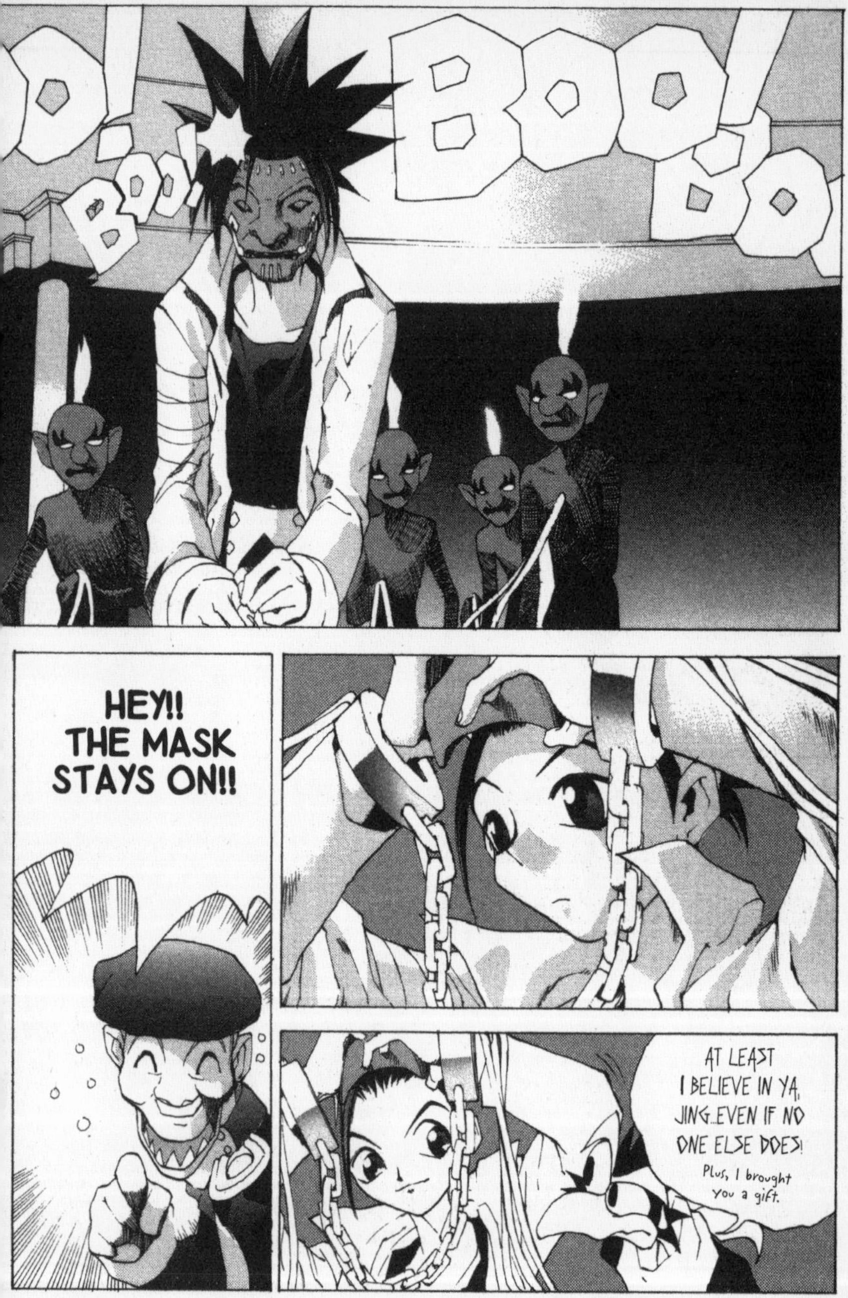
BOO! BOO!
BOO!
BOO!
BOO!
AT LEAST I BELIEVE IN YA, JING...EVEN IF NO ONE ELSE DOES!
Plus, I brought you a gift.
HEY!! THE MASK STAYS ON!!

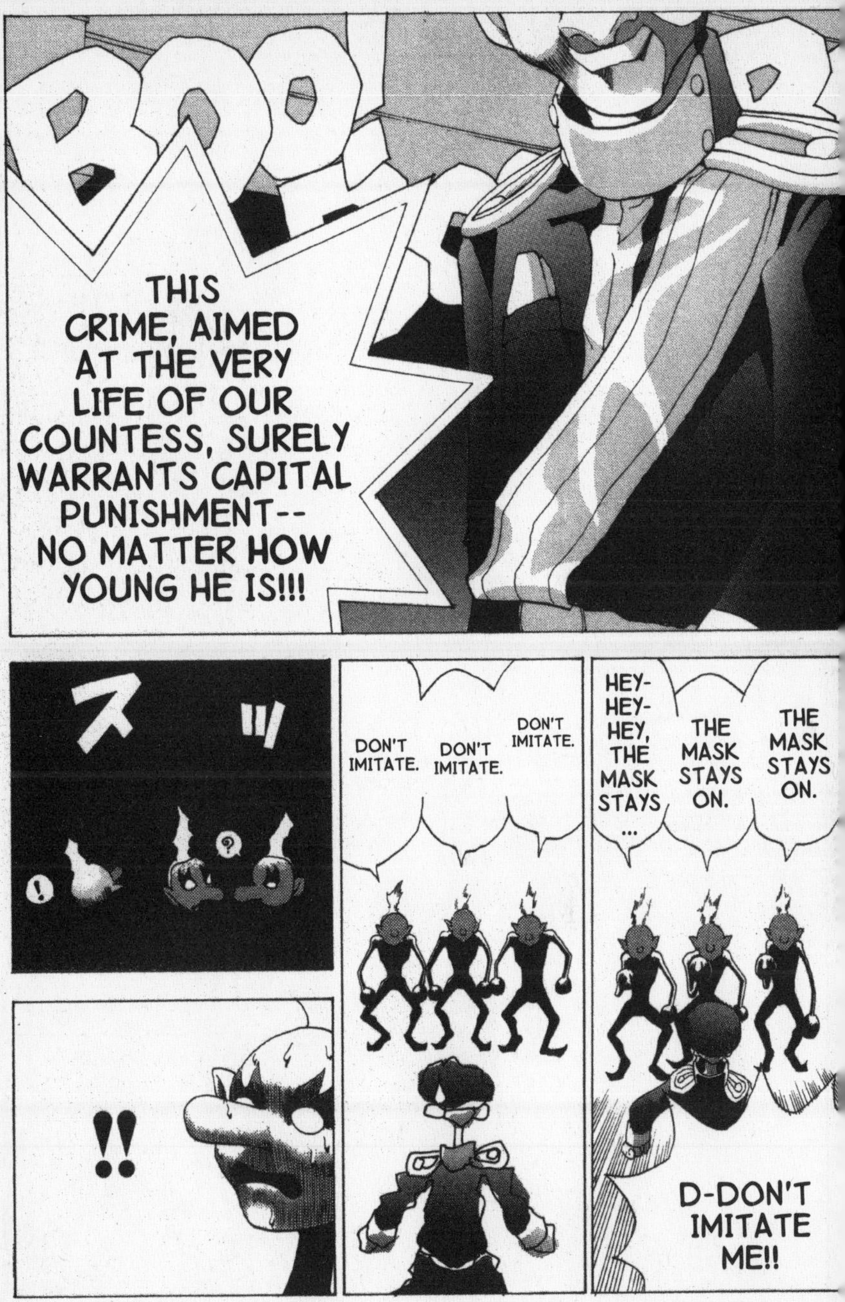
THIS CRIME, AIMED AT THE VERY LIFE OF OUR COUNTESS, SURELY WARRANTS CAPITAL PUNISHMENT-- NO MATTER HOW YOUNG HE IS!!!
THE MASK STAYS ON.
THE MASK STAYS ON.
HEY-HEY-HEY, THE MASK STAYS...
D-DON'T IMITATE ME!!
DON'T IMITATE.
DON'T IMITATE.
DON'T IMITATE.
スッ
!
?
!!

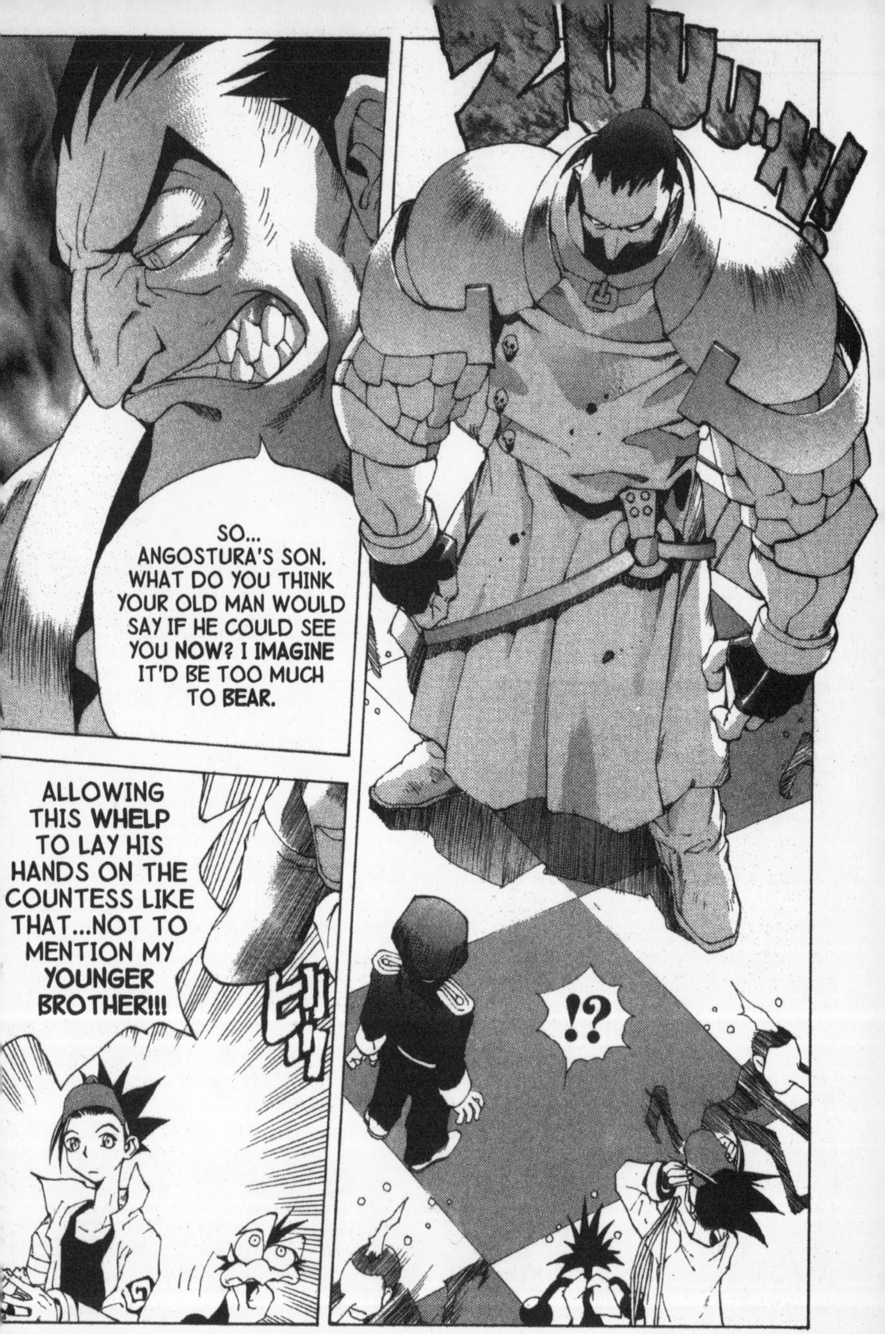
ZUUUU...N!!
!?
SO... ANGOSTURA'S SON. WHAT DO YOU THINK YOUR OLD MAN WOULD SAY IF HE COULD SEE YOU NOW? I IMAGINE IT'D BE TOO MUCH TO BEAR.
ALLOWING THIS WHELP TO LAY HIS HANDS ON THE COUNTESS LIKE THAT...NOT TO MENTION MY YOUNGER BROTHER!!!

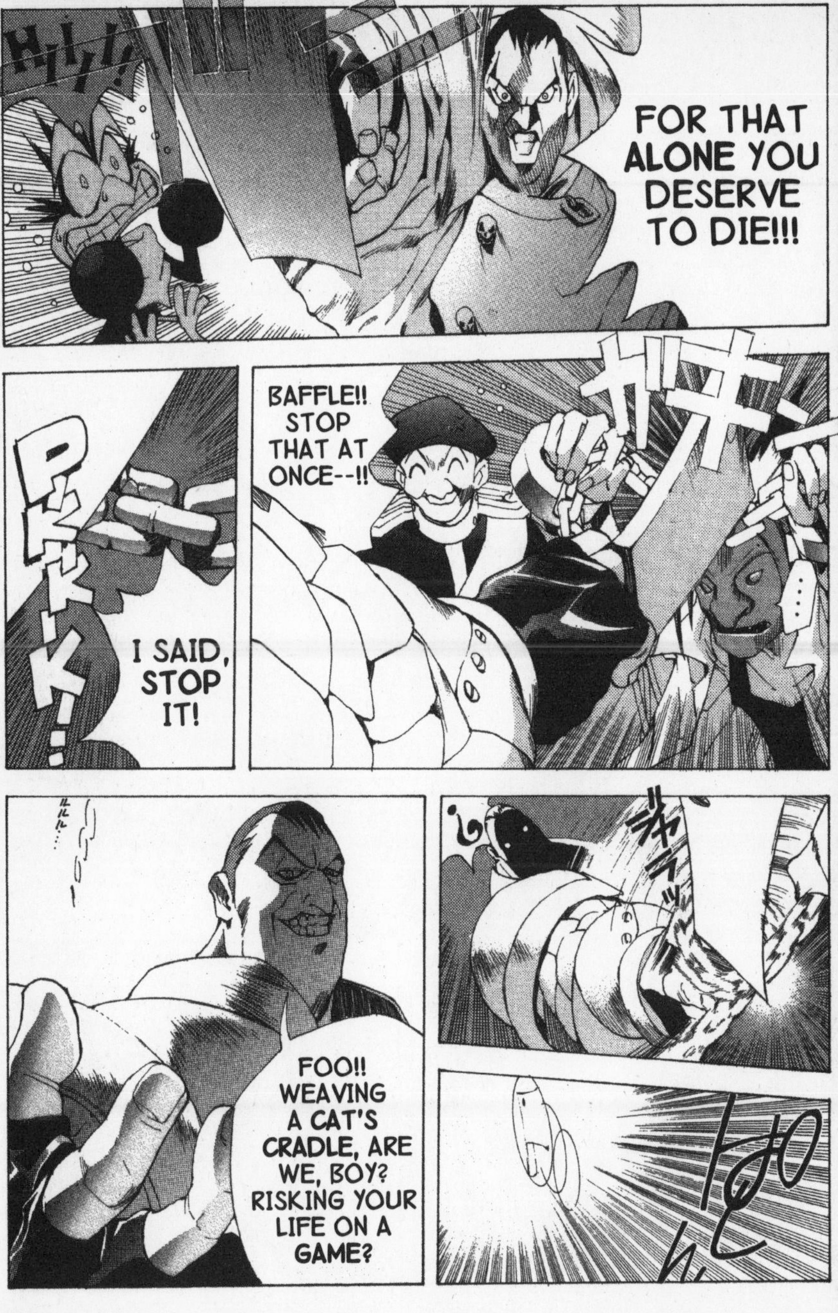
FOR THAT ALONE YOU DESERVE TO DIE!!!
BAFFLE!! STOP THAT AT ONCE--!!
...
I SAID, STOP IT!
FOO!! WEAVING A CAT'S CRADLE, ARE WE, BOY? RISKING YOUR LIFE ON A GAME?

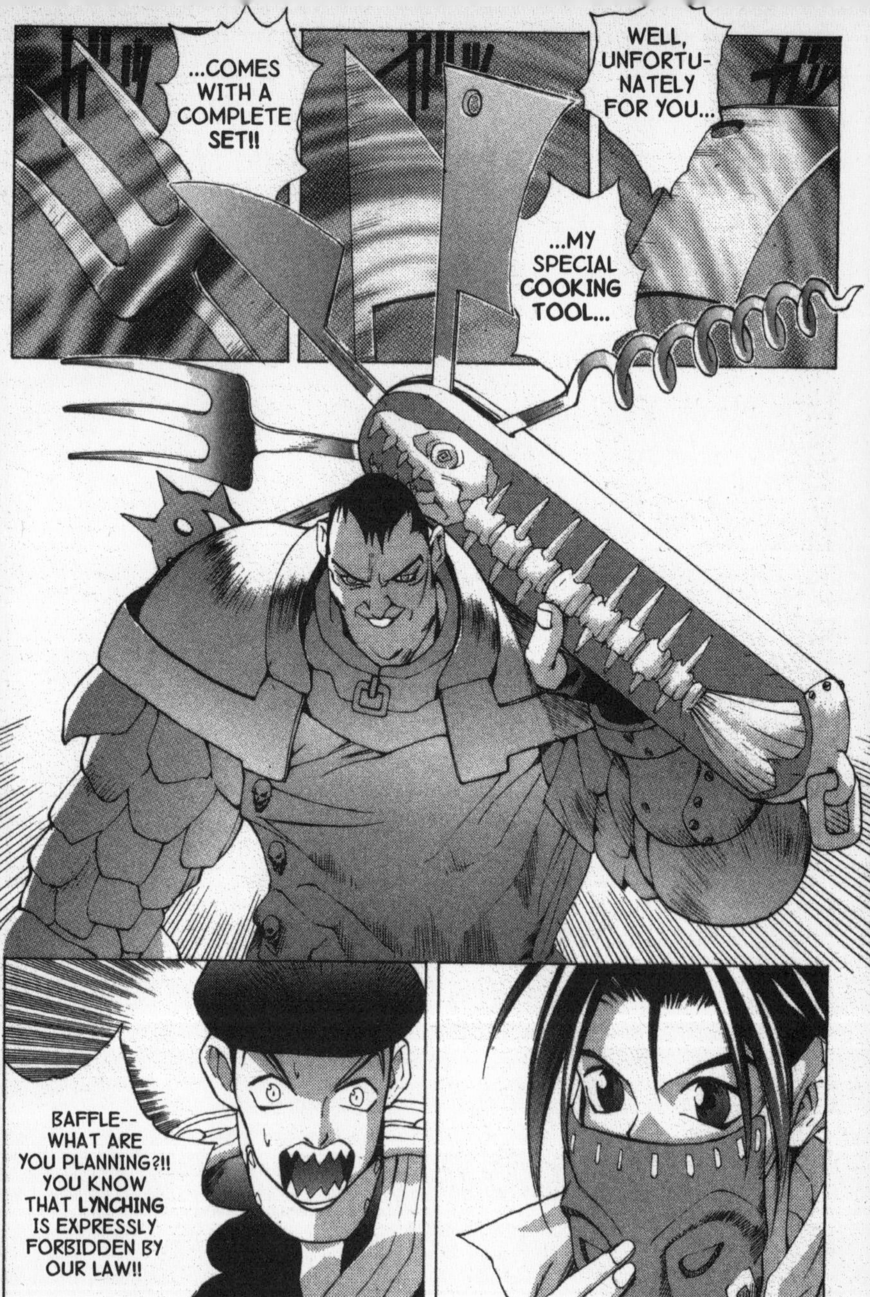
WELL, UNFORTUNATELY FOR YOU...
...MY SPECIAL COOKING TOOL...
...COMES WITH A COMPLETE SET!!
BAFFLE-- WHAT ARE YOU PLANNING?!! YOU KNOW THAT LYNCHING IS EXPRESSLY FORBIDDEN BY OUR LAW!!

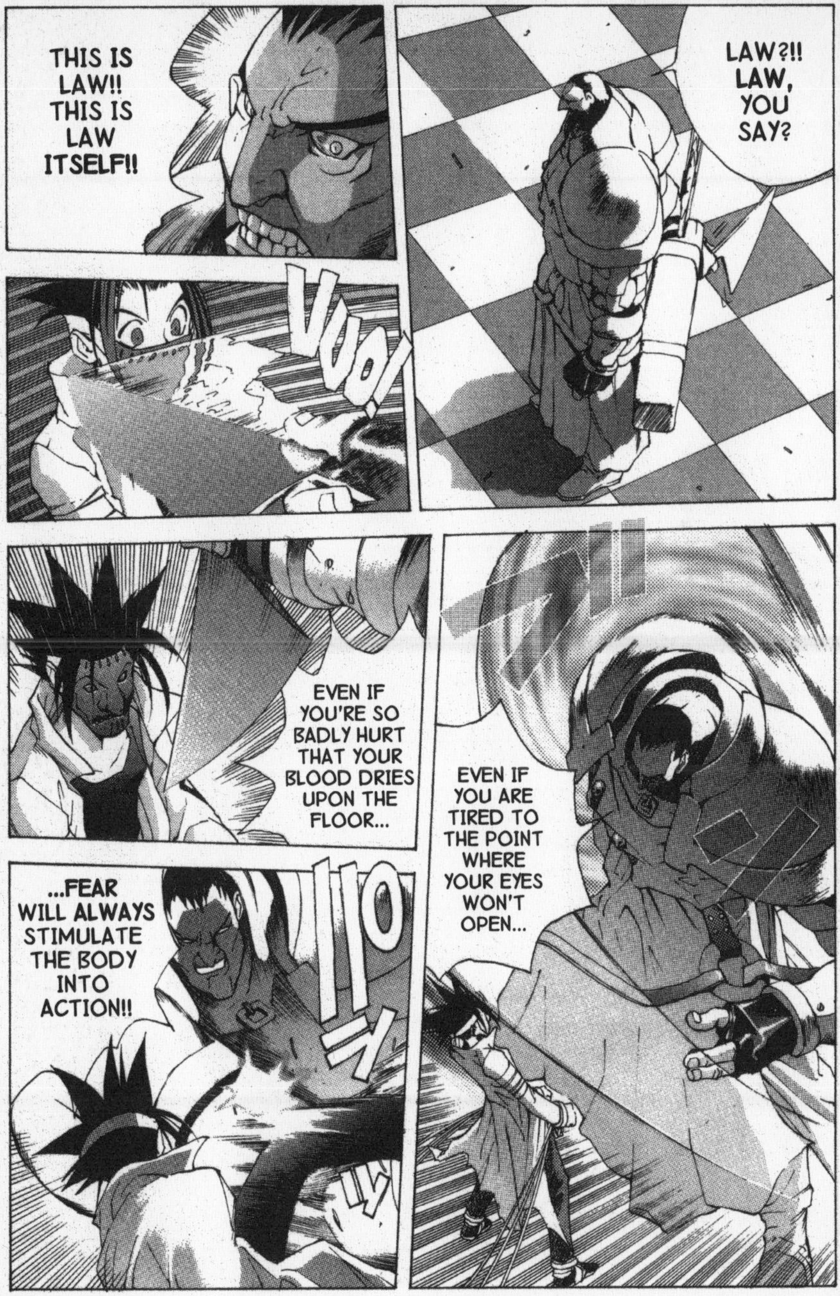

LAW?!! LAW, YOU SAY?
THIS IS LAW!! THIS IS LAW ITSELF!!
VUO!
EVEN IF YOU ARE TIRED TO THE POINT WHERE YOUR EYES WON'T OPEN...
EVEN IF YOU'RE SO BADLY HURT THAT YOUR BLOOD DRIES UPON THE FLOOR...
...FEAR WILL ALWAYS STIMULATE THE BODY INTO ACTION!!

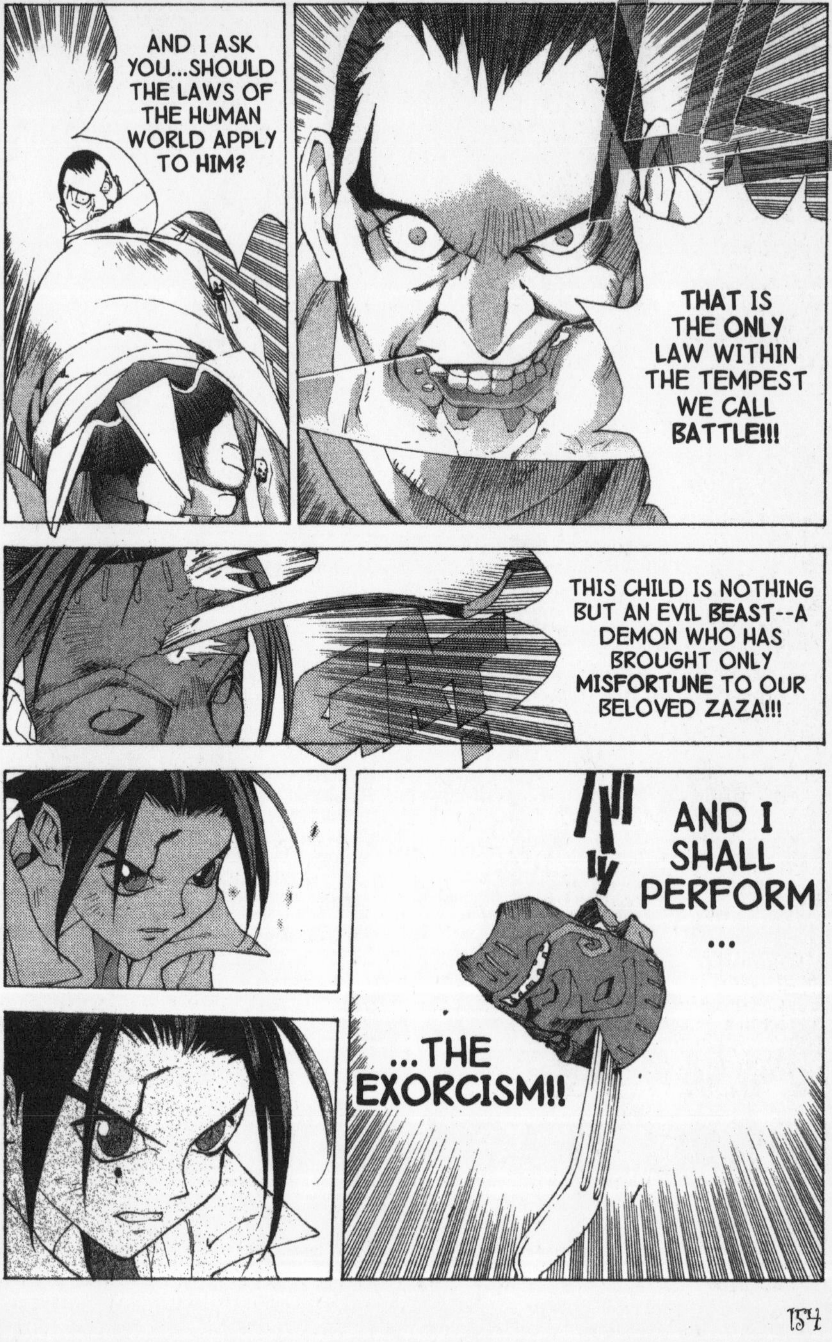
THAT IS THE ONLY LAW WITHIN THE TEMPEST WE CALL BATTLE!!!
AND I ASK YOU...SHOULD THE LAWS OF THE HUMAN WORLD APPLY TO HIM?
THIS CHILD IS NOTHING BUT AN EVIL BEAST--A DEMON WHO HAS BROUGHT ONLY MISFORTUNE TO OUR BELOVED ZAZA!!!
AND I SHALL PERFORM ...
...THE EXORCISM!!

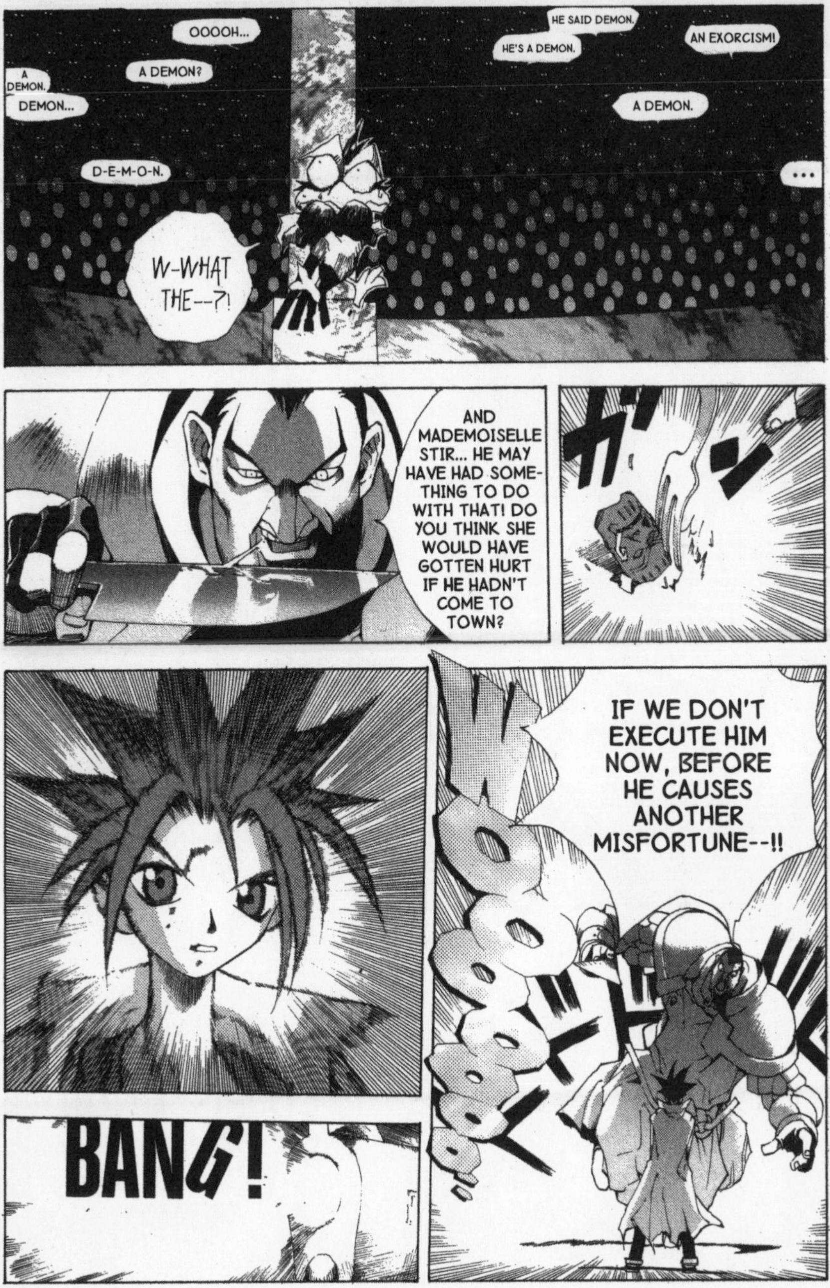
AN EXORCISM!
HE SAID DEMON.
HE'S A DEMON.
A DEMON.
...
OOOOH...
A DEMON?
A DEMON.
DEMON...
D-E-M-O-N.
W-WHAT THE--?!
AND MADEMOISELLE STIR... HE MAY HAVE HAD SOMETHING TO DO WITH THAT! DO YOU THINK SHE WOULD HAVE GOTTEN HURT IF HE HADN'T COME TO TOWN?
IF WE DON'T EXECUTE HIM NOW, BEFORE HE CAUSES ANOTHER MISFORTUNE--!!
BANG!

Y-YOU DON'T HAVE FREE REIN HERE, BAFFLE! IF... IF YOU ATTEMPT TO ENFORCE A PUBLIC EXECUTION WITHOUT THE LAW'S APPROVAL...

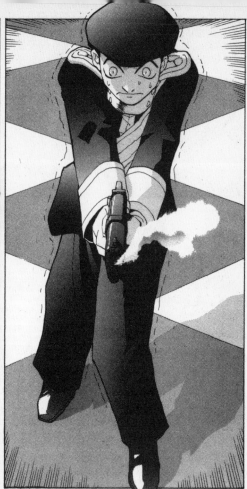

...I-I'LL HAVE TO ARRANGE... CONFISCATION... OF YOUR MASK... FROM YOUR HEAD!!

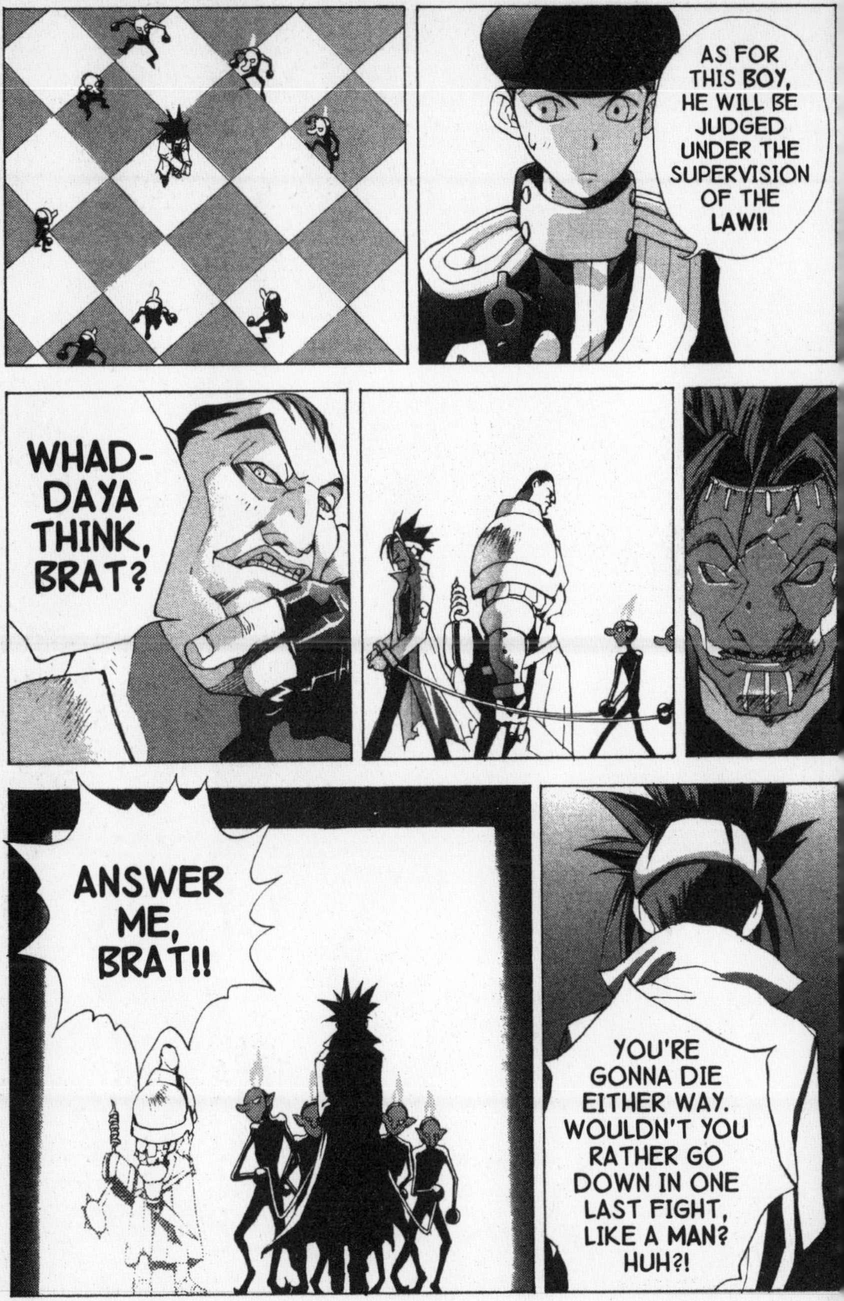
AS FOR THIS BOY, HE WILL BE JUDGED UNDER THE SUPERVISION OF THE LAW!!
WHAD-DAYA THINK, BRAT?
YOU'RE GONNA DIE EITHER WAY. WOULDN'T YOU RATHER GO DOWN IN ONE LAST FIGHT, LIKE A MAN? HUH?!
ANSWER ME, BRAT!!

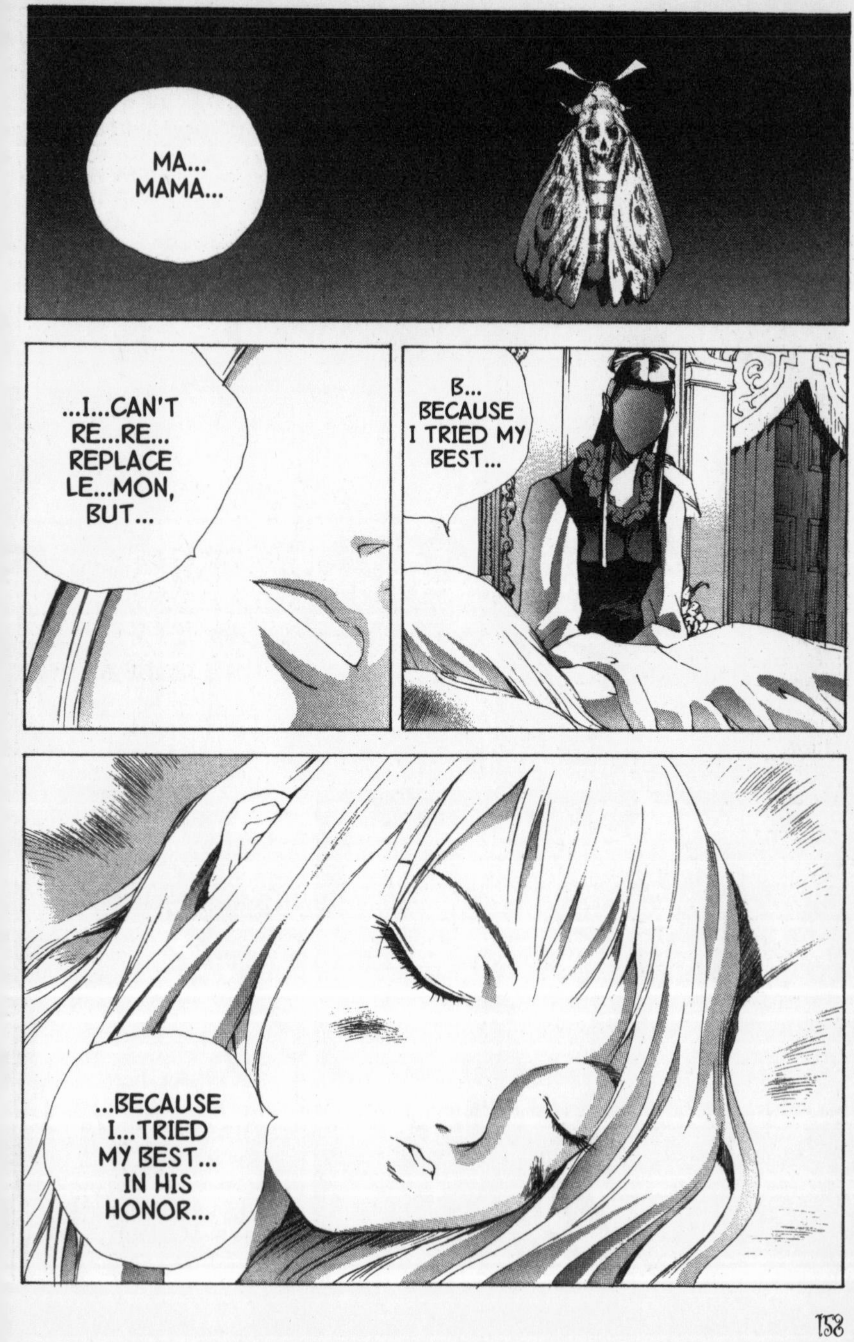
MA... MAMA...
B... BECAUSE I TRIED MY BEST...
...I...CAN'T RE...RE... REPLACE LE...MON, BUT...
...BECAUSE I...TRIED MY BEST... IN HIS HONOR...

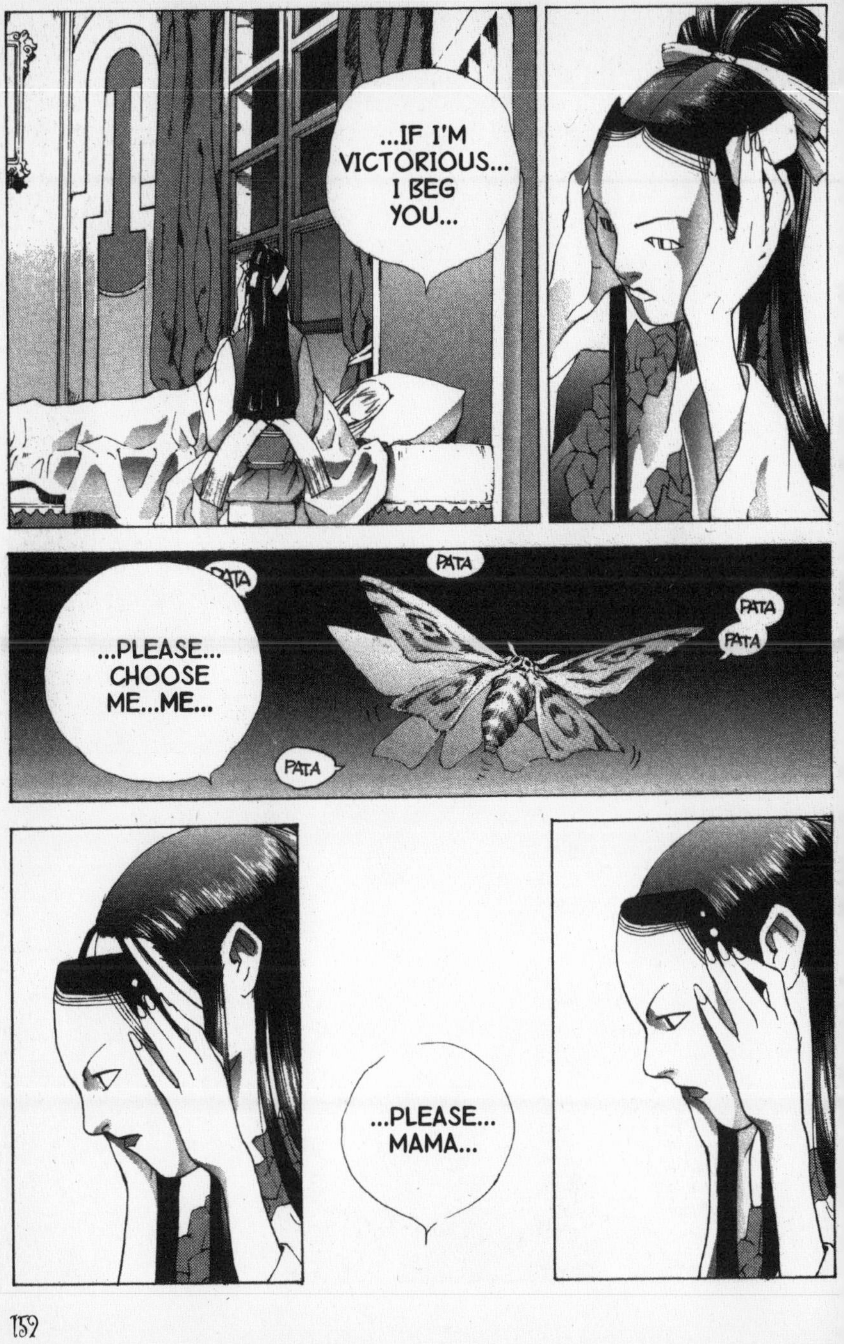
...IF I'M VICTORIOUS... I BEG YOU...
PATA
PATA
PATA
PATA
...PLEASE... CHOOSE ME...ME...
PATA
...PLEASE... MAMA...

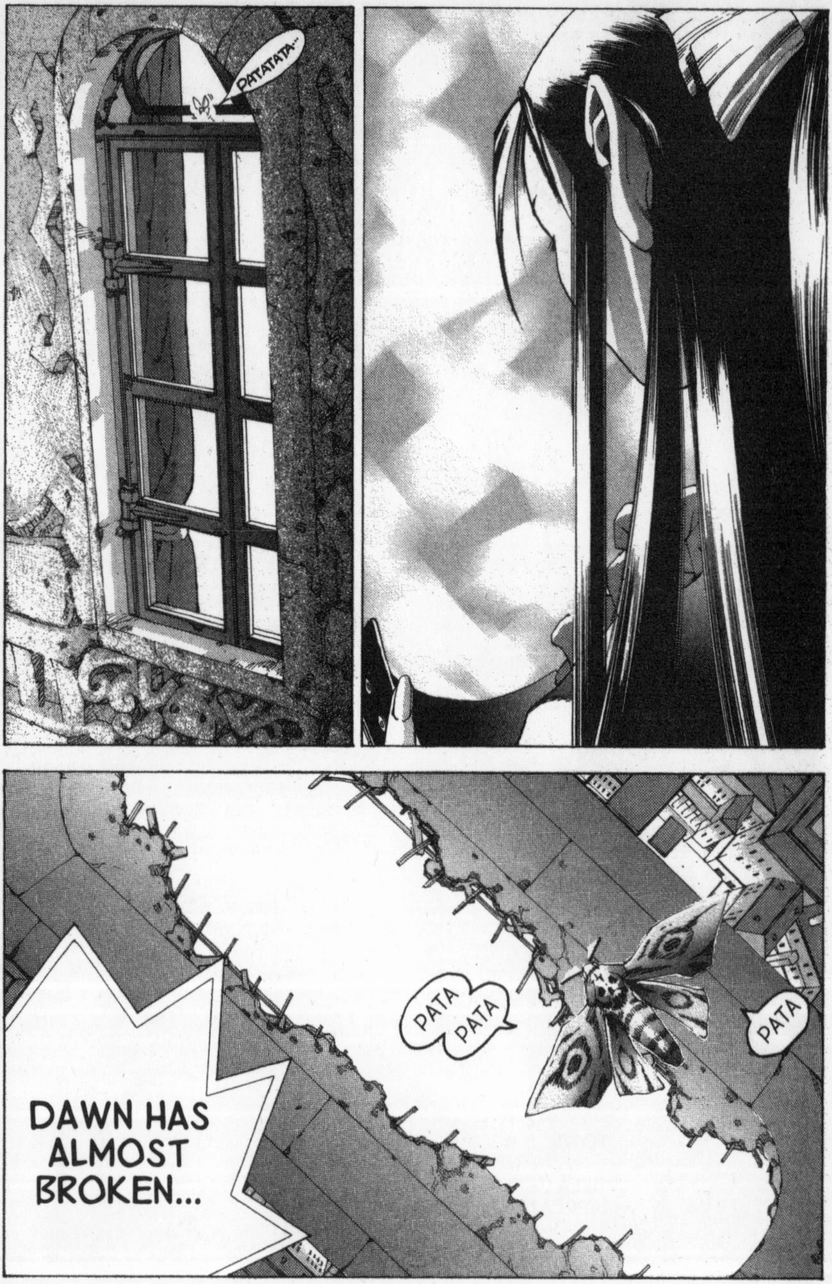
PATATATA...
PATA
PATA PATA
DAWN HAS ALMOST BROKEN...

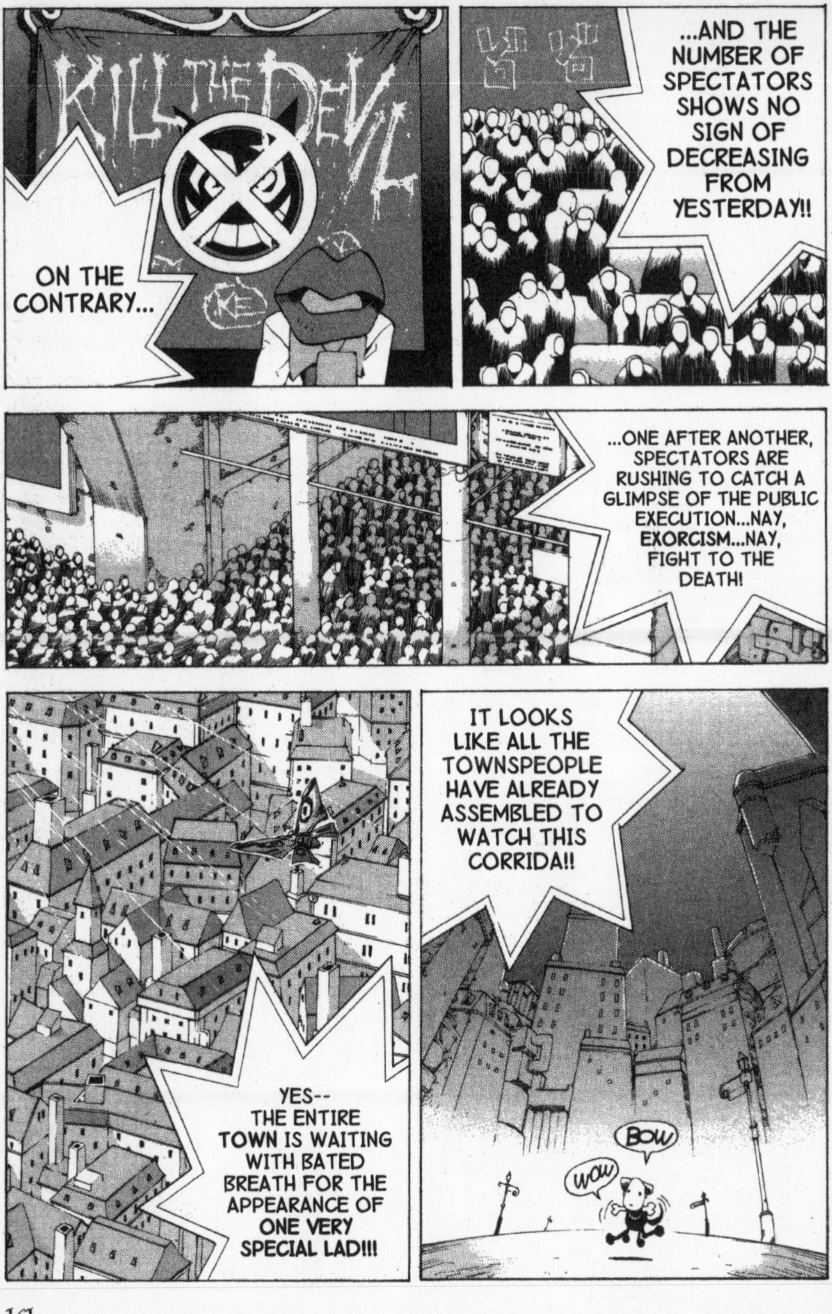
...AND THE NUMBER OF SPECTATORS SHOWS NO SIGN OF DECREASING FROM YESTERDAY!!
ON THE CONTRARY...
...ONE AFTER ANOTHER, SPECTATORS ARE RUSHING TO CATCH A GLIMPSE OF THE PUBLIC EXECUTION...NAY, EXORCISM...NAY, FIGHT TO THE DEATH!
IT LOOKS LIKE ALL THE TOWNSPEOPLE HAVE ALREADY ASSEMBLED TO WATCH THIS CORRIDA!!
BOW
WOW
YES-- THE ENTIRE TOWN IS WAITING WITH BATED BREATH FOR THE APPEARANCE OF ONE VERY SPECIAL LAD!!!

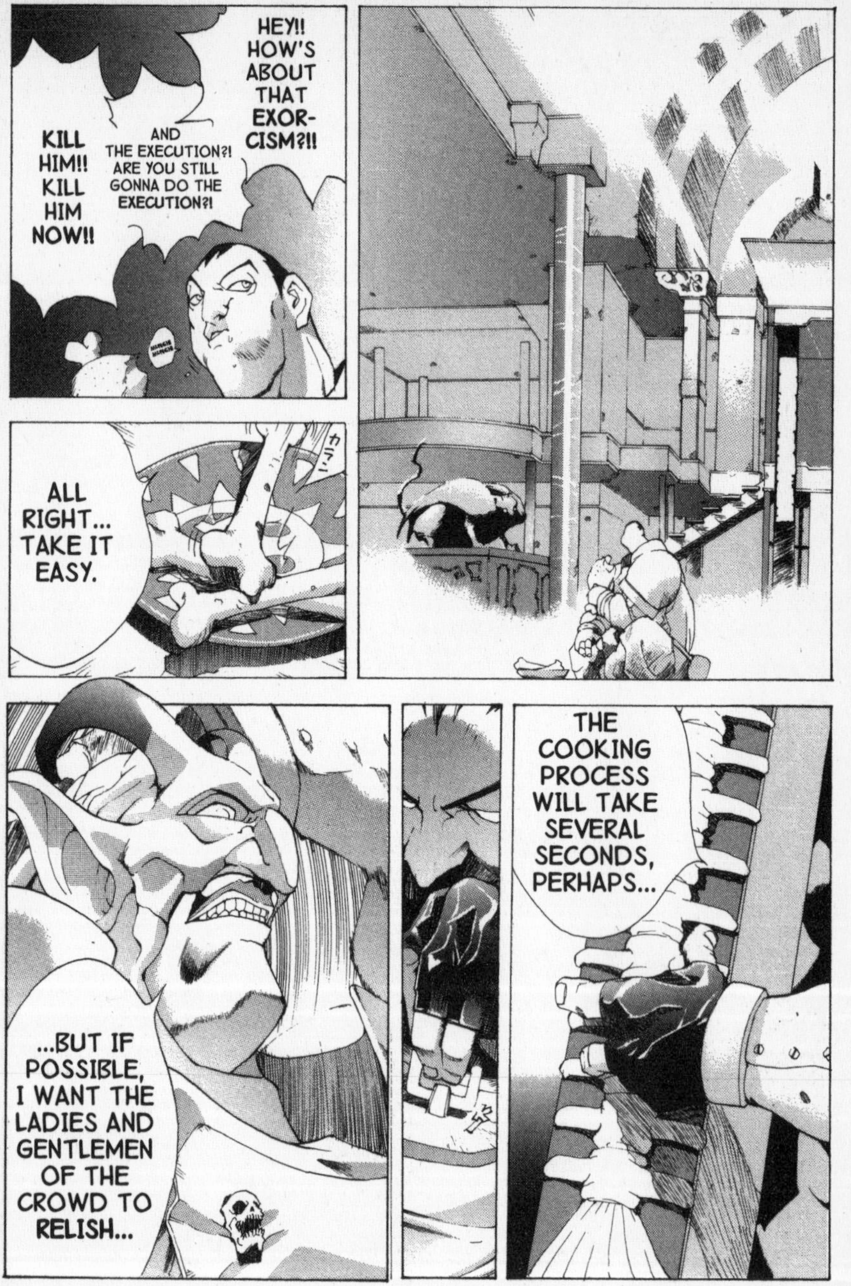
HEY!! HOW'S ABOUT THAT EXORCISM?!!
AND THE EXECUTION?! ARE YOU STILL GONNA DO THE EXECUTION?!
KILL HIM!! KILL HIM NOW!!
カラン
ALL RIGHT... TAKE IT EASY.
THE COOKING PROCESS WILL TAKE SEVERAL SECONDS, PERHAPS...
...BUT IF POSSIBLE, I WANT THE LADIES AND GENTLEMEN OF THE CROWD TO RELISH...

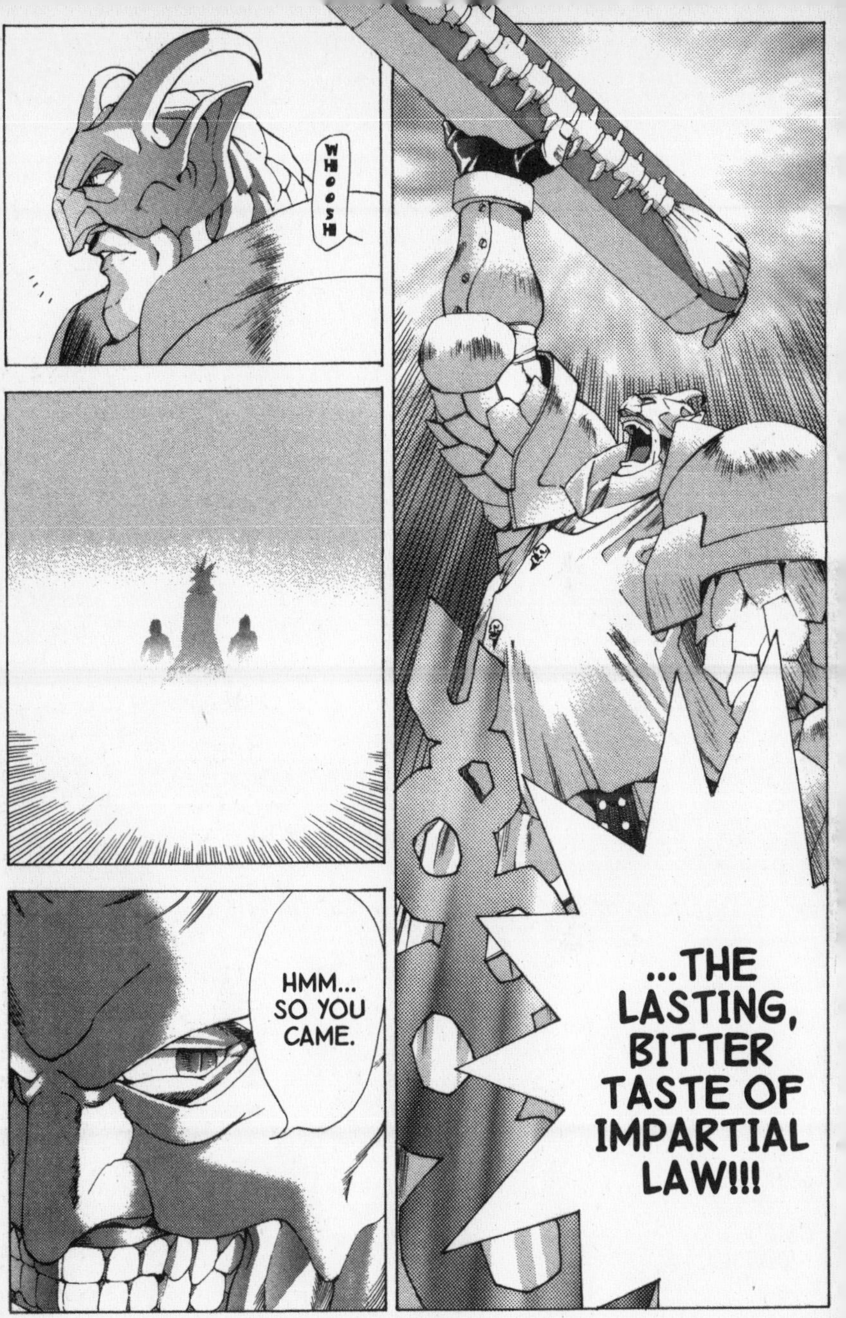
...THE LASTING, BITTER TASTE OF IMPARTIAL LAW!!!
WHOOSH
HMM... SO YOU CAME.

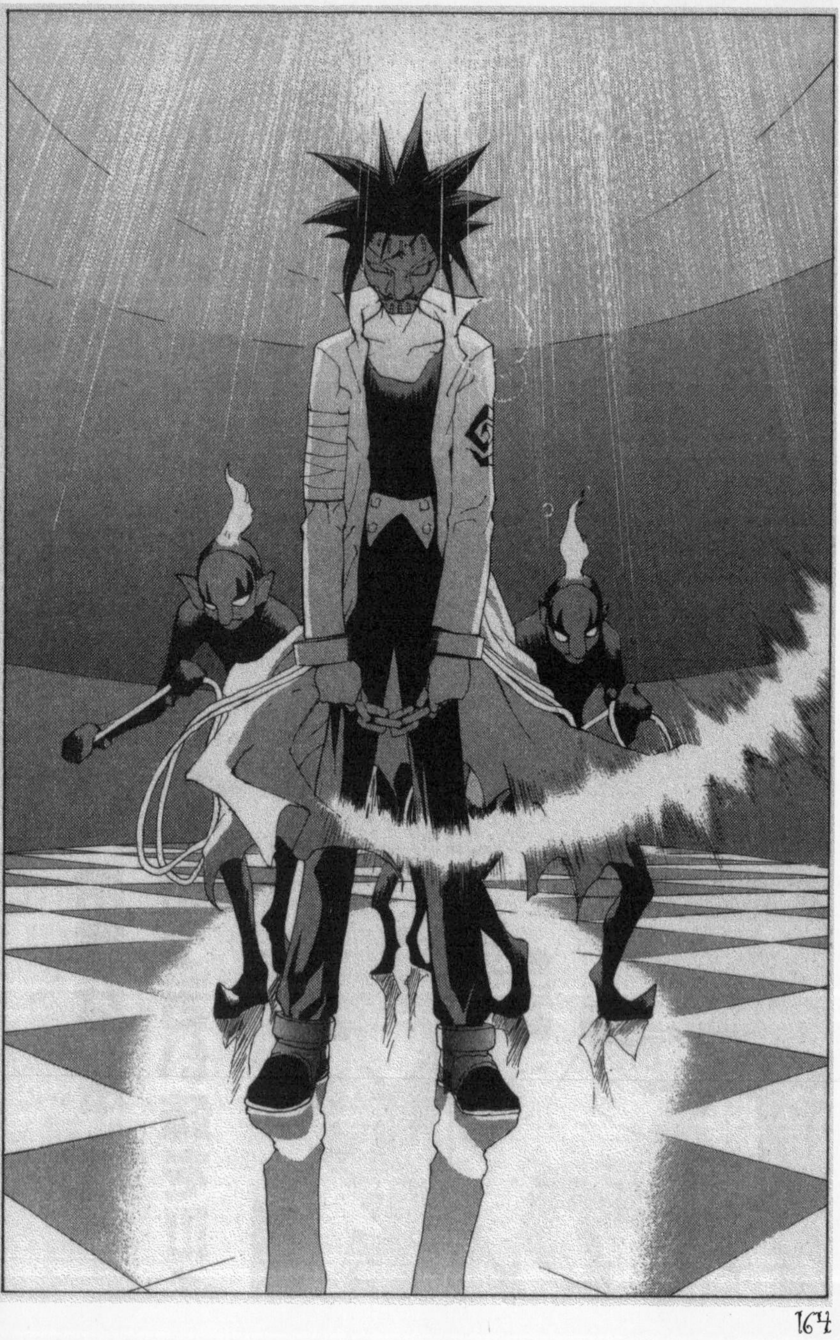

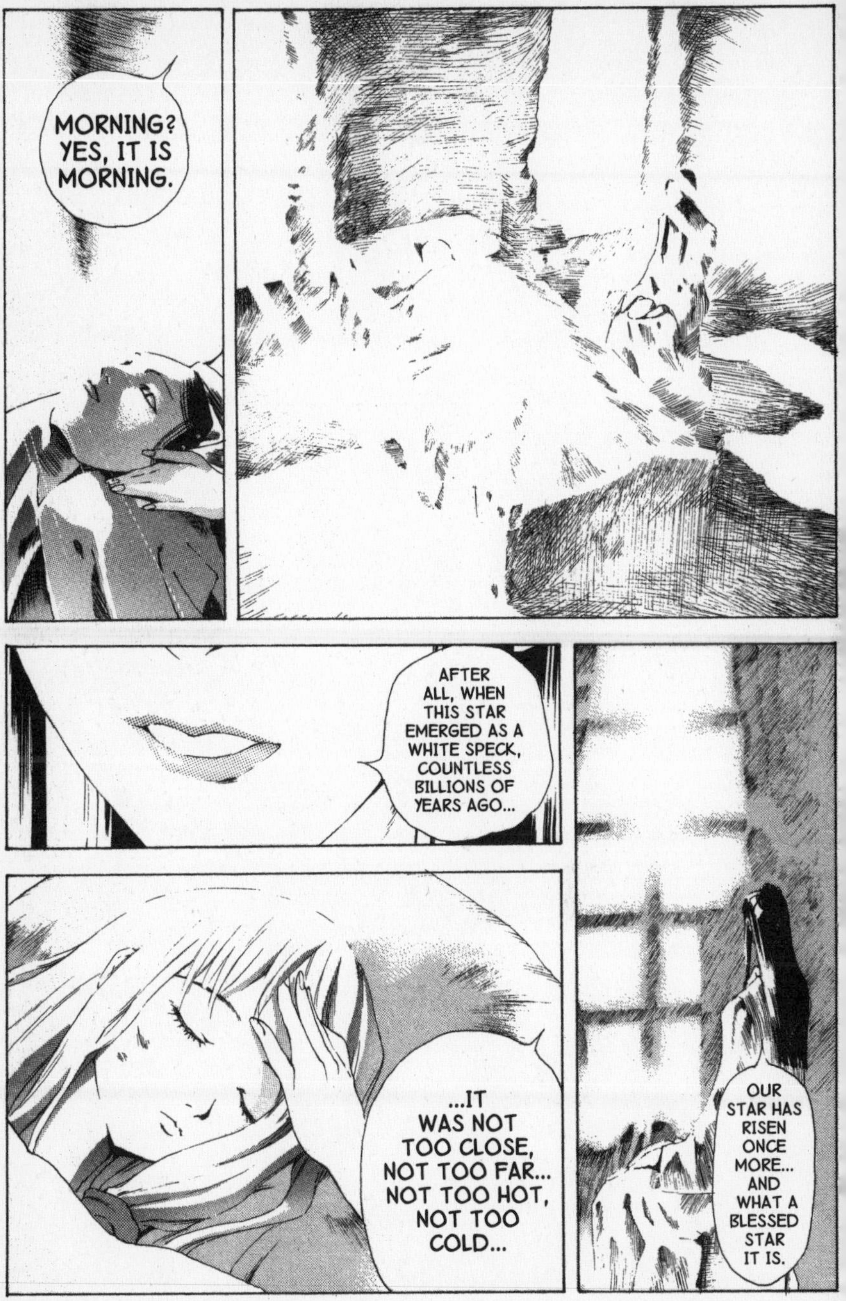
MORNING? YES, IT IS MORNING.
OUR STAR HAS RISEN ONCE MORE... AND WHAT A BLESSED STAR IT IS.
AFTER ALL, WHEN THIS STAR EMERGED AS A WHITE SPECK, COUNTLESS BILLIONS OF YEARS AGO...
...IT WAS NOT TOO CLOSE, NOT TOO FAR... NOT TOO HOT, NOT TOO COLD...

...AND SO WE WERE ABLE TO SNUGGLE UP CLOSE TO IT, AND IT CONTINUES TO GAZE DOWN UPON US.

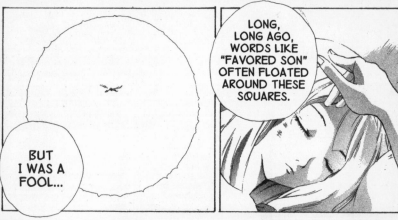

LONG, LONG AGO, WORDS LIKE "FAVORED SON" OFTEN FLOATED AROUND THESE SQUARES.

BUT I WAS A FOOL...

...TO HOLD ONLY THE SETTING SUN DEAR.

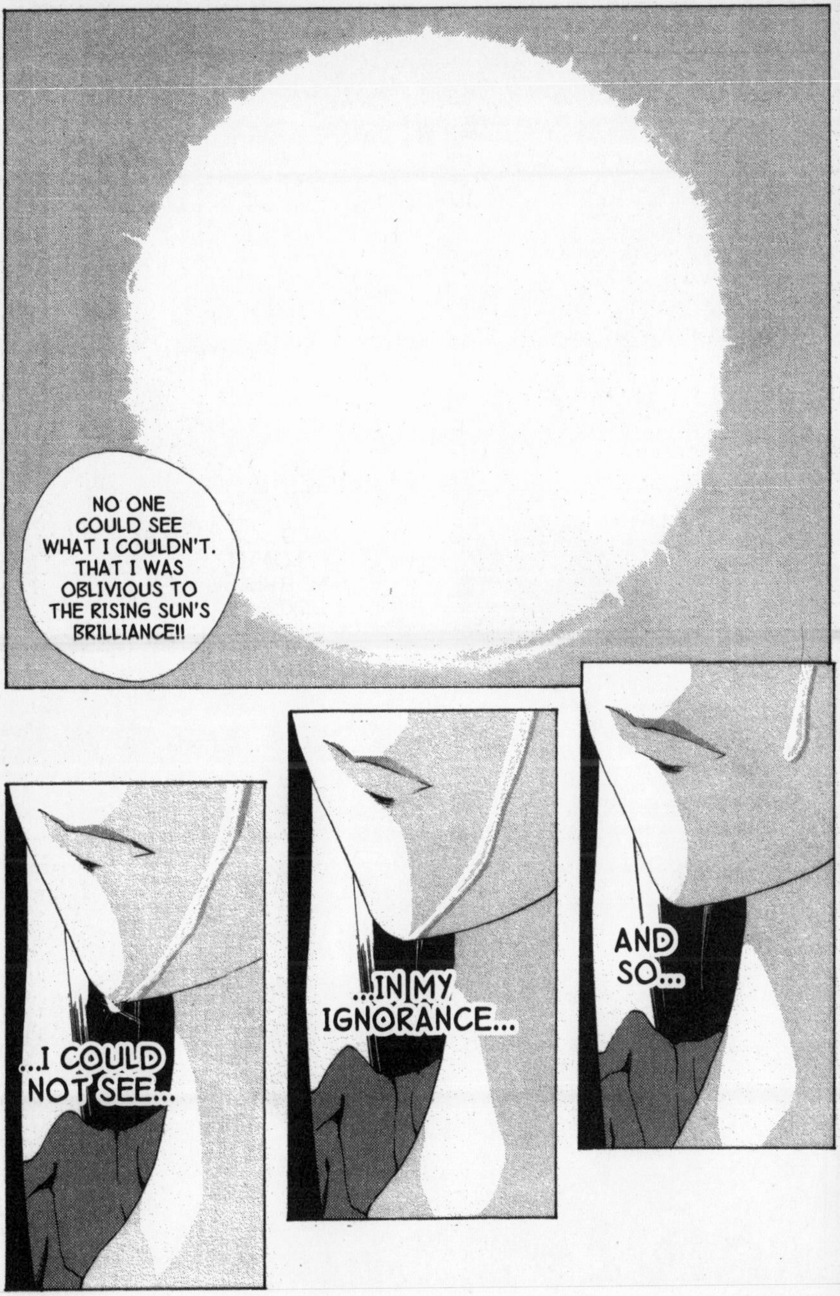
NO ONE COULD SEE WHAT I COULDN'T. THAT I WAS OBLIVIOUS TO THE RISING SUN'S BRILLIANCE!!
AND SO...
...IN MY IGNORANCE...
...I COULD NOT SEE...

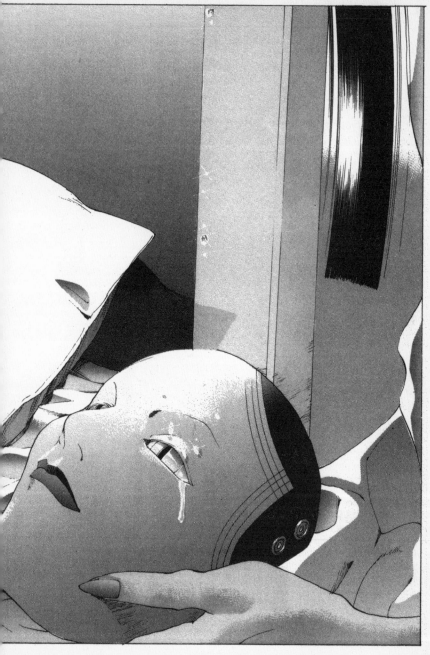

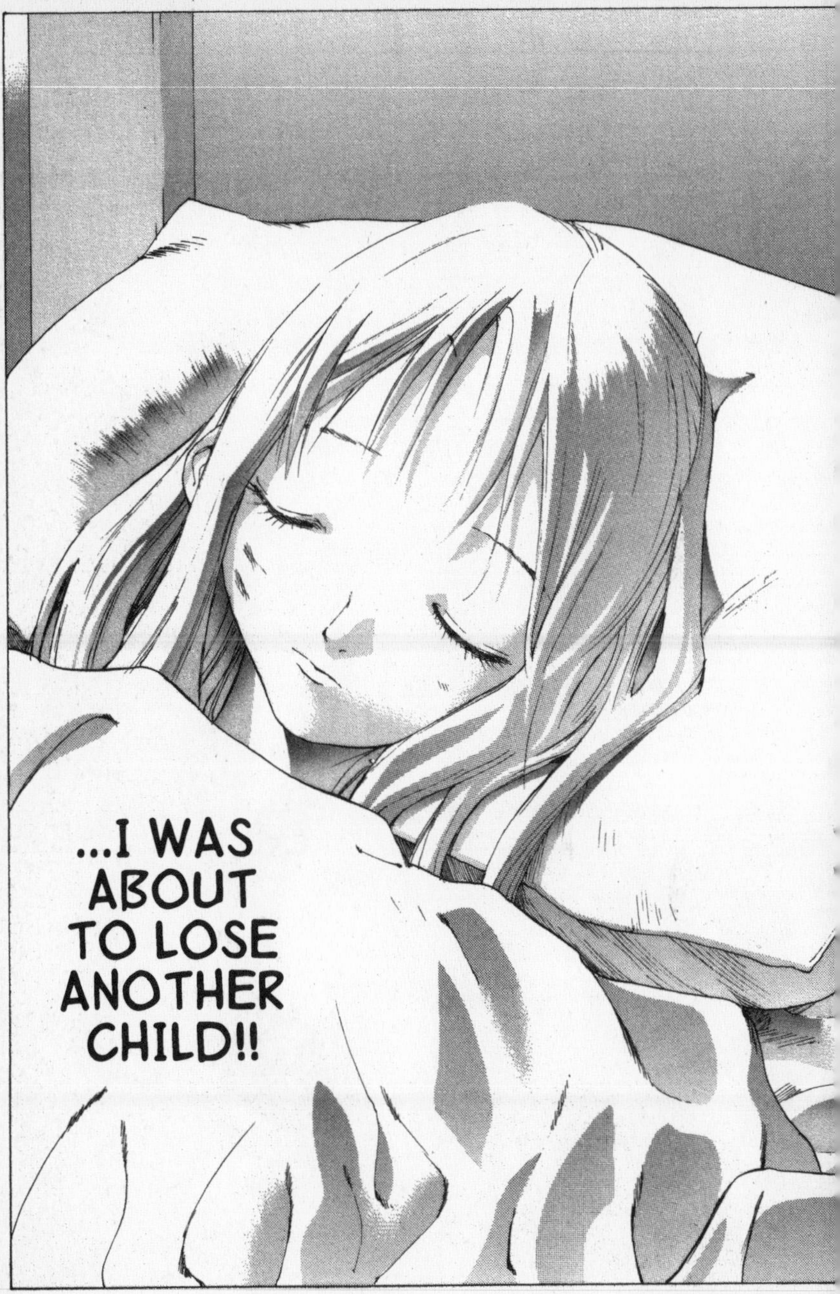
...I WAS ABOUT TO LOSE ANOTHER CHILD!!

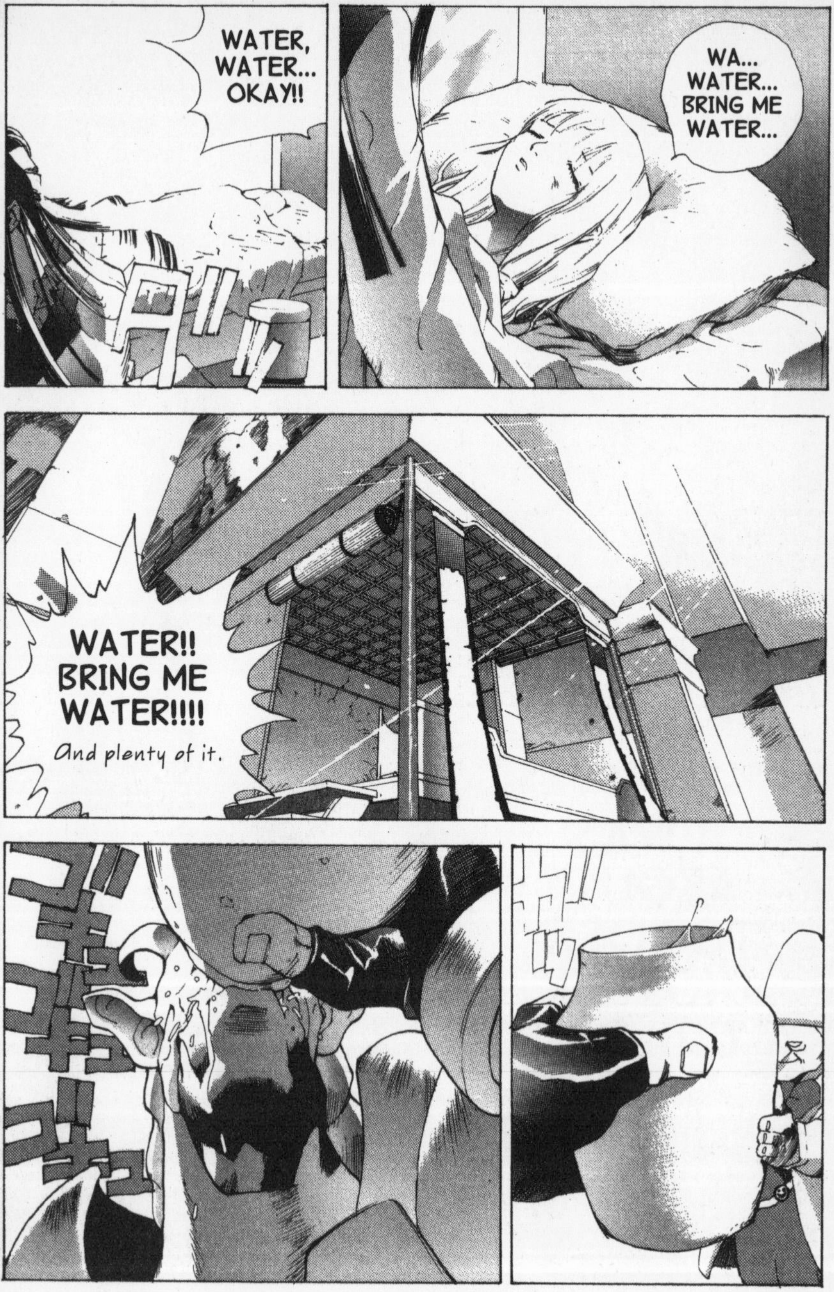
WA... WATER... BRING ME WATER...
WATER, WATER... OKAY!!
WATER!! BRING ME WATER!!!!
And plenty of it.

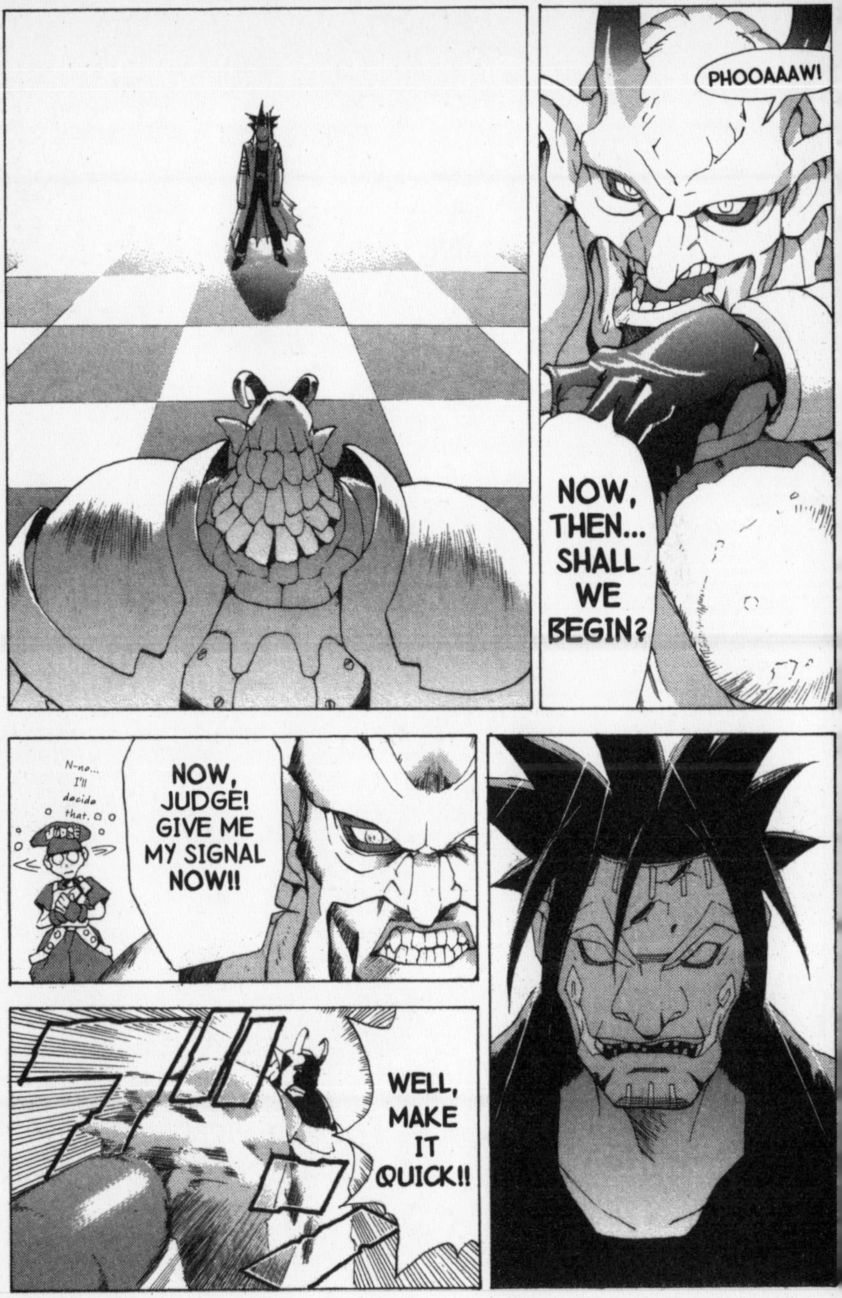
PHOOAAAW!
NOW, THEN... SHALL WE BEGIN?
NOW, JUDGE! GIVE ME MY SIGNAL NOW!!
N-no... I'll decide that.
JUDGE
WELL, MAKE IT QUICK!!

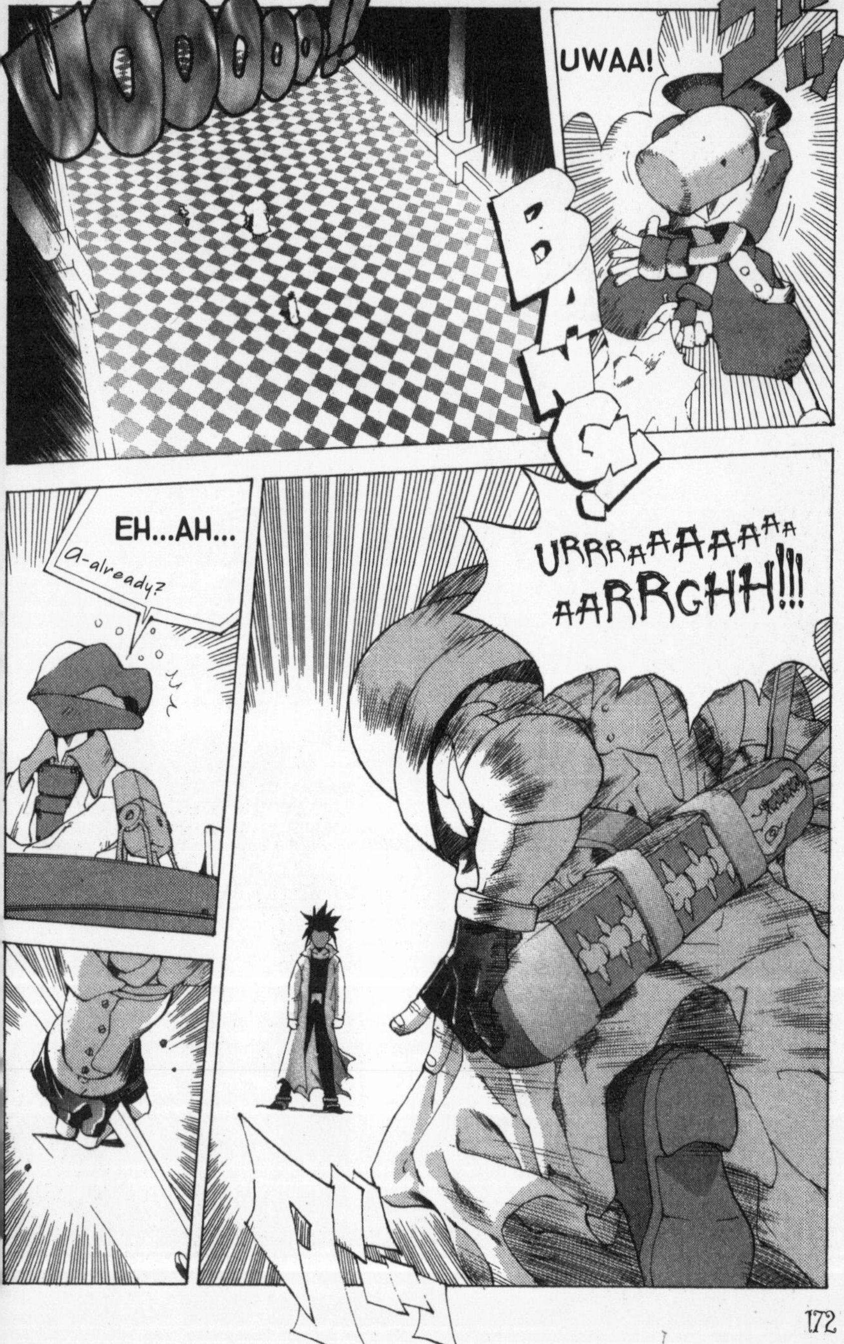
UWAA!
BANG!
UOOOOOo!!
URRRAAAAAAA
AARRGHH!!!
EH...AH...
a-already?

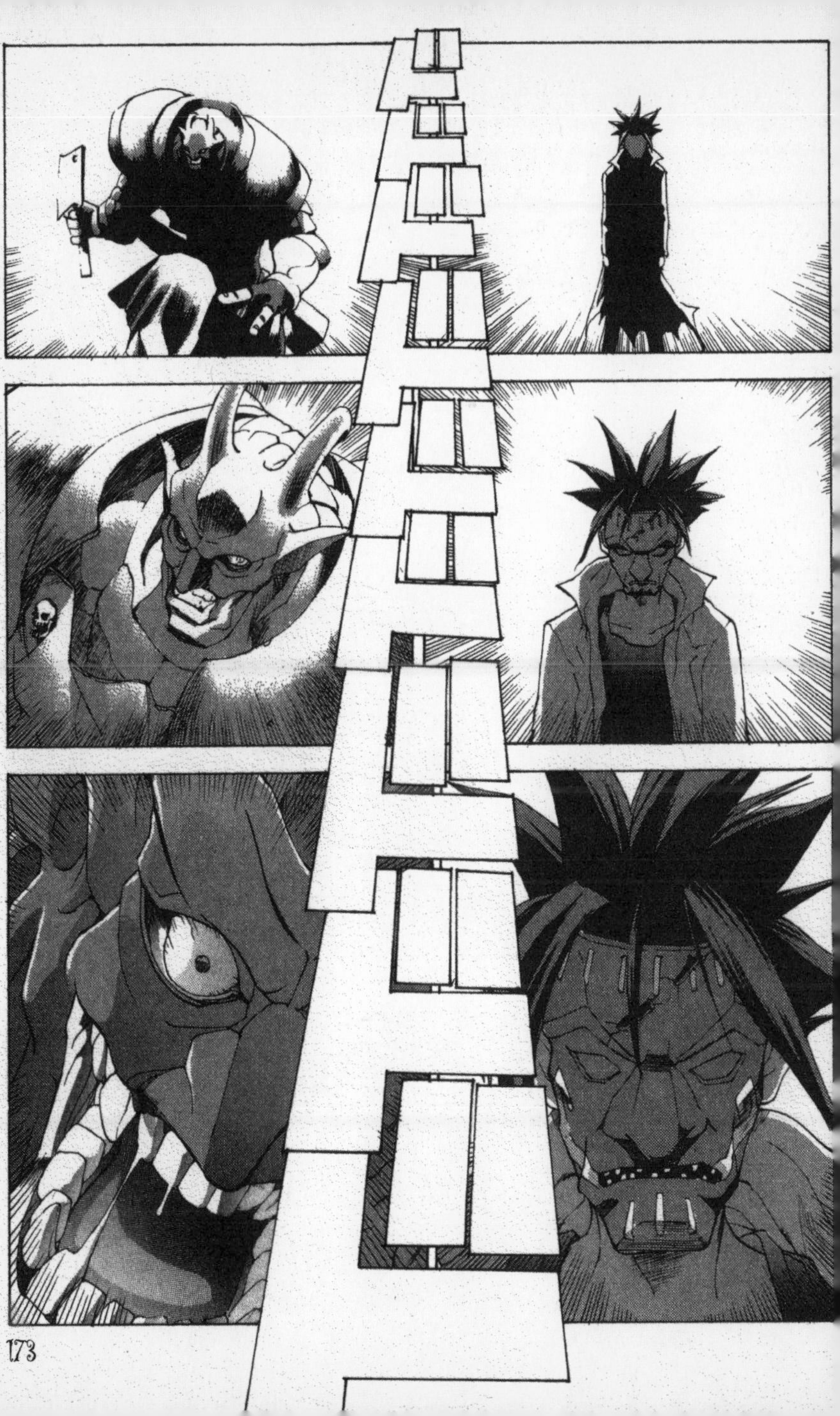

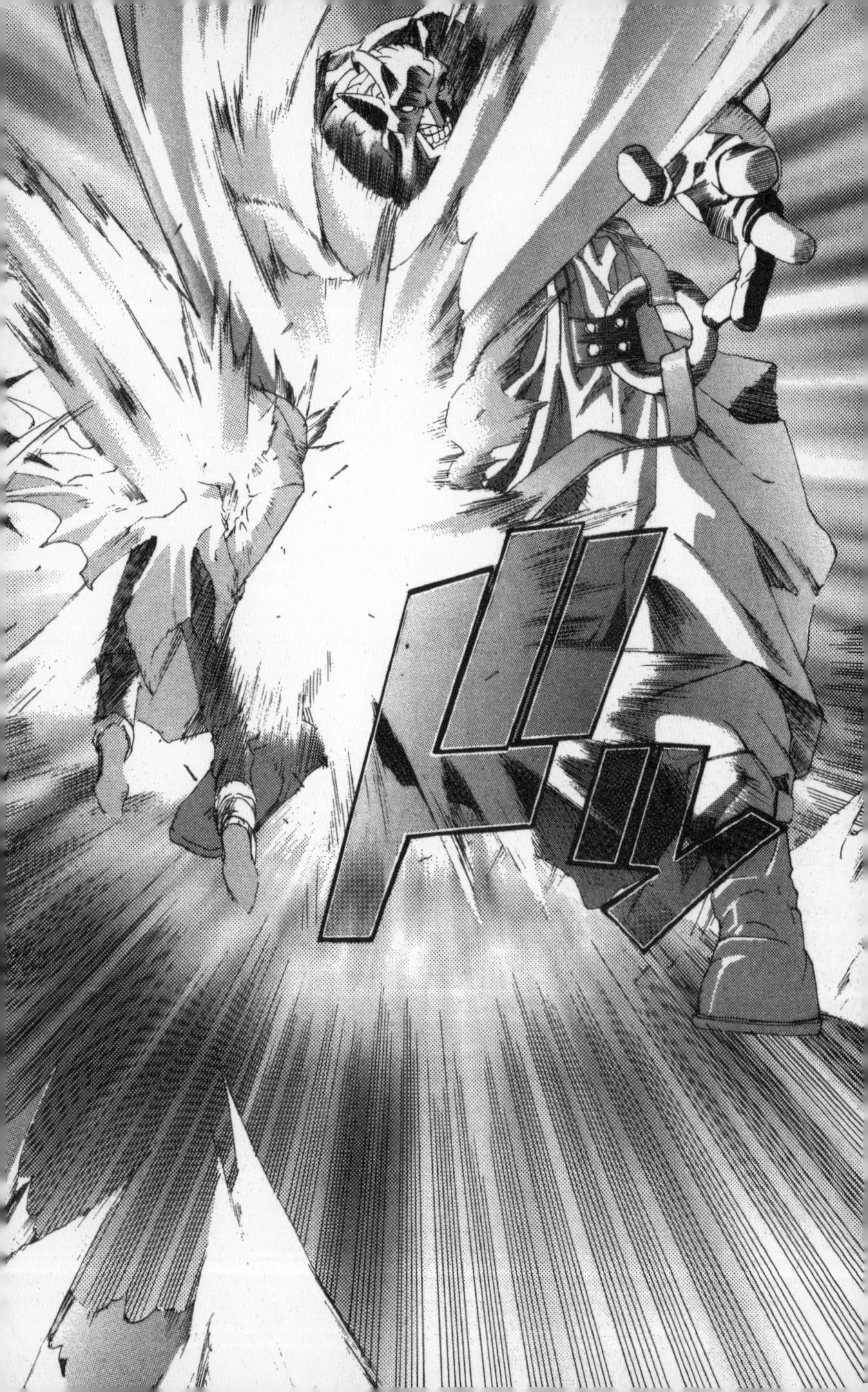

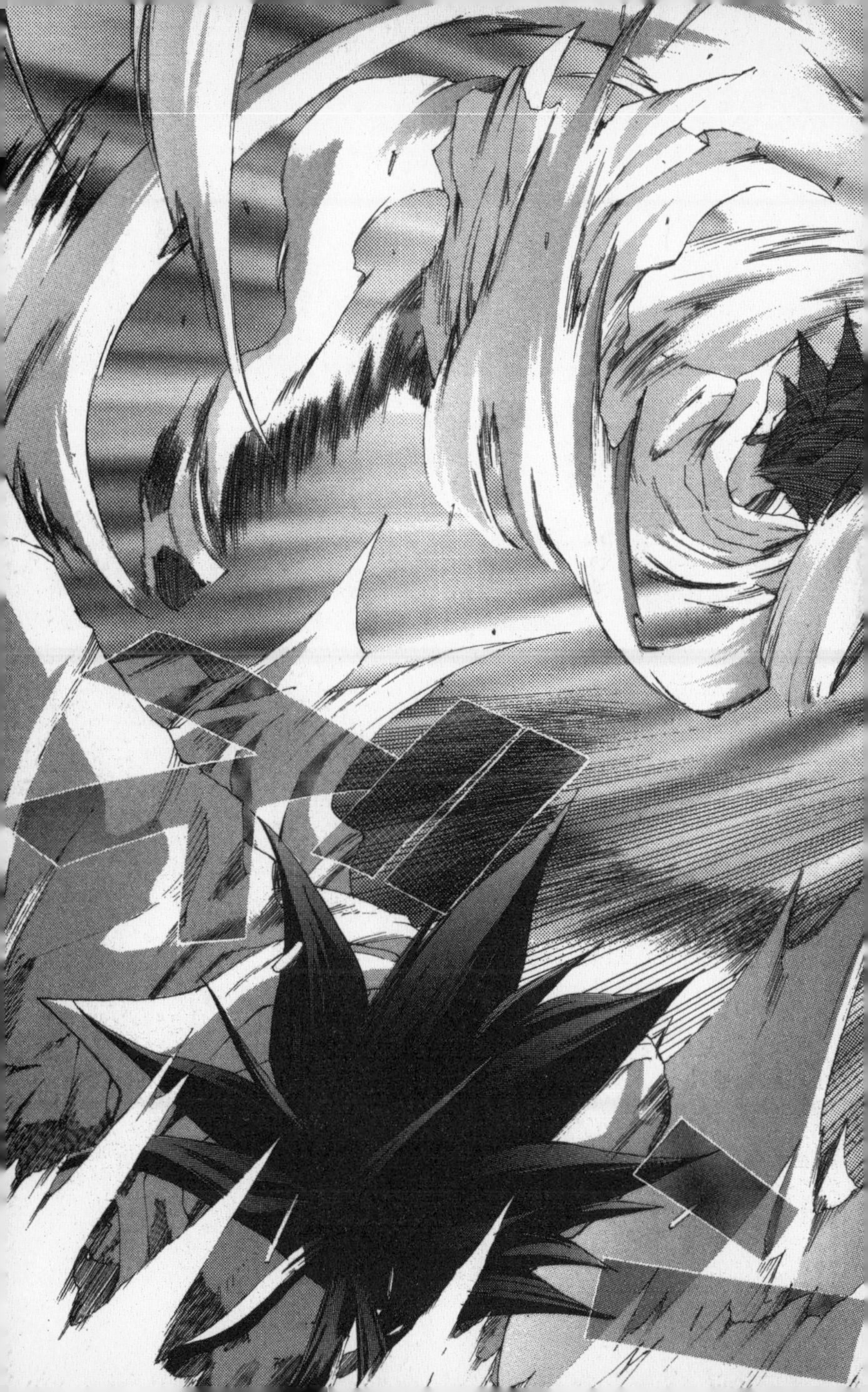

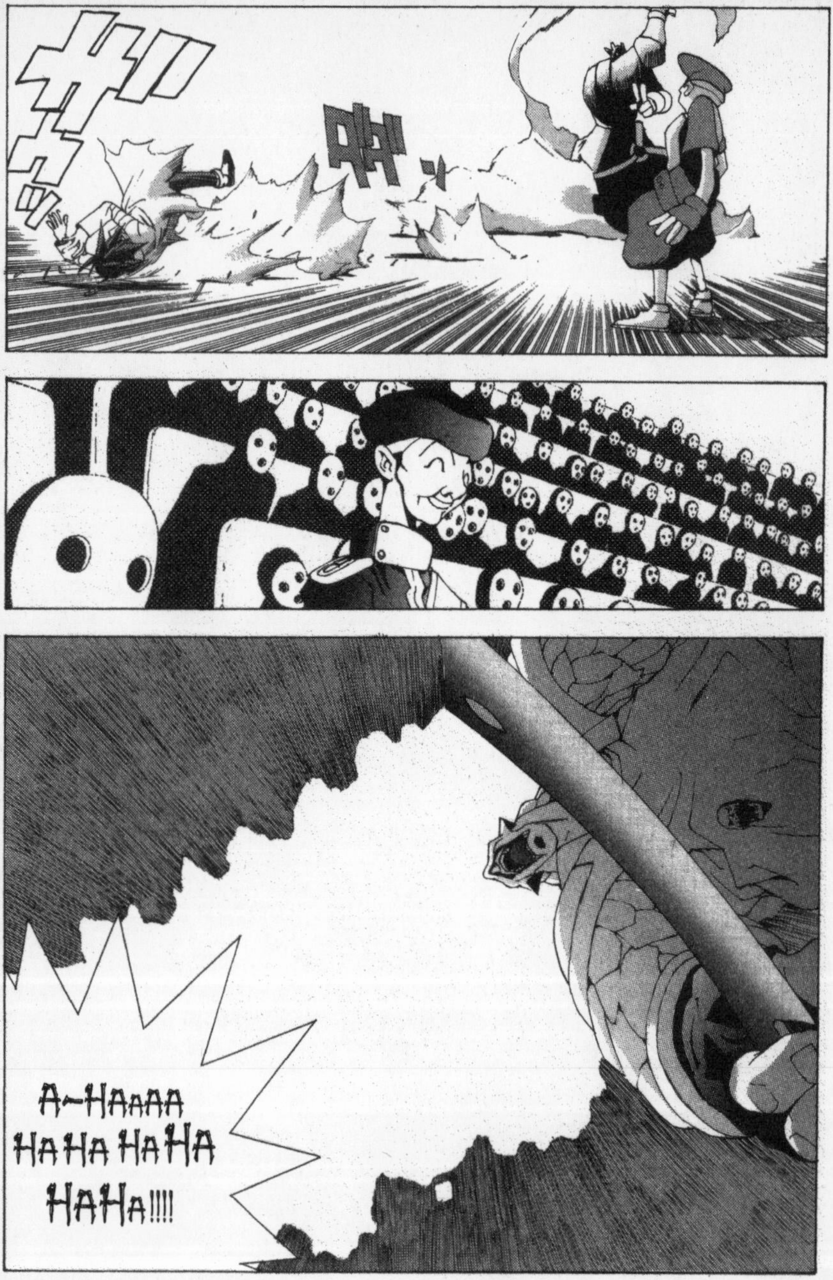
A-HAAAA
HA HA HA HA
HAHA!!!!

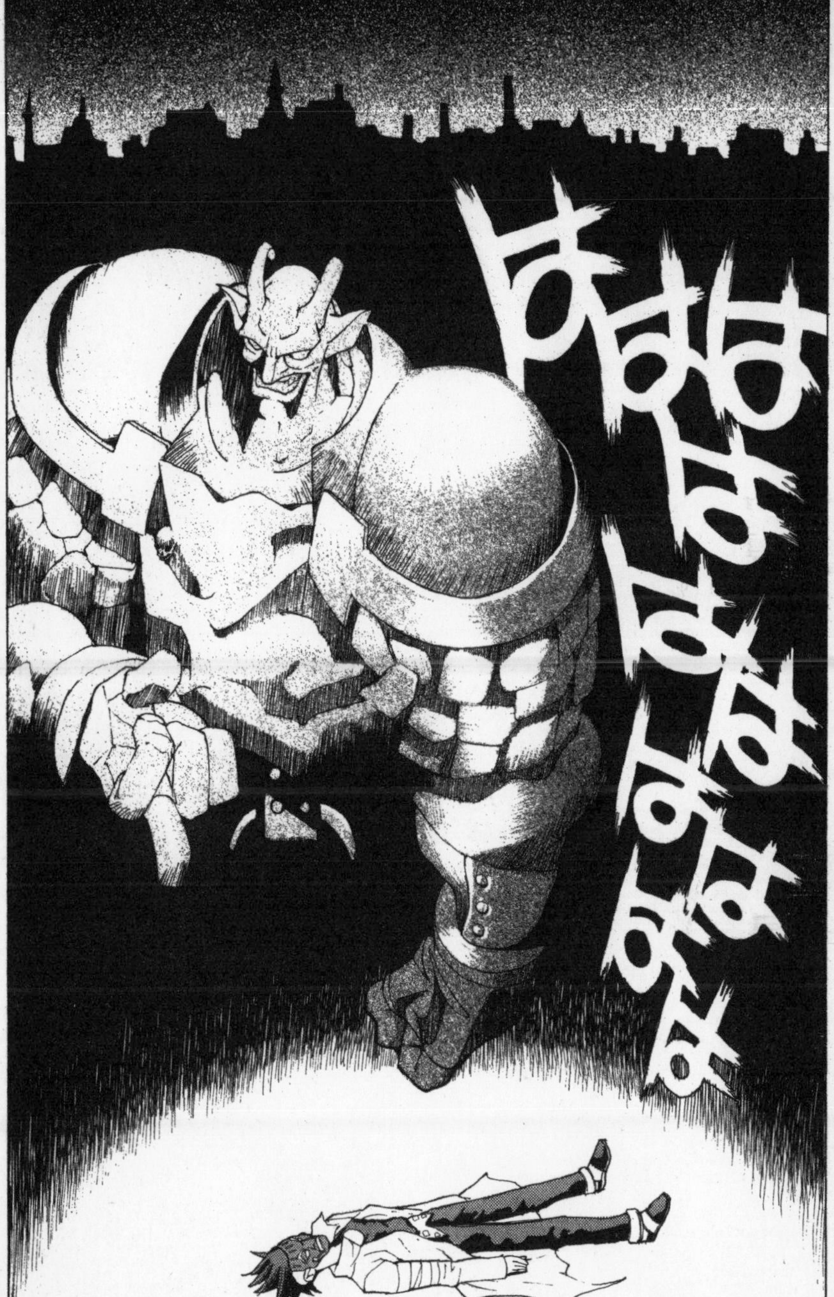
ははははははは
ははははははは

24th SHOT - WALTZ OF THE WIND

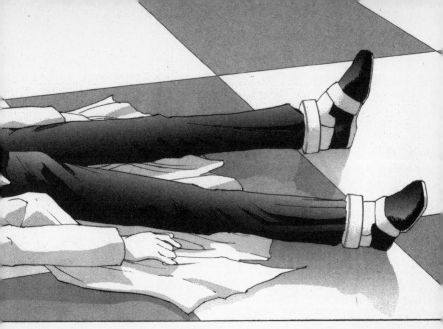

GOOD COOKING IS AN ART, I TELL YOU--AN ART!!

HA HA HA HA HA HA HA HA HA HA HA HA!

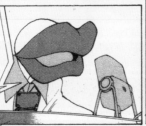

I DON'T BELIEVE IT--THE FIGHT THAT EVERYONE EXPECTED TO BE SO **THRILLING** HAS BEEN CUT DISAPPOINTINGLY SHORT! WHO EXPECTED THIS TO TURN INTO AN OUTRIGHT TRAGEDY?

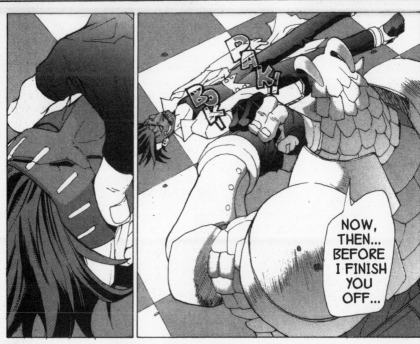

NOW, THEN... BEFORE I FINISH YOU OFF...

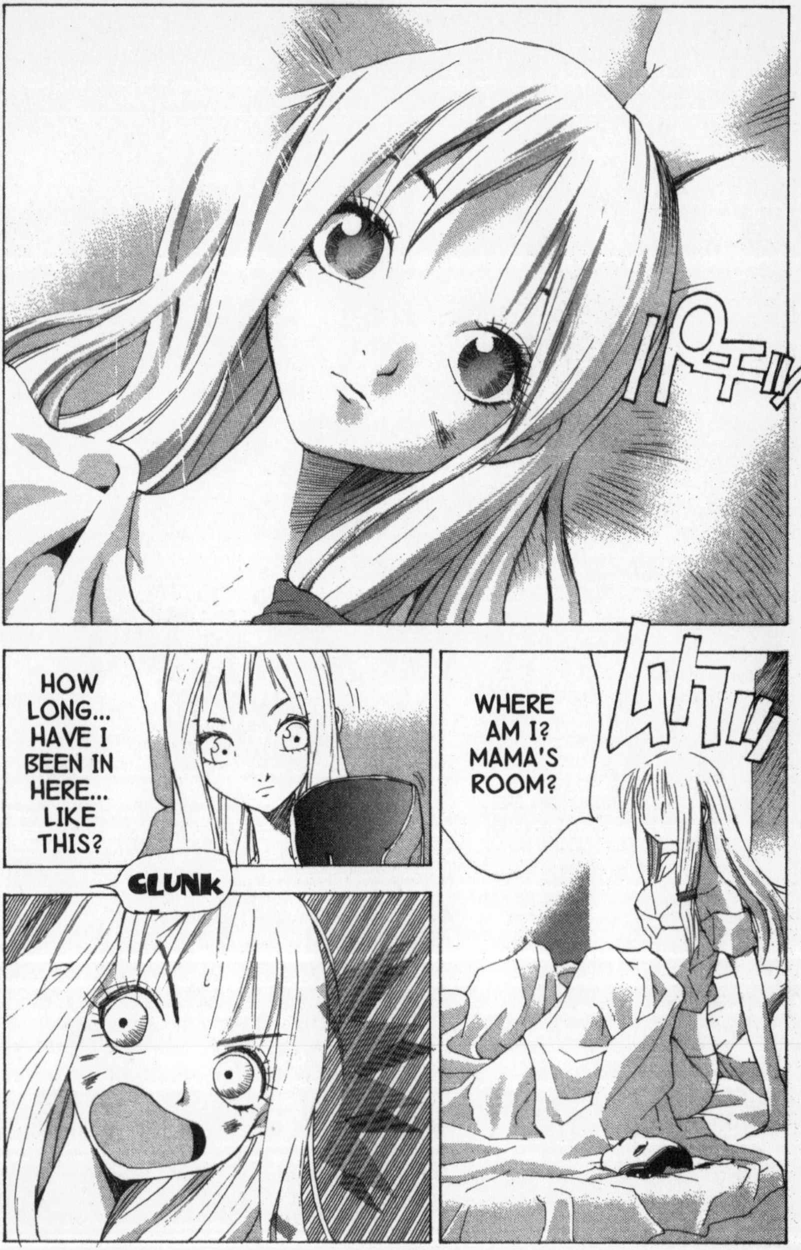
パチッ
ムクッ
WHERE AM I? MAMA'S ROOM?
HOW LONG... HAVE I BEEN IN HERE... LIKE THIS?
GLUNK

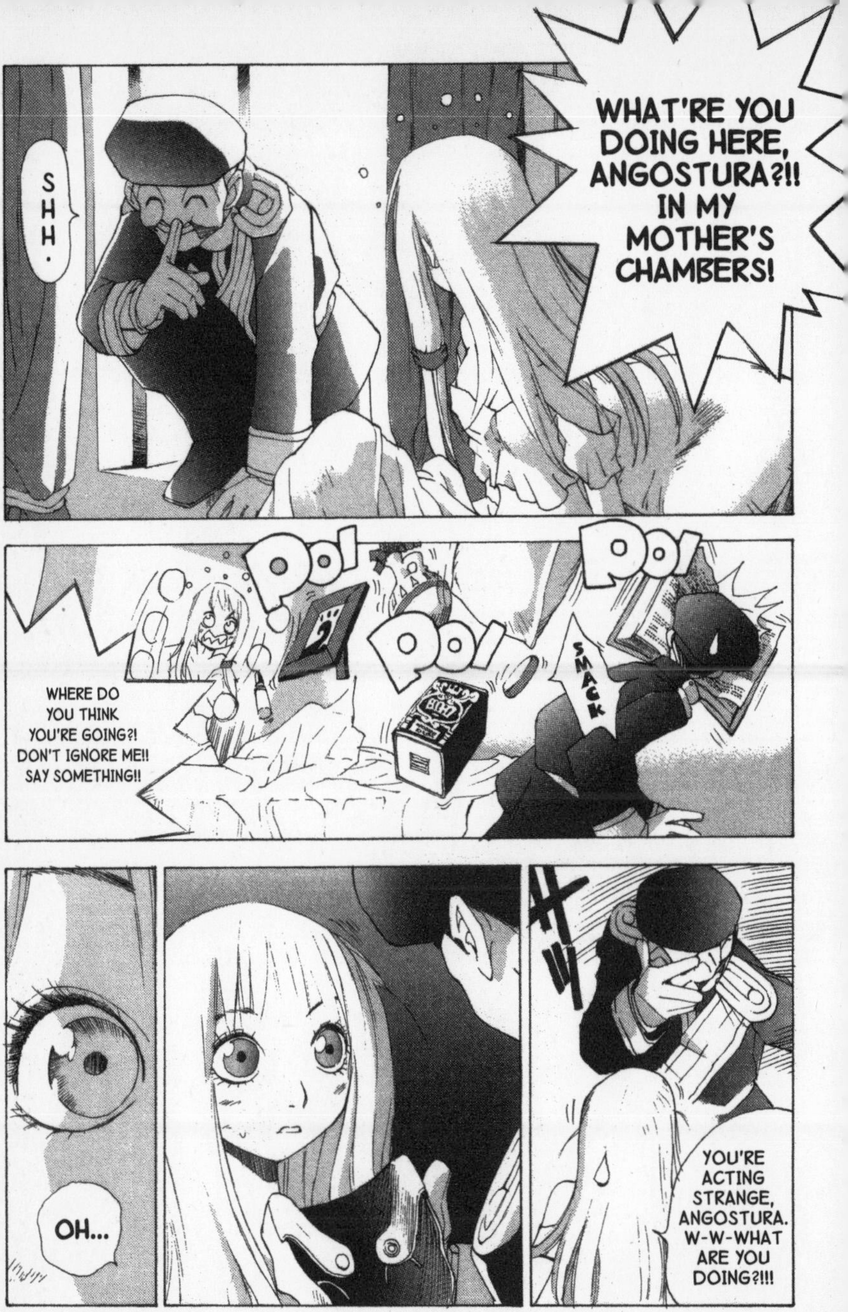
WHAT'RE YOU DOING HERE, ANGOSTURA?!! IN MY MOTHER'S CHAMBERS!
SHH.
POI
POI
POI
SMACK
WHERE DO YOU THINK YOU'RE GOING?! DON'T IGNORE ME!! SAY SOMETHING!!
YOU'RE ACTING STRANGE, ANGOSTURA. W-W-WHAT ARE YOU DOING?!!!
OH...

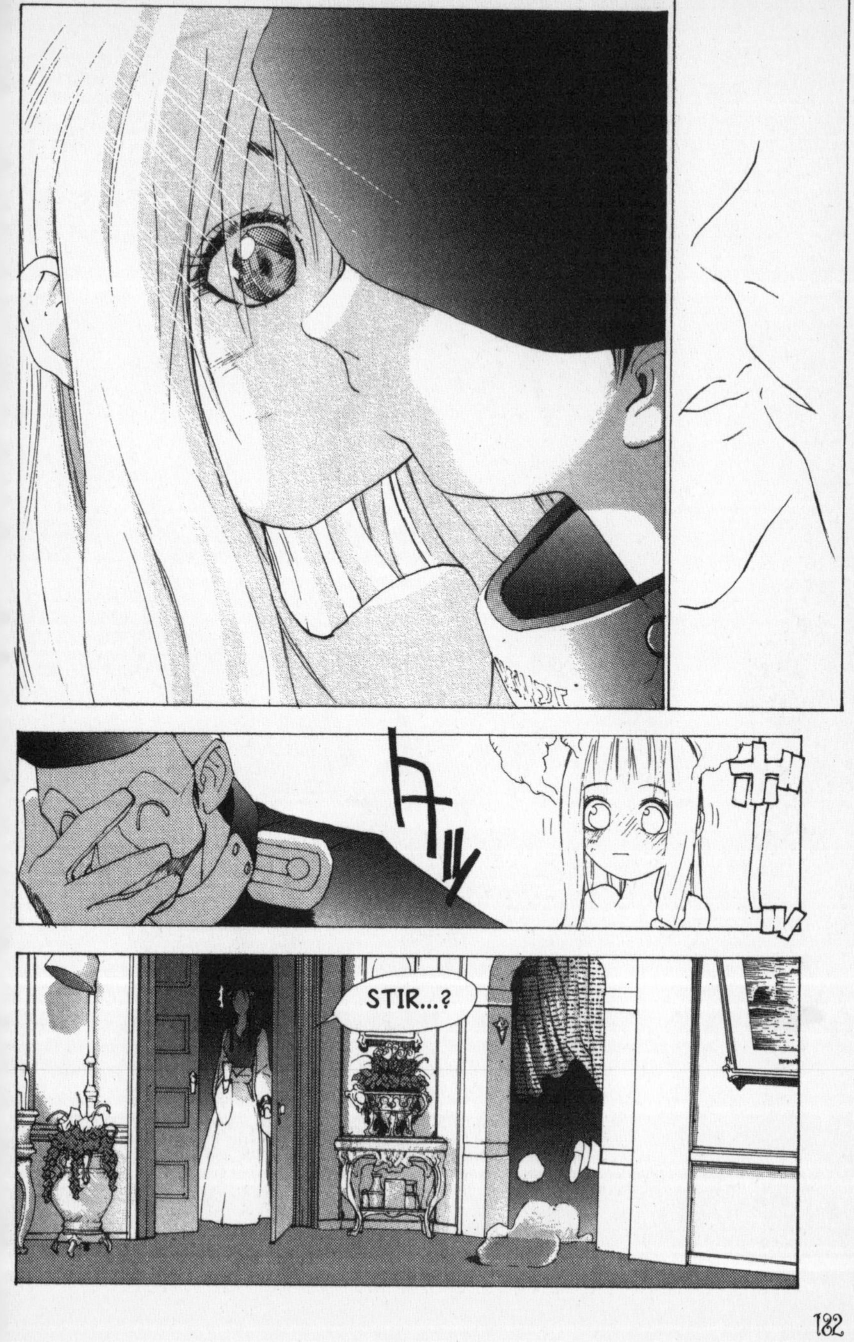
ボッ
カッ
STIR...?

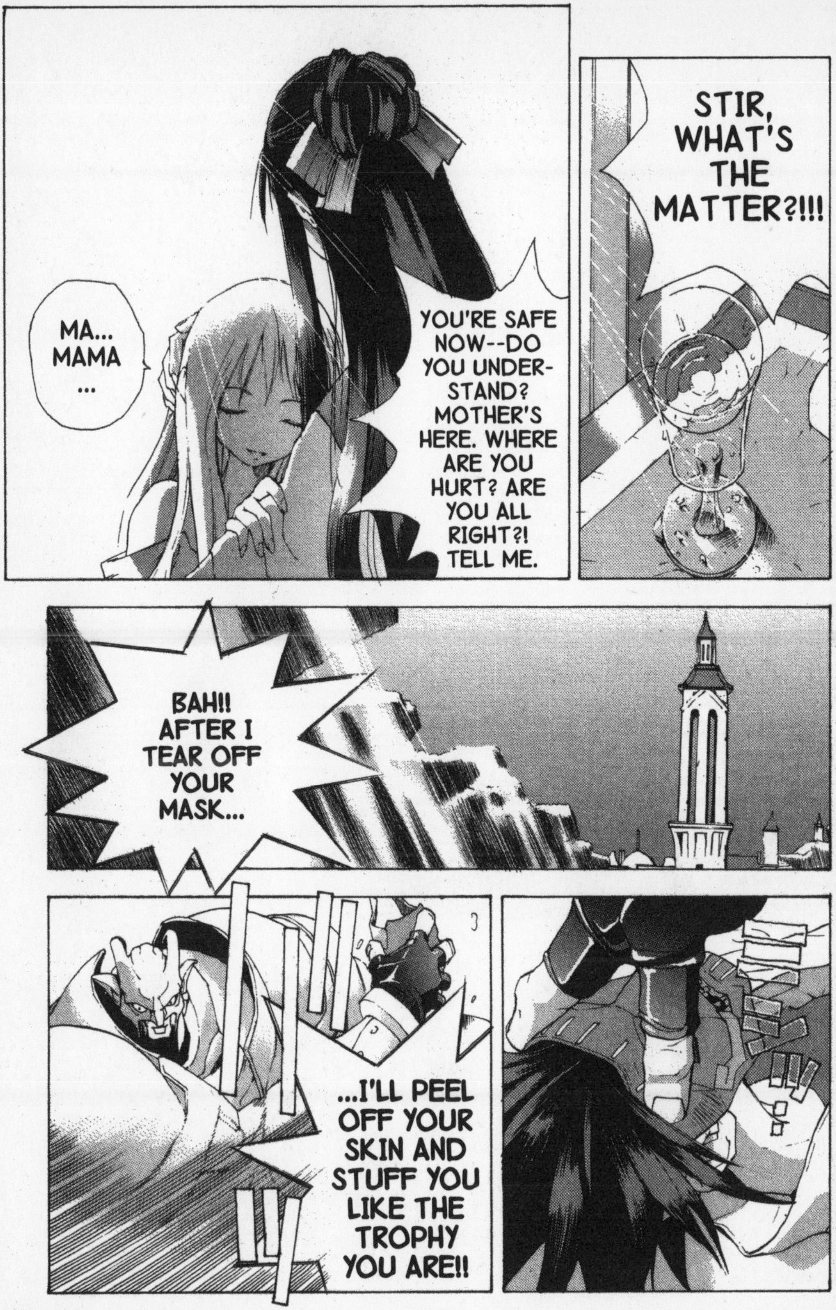
STIR, WHAT'S THE MATTER?!!!
YOU'RE SAFE NOW--DO YOU UNDER-STAND? MOTHER'S HERE. WHERE ARE YOU HURT? ARE YOU ALL RIGHT?! TELL ME.
MA... MAMA ...
BAH!! AFTER I TEAR OFF YOUR MASK...
...I'LL PEEL OFF YOUR SKIN AND STUFF YOU LIKE THE TROPHY YOU ARE!!

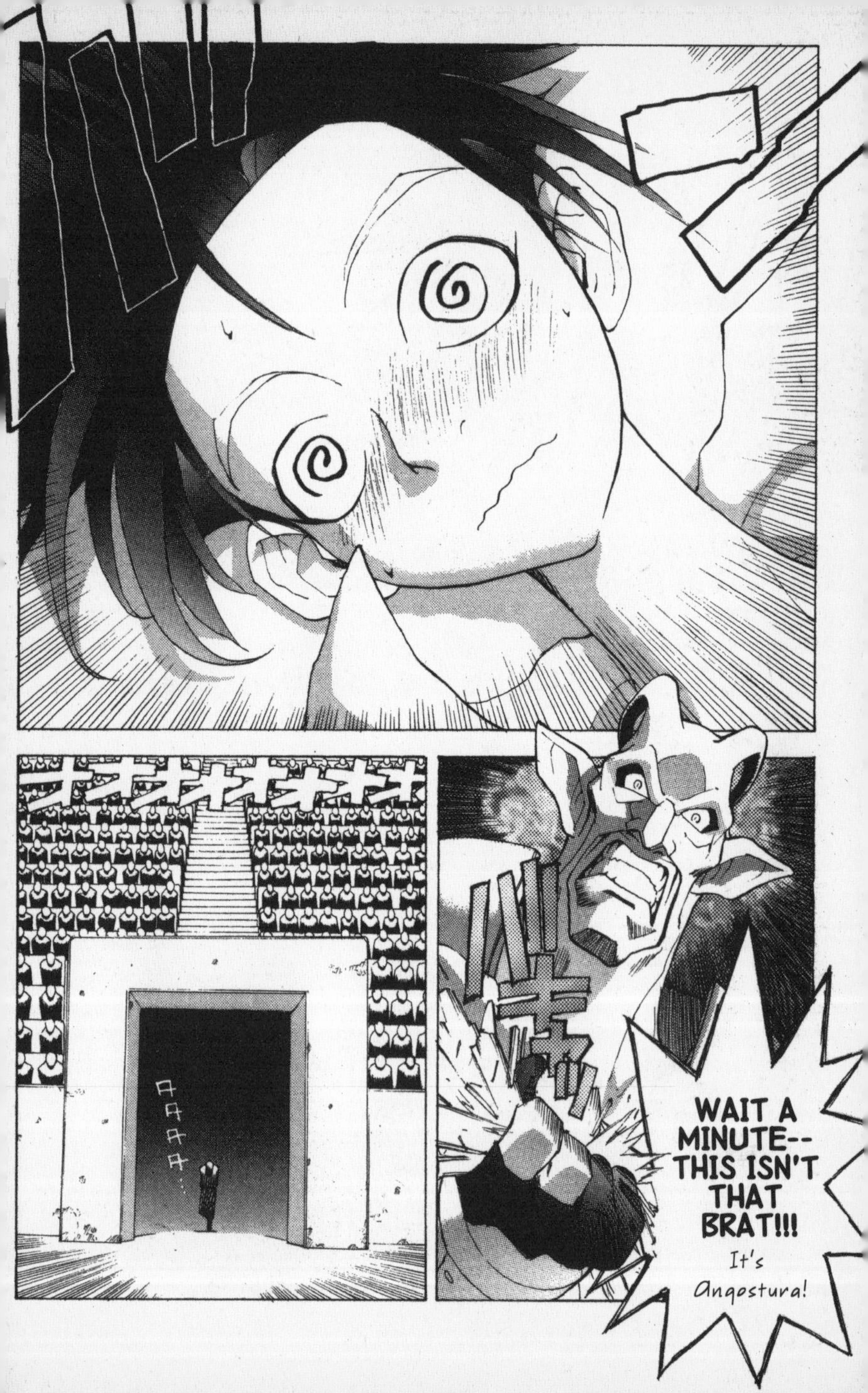
WAIT A MINUTE-- THIS ISN'T THAT BRAT!!!
It's Angostura!

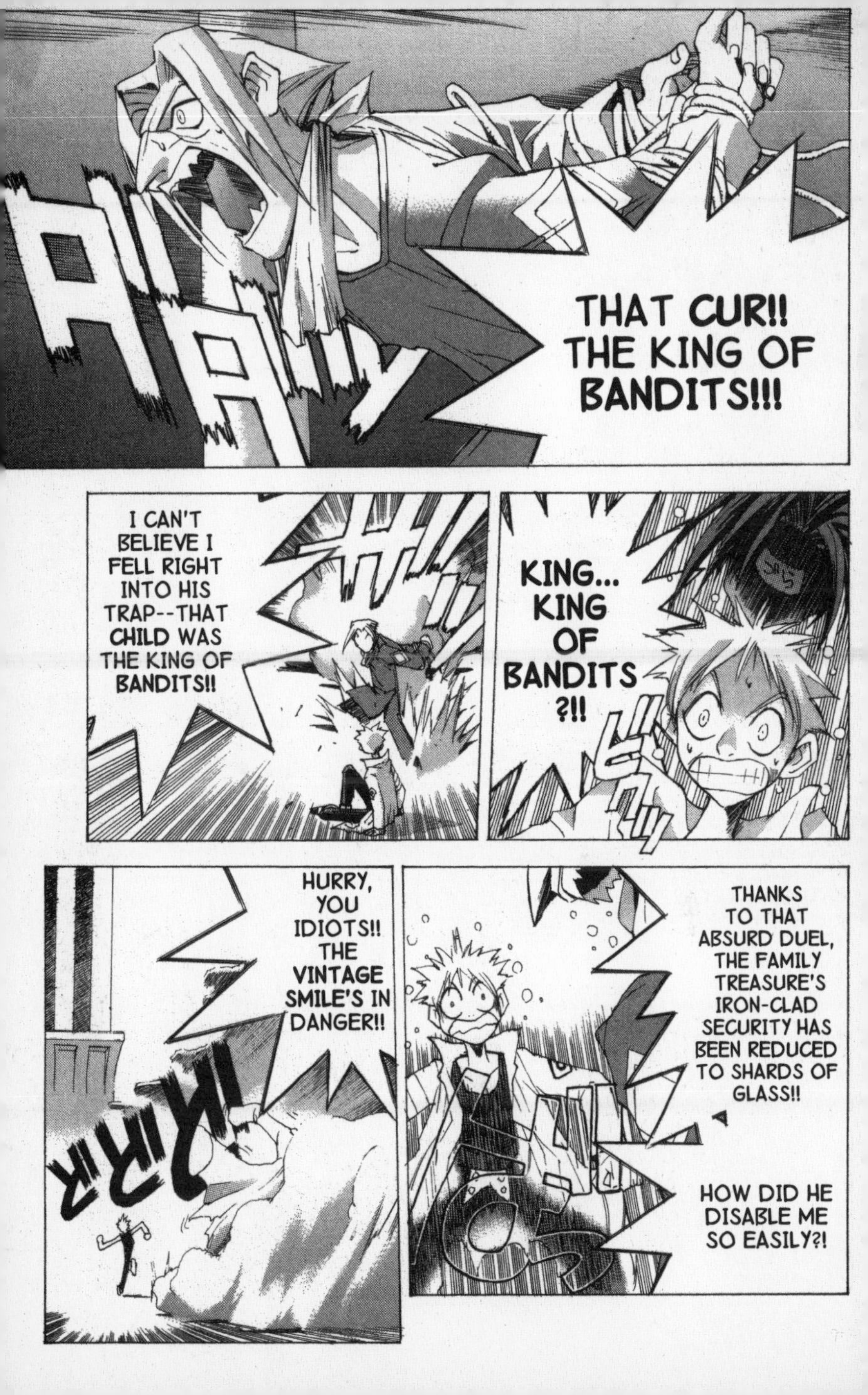
THAT CUR!! THE KING OF BANDITS!!!
KING... KING OF BANDITS ?!!
I CAN'T BELIEVE I FELL RIGHT INTO HIS TRAP--THAT CHILD WAS THE KING OF BANDITS!!
THANKS TO THAT ABSURD DUEL, THE FAMILY TREASURE'S IRON-CLAD SECURITY HAS BEEN REDUCED TO SHARDS OF GLASS!!
HOW DID HE DISABLE ME SO EASILY?!
HURRY, YOU IDIOTS!! THE VINTAGE SMILE'S IN DANGER!!

OH...
MY...
NOOO
OOO
!!!

I-I THOUGHT HE WAS YOU, MASTER ANGOSTURA.

OH!! HOW IS THE COUNTESS? AND THE MADEMOISELLE-- IS SHE SAFE?!!

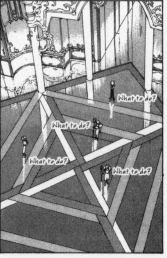

What to do?

What to do?

What to do?

What to do?

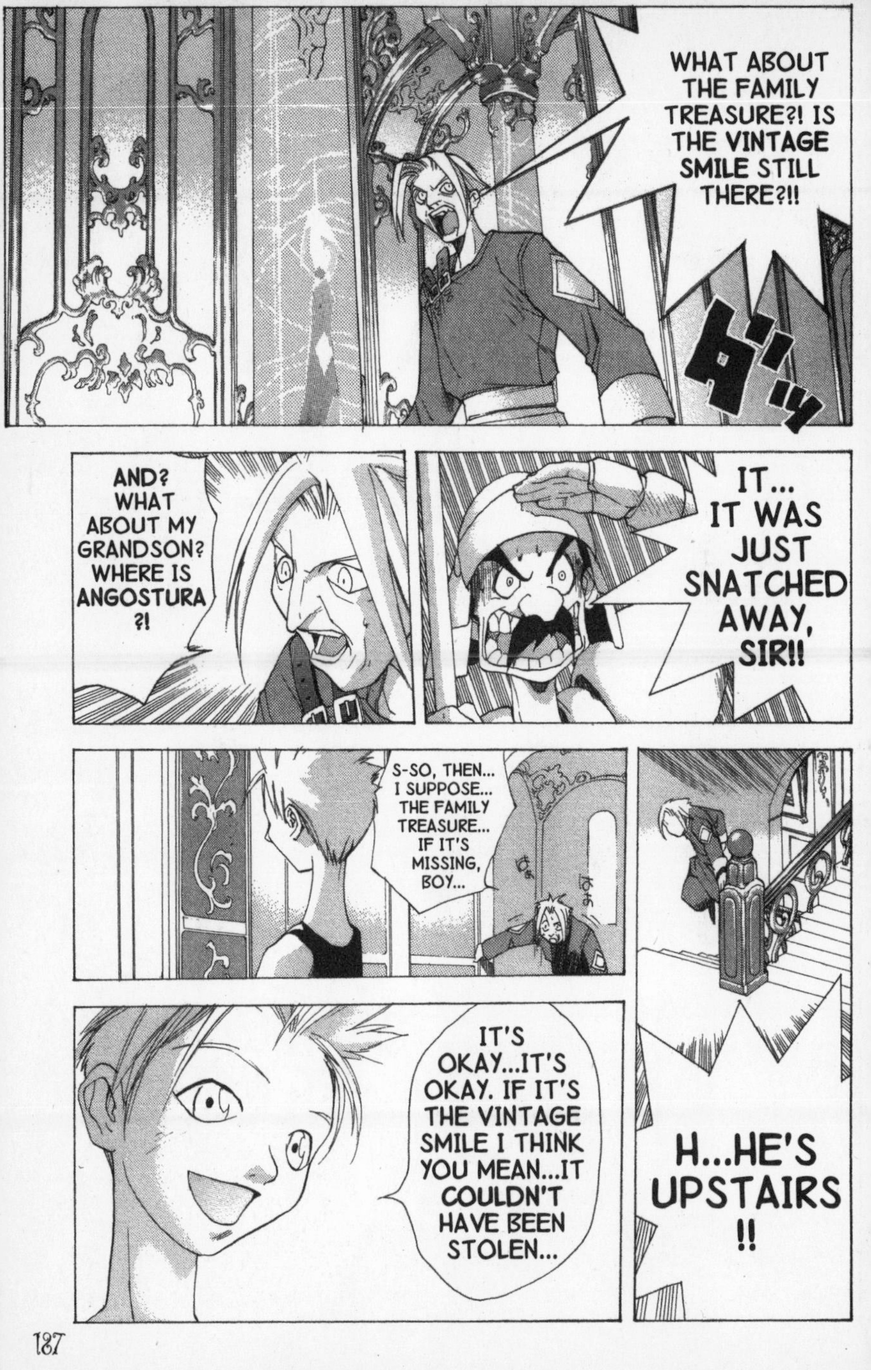
WHAT ABOUT THE FAMILY TREASURE?! IS THE VINTAGE SMILE STILL THERE?!!
ダッ
IT... IT WAS JUST SNATCHED AWAY, SIR!!
AND? WHAT ABOUT MY GRANDSON? WHERE IS ANGOSTURA?!
H...HE'S UPSTAIRS!!
S-SO, THEN... I SUPPOSE... THE FAMILY TREASURE... IF IT'S MISSING, BOY...
IT'S OKAY...IT'S OKAY. IF IT'S THE VINTAGE SMILE I THINK YOU MEAN...IT COULDN'T HAVE BEEN STOLEN...

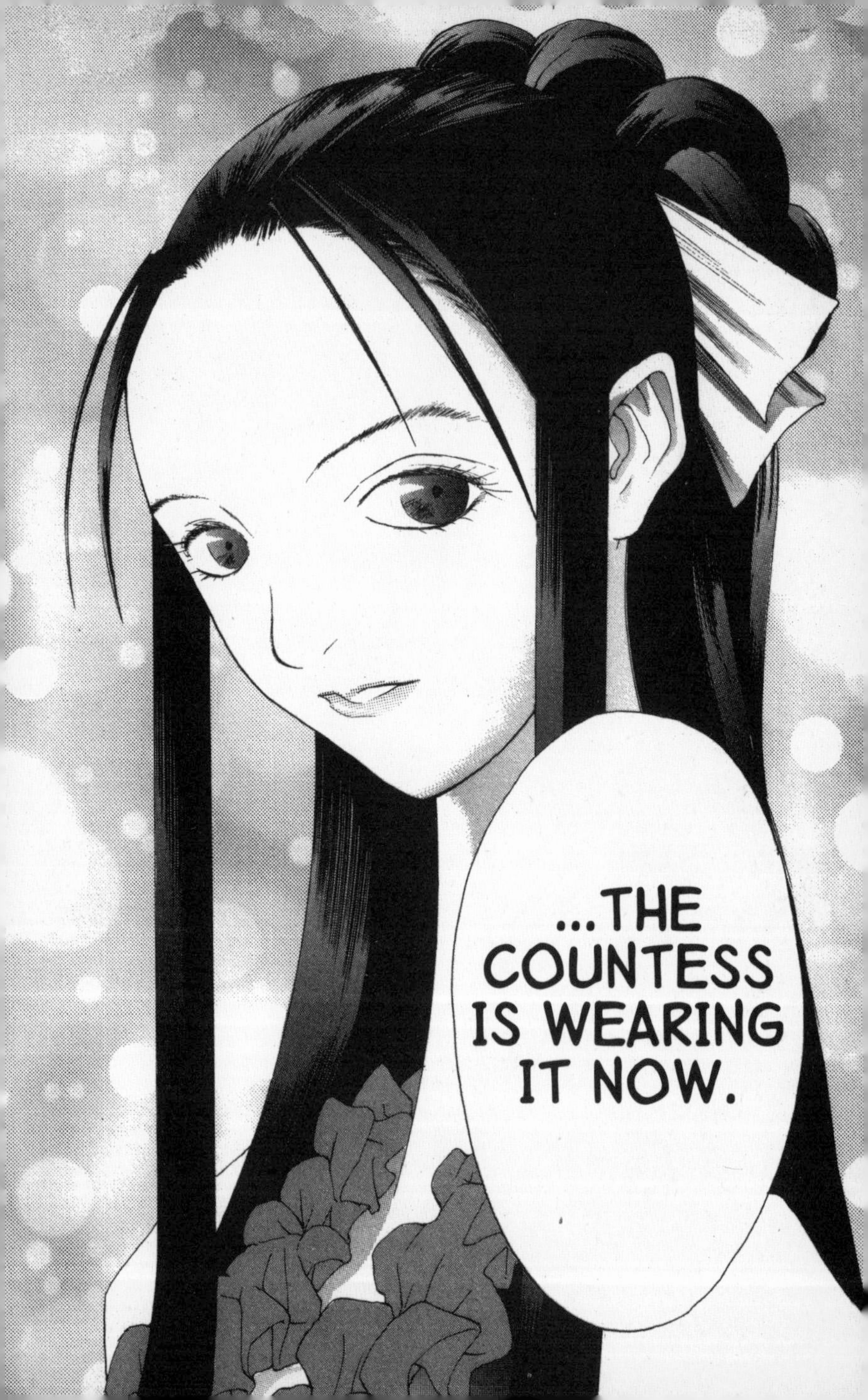
...THE COUNTESS IS WEARING IT NOW.

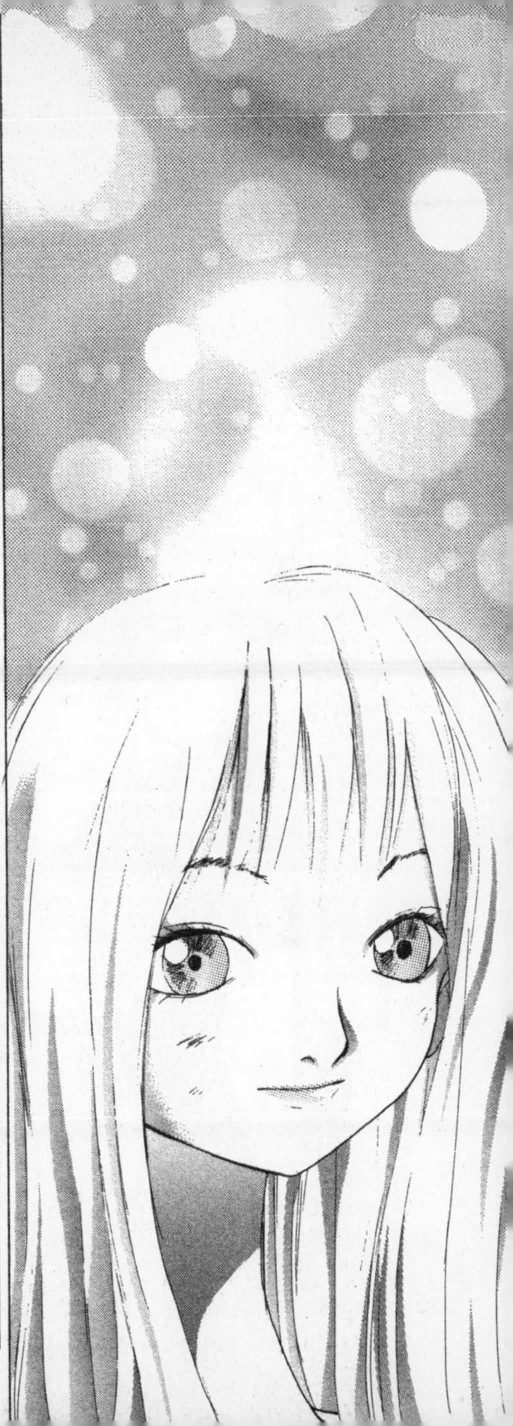

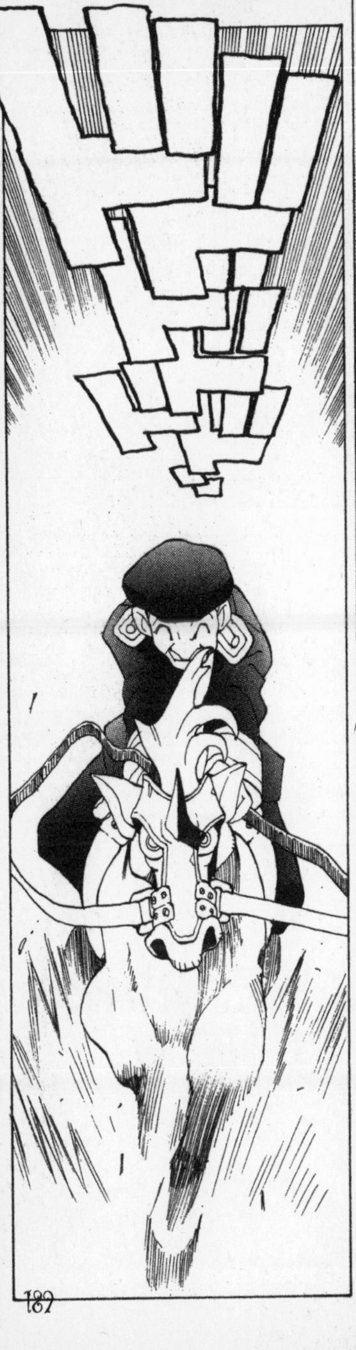

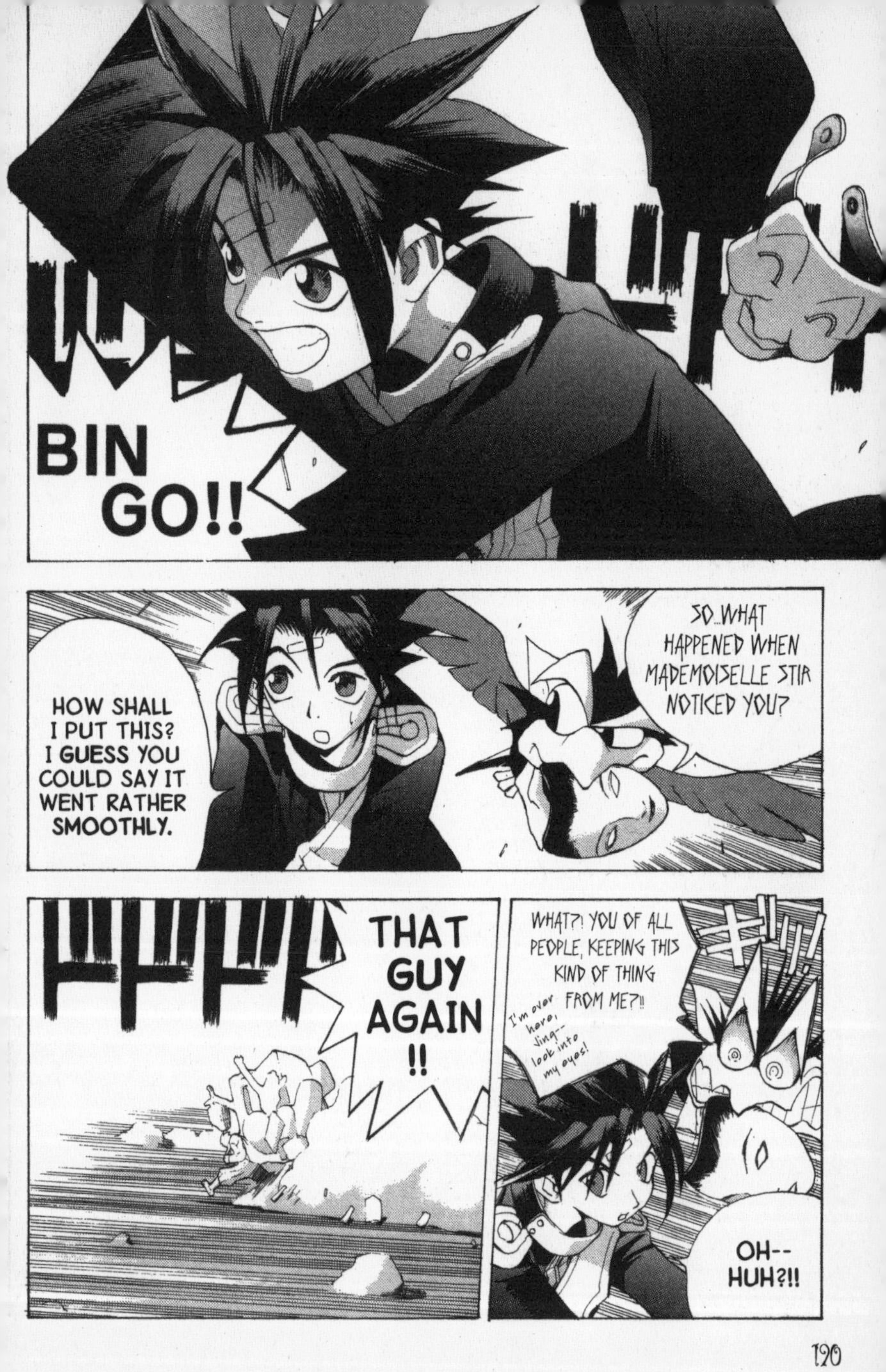
BIN GO!!
SO...WHAT HAPPENED WHEN MADEMOISELLE STIR NOTICED YOU?
HOW SHALL I PUT THIS? I GUESS YOU COULD SAY IT WENT RATHER SMOOTHLY.
WHAT?! YOU OF ALL PEOPLE, KEEPING THIS KIND OF THING FROM ME?!!
I'm over here, Jing-- look into my eyes!
OH-- HUH?!!
THAT GUY AGAIN !!

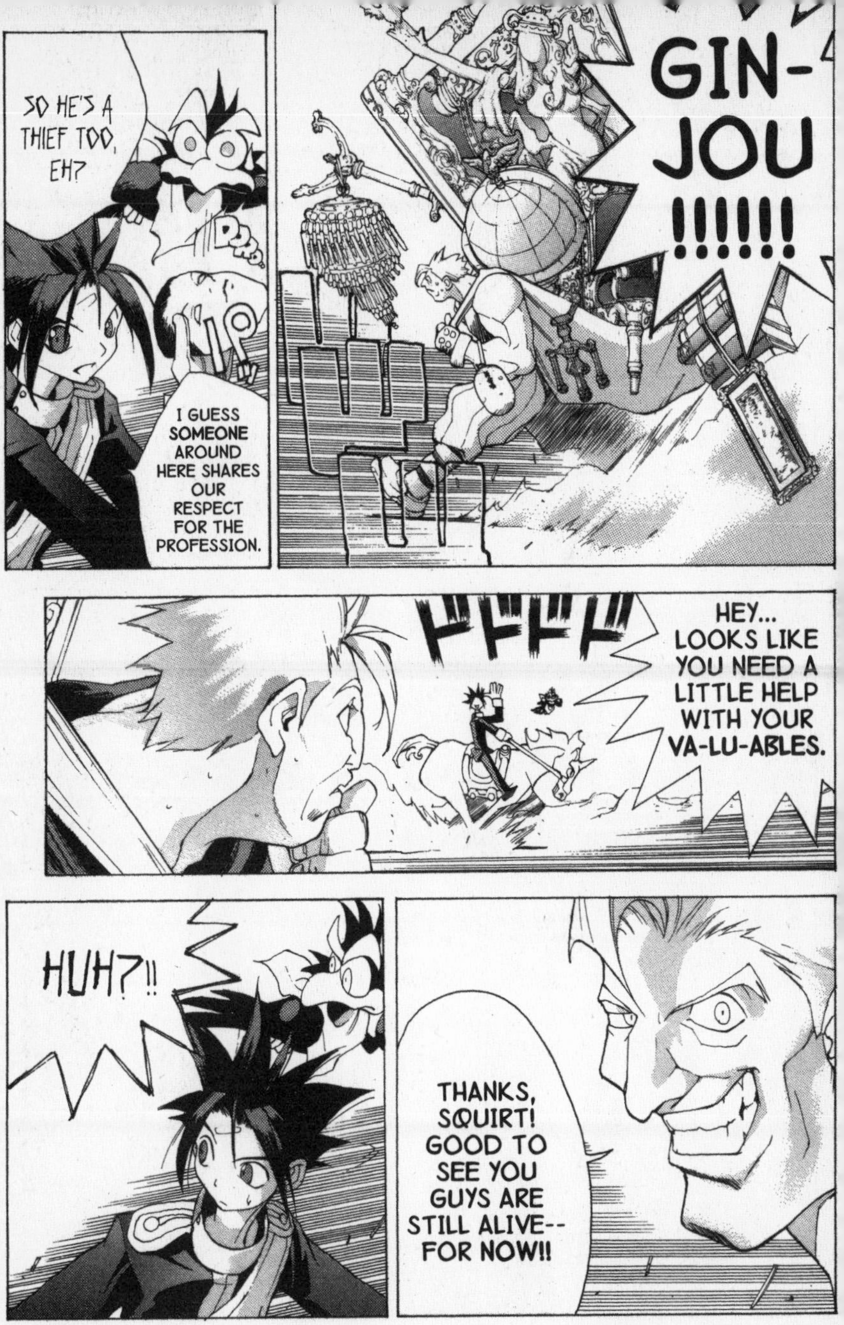
GIN-JOU!!!!!!
SO HE'S A THIEF TOO, EH?
I GUESS SOMEONE AROUND HERE SHARES OUR RESPECT FOR THE PROFESSION.
HEY... LOOKS LIKE YOU NEED A LITTLE HELP WITH YOUR VA-LU-ABLES.
THANKS, SQUIRT! GOOD TO SEE YOU GUYS ARE STILL ALIVE--FOR NOW!!
HUH?!!

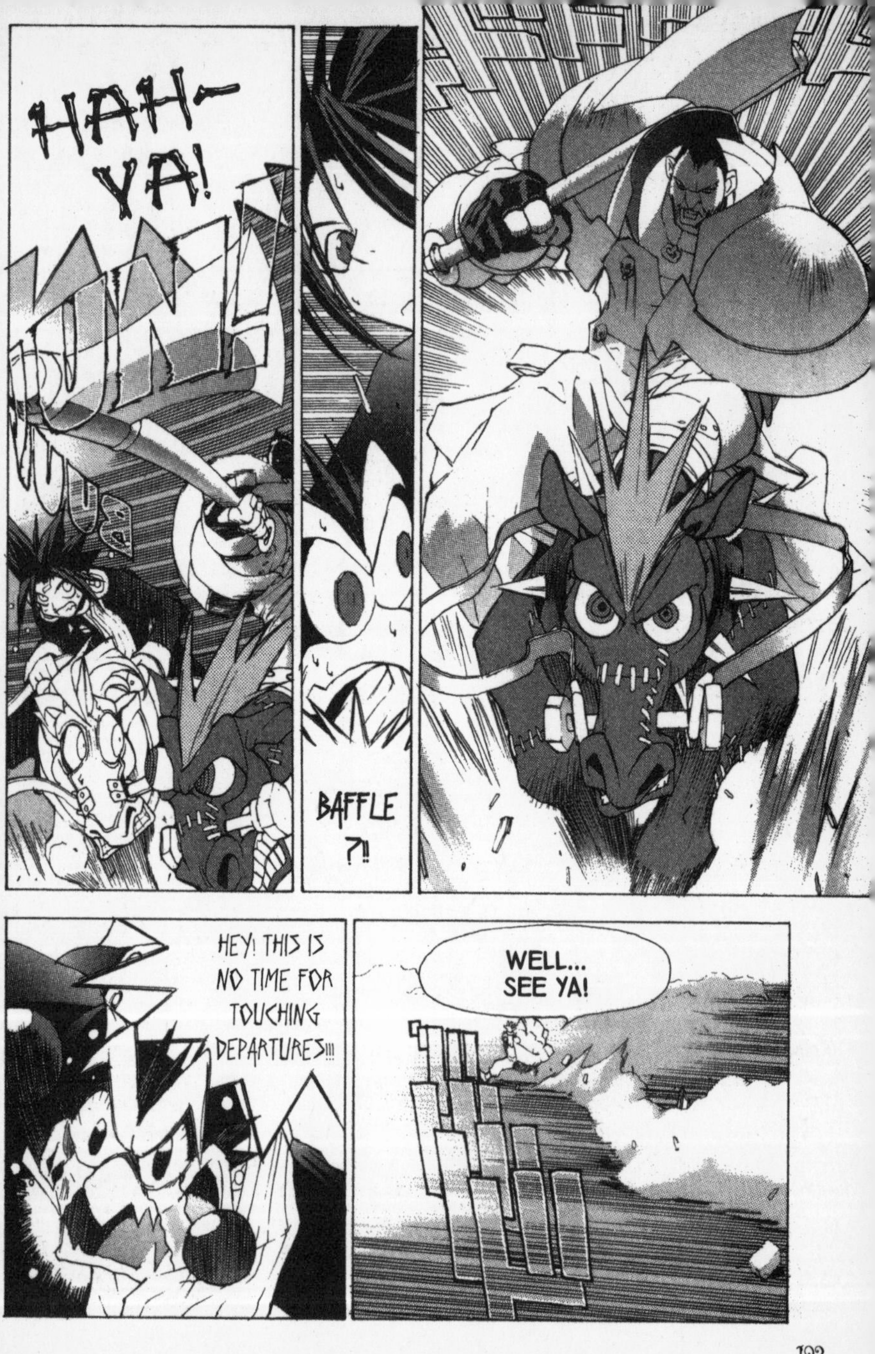
BAFFLE ?!!
HAH-YA!
WELL... SEE YA!
HEY! THIS IS NO TIME FOR TOUCHING DEPARTURES!!!

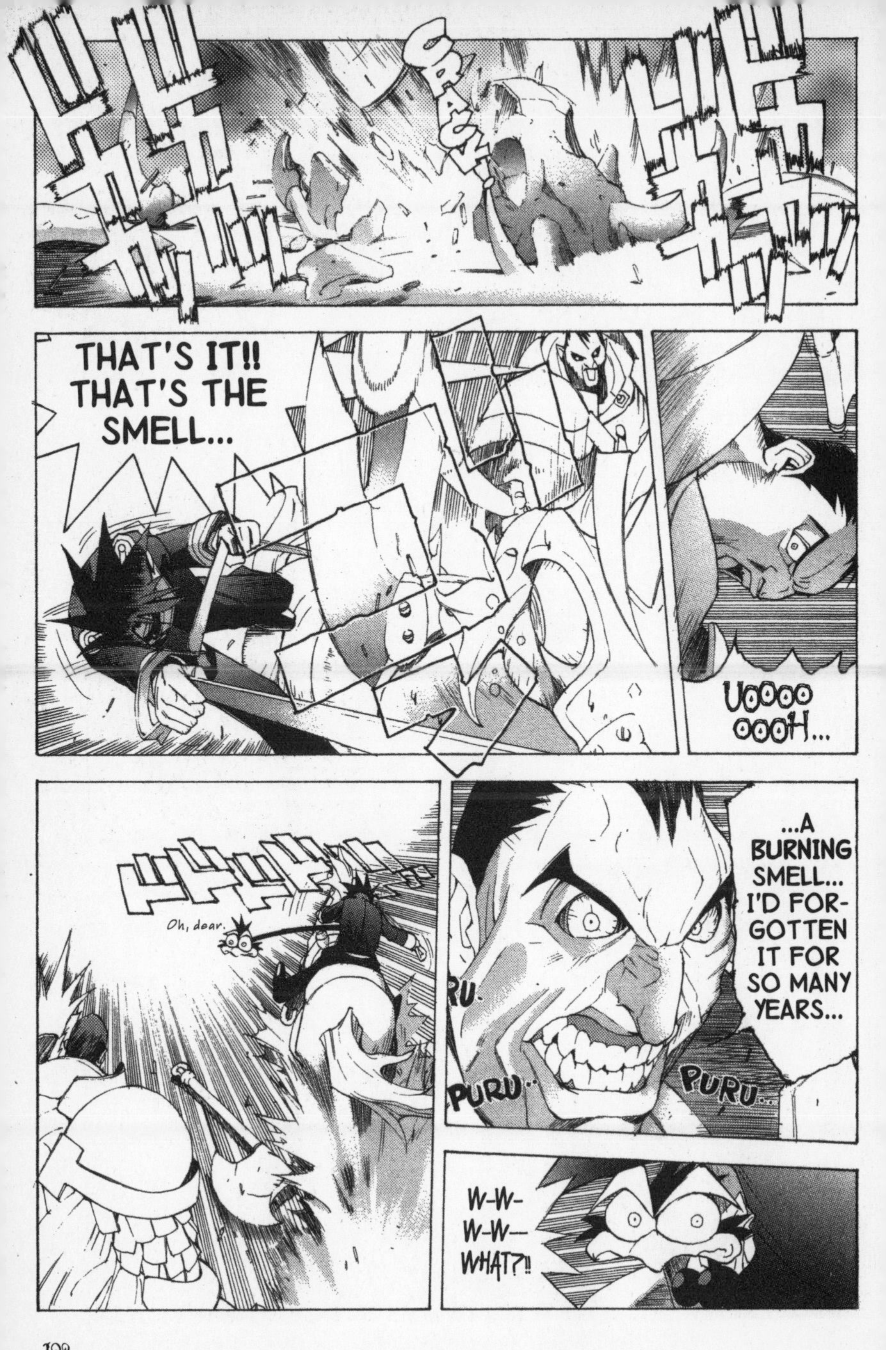
CRACK!
UOOOO OOOH...
THAT'S IT!! THAT'S THE SMELL...
...A BURNING SMELL... I'D FORGOTTEN IT FOR SO MANY YEARS...
PURU..
PURU..
PURU...
W-W-W-W-WHAT?!!
Oh, dear.

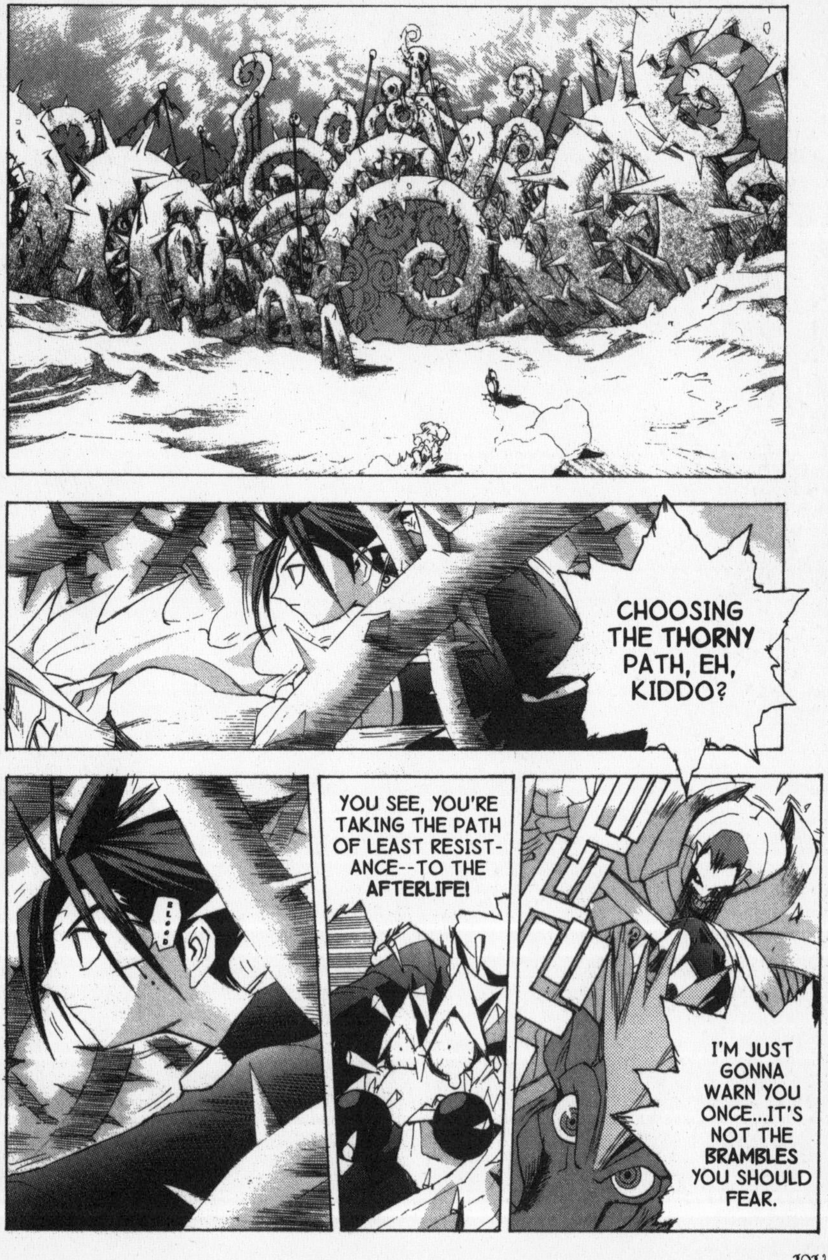
CHOOSING THE THORNY PATH, EH, KIDDO?
I'M JUST GONNA WARN YOU ONCE...IT'S NOT THE BRAMBLES YOU SHOULD FEAR.
YOU SEE, YOU'RE TAKING THE PATH OF LEAST RESIST-ANCE--TO THE AFTERLIFE!
BLOOD

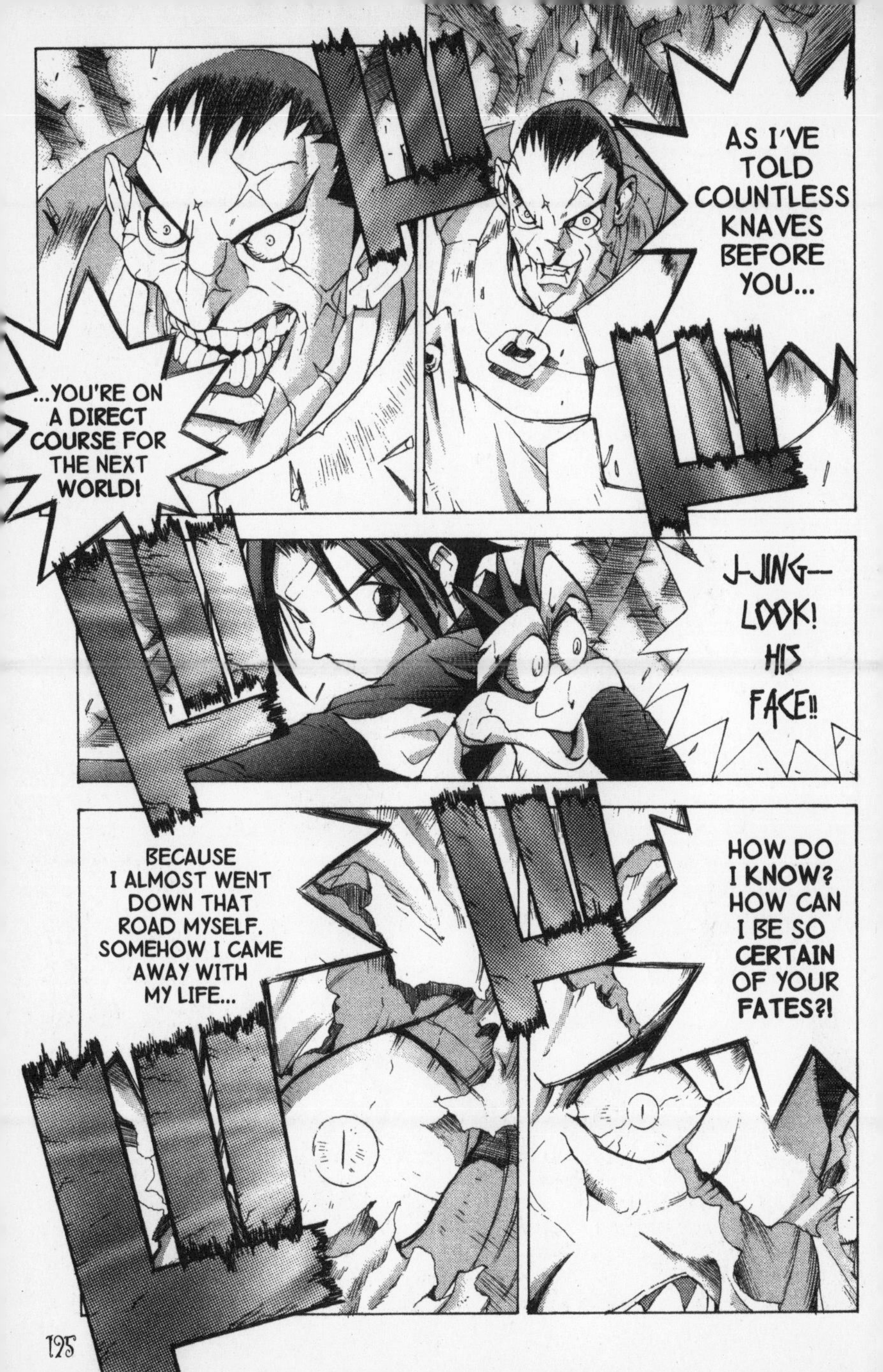
AS I'VE TOLD COUNTLESS KNAVES BEFORE YOU...
...YOU'RE ON A DIRECT COURSE FOR THE NEXT WORLD!
J-JING-- LOOK! HIS FACE!!
HOW DO I KNOW? HOW CAN I BE SO CERTAIN OF YOUR FATES?!
BECAUSE I ALMOST WENT DOWN THAT ROAD MYSELF. SOMEHOW I CAME AWAY WITH MY LIFE...

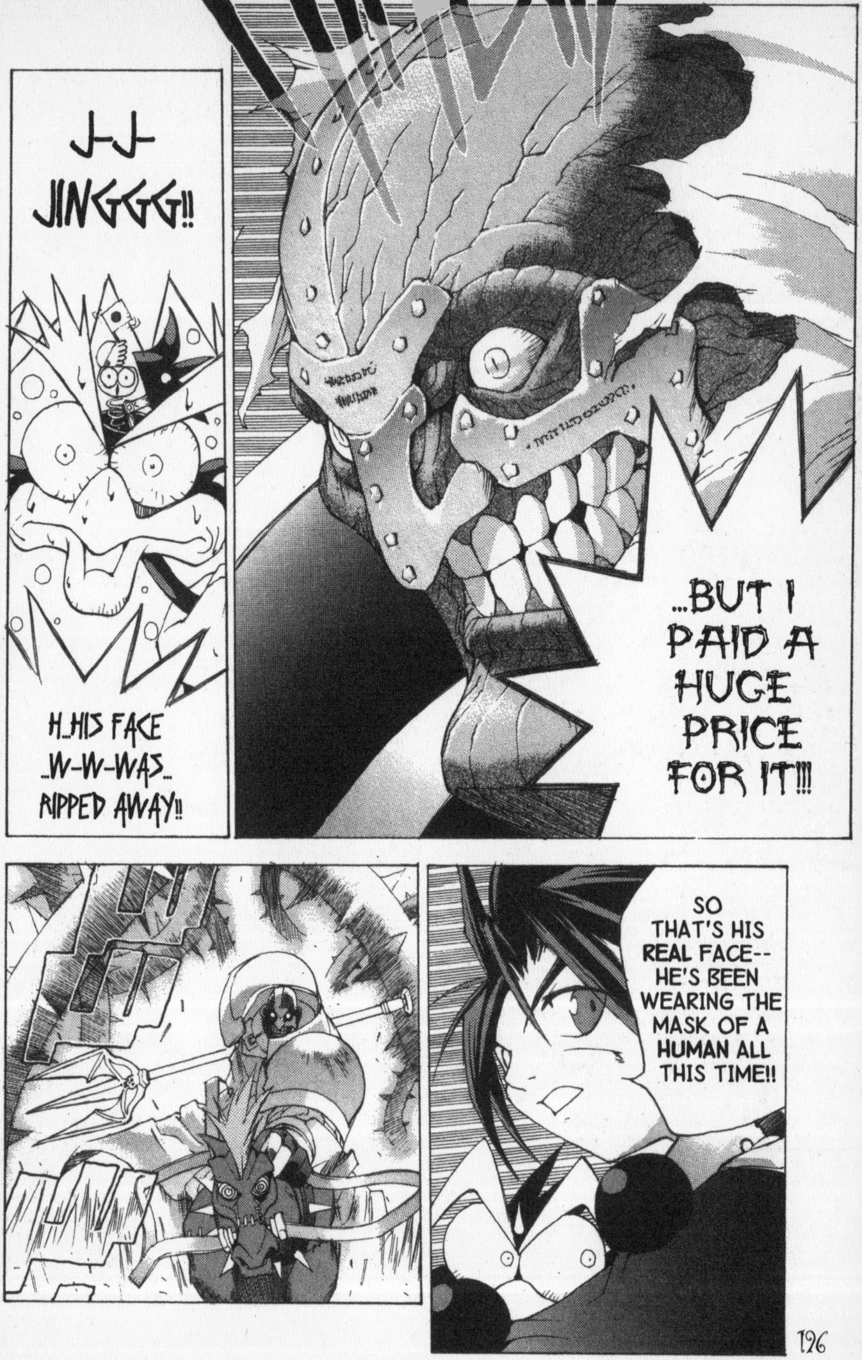
...BUT I PAID A HUGE PRICE FOR IT!!!
J-J-JINGGG!!
H...HIS FACE ...W-W-WAS... RIPPED AWAY!!
SO THAT'S HIS REAL FACE-- HE'S BEEN WEARING THE MASK OF A HUMAN ALL THIS TIME!!

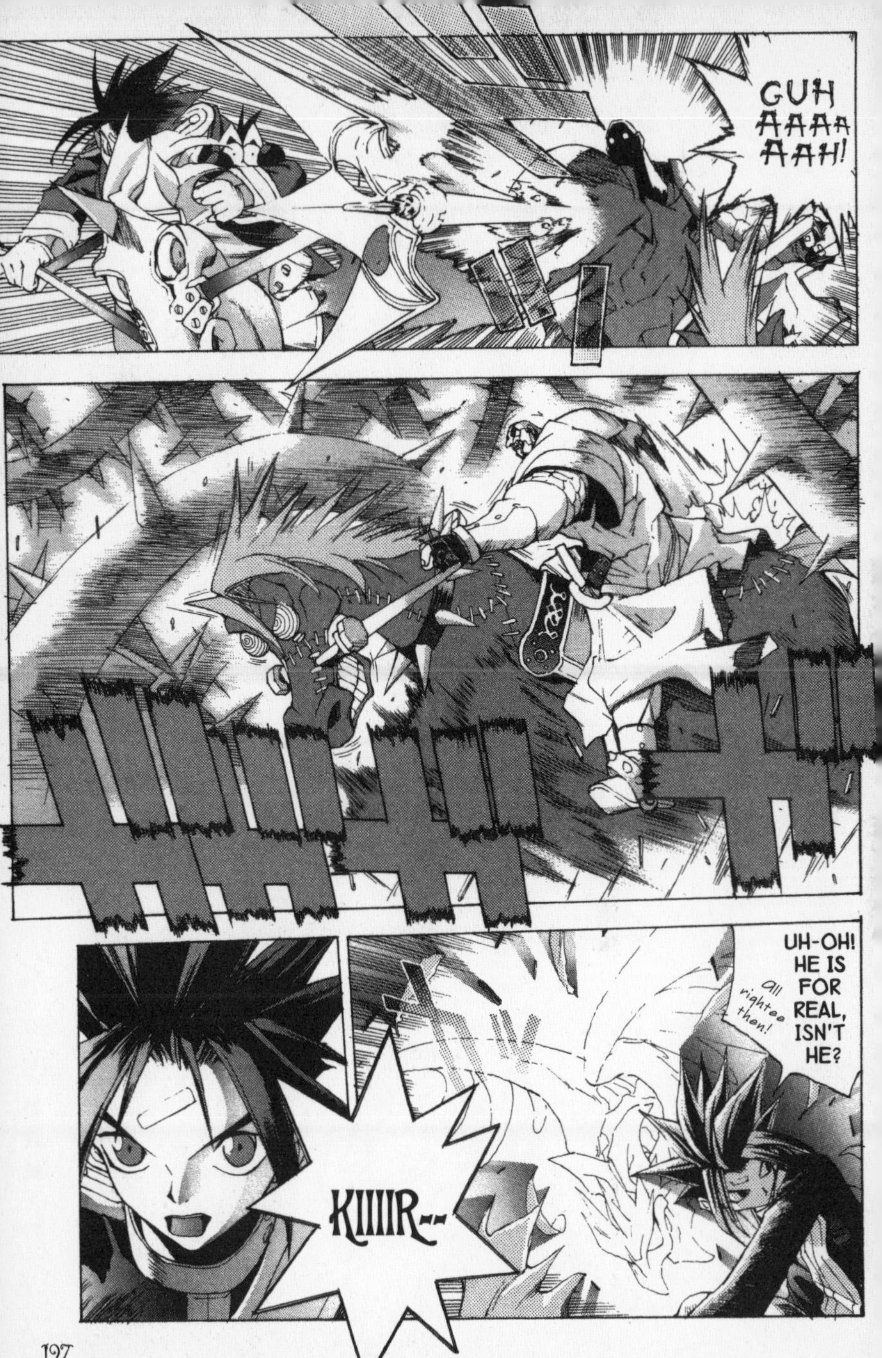
GUH AAAA AAH!
UH-OH! HE IS FOR REAL, ISN'T HE?
all rightee then!
KIIIIR--

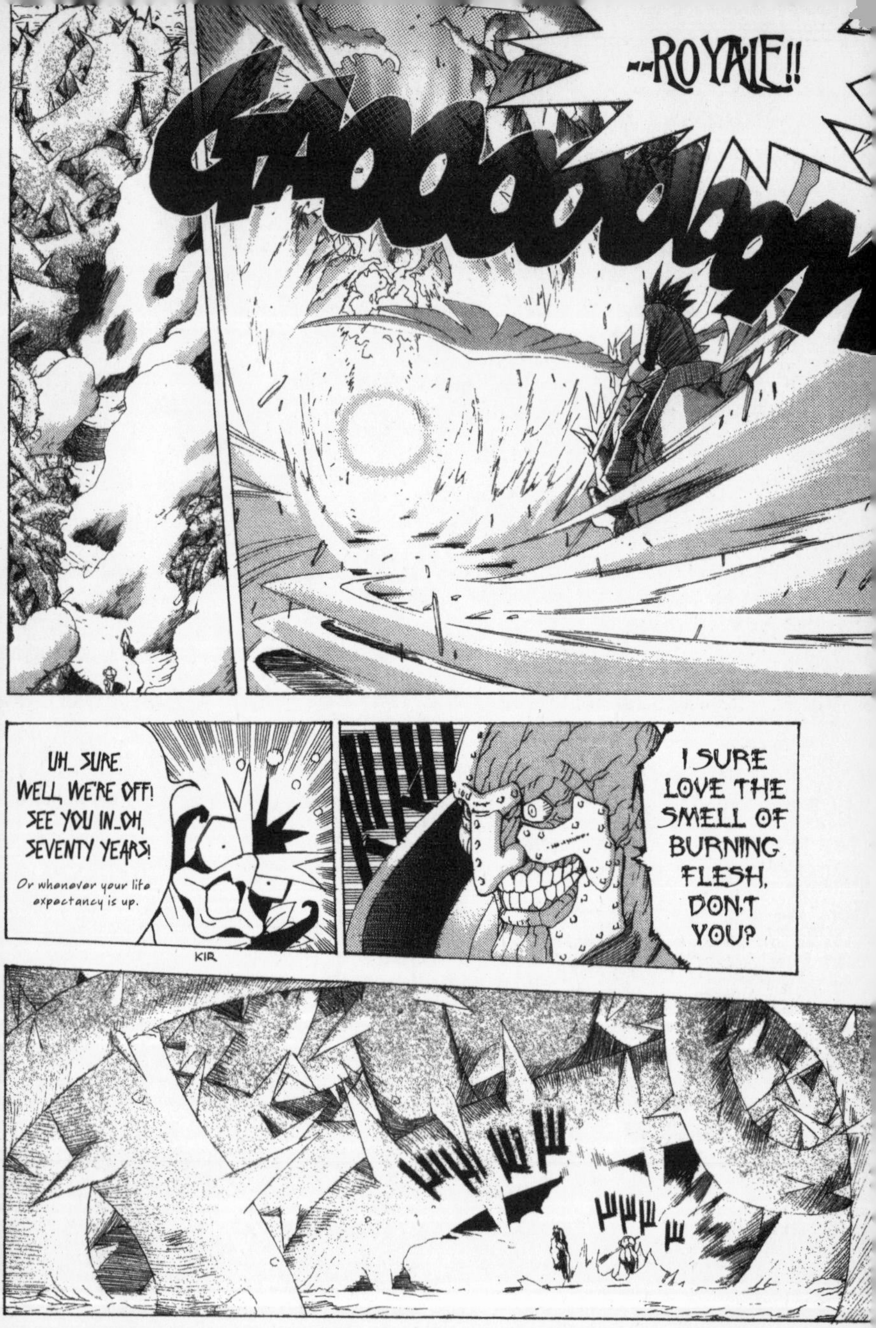
--ROYALE!!
I SURE LOVE THE SMELL OF BURNING FLESH, DON'T YOU?
UH... SURE. WELL, WE'RE OFF! SEE YOU IN...OH, SEVENTY YEARS!
Or whenever your life expectancy is up.
KIR

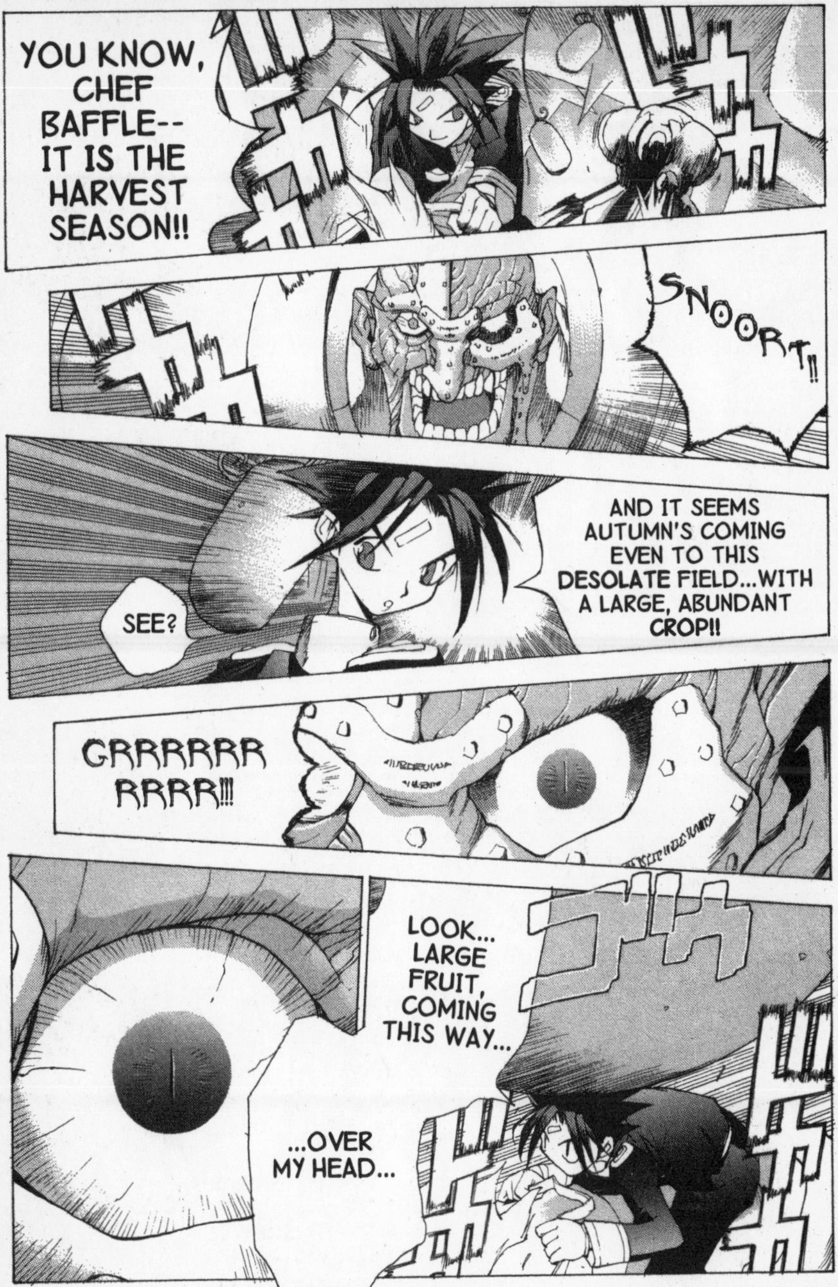
YOU KNOW, CHEF BAFFLE-- IT IS THE HARVEST SEASON!!
SNOORT!!
AND IT SEEMS AUTUMN'S COMING EVEN TO THIS DESOLATE FIELD...WITH A LARGE, ABUNDANT CROP!!
SEE?
GRRRRRR RRRR!!!
LOOK... LARGE FRUIT, COMING THIS WAY...
...OVER MY HEAD...

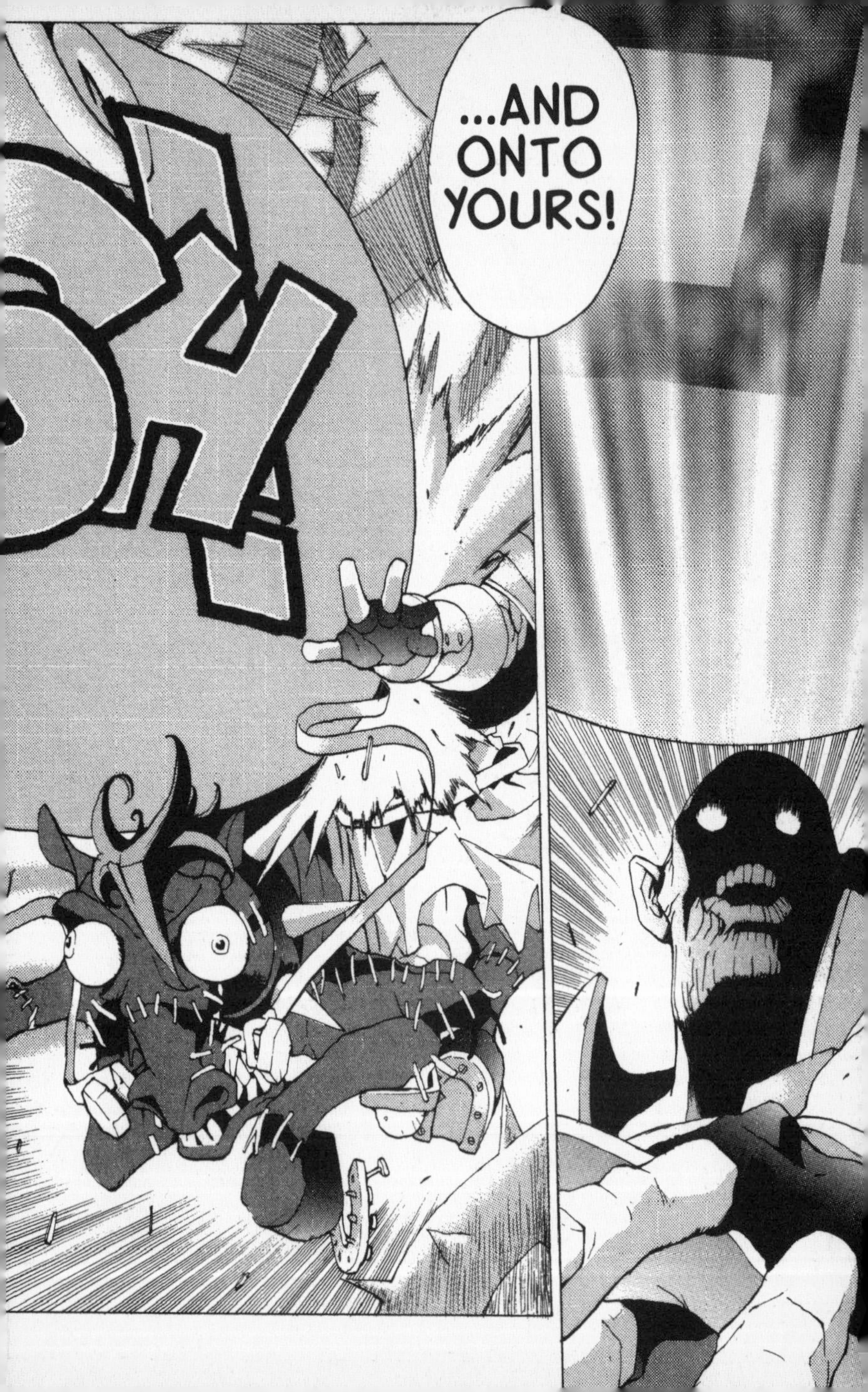
...AND ONTO YOURS!

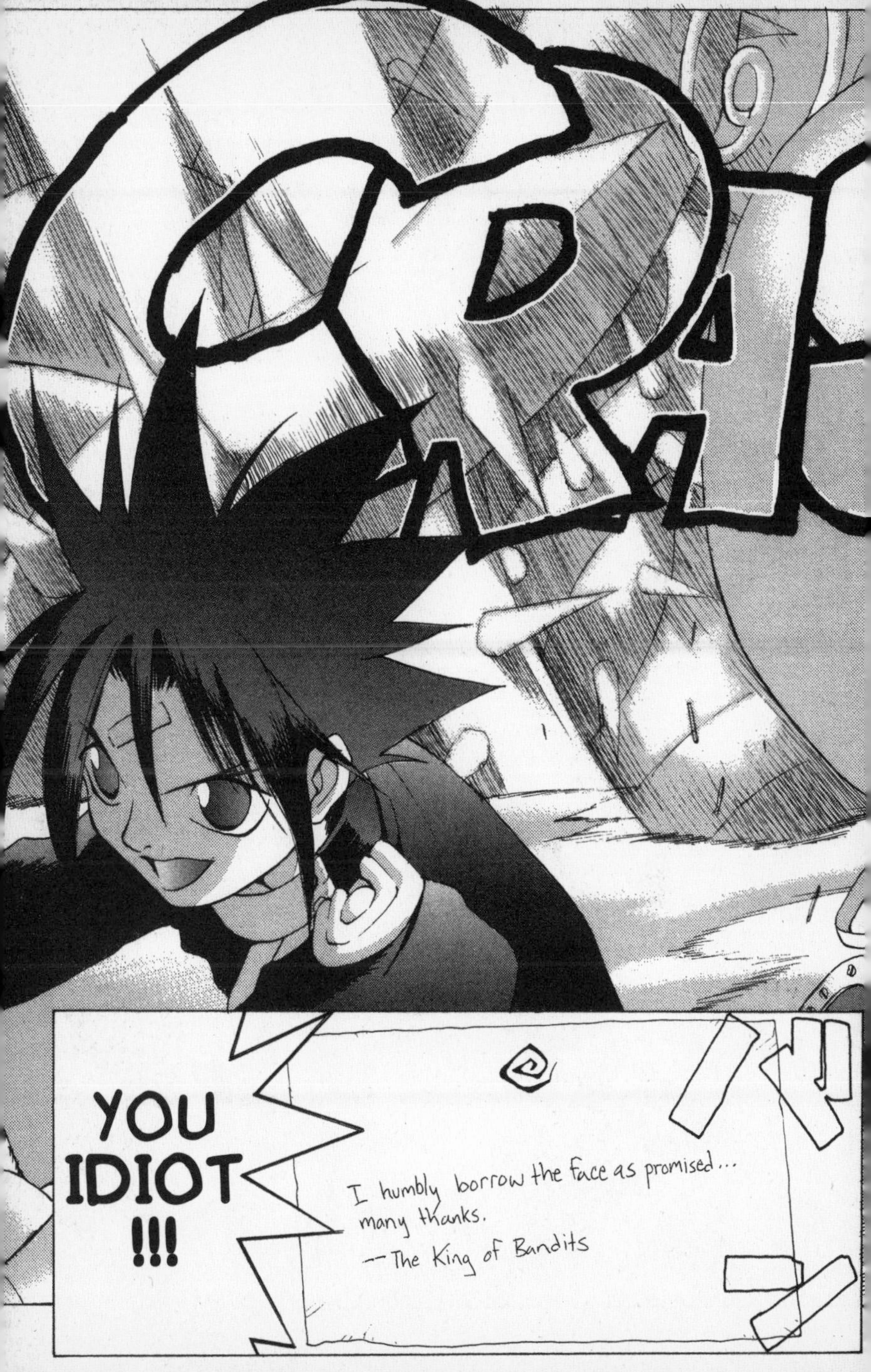
I humbly borrow the face as promised... many thanks.
--The King of Bandits
YOU IDIOT !!!

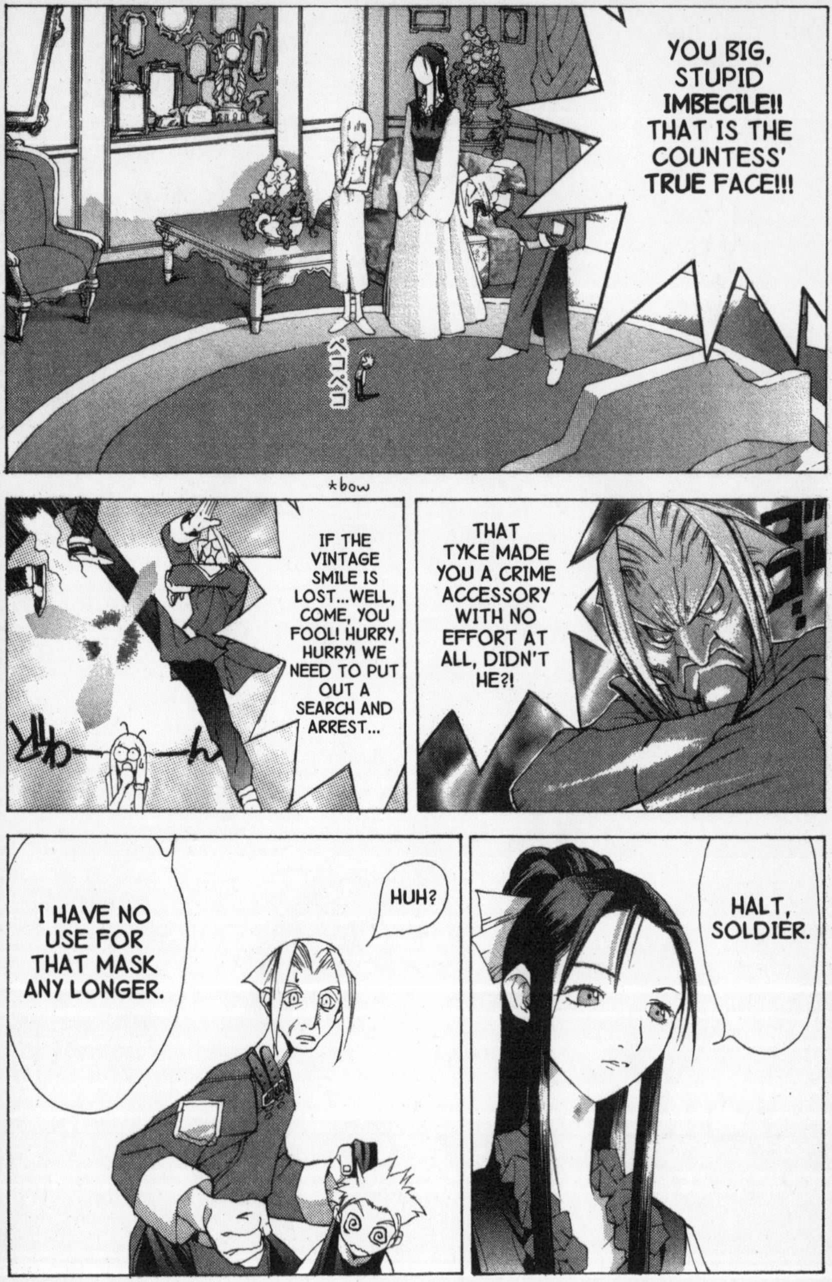
YOU BIG, STUPID IMBECILE!! THAT IS THE COUNTESS' TRUE FACE!!!
*bow
THAT TYKE MADE YOU A CRIME ACCESSORY WITH NO EFFORT AT ALL, DIDN'T HE?!
IF THE VINTAGE SMILE IS LOST...WELL, COME, YOU FOOL! HURRY, HURRY! WE NEED TO PUT OUT A SEARCH AND ARREST...
HALT, SOLDIER.
HUH?
I HAVE NO USE FOR THAT MASK ANY LONGER.

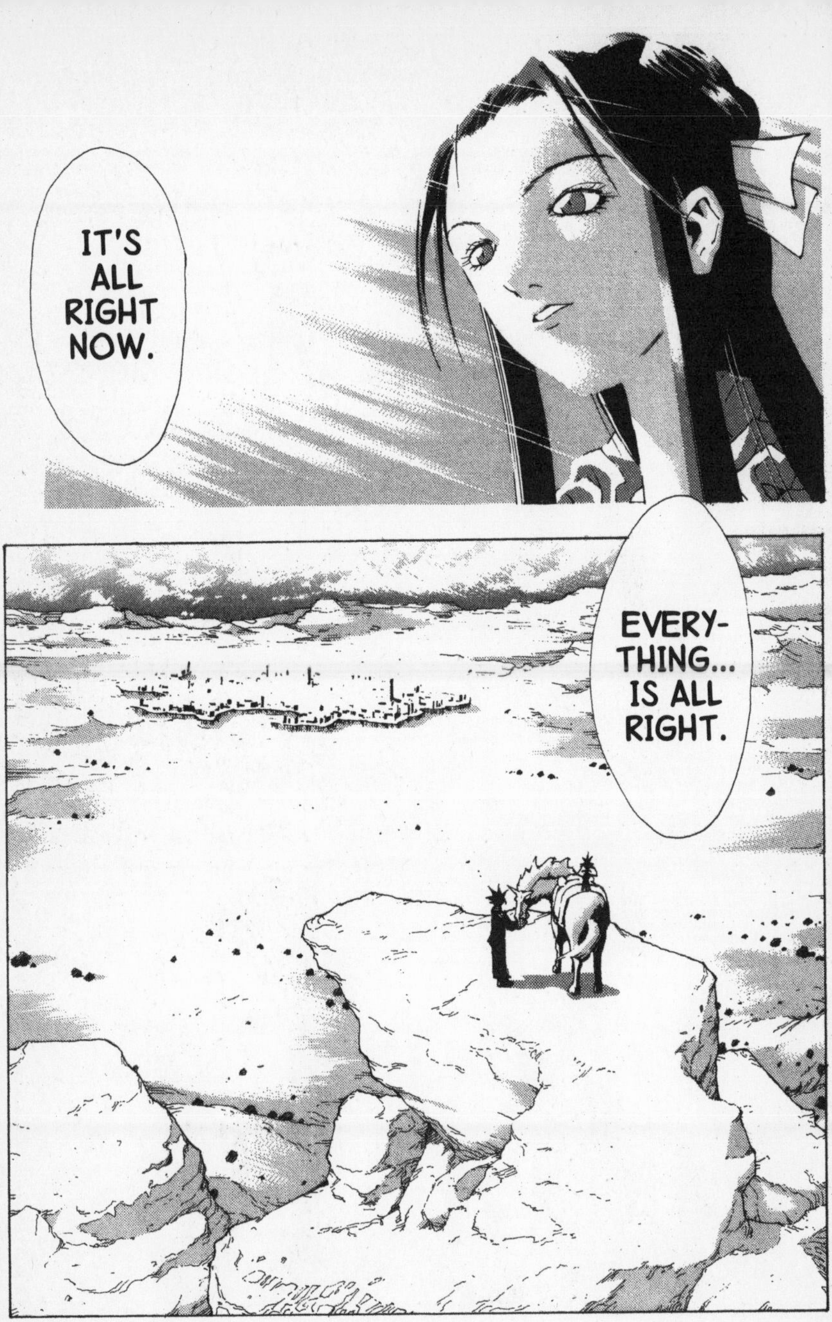
IT'S ALL RIGHT NOW.
EVERY-THING... IS ALL RIGHT.

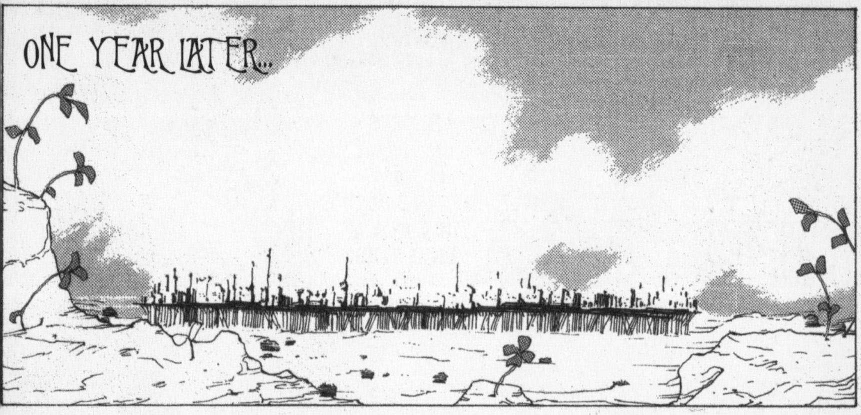
ONE YEAR LATER...
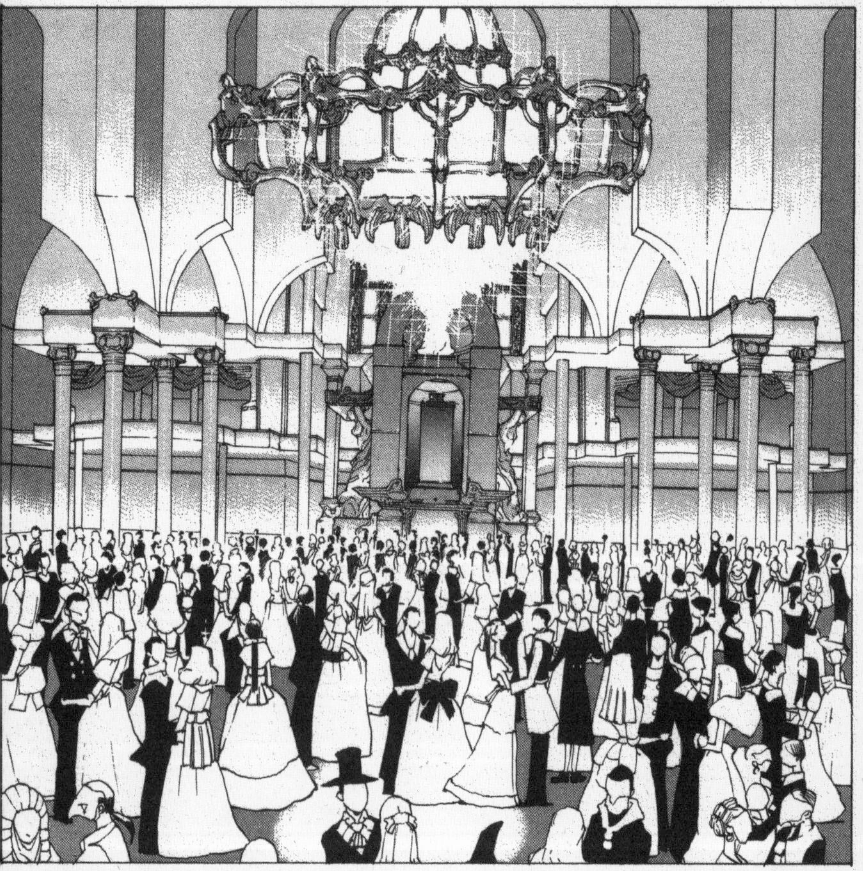

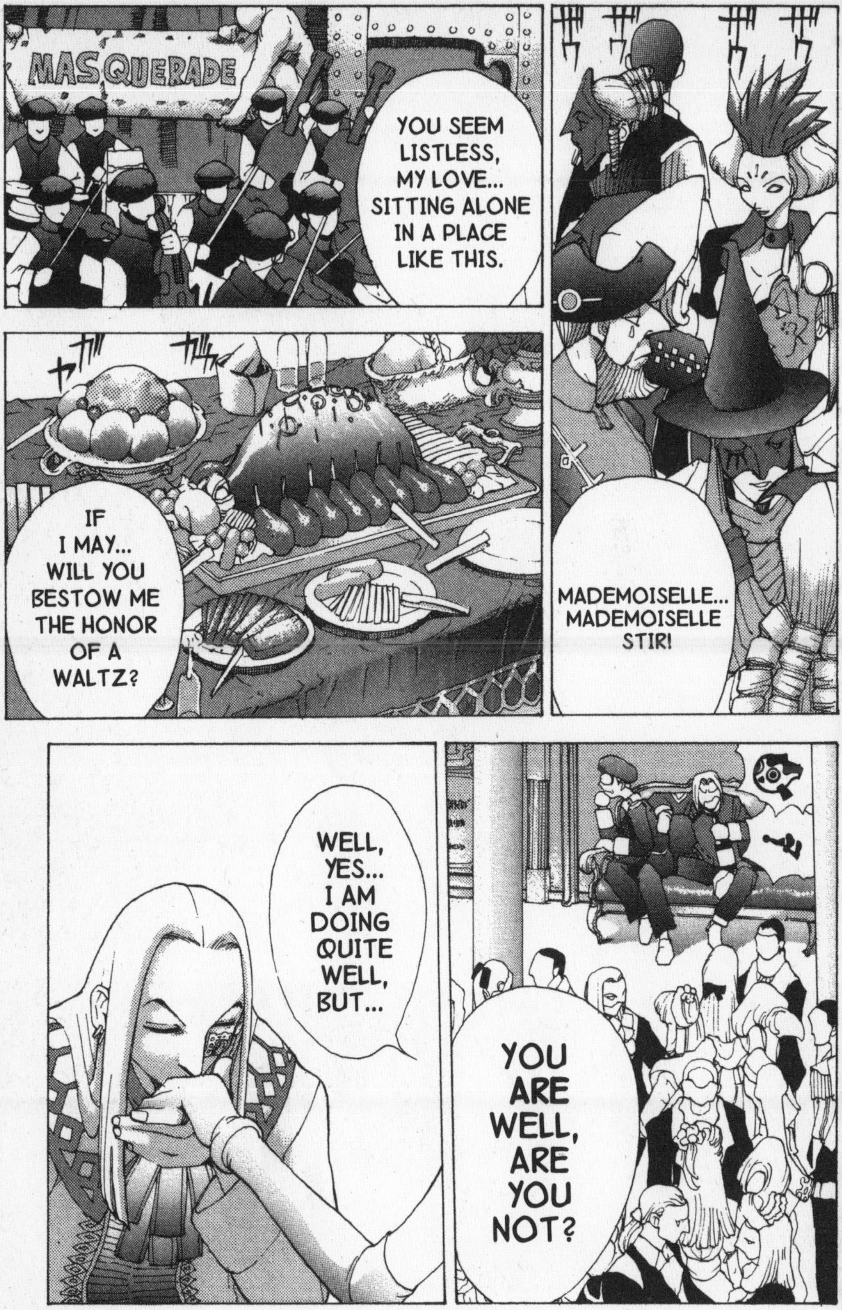
MADEMOISELLE... MADEMOISELLE STIR!
MASQUERADE
YOU SEEM LISTLESS, MY LOVE... SITTING ALONE IN A PLACE LIKE THIS.
IF I MAY... WILL YOU BESTOW ME THE HONOR OF A WALTZ?
YOU ARE WELL, ARE YOU NOT?
WELL, YES... I AM DOING QUITE WELL, BUT...

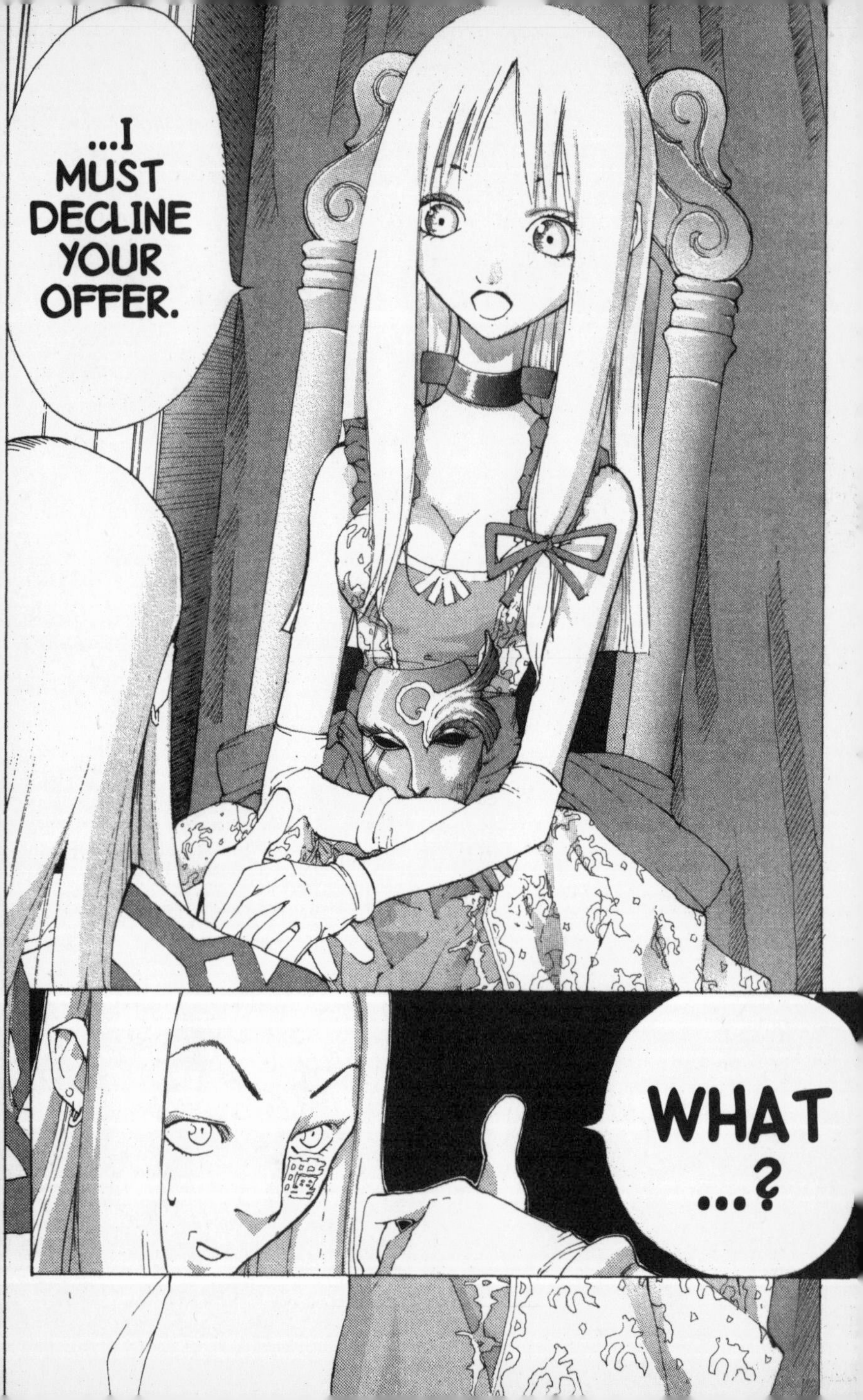
...I MUST DECLINE YOUR OFFER.
WHAT ...?

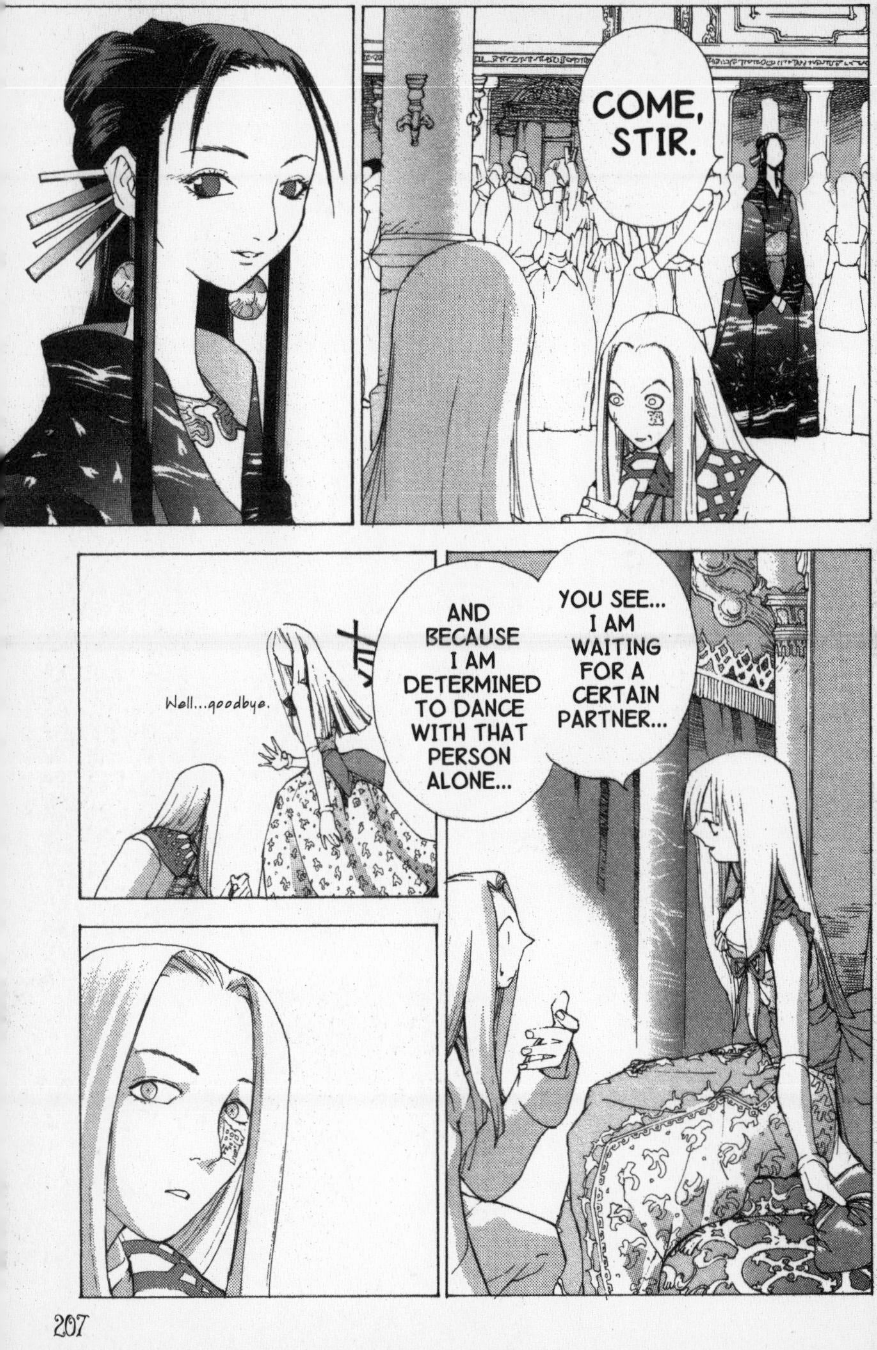
COME, STIR.
YOU SEE... I AM WAITING FOR A CERTAIN PARTNER...
AND BECAUSE I AM DETERMINED TO DANCE WITH THAT PERSON ALONE...
Well...goodbye.

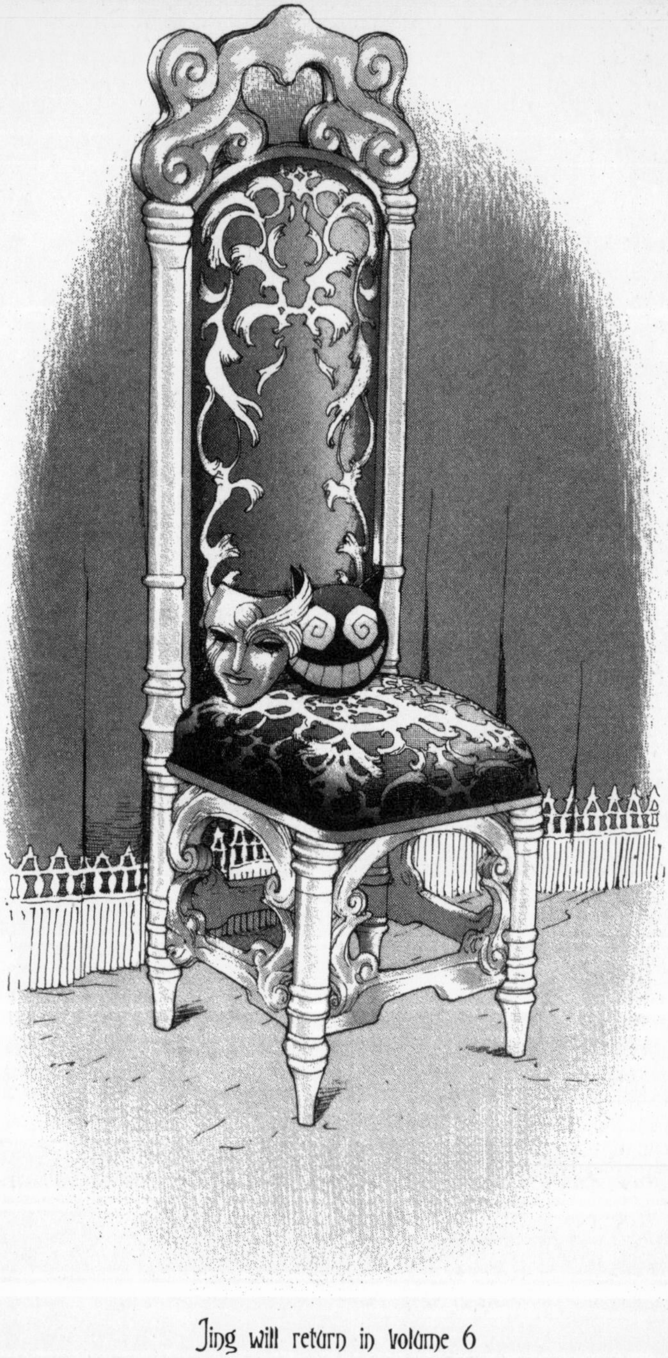

Jing will return in volume 6

熊倉裕一
完全監修

who the hell is he !!?

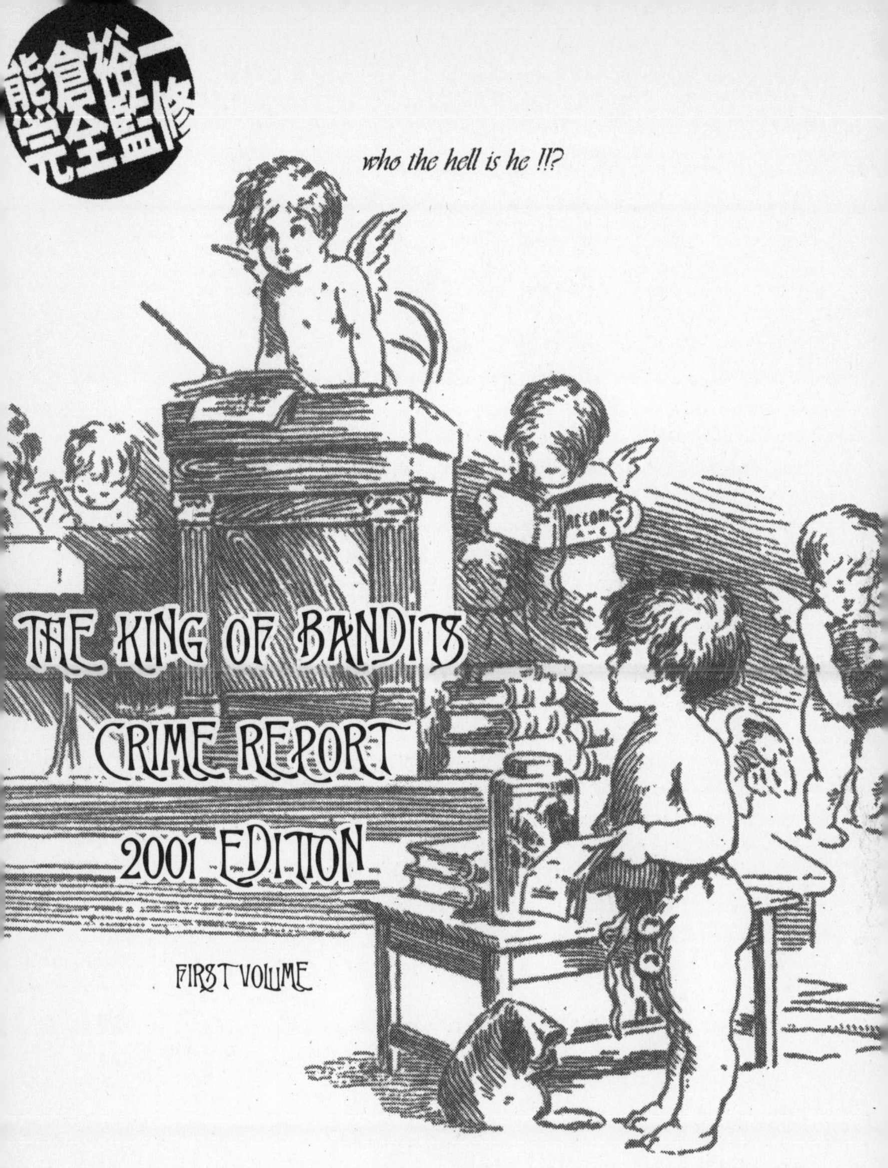

THE KING OF BANDITS CRIME REPORT 2001 EDITION

FIRST VOLUME

On the surface, Jinq: King of Bandits appears to be merely an action series about a master thief in a fantasy world. But at second glance, the series is full of hidden puns and inside jokes that occur on many different levels. Here, author Yuichi Kumakura helps us plumb the depths of this deceptively simple series.

characters

It is well-known among King of Bandits fans that the names of almost all characters in the Jing world are taken from the names of alcoholic beverages. Furthermore, all of the towns that Jing and Kir visit carry the names of cocktails--mixtures of said alcohol. In this "crime report," we will explore the origins of these zingy characters and settings. Oh, and while we're on the subject, let's address one of the most common questions asked in fan letters to Yuichi Kumakura: "Do you really drink?" We assure you, Kumakura does not drink nearly as much alcohol as these books would imply—seems he's just not the type.

Jin [Gin=Jing]

Gin is a distilled alcohol made by drenching the contents of the needle juniper in alcohol. Actually, it was originally used in Holland for medical purposes; specifically, as a fever reducer. Today, it is distinguished among the hard liquors by its unique flavor. Jing was originally spelled "Ging," but when the title was incorporated into the logo, it was decided that Japanese people might be confused as to how to pronounce it, since "G" has both a hard and a soft sound in English. Thus, we have the current spelling: "JING."

Ki-Ru [Kir]

Kir is a cocktail made by filling a glass of Créme de Cassis (an alcohol distilled from Cassis, a black berry native to Eurasia) with chilled white wine. It is said the name comes from the then-mayor of Dijon, a city in Burgundy, France. So why was this name chosen for Kir? Can't tell you that, but many believe the name is intricately tied to his mysterious origins.

Ki-Ru Rowaiyaru [Kir Royale]

A specific variation of the above Kir where champagne is added instead of ordinary white wine. In other words, it's a Kir with a high-class connotation. Then again, it seemed like a good idea to add "Royale" (meaning of the king, or of the crown), since it goes with the whole "King" of Bandits theme.

Konyakku [Cognac]

A brandy specifically manufactured in the Cognac region of France. Many believe this particular drink gave rise to the practice of field-dilapidation during religious wars, but looking through the cynical eye of history, one notices that miserable times tend to produce mellow drinks. With that in mind, is Cognac not an appropriate moniker for the mayor of an entire city of ill-intentioned thieves?

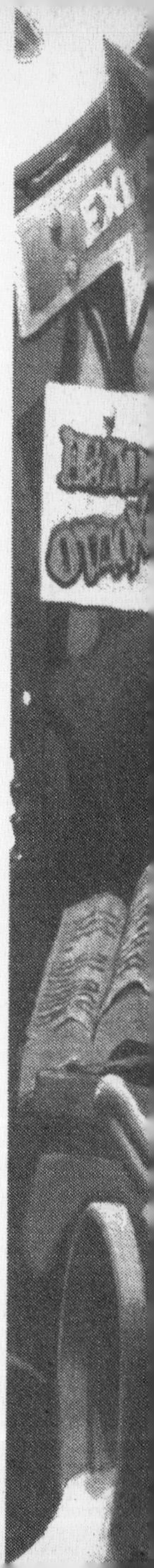

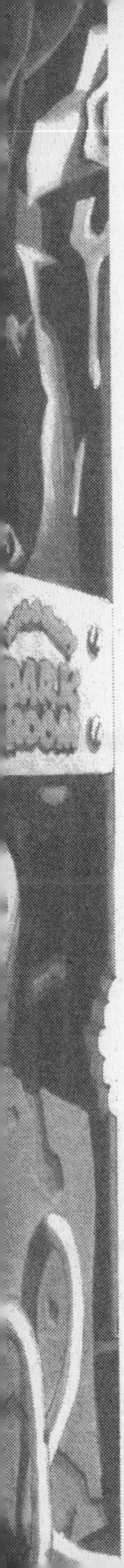

Vokka [Vodka]

An alcohol distilled from potatoes, as well as grains such as rye and barley, fermented in malt. It has become an integral part of the culture in cold nations like Russia, and is known for its tendency to produce alcoholics. Speaking of Russia, is it just me or does Vodka, the boss of the first gang of thieves Jing encounters, look like an old man from the northern meridian passage?

Shi-Doru [Cidre]

The name of Cidre, whose heart is the very first treasure captured by Jing, is taken from fruit wine fermented from apple juice. A cheap alcohol that has recently become available in convenience stores, its alcohol content is pretty low. So it is well-suited to such a fragile, crystalline creature.

Roze [Rose]

White and red wines are well-known, but there is another type of wine known as Rosé. Its beautiful pink color makes for an impressive appearance--"Rosé" actually just means rose-colored. The perfect name for a feisty, optimistic policewoman! Her father's name is never mentioned, by the way.

Gurappa [Grappa]

A huge piggy bank full of suspicious gold coins, as it turned out. Grappa's name comes from another type of brandy that is fermented from wine grapes, but is made in Italy. So, naturally, its dignified taste immediately caused the image of a casino boss, wearing steam-armor, to flash before my eyes!

Tomu & Jeri [TOM & JERRY]

Speaking of cartoons, this name also refers to the two main characters of another globally recognized cartoon. But while it does cause two particular animals to come to mind, there is also a drink crowned with this name. It is a mixture of rum, brandy, sugar and egg, and I understand that people often drink it on Christmas Day.

Buru-Hawai [Blue Hawaii]

A shaker-style cocktail using rum as a base and adding orange-flavored liqueur, Blue Curaçao, pineapple juice and lemon juice. This town, as it appears in the series, is a far cry from the image Hawaii usually brings to mind--it was conceived more as a bluish, chilling former resort town.

Morutekaron [Mortecalon]

This is an anagram of the famous Monte Carlo, which is basically a government-run casino. But "Morte" connotes death in French, so it is a very meaningful name when you consider this casino's true colors.

Adonisu [Adonis]

This drink, which takes its name from a pretty-boy loved by Venus in ancient mythology, is a stir-type cocktail (mixed with a bar spoon) using vermouth and orange bitters in dry sherry. That's why it was chosen as this city's name: it symbolizes the parallel of the mythological story with the strange relationship between a nine-tailed fox who possesses a mysterious mind-control technique, and the city's beautifully formed young lord.

Miraberu [Mirabelle]

A type of brandy made from plums. When this character is about to be executed, even as they are about to cut off her head, her braids are reminiscent of an episode that Thomas Moore, author of the 16th-century novel "Utopia," wrote about not cutting his hair before his death sentence.

Van Musu [Vins Mousseux]

This French term is a general reference to sparkling wine, so it is quite suitable as a name for a ruler of a town famous for the cultivation of clockwork grapes. His popular name, of course, is "Mastergear," but that, of course, was just to express his being the most important "gear" controlling a town entirely run by gears.

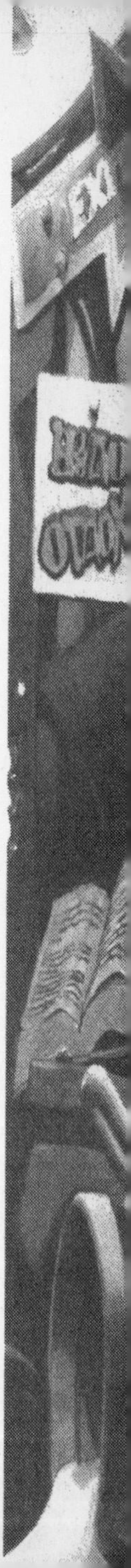

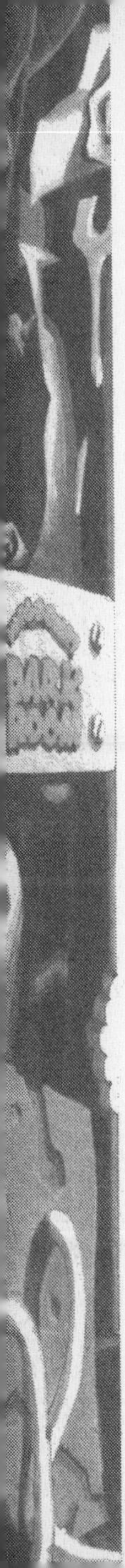

Eeggunoggu [Egg Nogg]

A shake-style cocktail that combines brandy with milk, eggs, sugar and often various other liqueurs. Since it is the name of a group of characters, a cocktail name seemed more appropriate than any single type of drink. I can also say that since it is actually a group of steel roosters, choosing a drink with the word "egg" in it seemed natural.

Sheri [Sherry]

Refers to a type of strongly alcoholic wine made around Jerez, a city in the south of Spain. It is mainly known for its unique taste, which comes from the addition of yeast. Also, this spelling is similar to "Shelley," the name of the author of "Frankenstein." As if any sort of connection could be made between a female fox and the founder of modern-day horror.

Kurokkudairu [Clockdile]

wani = crocodile, and tokei = a juxtaposition of clocks.

Sanguria [Sangria=Sungria]

A popular Spanish wine with the added sweetness of orange and lemon juices. The spelling became "Sungria" in the series, but it was quite intentional, as the addition of the "Sun" suggests a more fitting destination for Jing's gang and the porvoras, who set out from Neptune.

Sharutoryu-Zu [Chartreuse]

A liqueur originally distilled from medicinal plants at the Chartreuse Monastery in France. A great amount of this liqueur, said to be an elixir for long life, was made by the monks. Izarra's father, on the other hand, would probably have been dealing in star gems...but the details of his life are unknown.

Izara [Izarra]

Izarra is in the same group of herb-based liqueurs as Chartreuse. No accident--it reflects Chartreuse and Izarra's parent-child relationship. Made in the region of Basque, situated in the Pyrenees mountains between France and Spain where it is said that Heminqway loved to drink. By the way, Izarra means "star" in the Basque language. What a coincidence...

Tanbura [Tumbler]

A tumbler, aside from being Izarra's family name, is a cylindrical cocktail glass. It is used for gin and tonics and the like. Another name for it is a highball glass. It can hold anywhere from 180-300ml of liquid. On (or in? hyuk, hyuk) the other hand...

Goburetto [Goblet]

This is a type of glass with legs that is used for beer and such. It has a capacity of around 300ml. In a nutshell, this episode is pretty much a showdown of the "glasses." Incidentally, the glass Goblet holds during the meal scene is somewhere roughly between a wine glass and a goblet.

Rojo [Rojo]

One of Goblet's twin sons is called Rojo, which means "red" in Spanish (it's pronounced "ro-ho"). So, one would only assume that the other son would be named Blanco ("white")!

Poruvo-Ra [Porvora]

Particularly popular, maybe because one or two of them were a struggle even for Jing, were the Porvoras. However, "Porvora" is one of the few names in the series that are not alcoholic in origin--it actually means "gunpowder" in Spanish!

Ko-Pusu Ribaiba [Corpse Reviver]

Jing and Kir set off from the town of Corpse and arrive in the town of Reviver...together, these towns make up the cocktail name of Corpse Reviver. This stir-type beverage, touted by some as a hangover cure, is made with vermouth, brandy, and small amounts of liqueurs such as Cointreau, China Lilet, Pernod, etc. in a base of dry gin.

Berumotto [Vermouth]

A type of flavored wine with added spice, fruits, and sugar. France and Italy are its main production centers. When the series came out, its author was reported as saying that Vermouth was designed after Natalie Portman's character in Luc Besson's film, "The Professional." There's definitely similarity in the hair...

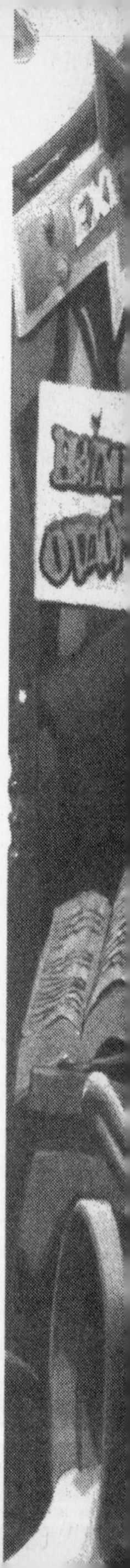

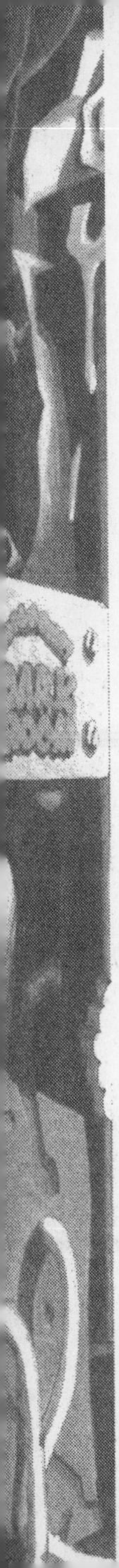

Peruno [Pernod]

Pernod was once synonymous with Absente, called the "Devil's alcohol," because of its inclusion of absinthe, a powerful hallucinogen that invades the nervous system. Now that Absente is no longer in production, a new production method has been discovered using medicinal plants. The inspiration for Pernod in this series was apparently Malcolm MacDowell of "Clockwork Orange," directed by Stanley Kubrick (this is especially apparent on page 106 of Volume Three). You see what I mean, right? The unnerving gaze...the makeup around the eyes...

Kinarire [China Lilet]

China Lilet is a flavored wine made from the bark of herbs in the China family. This wine was once used for the medical treatment of malaria. It goes particularly well with Pernod--in fact, the relationship between these two characters seems similar to the dynamic between the two main characters in my personal manga masterpiece! Speaking of which, the makeup on China Lilet's face is kind of familiar...

Koantoro [Cointreau]

An orange, spicy fruit liqueur, produced by the Cointreau company in France. This immortal king may wear a crown, but he is not necessarily at the height of fashion. This manga really does defy traditional fantasy stereotypes, eh?

Vila-Ru [Vilare]

A huge but obedient robot. Its name comes not from alcohol, but the name of a developer of everlasting engines which were carried on the back of the shoulders (history verifies this). It is interesting to note that the passage Vilare reads to the dead Cointreau is the opening paragraph of an actual book. Those readers who are interested may have fun trying to find it.

Senbunsu Hebun [Seventh Heaven]

Seventh Heaven is where the highest-ranking angels reside in Islam. This name, however, refers to a shake-type cocktail that adds Maraschino and grapefruit juice to dry gin. It seems that the historic Castel Sant'Angelo, located in central Rome, became the model for this giant prison. The real castle actually was used as a prison, and also has a story attached to it about a man who somehow broke out of the place! With that man was the 14th-century chaser (or metal engraver) of Firenze, Benvenuto Cellini!! His detailed autobiography was recently assembled, and the first and last volumes are currently being sold by Iwanami Books in Japan. If you read it, I am fairly certain you will discover a surprising parallel with the story behind Seventh Heaven...

Aka Shia [Acacia]

Campari's hometown is named for a cocktail that involves adding Benedictine and Kirschwasser to dry gin and shaking well. Acacia may also sound familiar if one has heard of the "Dalian of Acacia," series, a sequence of novels by Takayuki Kiyooka. It evokes a very nostalgic image for me, so I felt it was a suitable name for the village sleeping within Campari's heart. Also, the clothing of the younger Campari, whom Jing and the gang come across during the dream sequence, makes me think of national clothes during the war in Japan. And the people who send him off are sort of like the people who lamented the young men's departure to the front. The image of a sorrowful people who could not avoid destruction hangs densely in the air...

Benedikutin [Benedictine]

Comparable to the aforementioned Chartreuse, this is another liqueur made in monasteries from medicinal plants. Benedictine's holding a stick and a hula-hoop soon after entering the prison of dreams, along with much of the scenery that follows, was inspired by "Mystery and Melancholy of a Street," the work of an Italian painter, Giorgio de Chirico. The eerie dolls that chase Jing and the gang afterwards, and in fact most of the images of the prison of dreams, were largely inspired by de Chirico's works.

End of King of Bandits Crime Report, First Volume

Continued in Volume 6

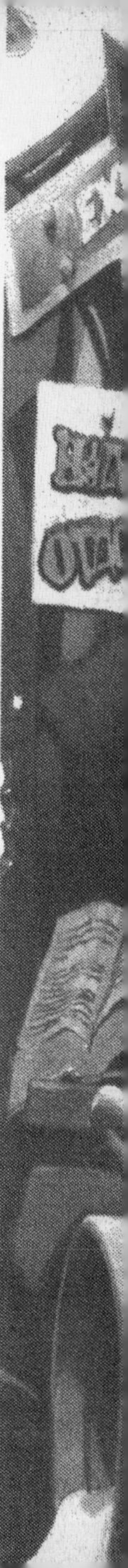

KING OF BANDITS

王ドロボウJING

The sky is the limit when
Jing and Kir end up on cloud nine...
after stealing a map of Fuzzy Navel.
The terrible twosome receive a shock
from worshipers of electricity, run into
a very pretty little kitty, and try to
avoid sleeping with the flying fishes.

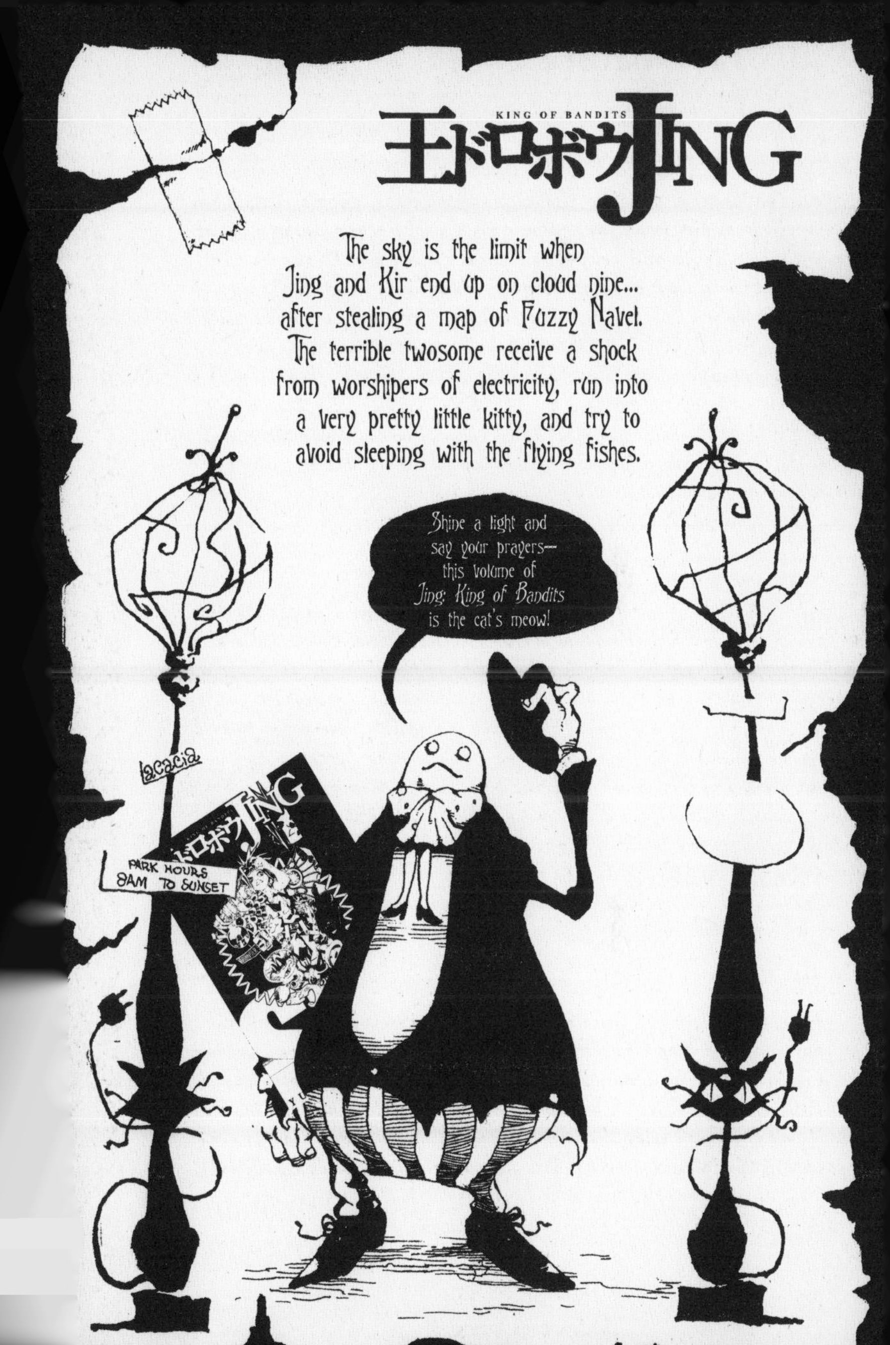
Shine a light and say your prayers— this volume of *Jing: King of Bandits* is the cat's meow!
lacacia
PARK HOURS 9AM TO SUNSET
王ドロボウJING

ALSO AVAILABLE FROM TOKYOPOP®

**For more
information visit
www.TOKYOPOP.com**

01.09.04T

ALSO AVAILABLE FROM TOKYOPOP

MANGA

.HACK//LEGEND OF THE TWILIGHT
@LARGE
ABENOBASHI
A.I. LOVE YOU
AI YORI AOSHI
ANGELIC LAYER
ARM OF KANNON
BABY BIRTH
BATTLE ROYALE
BATTLE VIXENS
BRAIN POWERED
BRIGADOON
B'TX
CANDIDATE FOR GODDESS, THE
CARDCAPTOR SAKURA
CARDCAPTOR SAKURA - MASTER OF THE CLOW
CHOBITS
CHRONICLES OF THE CURSED SWORD
CLAMP SCHOOL DETECTIVES
CLOVER
COMIC PARTY
CONFIDENTIAL CONFESSIONS
CORRECTOR YUI
COWBOY BEBOP
COWBOY BEBOP: SHOOTING STAR
CRESCENT MOON
CULDCEPT
CYBORG 009
D.N. ANGEL
DEMON DIARY
DEMON ORORON, THE
DEUS VITAE
DIGIMON
DIGIMON ZERO TWO
DIGIMON TAMERS
DOLL
DRAGON HUNTER
DRAGON KNIGHTS
DREAM SAGA
DUKLYON: CLAMP SCHOOL DEFENDERS
ERICA SAKURAZAWA COLLECTED WORKS
EERIE QUEERIE!
ET CETERA
ETERNITY
EVIL'S RETURN
FAERIES' LANDING
FAKE
FLCL
FORBIDDEN DANCE
FRUITS BASKET
G GUNDAM
GATE KEEPERS

GETBACKERS
GIRL GOT GAME
GRAVITATION
GTO
GUNDAM SEED ASTRAY
GUNDAM WING
GUNDAM WING: BATTLEFIELD OF PACIFISTS
GUNDAM WING: ENDLESS WALTZ
GUNDAM WING: THE LAST OUTPOST (G-UNIT)
HAPPY MANIA
HARLEM BEAT
I.N.V.U.
IMMORTAL RAIN
INITIAL D
ISLAND
JING: KING OF BANDITS
JULINE
KARE KANO
KILL ME, KISS ME
KINDAICHI CASE FILES, THE
KING OF HELL
KODOCHA: SANA'S STAGE
LAMENT OF THE LAMB
LES BIJOUX
LEGEND OF CHUN HYANG, THE
LOVE HINA
LUPIN III
MAGIC KNIGHT RAYEARTH I
MAGIC KNIGHT RAYEARTH II
MAHOROMATIC: AUTOMATIC MAIDEN
MAN OF MANY FACES
MARMALADE BOY
MARS
MINK
MIRACLE GIRLS
MIYUKI-CHAN IN WONDERLAND
MODEL
ONE
PARADISE KISS
PARASYTE
PEACH GIRL
PEACH GIRL: CHANGE OF HEART
PET SHOP OF HORRORS
PITA-TEN
PLANET LADDER
PLANETES
PRIEST
PRINCESS AI
PSYCHIC ACADEMY
RAGNAROK
RAVE MASTER
REALITY CHECK
REBIRTH

01.09.04T

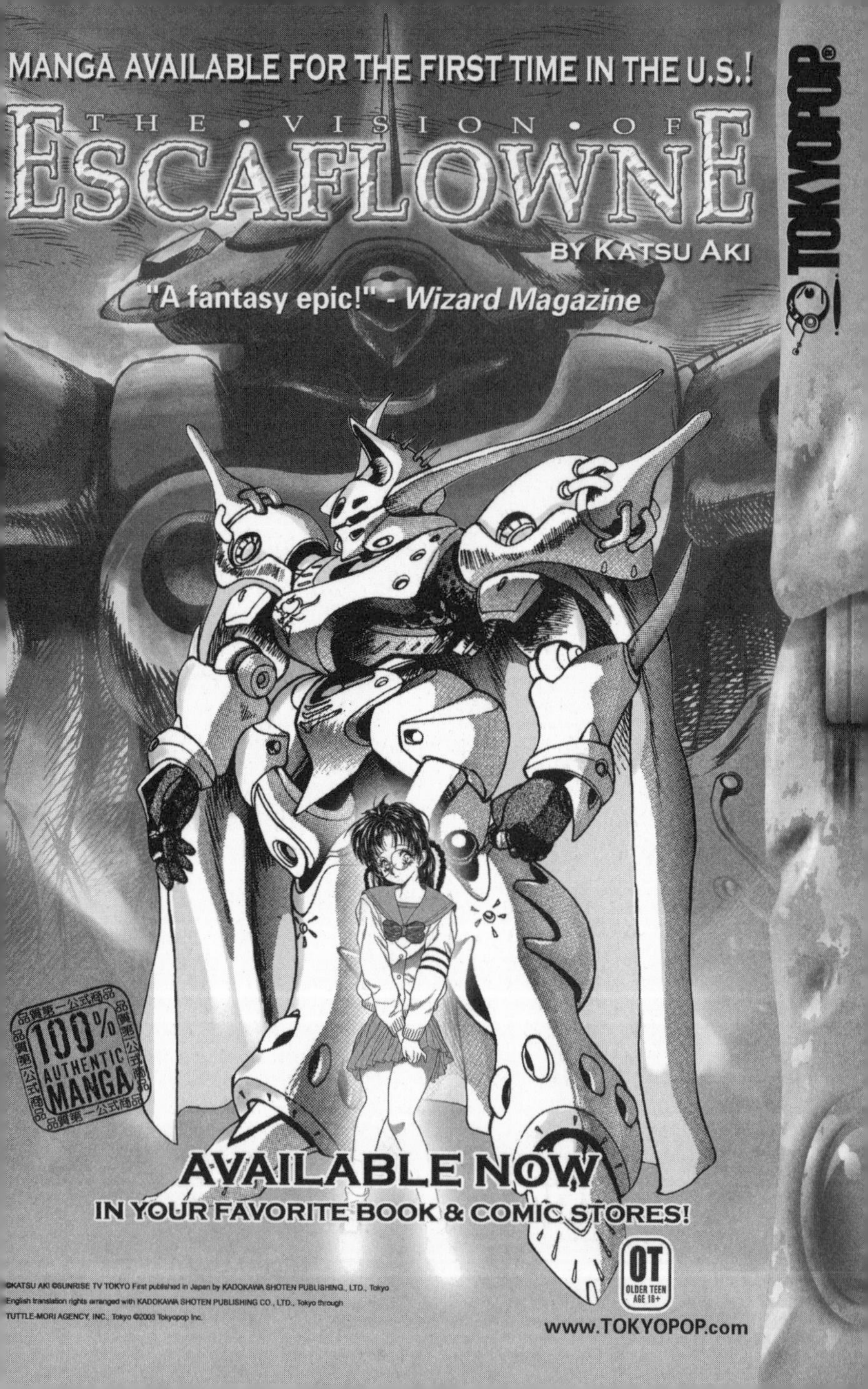
MANGA AVAILABLE FOR THE FIRST TIME IN THE U.S.!
THE • VISION • OF
ESCAFLOWNE
BY KATSU AKI
"A fantasy epic!" - Wizard Magazine
TOKYOPOP
100% AUTHENTIC MANGA
品質第一公式商品
AVAILABLE NOW
IN YOUR FAVORITE BOOK & COMIC STORES!
OT OLDER TEEN AGE 16+
©KATSU AKI ©SUNRISE TV TOKYO First published in Japan by KADOKAWA SHOTEN PUBLISHING., LTD., Tokyo
English translation rights arranged with KADOKAWA SHOTEN PUBLISHING CO., LTD., Tokyo through
TUTTLE-MORI AGENCY, INC., Tokyo ©2003 Tokyopop Inc.
www.TOKYOPOP.com

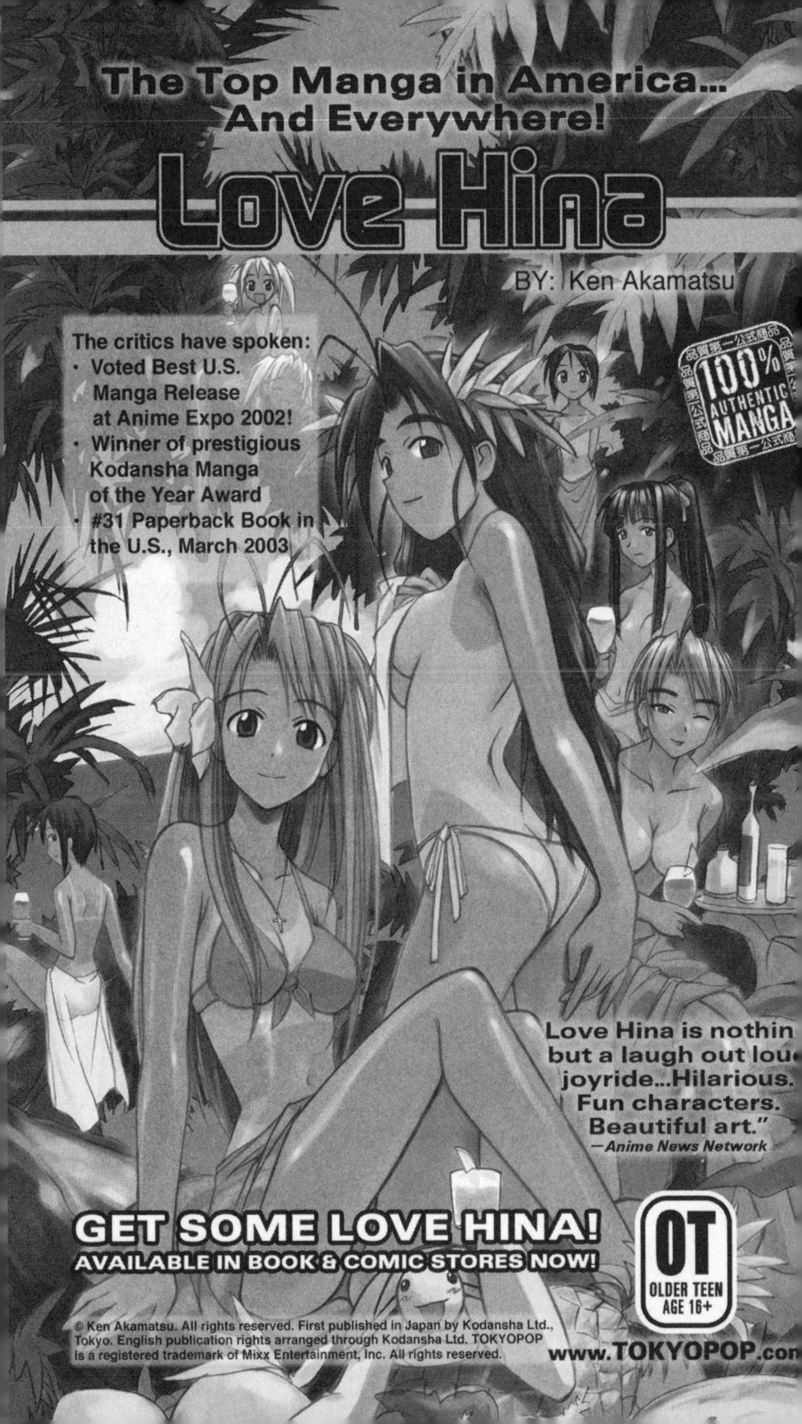
The Top Manga in America... And Everywhere!
Love Hina
BY: Ken Akamatsu
The critics have spoken:
• Voted Best U.S. Manga Release at Anime Expo 2002!
• Winner of prestigious Kodansha Manga of the Year Award
• #31 Paperback Book in the U.S., March 2003
100% AUTHENTIC MANGA
Love Hina is nothin
but a laugh out lou
joyride...Hilarious.
Fun characters.
Beautiful art."
—Anime News Network
GET SOME LOVE HINA!
AVAILABLE IN BOOK & COMIC STORES NOW!
OT OLDER TEEN AGE 16+
© Ken Akamatsu. All rights reserved. First published in Japan by Kodansha Ltd., Tokyo. English publication rights arranged through Kodansha Ltd. TOKYOPOP is a registered trademark of Mixx Entertainment, Inc. All rights reserved.
www.TOKYOPOP.con

A.I.
LOVΣ YOU ™
by Ken Akamatsu

A.I. Program Thirty became a real girl...

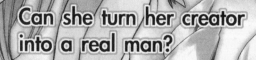

Can she turn her creator into a real man?

OT
OLDER TEEN
AGE 16+

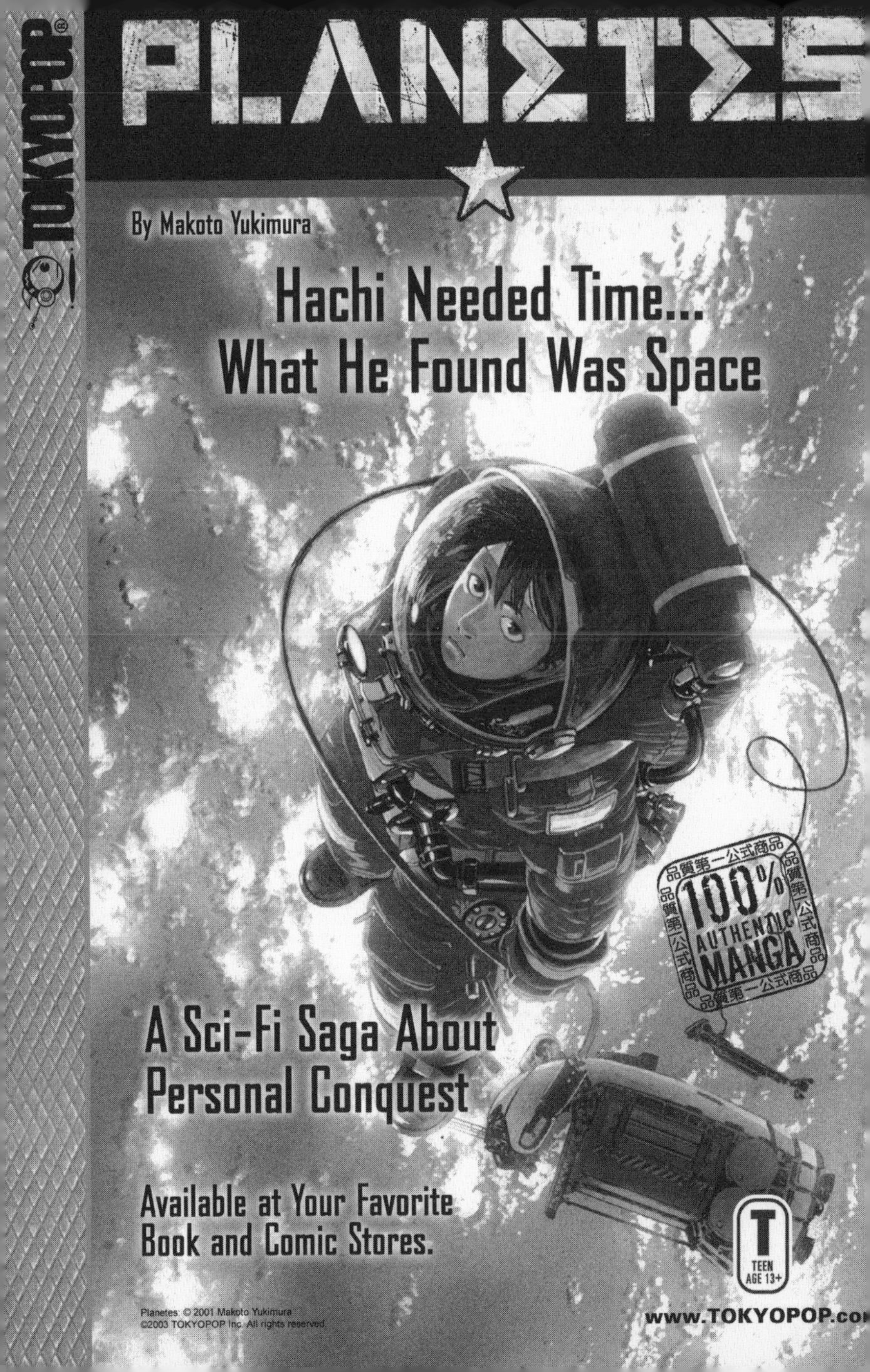
TOKYOPOP®
PLANETES
By Makoto Yukimura
Hachi Needed Time...
What He Found Was Space
100% AUTHENTIC MANGA
品質第一公式商品
A Sci-Fi Saga About
Personal Conquest
Available at Your Favorite
Book and Comic Stores.
T
TEEN AGE 13+
Planetes © 2001 Makoto Yukimura
©2003 TOKYOPOP Inc. All rights reserved.
www.TOKYOPOP.com

STOP!

This is the back of the book.
You wouldn't want to spoil a great ending!

This book is printed "manga-style," in the authentic Japanese right-to-left format. Since none of the artwork has been flipped or altered, readers get to experience the story just as the creator intended. You've been asking for it, so TOKYOPOP® delivered: authentic, hot-off-the-press, and far more fun!

DIRECTIONS

If this is your first time reading manga-style, here's a quick guide to help you understand how it works.

It's easy... just start in the top right panel and follow the numbers. Have fun, and look for more 100% authentic manga from TOKYOPOP®!